Implementation of
Soviet Economic Reforms

Karl W. Ryavec

The Praeger Special Studies program—utilizing the most modern and efficient book production techniques and a selective worldwide distribution network—makes available to the academic, government, and business communities significant, timely research in U.S. and international economic, social, and political development.

Implementation of Soviet Economic Reforms
Political, Organizational, and Social Processes

PRAEGER SPECIAL STUDIES IN INTERNATIONAL POLITICS AND GOVERNMENT

Praeger Publishers   New York   Washington   London

Library of Congress Cataloging in Publication Data

Ryavec, Karl W
 Implementation of Soviet economic reforms.

 (Praeger special studies in international politics and government)
 Bibliography: p.
 Includes index.
 1. Industrial management—Russia.   2. Russia—Economic policy—1966-
 HD70.R9R868   658.4'00947   75-3627
 ISBN 0-275-05240-0

PRAEGER PUBLISHERS
111 Fourth Avenue, New York, N.Y. 10003, U.S.A.

Published in the United States of America in 1975
by Praeger Publishers, Inc.

All rights reserved

© 1975 by Praeger Publishers, Inc.

Printed in the United States of America

ACKNOWLEDGMENTS

The original impetus for this book came from Professor John N. Hazard of Columbia University. His aid did not end there but included reading and commenting on earlier versions. Professors Grey Hodnett of York University and Peter Juviler of Barnard College and Columbia deserve credit for suggesting the topic itself and devising aspects of the approach I have used. I am grateful as well for the suggestions offered me by Professors Alexander Erlich and Loren Graham, also of Columbia.

Research for a second, fuller version, differing in many respects from the first, was facilitated by a research fellowship granted me during a sabbatical year, 1970-71, by the Russian Research Center of Harvard University, then directed by Professor Richard Pipes. My attendance at Professor Abram Bergson's weekly meetings of economists helped attune me to several issues and processes important for this study. Associates and fellows of the Center who read initial versions of parts of the book and offered valuable comments include Professors Joseph Berliner, Paul Cocks, Earl Brubaker, and Martin Spechler.

Several present and former colleagues of the Political Science Department of the University of Massachusetts at Amherst--Professors Ferenc Vali, Andrew Martin, Gerard Braunthal, and Fred Kramer--also aided me, as did Professor Vaclav Holesovsky of the University's Economics Department and Professor Curt Tausky of the Sociology Department.

I also wish to thank the editors of three journals--<u>Canadian Slavic Studies</u>, <u>Soviet Studies</u>, and <u>Western Political Quarterly</u>--for granting permission to reprint parts of my articles that appeared therein: "Soviet Industrial Managers, Their Superiors and the Economic Reform: A Study of an Attempt at Planned Behavioural Change," <u>Soviet Studies</u> 21, no. 2 (October 1969): 208-29; "Soviet Industrial Management, the Communist Party, and the Economic Reform," <u>Western Political Quarterly</u> 3 (September 1970): 589-99 (reprinted by permission of the University of Utah, copyright holder); "Soviet Industrial Management, 1965-1970: Challenge and Response," <u>Canadian Slavic Studies</u> 5, no. 2 (Summer 1971): 151-77.

CONTENTS

	Page
ACKNOWLEDGMENTS	v
LIST OF TABLES	ix
LIST OF FIGURES	ix
LIST OF ABBREVIATIONS	ix
GLOSSARY	x
INTRODUCTION	1
Basic Definitions	2
Significance	4
Theoretical Framework	5
Notes	13

Chapter

1	THE ORIGINS AND CONCEPT OF THE REFORM	17
	The Old System	17
	Earlier Stirrings of Reform	23
	Intended Goals of the Economic Reform	30
	The Goals of Managerial Change	46
	Conclusion	48
	Notes	49
2	MANAGERS AND MINISTERIAL SUPERIORS	56
	Issues	56
	The Ministries: Personnel, Powers, Structure, and the Challenge of Change	60
	Behavior	77
	Notes	92
3	THE ROLE OF NONMINISTERIAL AGENCIES IN THE IMPLEMENTATION PROCESS	101
	Gosplan	101
	The State Bank	110

Chapter		Page
	The Ministry of Finance	114
	The Interstices: Obedineniia	116
	Conclusion	135
	Notes	136
4	THE COMMUNIST PARTY AND INDUSTRIAL MANAGEMENT	145
	Introduction	145
	The Party, Industrial Management, and the Economic Reform: The First Two Years	152
	The Party and the Ministries: An Uncompleted Attempt at Change	158
	The Party and the Manager: Recent Developments	165
	Obedineniia and the Party	174
	Conclusion	175
	Notes	179
5	THE MANAGER AND INDUSTRIAL WORKERS: THE EFFECT OF THE REFORM ON LABOR	186
	Introduction	186
	Managerial Power: Edinonachalie and Discipline	190
	Countervailing Forces?	198
	The Availability of Labor	202
	The Reform, Automation, and Unemployment	206
	The Shchekino Experiment	209
	Amelioration or Solution?	211
	The Young Workers	213
	Conclusion	214
	Notes	216
6	THE MANAGER-MANAGER RELATIONSHIP	225
	Introduction	225
	Direct Ties	227
	Contracts and Inter-Enterprise Obligations: Ideal and Actuality	230
	Proposed Solutions	233
	Ministries, Supply, and Arbitration	236
	Summary and Conclusion	241
	Notes	241

Chapter	Page
7 MANAGERS AND MANAGEMENT	246
Significance, Problems, and Politics	246
The Challenge	252
The Response	258
Conclusion	272
Notes	273
8 THE INCOMPLETE REFORM: EFFECTS AND SIGNIFICANCE	281
Fundamental Significance	281
Results and Effects	282
Causal Factors	289
The Significance and Implications of the Soviet Economic Reform	303
Notes	308
BIBLIOGRAPHY	313
INDEX	350
ABOUT THE AUTHOR	361

LIST OF TABLES

Table		Page
1.1	Party Functions in Industry	38
2.1	Transfer of Industrial Enterprises, 1966-70	79
4.1	List of Party Functions in Industry	153

LIST OF FIGURES

Figure		Page
1.1	Major Managerial Relationships	7
8.1	Results of the Reform by Topic	285

LIST OF ABBREVIATIONS

ABSEES	Soviet and East European Abstracts Series
CASP	Current Abstracts of the Soviet Press
CDSP	Current Digest of the Soviet Press
FBIS	Foreign Broadcast Information Service
JPRS	(U.S.) Joint Publications Research Service

GLOSSARY

Administirovanie	Inflexible and forced administration of an organization
Aktiv	The most active and politicized members of an organization
Apparat	The administrative machinery of any organization (usually of the Communist Party)
Apparatchik	A full-time paid functionary (usually of the Party apparatus) (plural, apparatchiki)
Amalgamation (industrial)	See obedinenie
Association (industrial)	See obedinenie
Blat	Personal influence and its use (at times with special favors) or bribes to accomplish work or obtain special treatment
Bronia	("armor") The quota of recent high-school graduates that industrial managers are required to hire
Druzhina	A body of the people's militia
Edinonachalie	"One-man control." The principle of assigning fundamental responsibility for an industrial enterprise to its single director (manager)
Filial	A branch of an enterprise (plural, filialy)
Firma	See obedinenie (plural, firmy)
Gavk	Acronym for Glavnoe Upravlenie (Chief Administration), a level of administration between the ministry and the individual industrial enterprises. Now being eliminated as part of the creation of obedineniia (plural, glavki)
Gos-	A prefix meaning "state"

Gosarbitrazh	State Arbitration System, a network of institutions for arbitrating disputes (often concerning contracts) among industrial enterprises
Gosbank	State Bank
Gosplan	State Planning Commission (plural, Gosplany)
ITR	(Inzhinerno-tekhnicheskie rabotniki) White-collar, nonmanagerial specialists in industry
Khozraschet	Economic or business accounting and accountability
Komandirovka	Business trip (plural, komandirovki)
Kombinat	Combine (now rare), a complex of plants producing a wide range of goods (plural, kombinaty)
Kontrol' rublem	("control by the ruble") The process by which Gosbank supervises enterprises' credit, expenditures, and accounts
Krugovaia poruka	("mutual guarantee") Mutual support by officials in covering up deficiencies or illegalities
Mestnichestvo	Localism; disregard of the natural interest in and concentration on local needs, particularly in matters of supply
Nariad	Allocation certificate indicating the terms of obtaining goods, particularly quantity and supplier; it serves as a basis for interenterprise contracts
NEP	New Economic Policy, a period (1921-28) of somewhat relaxed political climate; free markets and limited capitalistic forms existed
Nomenklatura	List of appointments subject to Party initiation or ratification

NOT	(Nauchnaia organizatsiia truda) Scientific organization of work
ob-	Abbreviation for oblast (region or province) (plural, oblasty)
Obedinenie	Association, amalgamation, firm (plural, obedineniia)
Obkom	oblast Party committee
Orgnabor	A state system for labor recruitment and allocation
Orgtekhplan	The scheme or plan of organizational and technical measures of an industrial enterprise; part of the <u>tekhpromfinplan</u>
Otdel	Section (for instance, of a ministry)
Part-	Abbreviation for Party (Communist)
Partburo	Party bureau; the executive organ of a Party organization
Partkom	Party Committee
Partiinost'	"Party spirit" or conformance to Party principles and policy in thinking and acting
Partorg	Party organizer
Piatiletka	Five-year plan
Predpriiatie	Enterprise (industrial), often translated as "plant" (plural, predpriiatiia)
Rai-	Abbreviation for raion (district, county)
Raikom	District Party Committee (plural, raikomy)
Shchekino	Name of a town and chemical plant in the Ukraine that also symbolizes reductions in labor forces and their upgrading in job capabilities

Shturmovshchina	("storming") The practice of rapidly completing work at the end of a planning period, particularly at the end of a month (of military derivation)
Snab-	Abbreviation for supply (as in Gossnab)
Sov-	Abbreviation for Soviet (Council)
Sovnarkhoz	Acronym for Council of National Economy, the regional organizations that made many planning and industrial decisions between 1957 and 1965 (plural, sovnarkhozy)
Stroibank	Construction Bank
Tekhpromfinplan	The annual operating plan of an industrial enterprise
Tolkach	Literally, "pusher"; in usage, "expediter" or "fixer"--unofficial supply agents of enterprises (plural, tolkachi)
VAL	(from _valovoi_, gross) The former main success indicator for an enterprise, gross output
Vedomstvennost'	"Departmentalism," following the narrow interests of a particular bureaucratic office
Zaiavka	A statement of needs or requests for supplies; indents (plural, Zaiavki)

Implementation of
Soviet Economic Reforms

INTRODUCTION

As change is inevitable, so is resistance to it; and in the Soviet system it assumes a political character. The combination of attempts at change and resistance may modify the original policy, perhaps even fundamentally alter the relationship between the forces attempting change and those opposing it. Such alteration may even transform the political system. The particular change examined here is the complex of alterations brought about in order to facilitate the implementation in Soviet industry of the economic reform formally begun in 1965. The time period under consideration is from the beginning of 1966 through 1973.

The reform has given a powerful impetus to a variety of new departures in the industrial sector and has strongly affected groupings involved with industry. Such developments as the rise in unemployment (mostly short-term) and the consequent beginning of means to cope with it, and the recent establishment of schools of management modeled upon Western business schools, are notable examples of the reform's effects.

Some writers argue that the reform is dead. This is true only in the most narrow economic sense. Although what might be labeled the first stage of the reform has not had the effect that Aleksei Kosygin and others seem to have intended, it has made possible and necessitated a number of both corrective moves and innovations. (The singular "reform" is used here to emphasize the essential interrelationship of many of the economic, social, and political events and processes of the period under review.) Whether the leadership will be able to rationalize and modernize the Soviet economy without political changes occurring in the process is an important political question.

This study is not an appraisal of the economic effectiveness of the reform[1] but an examination of the political, organizational, and social prerequisites and effects of Soviet economic change, in this case the economic reform of 1965. The economic reform is actually a behavioral reform, an attempt to change the economic behavior of part of the Soviet population. The Soviet economy could produce more and better products without technical improvement or replacement if material components were utilized more efficiently. Any rise in productivity requires a change in "process," that is, the reorganization of the entire matrix of variable inputs, including work behavior, that determine a specific output. "A 'higher' process is one where for identical or equivalent outputs there is a lesser real value of inputs."[2] Final judgment upon the effectiveness of the reform cannot yet be pronounced. However, although the behavioral changes begun in 1965 have not caused Soviet industry to be run in a fashion significantly different from the one that has characterized its operation since the 1930s, they have begun to increase labor productivity and the assimilation of new technology. In addition, the drive to modernize the Soviet economy clearly will continue until a high degree of success is achieved. In the process, reform will have to extend into the societal and political spheres.

This is primarily a study of the implemental stage of a policy, the stage at which disequilibrium is greatest and conflicts are most numerous.[3] The earlier "evaluation" and "initiation" stages involved mainly the political elite, but actual implementation brings forth visible and significant "politics at the lower level."[4]

This examination of behavioral change in industry involves reference to a number of areas of intellectual inquiry because the Soviet industrial "system" interacts with several sectors of Soviet society, being affected by inputs from them and affecting them with its outputs. The goal of the change is a more efficient industry producing more goods of higher quality. Success in this venture might include a more powerful Soviet strategic position in international affairs and an increase of domestic support for the political system. But, on the other hand, success might also accelerate the erosion of Soviet authoritarianism by injecting more rationality and new thought patterns into a major area of its operation.

BASIC DEFINITIONS

The main aspect of the reform has two features: (1) recentralization of the state system of planning and administrative control through termination of the decentralized sovnarkhoz system (begun by Nikita Khrushchev in 1957) and reconstitution of the ministries and the "branch" system of industrial administration; and (2) change of the emphasis in the calculation of industrial enterprises' accomplishments from the value of gross output (the VAL) to profits or sales

INTRODUCTION

and profitability (rentabel'nost'), accompanied by a significant reduction in the numbers of centrally set enterprise indicators from approximately forty to eight or nine and by an increase in the powers of industrial managers over personnel, operations, and material resources.[5] Thus, the core of the reform is a reestablishment of centralized, authoritative organizational structure, but with fewer powers for the major units in this structure and the intended decentralization of decision-making in some areas--for instance, choice of supplies, determination of detailed product mix, and making of contracts through their devolution to enterprise directors. This pattern is not without contradictions that may undermine the attainment of the reform's goals. It constitutes an attempt to merge bureaucratic centralism with entrepreneurial decentralization, and is the most recent variant in the Russian tradition of trying to institute major changes, and even innovations, from the top down through the use of political power and bureaucratized instrumentalities. The policies of Count Sergei Witte constitute a historical example.[6]

One of my purposes here is to determine the degree to which the present reforms, in their behavioral and organizational aspects, affect the political, economic, and social milieu into which they have been introduced and to elucidate the interaction between this milieu and the policies of reform. Another issue is the extent to which ideas and behavior from outside the Soviet Union can be introduced into processes inside it while the sociopolitical elements always closely associated with these ideas and behavior in their original settings are rejected. As Robert Conquest notes, "Russia is now, for the third time, seeking to obtain the technological developments of Western culture, while rejecting its whole civic and political content--as under Peter the Great and Stalin."[7] The reform also attempts to combine different Soviet models of the administration of industry: the rigid ministerial centralism of the Stalinist period and the more decentralized administration of the earlier New Economic Policy (NEP) period, with its entrepreneurial features and atmosphere.

Although the reform is important for the management of industry, for the quantity and quality of industry's output, and for Soviet society and its politics, it does not constitute a thoroughgoing and logically based or radical reorientation of fundamental assumptions, beliefs, or principles concerning the economy. Certainly "capitalism" is not being reintroduced, Chinese Communist propaganda charges and some Western newspaper accounts notwithstanding. No complete second NEP is officially envisioned. Prices, despite the significant revisions of 1967, continue to be set bureaucratically and lack a consistent relationship to actual costs;[8] enterprises are still given output plans; profits do not go to individual managers, much less stockholders or workers, but are divided between the enterprise and the state; managers still must meet seven or eight centrally set major indices (not to mention some "additional conditions" or <u>dopolnitel'nye usloviia</u>) and do not, for example, determine their enterprises' wage funds; workers do not have the right to strike and almost never do; and consumers are able to influence industrial output and politics only indirectly, insofar as the political leadership deems it necessary to respond favorably to the blunt, undifferentiated desires of an "amorphous social force."[9] The major differences between the Soviet and American (and the West European) economies are still those of kind, not only of degree, despite John Kenneth Galbraith's argument that the Soviet and American economies are similar in their "convergence to . . . planning."[10]

SIGNIFICANCE

The political significance of the reform lies in its threat to the continuation of the Party's dominance of industrial administration and thereby poses a long-term challenge to the Party's position in related spheres of social life: science, engineering, education, and the activities of the trade unions.

Any definite alteration of the network of human relationships put together by Lenin and Stalin would constitute a threat to the ideology, structure, role, and leading personnel of the Communist Party of the Soviet Union (CPSU). The CPSU has faced greater "threats," such as the German invasion, and has survived and prospered. But notwithstanding the undeniable strengths of the Leninist style and form of organization, it cannot retain its present preeminence in a different socioeconomic setting. The Party and the setting interlock into a powerful political unit. To change that setting in some definite way is to begin the relegation of the Party apparatus to a lesser role. (This would not be an insignificant status, however.)

The economic reform threatens such a change in setting. Although the Party apparatus has reasserted its prerogatives in industrial management, the threat still exists and may even be increasing, particularly if the effects of the several spin-offs of the reform are considered. The assertive actions of the Party apparatus in the face of the reform indicate that a threat was perceived, and correctly so.

The Soviet political system has a fragile strength and a particular form that is derived not from rule by the CPSU alone but from the unique fit of the CPSU with the society and its particular traditions. But, although this interlocking makes for an unusual political system if it is viewed as a whole, the political processes operating within it are similar to those in other systems, including liberal democratic ones. One authority on the Soviet Party's role

INTRODUCTION

in industry notes that "the central question of the present period surely is that of economic reform."[11] Consideration of the 1965-73 period shows that the broad political processes did not overwhelm the economic reform, although the rise of Leonid Brezhnev and the quasi re-Stalinization did impede the reform and limit its scope.

Even before 1965, discussion of reform tacitly called into question the correctness of the command economy, openly implying that something else would be better. In addition, some of the processes criticized are elements of the normal assumptions and activities of the Party.[12] The reform's implementation is inescapably political. First, it is being implemented by the political leaders and through the political structure. Second, implementation has become inextricably intertwined with important political questions, such as the cohesion of the top political leadership, that leadership's ability to implement the reform (even with modifications), and the utility to the reform of some of the organizational means available to the leadership (such as the local Party organs and the agencies of the state bureaucracy). Third, other political issues are involved: the capacity of interest groups and other social forces to resist implementation and in effect modify the reform, the prospect of change in the established network of key relationships among elites, the tension between the decentralized and centralized patterns of planning and management, the problems for party rukovodstvo (guidance, leadership) and kontrol' (supervision, checking) posed by the creation of the new obedineniia (amalgamations) and the possibility of managers' establishing economic contacts among themselves, and the crucial test of whether the reform can substantially aid in providing the population with a large quantity of high-quality consumer goods.

THEORETICAL FRAMEWORK

"The blinkers that have been inserted between the so-called disciplines into which the study of human affairs has been arbitrarily partitioned are as much against the interests of mankind as any political iron curtain is."[13]

Multidisciplinary and comparative studies have been called for quite frequently in recent years but, interestingly, they are an almost nonexistent phenomenon both in political science in general and in Soviet studies specifically. The call for new approaches has been justified. Marshall Shulman has listed several problems that are treated here as "most interesting" ones requiring interdisciplinary study: the "complex political and social problems involved in economic planning and administration, . . . elites and interest groups, bureaucratic politics and organization theory, [and] decision-making processes. . . ."[14] In addition, there is decreasing sense in trying to draw a sharp line between the concerns of the political scientist and the economist. "In centrally planned societies economic decisions are not taken independently of political decisions."[15]

Key Managerial Relationships

If one considers the four major relationships of the Soviet enterprise director at work, one realizes that for the reform to be effective, meaningful change must occur in these relationships and in others, such as between the Party apparatus and the ministries.

Although we are using the concept of role relationship,[16] it is sufficient here to use the term "relationship." The specialized literature on role relationships is not developed; the concept is utilized as an aid in specifying certain goals, in judging important aspects of the attempt at change embodied in the reform, and in categorizing data and assessing their significance. The fundamental elements of the concept are status and role. This study is concerned with four major role relationships or behavioral interactions of Soviet industrial managers qua managers.

The political significance of managerial relationships arises from the conflict between the leadership's views of what ought to be and the facts of what behavior is, a conflict of wills, attitudes, and behaviors.

The Soviet manager's four relationships emphasized here are manager-superior, manager-Party (local and enterprise Party organs), manager-subordinates, and manager-manager. (See Figure 1.1.)

Several Soviet sources, including Kosygin, have said that for meaningful economic progress to take place in Soviet industry, changes must take place within its human relationships. In other words, the leadership is concerned precisely with those aspects of managerial behavior that can be analyzed by using role relationships. For example, Kosygin notes that it is in enterprises that "the success of the matter will be decided" and "the development of economic methods of guiding industry changes the very nature of the interrelations between the enterprises and superior bodies."[17] The other main role relationships of the manager are also to undergo change. One Soviet commentator says:

> This involvement [of the enterprise in the economy] is carried out with the help of planning and incentives in three absolutely concrete forms of economic relations: the enterprise with society,

FIGURE 1.1

Major Managerial Relationships

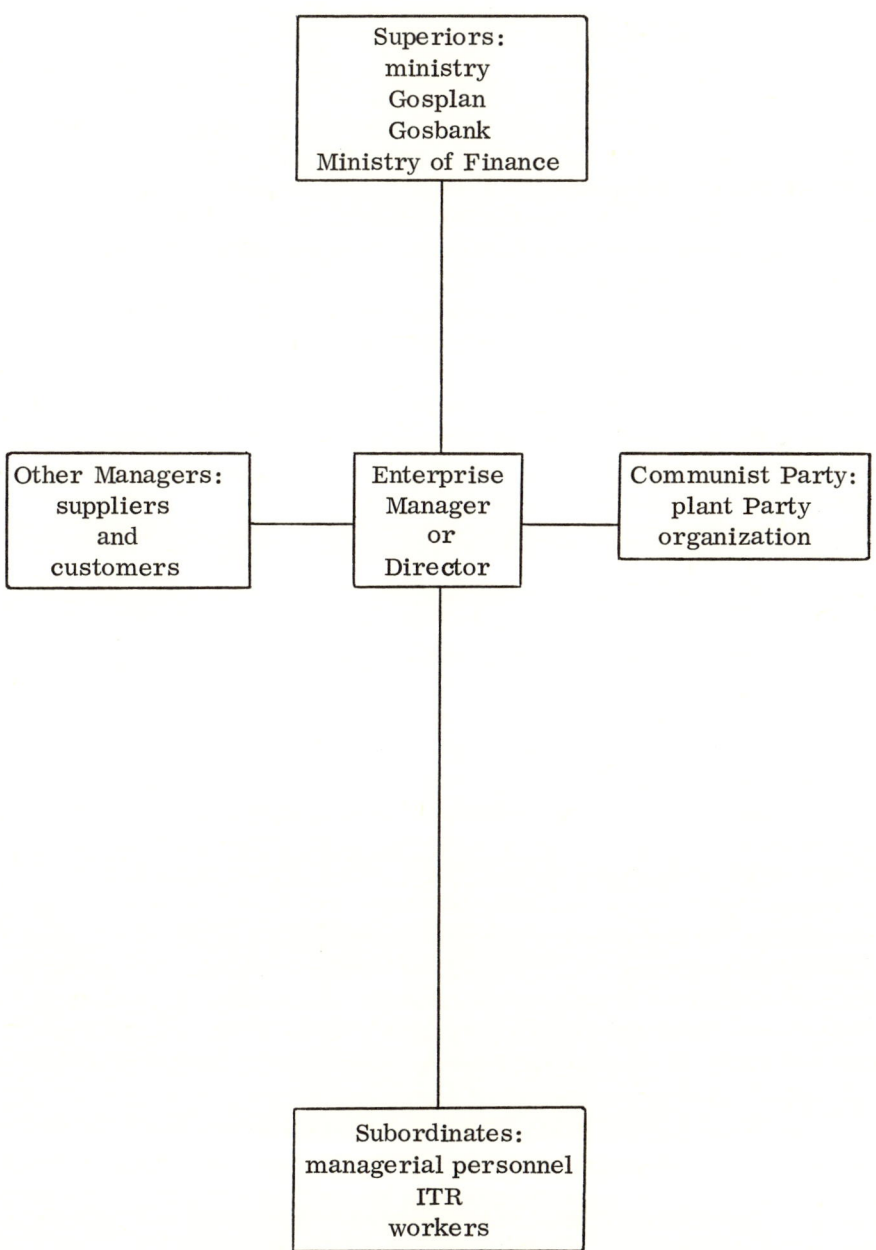

enterprises with each other, and the enterprise with the workers employed in it. <u>Proper organization of these relations is the key to development of the most effective system of economic stimulation of production and full use of the advantages of socialism and its objective economic laws and categories.</u>[18]

A. Rumiantsev, the editor of <u>Ekonomicheskaia gazeta</u>, adds: "The problems of management are above all problems of economic and production relations."[19]

Although publicly stated, the intent to change managers' relationships cannot be easily carried out. Key industrial cadres must be persuaded to act and think in a new way. The Stalinist way out-- a purge--would be too disruptive of the complex Soviet economy to be seriously contemplated. And perhaps it is rendered impossible. As Jeremy Azrael says, "There can be little question that there was a more or less steady increase in the political influence of the managerial elite, relative to that of other key elite groups, throughout the last decade or so of Stalin's rule."[20] This process has not been reversed.

Bureaucracy

Large organizations are inevitably bureaucratic and thus conflictful and informalist in their activity.[21] Since the expertise and interests of different groupings within an organization differ, so do the groupings' points of view, suggestions for policy, and claims and demands made upon the organization as a whole.

Externally, or between bureaucracies, conflict seems also to be endemic. "<u>Every large organization is in partial</u> conflict with every other social agent it deals with."[22] Even attempts to be "conservative" and merely maintain the status quo lead to disputes. Accordingly, bureaucracies can be considered small political systems.[23] The Soviet Union may be a "model" of "bureaupathology," perhaps because the absence of many countervailing groups and of a relatively free-flowing political process prevents both the state and the Party bureaucracies from facing the types of limitations that bureaucracies in "open societies" encounter.[24]

Conflict within the Soviet industrial bureaucracy has been described by a French scholar, who says:

> Within each ministry, enterprises competed
> fiercely for a privileged status, for reasonable

quotas, and for easy orders. The same sort of competition existed on a lower level within each enterprise and on a higher level among ministries. The jungle of liberal capitalism of the past looks like a fencing tournament in comparison with this sordid infighting for influence interspersed with negotiations, shady deals, and blackmail.[25]

"Bureaucracy" is often understood only as a simplistic Weberian model: rational, efficient, politically neutral, and just.[26] Actual bureaucratic behavior deviates noticeably from what is formally prescribed. This has been labeled "bureaucratic informalism," a term encompassing bureaucratic activity that has in common elements such as a multiplicity of informal (and occasionally illegal) personal arrangements among bureaucrats and between them and superiors and clientele. Perhaps "no formal organization will operate effectively without an accompanying informal organization."[27] Efficient administration demands that bureaucrats adapt their behavior to changing and particular circumstances.

The institutions of blat, shturmovshchina, and the tolkach are indicators of widespread Soviet informalism. The overall pattern of administration in the Soviet Union is non-Weberian. Its striking general feature is the presence of parallel and even competing chains of command engaged in the performance of similar, or often even the same, functions. Such a pattern is highly useful for purposes of political control as long as the Politburo (political bureau) retains ultimate control of each hierarchy. The Soviet Union's rejection of the "monistic concept" of bureaucracy may have been beneficial to economic development, which requires the presence of a "prefect"-like person or organization (the Communist Party in the Soviet case) to establish effective coordination in dynamic programs of development.[28]

On the other hand, some heavy managerial responsibilities--maintenance, efficient operation, and the sale of quality products--could be well served by some additional degree of routine. Some informalism is, therefore, not conducive to better functioning of an organization. Both kinds can have political significance because they are unapproved, indicate the presence of conflict, and involve the positing of alternatives to official or top-level programs, policies, and assumptions.

Political Implications

Informalism in a bureaucracy's own interests may have political meaning. Rules cannot be applied abstractly; in particular cases, reference must be made to political and social values. In adhering to values, politics enters as political ideology or political act or alliance. And bureaucratic interaction with the larger society is inevitably a political process. Public decisions and their implementation are involved with power and its application. As Wallace Sayre writes: "The experience of discretionary power, the making of value choices, is a characteristic and increasing function of administrators and bureaucrats; they are thus importantly engaged in politics."[29]

This exists along with a politics of bureaucracy, or a "politics of the lower level." As Gordon Tullock points out, "political activity, as such, is quantitatively far more significant in almost any of the . . . large organizations than it is among the strictly limited group of individuals assumed to be engaged in national politics at any one time. Traditional political theory seems to have neglected, in a relative sense, this extremely important 'politics of bureaucracy. . . .'"[30] Similarly, Brian Chapman notes: "The boundary line between politics and administration is not at all clearly drawn. . . . The determination of ends, the choice of means, the balance of social forces, are the stuff of politics. In these terms it is clear that some civil servants are engaged in politics."[31] In other words, politics and administration are interwoven and interdependent aspects of the larger political process.

Bureaucracy's "domination of the output end of the political conversion process" results in the dependence of all other governmental structures upon it. In effect, the "outputs" fashioned by a bureaucracy become "inputs" affecting the political system as a whole and sometimes, of course, acting in the bureaucracy's favor.[32] Bureaucracies can even act against the wishes and policies of political leaderships.[33] This applies also to the industrial bureaucracy of the USSR. The ministerial bureaucracy's stubborn but quiet refusal to implement the present economic reform as it was presented at the top levels of the leadership testifies to the existence of political authority and power in the Soviet industrial bureaucracy.

This study presents and analyzes the way in which the independent authority and power of the planning and ministerial bureaucracy and the industrial managers were applied during the implemental stage of the reform, and states its political and administrative significance. In so doing, the issue of the relative weights to be assigned in the outcome to the conflicting demands of bureaucracy, ideology, and science is discussed. Each pulls in a different direction and with a different intent. "Bureaucracy" emphasizes the self-defined needs of the operating "bureaus" and groupings in industrial administration. "Ideology" assigns priority to the continuation of central planning under the direction of the Party leadership; the emphasis upon growth,[34] particularly of the means of production; and

INTRODUCTION 11

the relegation to the background of the desires of consumers and the claims of efficiency. "Science" emphasizes the values of rationality, efficiency, specialized knowledge, and an economy in which central planning no longer strives for total coverage but instead supplies only periodic and essential corrective stimuli.

The political leadership ("politics"?) eventually is faced with a general resolution of these three kinds of demands that does not fully agree with its goals in the initiation stage of the reform--in other words, a compromise. The question of beginning a new reform arises, including the prospect of beginning the political cycle anew.

Despite its effect on policy, an explicit political opposition is not present within Soviet industrial management. Its existence would presuppose the defense of general principles, not an overall concern of Soviet management personnel.[35] But in the USSR, managerial actions that lead administrative personnel into effective patterns of mutual responsibility and of planning and acting in concert, independent of the Party apparatus, are as political as opposition based on the protection and furtherance of a general principle. If an "instrumental" system serving long-standing social patterns operates in violation of its norms as expressed in the unstructured ideology, no or few significant effects may result. On the other hand, if an ideological system with a few overriding goals regularly operates in a deviant or unspecified manner, the effects may well be of profound importance. Through time the ideology may become so weakened and distorted that the political system may be transformed into an instrumental one. When the process of change has reached this point, the political leadership that formerly provided guidance in accordance with the ideology either has to find a new basis for its dominant role or submit to a relationship of equality with other groups.[36] It is therefore not surprising that the Party apparatus has brought the Party as an organization directly into the implementation of the reform as a counterweight to the managerial bureaucracy.

Political Culture and Administrative Tradition

Throughout this book there are various indications of an identifiable Russian pattern of response to political, social, and organizational questions. Joseph La Palombara emphasizes the long-term continuity of political and administrative forms and practices, noting that "traditional ways have amazing survival power; they are capable of adapting to even the most radical changes in formal organizational structure."[37] Certainly the shift from tsarism to Bolshevism is a radical change, yet some bureaucrats served both--in the same offices or manner. So-called bourgeois specialists "remained an important element in the Soviet industrial establishment throughout the

1930's" and retained "virtually monopolistic control over many of the most fundamental 'premises' of policy decisions." Even instances of patterning Soviet administrative decrees upon tsarist decrees were noted.[38] Lenin's comment that the Soviet state apparatus was the old tsarist bureaucratic machine anointed with a little "Soviet holy oil" seems most appropriate. The present Soviet bureaucratic resistance to official directives also has historical roots.[39]

The Soviet pattern of parallelism in structures and functions has a Russian historical origin, perhaps originally stemming from the great dualism of Tatar and native rule. There has been a continuing tendency in Russian political history to use more than one agency to cope with the same question. Before 1917, Bernard Pares wrote of the bureaucracy, "There is overlapping of every kind."[40]

Elites and Interest Groups

In order for the reform to be implemented, each key grouping in industry has to be brought "on board," because the reform presupposes change in their collective behavior. Politically significant groupings now exist "with which the governing elite must bargain. . . ."[41] We shall show some of the features of the operation of specialized groups in the implemental or "rule-application" stage of the reform and discuss the configuration of power relationships now existing among them.

Public Administration and Administrative Reform

Considerations involving administration and administrative change are also taken into account. These are numerous, since "at its fullest range, public administration embraces every area and activity governed by public policy. . . ."[42] A major such consideration here is administrative reform, which realistically can be defined as "the artificial inducement of administrative transformation against resistance," a form of "power politics in action. . . ."[43]

An attempt is made here to ascertain which of the elements and "rules" of effective administrative reform have been adopted and which violated in this case, and also to state what the implications may be for other attempts at administrative reform in the Soviet Union.

Having presented the theoretical foundations, the study moves on to discussion of previous attempts at reform, the original official model of this reform, and an interpretation of its development and political significance.

NOTES

1. See Michael Ellman, Economic Reform in the Soviet Union (London: Political and Economic Planning, 1969); Theodore Frankel, "Economic Reform: A Tentative Appraisal," Problems of Communism 16, no. 3 (May-June 1967): 29-41; and Gertrude Schroeder, "Soviet Economic 'Reforms': A Study in Contradictions," Soviet Studies 20, no. 1 (July 1968): 1-21; and "Soviet Economic Reform at an Impasse," Problems of Communism 20, no. 4 (July-August 1971): 36-46.
2. Robert A. Solo, Economic Organizations and Social Systems (Indianapolis: Bobbs-Merrill, 1967), p. 101.
3. Jerald Hage and Michael Aiken, Social Change in Complex Organizations (New York: Random House, 1970), p. 100.
4. See Gordon Tullock, The Politics of Bureaucracy (Washington, D.C.: Public Affairs Press, 1965), p. 10.
5. See Rush V. Greenslade, "The Soviet Economic System in Transition," in U.S. Congress, Joint Economic Committee, New Directions in the Soviet Economy (Washington, D.C.: U.S. Government Printing Office, 1966), Pt. I, 13; and Schroeder, "Soviet Economic Reform at an Impasse," p. 46.
6. See Theodore H. von Laue, Sergei Witte and the Industrialization of Russia (New York: Columbia University Press, 1963), p. 144.
7. Robert Conquest, in U.S. Senate, Subcommittee on National Security and International Operations, International Negotiation (Washington, D.C.: U.S. Government Printing Office, 1971), Pt. 6, p. 189.
8. See Robert W. Campbell, Soviet Economic Power (2nd ed.; Boston: Houghton Mifflin Co., 1966), p. 105; Alec Nove, The Soviet Economy: An Introduction (rev. ed.; New York: Praeger, 1966), p. 149; Leon Smolinski, "The Soviet Economy: In Search of a Pattern," Survey 59 (April 1966): 98; and Marshall I. Goldman, The Soviet Economy (Englewood Cliffs, N.J.: Prentice-Hall, 1968), pp. 131-32.
9. See Zbigniew K. Brzezinski, "The Soviet Political System: Transformation or Degeneration," Problems of Communism 15, no. 1 (January-February 1966): 9, note; included in his Ideology and Power in Soviet Politics (rev. ed.; New York: Praeger, 1967), pp. 95-127.
10. See John K. Galbraith, The New Industrial State (Boston: Houghton Mifflin Co., 1967), pp. 107-08; and Conquest, op. cit., pp. 187-89.
11. Jerry Hough, "The Soviet Elite: I," Problems of Communism 16, no. 1 (January-February 1967): 31.
12. See Abraham Katz, The Politics of Economic Reform in the Soviet Union (New York: Praeger, 1972), p. 190; this is a published version of "The Politics of Economic Reform in the Soviet Union"

(Cambridge, Mass.: Center for International Affairs, Harvard University, May 1967) (mimeographed), see pp. 632-34. See also Moshe Lewin, Political Undercurrents in Soviet Economic Debates (Princeton, N.J.: Princeton University Press, 1974).

13. Arnold Toynbee, "Sorokin's Philosophy of History," in Philip J. Allen, ed., Pitirim A. Sorokin in Review (Durham, N.C.: Duke University Press, 1963), pp. 93-94.

14. See Marshall D. Shulman, "The Future of Soviet Studies in the United States," Slavic Review 29, no. 3 (September 1970): 583-84.

15. See Karl Schiller, "Can Economics and Politics Be Treated Separately?" German Tribune, January 21, 1971, p. 10 (reprinted from Der Volkswirt, December 23, 1970); and Joseph Berliner, "Some Propositions on Technological Progress," September 1970 (mimeographed: Cambridge, Mass.).

16. See Robert K. Merton, Social Theory and Social Structure (rev. and enl. ed.; Glencoe, Ill.: Free Press, 1957), p. 369; and Neal Gross, Ward Mason, and Alexander McEachern, Explorations in Role Analysis: Studies of the School Superintendency Role (New York: John Wiley & Sons, 1958), esp. pp. 51-53 and Figs. 4-2 and 4-3. Also see Bruce J. Biddle and Edwin J. Thomas, eds., Role Theory: Concepts and Research (New York: John Wiley & Sons, 1966).

17. A. N. Kosygin, "Ob uluchshenii upravleniia promyshlennost'iu, sovershenstvovanii planirovaniia i usilenii ekonomicheskogo stimulirovaniia promyshlennogo proizvodstva," Pravda, September 28, 1965, p. 4.

18. B. Sukharevskii, "Predpriiatie i material'noe stimulirovanie," Ekonomicheskaia gazeta 49 (December 1965): 12. This may be B. M. Sukharevskii, one of the two deputy chairmen of the State Committee for Questions of Wages and Labor. Emphasis in original.

19. A. Rumiantsev, "Ekonomicheskaia nauka i upravlenie narodnym khoziaistvom," Kommunist 1 (January 1966): 42.

20. Jeremy Azrael, Managerial Power and Soviet Politics (Cambridge, Mass.: Harvard University Press, 1966), p. 104.

21. See Victor Thompson, Modern Organization: A General Theory (New York: Alfred A. Knopf, 1961), ch. 5, "Conflict"; Samuel P. Huntington, "Interservice Competition and the Political Roles of the Armed Services," American Political Science Review 55, no. 1 (March 1961): 40-52; Robert Presthus, The Organizational Society (New York: Vintage Books, 1962), pp. 57-58; and Anthony Down, Inside Bureaucracy (Boston: Little, Brown & Co., 1967), pp. 50-54, 216, 276.

22. Downs, op. cit., p. 216. Emphasis in original.

23. Robert B. Denhardt, "The Organization as a Political System," Western Political Quarterly 24, no. 4 (December 1971): 678.

See also Herbert Kaufman, "Organization Theory and Political Theory," American Political Science Review 58, no. 1 (March 1964): 11, referring to Norton Long, "The Administrative Organization as a Political System," in S. Mailick and E. H. van Ness, eds., Concepts and Issues in Administrative Behavior (Englewood Cliffs, N.J.: Prentice-Hall, 1962), p. 125; and Joseph S. Berliner, "Bureaucratic Conservatism and Creativity in the Soviet Economy," paper delivered at the 1966 meeting of the American Political Association, New York City, September 1966, p. 17.

24. See Alfred Meyer, The Soviet Political System: An Interpretation (New York: Random House, 1965), p. 210; Merle Fainsod, How Russia Is Ruled (rev. ed.; Cambridge, Mass.: Harvard University Press, 1963), p. 579; and Jerry F. Hough, "The Bureaucratic Model and the Nature of the Soviet System," Journal of Comparative Administration 5, no. 2 (August 1973): 134-67.

25. Michel Collinet, "Une sociologie du pouvoir sovietique," Contrat social, September 1957, p. 248; quoted in Eugene Zaleski, Planning for Economic Growth in the Soviet Union, 1918-1932, trans. and ed. by Marie-Christine MacAndrew and G. Warren Nutter (Chapel Hill: University of North Carolina Press, 1971), pp. 296-97.

26. See Martin Albrow, Bureaucracy (New York: Praeger, 1970), pp. 61-66.

27. Herbert Simon, Administrative Behavior (2nd ed.; New York: Macmillan, 1961), pp. 148-49.

28. Jerry Hough, The Soviet Prefects (Cambridge, Mass.: Harvard University Press, 1969), pp. 292, 296; "The Bureaucratic Model," pp. 154, 161; and "The Prerequisites of Areal Deconcentration: The Soviet Experience," in James J. Heaphey, ed., Spatial Dimensions of Development Administration (Durham, N.C.: Duke University Press, 1971), pp. 132-75.

29. Wallace S. Sayre, "Premises of Public Administration," Public Administration Review 18, no. 2 (Spring 1958): 104; quoted in Felix A. Nigro, Modern Public Administration (New York: Harper & Row, 1965), p. 15.

30. Tullock, loc. cit.

31. Brian Chapman, The Profession of Government (London: Allen & Unwin, 1959), pp. 273-75.

32. Gabriel A. Almond and G. Bingham Powell, Comparative Politics (Boston and Toronto: Little, Brown & Co., 1966), pp. 157-58; and Fred W. Riggs, Administration in Developing Countries (Boston: Houghton Mifflin Co., 1964), p. 19.

33. See Peter Woll, American Bureaucracy (New York: W. W. Norton & Co., 1963), p. 161; and Richard E. Neustadt, Presidential Power (New York: John Wiley & Sons, 1964), ch. 3.

34. Abram Bergson, The Economics of Soviet Planning (New Haven and London: Yale University Press, 1964), p. 7; and

"Development Under Two Systems: Comparative Productivity Growth Since 1950," World Politics 23, no. 4 (July 1971): 605.

35. Jeremy R. Azrael, "Politics and Management," Survey 49 (October 1963): 99.

36. See Z. K. Brzezinski and S. P. Huntington, Political Power: USA/USSR (New York: Viking Press, 1964), pp. 75-76.

37. Joseph La Palombara, ed., Bureaucracy and Political Development (Princeton, N.J.: Princeton University Press, 1963), p. 13.

38. Barrington Moore, Soviet Politics (Cambridge, Mass.: Harvard University Press, 1951), p. 163. Moore's information comes from Alimov and Studenikin in Ye. B. Pashukanis, ed., 15 let Sovetskogo stroitelstva (Moscow, 1932).

39. Michael Florinsky, The End of the Russian Empire (New York: Collier, 1965), p. 14; and H. H. Gerth and C. Wright Mills, eds., From Max Weber (New York: Oxford University Press, 1958), p. 234.

40. Bernard Pares, Russia: Between Reform and Revolution (New York: Schocken, 1962), p. 136.

41. See H. Gordon Skilling, "Groups in Soviet Politics: Some Hypotheses," in H. Gordon Skilling and Franklyn Griffiths, eds., Interest Groups in Soviet Politics (Princeton, N.J.: Princeton University Press, 1971), p. 19.

42. Fritz M. Marx, ed., Elements of Public Administration (Englewood Cliffs, N.J.: Prentice-Hall, 1959), p. 6. See also Gerald E. Caiden, The Dynamics of Public Administration: Guidelines to Current Transformations in Theory and Practice (New York: Holt, 1971), pp. 12-22.

43. Gerald E. Caiden, Administrative Reform (Chicago: Aldine, 1969), pp. 8-9.

CHAPTER 1

THE ORIGINS AND CONCEPT OF THE REFORM

Although the economic reform was formally announced in 1965, it had actually been "simmering" for some time. It could have been announced earlier, the leadership and various other interests willing. Yevsei Liberman's ideas, often considered the guiding spirit of the reforms, first appeared in print in the mid-1950s.[1] However, they became widely publicized in the controlled press only in 1962.

THE OLD SYSTEM

Since the situation in industry and industrial management had been replete with difficulties, urgency was lent to the introduction of the reform. Most of the examples below are drawn from post-reform Soviet sources, and thus provide some candid "inside" views of how serious conditions actually were. The leadership may have encouraged the publication of such information in order to make it more difficult for anti-reform groups to oppose implementation.

General and Basic Difficulties

Generally stated, the difficulty was essentially systemic in nature and stemmed from Stalin's views and actions. As one scholar describes it:

> The economy was treated as a single gigantic factory in which agriculture provided manpower as a kind of raw material for industry. Industry itself gave little or nothing in return, and concentrated

overwhelmingly on the production of capital equipment for its own use. Food and amenities were produced in quantities sufficient to keep the wheels turning, but consumer satisfaction as an end in itself had no place in the scheme of things.[2]

This resulted in an organizational restraint upon the economy. "An unchanging line of products with an unchanging technology" could be changed only by transforming economic organization.[3] The promise of this appeared in Premier Kosygin's report to a Central Committee plenum on September 27, 1965, the official announcement of the reform. In it he says, "The forms of management, planning and incentive now in effect in industry no longer conform to present-day technical-economic conditions and to the level of development of productive forces."[4] Kosygin also criticizes the financing of investments by the state through outright grants. As remedies he proposes the substitution of long-term credits and the introduction of a charge on fixed capital drawn from enterprise profits (that is, the introduction of interest--a revisionist act) to foster economic responsibility at the enterprise level. The decline in output per unit of capital of 17 percent from 1959 to 1965 alone must have prompted thoughts of reform.[5]

The prominent economist L. Leont'ev enumerated some of the past behavioral "shortcomings" of the Soviet economy: the "underestimation of economic methods of management and economic accountability, the incomplete use of material and psychological incentives, and a subjectivist approach to the solution of a number of economic problems."[6] The chief of a department of Gosplan said: "It is well-known that during the recent years the growth rate of production output and the productivity of labor have decreased somewhat. The growth rate of the national income has also slowed; its dimensions with reference to a ruble of fixed capital have also decreased."[7]

The situation was not amenable to solution by means of the principles then underlying the operation of the economy. The Seven-Year Plan came to a near standstill in 1963. "The steady drop in the growth rate of production, the diminishing effectiveness of investments and the chronic supply difficulties showed that the crisis was a built-in feature of the economic system itself."[8] V. Kantorovich, the eminent mathematical economist, notes that during 1962-64 there were a "slowdown in the growth rates of industrial output" and a "decrease in returns per unit of assets expressed in a gradual decline in output" that "alarmed" economists.[9]

Undoubtedly the most critical comments on the economic system by a Soviet source are those attributed to A. Aganbegian, a corresponding member of the USSR Academy of Sciences and the director of the Novosibirsk Economics Institute. He says that the principal features of the USSR's economic difficulties are two: the "mistaken direction" of economic development and the fact that the systems of planning, incentives, and management do not correspond to the economy's real requirements. According to Aganbegian:

> Our systems of planning, establishing incentives and managing industry were developed in the 1930's. Ever since then nothing has changed except the names given things. . . . The extreme centralization and the absence of economic democracy have a very serious effect on our economy.
> . . . . . .
> . . . our prices and our monetary-value relationships serve no purpose at all. The thing held most important is centralized distribution.[10]

He adds that there is an "absolute lack of information," the figures released by the Central Statistical Administration being worthless.

Caught up in this ultimately untenable situation were the industrial managers. They squirmed as best they could, often with some success by dint of scheming and hard work, to meet (or appear to meet) the goals set for them. A great deal of "informalist" behavior, some of it illegal, existed. The manager had to strike a precarious balance to be "successful."[11]

The Former Manager-Superior Relationship

Four subjects require examination here: sovnarkhozy (economic councils), planning, Gosbank, and the Ministry of Finance. The negative aspects of the economic councils' operation outweighed the positive, particularly their fostering of the common problem of mestnichestvo ("localism"). As Kosygin, seemingly in bleak exasperation, put it: "Guidance of a branch of industry that was a unified whole in the production-technical respect was broken up among numerous economic regions and turned out to be totally disrupted. The branches seemingly 'dissolved' in the economies of the economic regions."[12]

In other words, in a "multi-stage system of management" (mnogostupenchatyi) the center lost firm control of the extremities through the interposition of intermediate authority pursuing its own interests. Brezhnev also made several rather specific criticisms of the sovnarkhozy, pointing out that the guidance of research and design was too separate from production, the sovnarkhozy were interested only in their "own" consumers and not in inter-republic deliveries, and (of some political implication) the leaders of some sovnarkhozy were trying to organize production of some equipment in regions other than their own.[13] They were building up horizontal, interregional linkages independent of the center and, perhaps, of Party control. Finally, the state committees established for general coordination were limited to nonbinding recommendations. The ministerial pattern was therefore dusted off and reestablished.

As for planning, the situation is powerfully described by the deputy chairman of the RSFSR Gosplan, who says, "At present an enterprise often fulfills the role of an executor of 'alien' plans, quite frequently [splosh' i riadom] not having any regard for the results." Liberman states the former ruling formula as "fulfill the plan at any cost."[14] This was a "displacement of goals" with devastating results for efficiency and quality.

Aganbegian again is highly critical, writing:

> How are economic plans worked out and drawn up? . . . in the regional economic councils and in the republics. . . . Then [they] arrive at the USSR Gosplan which in actual practice takes no account of them and replaces them with a plan of its own which often has nothing in common with the actual plans drawn up by the sovnarkhozy and the republics. As a rule the Gosplany call for rates of development three times greater than those desired by the local organs.[15]

In the former system of planning, contracts exerted little influence on plan formation, since they were not of primary importance. Kosygin also points out that plans were often unsubstantiated and needlessly changed, with the major index, gross volume of production (the VAL) failing to direct enterprises toward the production of needed and high-quality goods.[16]

Another problem of planning was the inability to produce economies of scale. For example, plenty of crude steel was produced; but there was a limit to the amount of high-quality steel products, partly because of the failure to include enough production of specialized processing equipment in the plans. The great investment in lumbering and sawmills somehow resulted in a shortage of furniture. Technical innovation was not going forward because enterprise managers hoarded reserves in anticipation of the planners' continual practice of "ratcheting" plans upward each year. A. Birman notes realistically, "the interests of the individual, the enterprise, and society on the whole again had begun to come into conflict. . . . It became obvious that a reform was needed."[17]

ORIGINS AND CONCEPT OF REFORM

The former operation of Gosbank, the State Bank, is summed up well by an official of the bank who says that formerly bank control (kontrol' rublem) was permeated with "administrative elements" and its effectiveness was low. It was ineffective, of course, partly because the planned tasks of the enterprise were not always linked. Also, the measures taken by the bank to reduce the incidence of nonpayment often did not give the desired results because the "guilty" enterprises felt no economic consequences.[18]

As for the Ministry of Finance, it exercised a strict and stultifying regulation of the staffs of enterprises and their budgets.[19] A director could change the amounts of administrative and managerial expenses by no more than 10 percent.

The Former Manager-Communist Party Relationship

Deficiencies existed in the operations of Party organizations in industry--for example, "family relations" or mutually advantageous but informal alliances and criminal corruption. "It . . . happens . . . that a lack of principle is displayed . . . by entire primary Party organizations. The atmosphere of mutual tolerance that prevails in them has a pernicious effect on people and activities."[20] Also, there was a persistent tendency for Party organizations to take over, at least temporarily, some operational functions of management, thereby reducing managerial initiative over the long run. This was particularly true, of course, when it seemed possible that the plan would not be fulfilled.[21] Despite the close supervision of enterprise operations by local Party organizations, the Party was ultimately ineffective in reversing the tide of problems plaguing industrial management. It was engaged in a task beyond its capabilities.[22]

The system under which managers operated made great demands upon them, furnished them with supplies insufficient for meeting those demands, and threatened them with punishment at every turn. In addition, their narrow engineering education did not provide them with the knowledge and attitudes upon which a flexible, entrepreneurial pattern of managerial action could rest. Besides this, many managers and managerial personnel were not properly placed and motivated. Kosygin noted the existence of "major shortcomings" and "serious disproportions" in the training of cadres for industry, and said that cadres were often incorrectly used, adding that managers engaged in too many discussions and too much paper work.[23]

Problems of operation also existed. A most significant and prevalent example is that of shturmovshchina ("storming"), the practice of cramming much of the plant's work into a short period at the end of the month, when,

> ... in the last-minute rush period, no one cares about quality, just so long as the products pass the control check. ... There is simply no time to inspect every part with meticulous care. This would slow down output, which means plan fulfillment. And again, if you reject the output, the program will go unfulfilled. ... After all, our earnings are dependent upon plan fulfillment.[24]

The deputy chairman ot TsSU (Central Statistical Administration) wrote:

> What an evil nonrhythmical production can be. It often happened that many enterprises yielded 15-20 percent of the monthly output in the first ten days of the month, 25-35 percent in the second ten days, and up to 50-60 percent of the total monthly output in the third ten-day period.[25]

These descriptions indicate how Sisyphean industrial labor was. There was also widespread neglect of actual costs, and additional rigidities arose from the prohibition against managers' disposing of excess material, equipment, and even above-plan profits without permission.

The Former Manager-Subordinate Relationship

A most serious problem was that of material incentives for workers and white-collar employees. "The system of incentives that has been in use until now does not in its essence strengthen the interest of the enterprise in the raising of planned goals."[26] Because of this the manager's capacity to obtain better work from his labor force was limited.

The Former Manager-Manager Relationship

The manager was not allowed to establish stable economic relations with suppliers and customers, either state agencies or other enterprises. Since he could not do this freely, he was unable to find the best or most prompt supplier and the most payment-conscious customer; and thus he often had to deal with enterprises and organizations that had no interest in businesslike relations. As a result he had to buy standardized and sometimes inappropriate supplies, and he sold to customers who were as dissatisfied with him as he often was with his suppliers.

Contracts, though they existed, were not meaningful economically because they were made upon direction by superior but not knowledgeable authorities; and they were often violated by both these authorities and by the contracting enterprises. The real powers in the relationship were outsiders, the sovnarkhozy, the state supply agencies, and occasionally <u>Gosarbitrazh</u> (the State Arbitration system). The manager-manager relationship was one in which great constraints were operative over the main feature--supply.

In summary, a general review of the Soviet manager's main relationships prior to 1966 indicates significant, sometimes almost overwhelming, difficulties and highlights the atmosphere of massive but still partly futile effort made by managers to perform their tasks. Industrial management could no longer continue to deliver even the limited successes that had been its strength. As a result, reform became necessary.

EARLIER STIRRINGS OF REFORM

The Late Stalin Years

Despite Stalin's paranoiac and rigid hold over the processes of Soviet politics, even in his time there were hints of proposals for economic reform, some of which resulted in muted but serious controversy at high levels. The execution of N. A. Voznesensky in 1949 and the demotion of Kosygin in 1946 are examples. Part of Voznesensky's position is similar to aspects of the present reform--"that a 'socialist' economy could be relied on to balance itself reliably under market conditions, with the planners accepting a market verdict on whether or not a project was uneconomic."[27]

Significantly, the events of that time have a living link to the present reform: Premier Kosygin. He probably was involved in Voznesensky's plans, and he has a central position in the present reform. He has had long involvement with light industry; and during 1954 he seems to have been part of the pro-consumer program grouping with Georgi Malenkov, Anastas Mikoyan, and I. Benediktov. This was the period of the New Course, which stressed, within a context of relaxing Stalinist rule, a rise in the Soviet standard of living. It would have been necessary to introduce basic economic changes in order to continue.[28]

1953-64

After the death of Stalin, "the interests of rulers and managers again converged to set the stage for reform."[29] The managers desired freedom from terror and freedom to make the decisions demanded by their functional roles. Some of the Party leaders had come to see that some decentralization of administration was necessary. Between March 1953 and the industrial reorganization enacted on May 10, 1957, several moves were made to put industrial administration on a more rational and meaningful basis. The result was to transfer some operational decision-making downward, a modification of the Stalinist model although not a departure from it.

The fall of Malenkov (February 1955) was the beginning of a restriction of the process. Malenkov lost to Khrushchev, the Party's First Secretary. Leonard Schapiro, commenting on this struggle, writes that ". . . in a sense this conflict was . . . a conflict between the party machine and the government machine, in which the party machine won."[30]

The victory was impermanent. The year 1957 saw the advent of a new decentralized pattern of industrial reorganization that was characterized by the great restriction of central planning authority, the breakup of many of the industrial ministries, and the formation of sovnarkhozy. This significant limitation upon the authority of the state bureaucracy was part of a militant populistic attack by Khrushchev on the entire line of Soviet society. The druzhiny (people's militia), the comrades' courts, and penalties such as exile and shooting were emphasized. The security and authority of industrial managers and other state personnel were threatened.

However, there was no corresponding victory over the technical questions determining productivity of industry, despite some understanding on Khrushchev's part of what total victory would entail, as indicated by his stress on the production of chemicals and fertilizers and his virulent and ironic attacks upon single-minded "metal-eaters" and rigid bureaucrats. In his report on the new Party program at the 22nd Party Congress in 1961, Khrushchev said:

> Our task . . . is to make ever greater use of and to improve the finance and credit levers, ruble control, prices, and profits. We must enhance the role of profits, of profitability. It is in the interest of better plan fulfillment that enterprises be given greater opportunity to determine the use of their profits, to make broader use of them for encouraging their collectives to do good work and for expanding production.[31]

Despite the similarity to the reform of 1965, this was said before the public emphasis on Liberman's proposals, which included the points made by Khrushchev. It now appears that Liberman was more a creature of policy than an individual of independent significance. The much-publicized reappearance of Liberman's microeconomic proposals in the issue of Pravda of September 9, 1962, was followed by the supportive publication of a 1918 document by Lenin conveniently "discovered" only then.[32] Khrushchev had rediscovered the thread of reform.

The Liberman proposals were straightforward and even simple, except in the consequences of their implementation for the power of the Party and state bureaucracies. Liberman proposed the following: the enterprise incentive system would be based upon profits, with the rules governing enterprise operation and performance reflecting this; although enterprises would continue to be told what to produce, they could fill in their plans and make contracts with other enterprises themselves; the central authorities would not prescribe plans for labor, wages, costs, or productivity; central decisions relating to any enterprise would be in effect for years and thus not subject to frequent changes (to encourage the adoption of ambitious plans and innovational projects); and the enterprise incentive fund would be used for enterprise investment and bonuses. V. Nemchinov, the influential academician, supported Liberman's proposals and added two suggestions: a charge on enterprises' use of capital and the elimination of the centralized system of allocating materials. The entire "package," if adopted, would undoubtedly have had "the double effect of encouraging more rational behavior at the enterprise level and removing from the central planners much of the crushing burden of current work."[33] The Kosygin reform, as announced in 1965, included some of these provisions.

Kernels of the future reforms were in evidence. The decentralized nonsystem of sovnarkhozy was undergoing a hesitant but obvious recentralization, thus already revealing, though in shadowy outline only, the future major elements of the reform of 1965: a freer enterprise and manager operating within a centralized nationwide framework of industrial administration. Recentralization was prompted by the need to counter a mushrooming of mestnichestvo that developed as part of the operating style of the sovnarkhozy. A series of organizational shake-ups ensued, beginning in 1960.[34] By late 1962, except for the dualism in the Party at the local levels and the continued dominance of Khrushchev (though the latter was not secure after the Cuban "adventurism" and "capitulationism"), the stage was almost set for the introduction of the "new model" economic organization. All that was necessary was some experimentation, the floating of a tide of "Libermanism," and the running out of

Khrushchev's political stock--a process that culminated in his removal in October 1964.

Khrushchev's last year in power, 1964, saw further moves toward reform, including various experiments in which enterprises operated in a situation even more of a departure from past practices than the actual reform of 1965. The pilot projects at the Bolshevichka and Mayak plants were the examples most publicized. This experiment linked two concepts new to Soviet economic history: the use of profitability as a main "success indicator" and the use of consumers' preferences to guide the direct negotiation of contracts between producers and retailers.[35]

In August 1964, Pravda published for "discussion" an important article by academician V. A. Trapeznikov that was a signal for a third, more active, phase of "Libermanism." He called for

> ... replacing the set of obligatory norms governing the manager's every step by a system of economic levers that will channel the work of the enterprise. The manager must be provided with extensive financial powers and freed from petty tutelage, but also required to ensure economical operation of the enterprise and high quality of output; the cardinal indicator [profit] will compel him to cut down on excesses and seek out all possible ways to reduce the cost of output.[36]

Thus, Trapeznikov's article was an accurate reflection of the content of the 1965 reforms, even giving a hint of the abolition of the sovnarkhozy and the reestablishment of the branch system of ministerial chains of command. It clearly indicated that the reform was well-developed intellectually and widely accepted in important political and other circles a year or more prior to its formal launching; and also showed how slowly the Soviet bureaucratic mill grinds. However, Khrushchev's removal was necessary for the new departure to begin. He would have hobbled the reform with stronger Party controls than those that materialized.

The same period, 1964-65, saw the emergence of ideas that went beyond those allowed in the official version of the reform. For example, some discussion of workers' rights and powers vis-a-vis management appeared, and the idea of workers participating in the selection of managerial personnel was raised. The Yugoslav workers' councils seem to have triggered a response in the Soviet Union. The idea of "direct production relations" between enterprises in the machine-building industries was also broached in print by mid-1965, as were the ideas of introducing political science as a discipline, having more than one candidate on a ballot for a single office, and increasing the number of people's assessors (in effect, the idea of a jury).[37] Such suggestions indicate the political impact of the atmosphere of experimentation. It is evident, therefore, that an economic reform with profits as the main success indicator was emerging a year and more prior to its announcement.

Announcement

Premier Kosygin's report at the September 1965 plenum of the Central Committee was both an official announcement of, and an authoritative commentary upon, the introduction of the reform, although much was left unclear. The day after the publication of Kosygin's report, a resolution of the Central Committee plenum ordering implementation was published. The sovnarkhozy were soon dissolved, and the industrial ministries reestablished. Later in October a new enterprise "statute" appeared, containing a new set of basic guidelines for the operation of industrial enterprises. This was followed in January 1966 by the placing of 43 enterprises under the new system; the issuance, in February 1966, of detailed instructions on incentives; and the transfer, in the spring and summer of 1966, of additional enterprises to the reformed system.[38] As a result, by the end of 1966, 673 enterprises employing 2 million employees had been transferred.[39]

Although 28 new ministries were formally created, in many cases it was an exercise in renaming, although real change did occur. About 50 sovnarkhozy, each with more than a thousand functionaries, were abolished; and in some cases the personnel was reassigned. Many of the ministries, however, had existed all along as state committees. In such cases an upgrading in status, pay, and privileges took place. Only five of the "new" ministries were genuinely new. The change-over cannot be viewed as part of a power struggle within the Party leadership. Only eight heads of all the top-level organizations involved were replaced.[40]

The statute (polozhenie) on the industrial enterprise, a document of fundamental legal importance and constituting the major directive of the reform, is an outline of mutual rights and obligations for agencies in industry; but although many of the articles are not of much importance for either the functions or the relationships of the manager, in a formal sense

> The Statute is an advance in several ways. It gives managers more room for initiative, enables them to manipulate their working

capital . . ., urges them to encourage direct
horizontal links with other enterprises, and frees
their hand concerning average wages and number
of workers.[41]

But an implicit limitation on implementation arose before the end of 1965: Only the most efficient enterprises had been picked for early transfer. "Among those transferred were the best enterprises."[42]

Thus, the implementation was governed by an air of both reality and unreality. Reality, or a concern for good operation, dictated which enterprises were initially switched over to the new system; unreality, or an unwillingness to face the economy's need for sweeping changes, underlay the caution. The reform's proponents, by selecting the better enterprises, may have been trying to make certain that the chances for failure were minimal, thus seeking to avoid conservatives' criticisms.

The first actual shift of a group of enterprises (among which those mentioned above probably can be numbered) was announced at the end of January 1966. This group consisted of 43 enterprises in 17 industrial ministries. The emphasis was on heavy industry and reflects two factors: the previous long-term favoring of group A industry and a desire to improve the productivity of heavy industry still further. Despite propaganda to the contrary, a primary goal of reform was actually the improvement of heavy industry. Thus Stalinist tradition lived on, suffering only modification.

Other difficulties in implementation soon became apparent. In early 1966 the USSR Council of Ministers noted that more care was to be taken during future change-overs of enterprises. Mention was made of "insufficient thought" in the transfer of the first 43. The difficulties involved supply and planning arrangements. But by this time service enterprises, such as railroads, were also undergoing reform; and a general process of extension of the reform to various kinds of operating economic organization was in effect. By May 1966 it was revealed that henceforth ministries themselves would shift enterprises to the new arrangement.[43]

By mid-1966 at least 653 enterprises had been converted--not a large number of the Soviet Union's approximately 45,000 industrial enterprises but still a significant figure, since those 653 enterprises employed 10 percent of the Soviet industrial-production staff and accounted for more than 12 percent of total industrial production.[44]

Despite this noticeable degree of progress, further advance, particularly the transfer of entire ministries, had to await the revision of wholesale prices on July 1, 1967. Other factors standing in the way of large-scale implementation included attempts to incorporate inefficient enterprises and the increase in military expenditures that began in 1965.

Since mid-1966 the process of adding enterprises to the reform has continued, but with less publicity. By the beginning of 1967 the enterprises of the Instrument Making, Means of Automation, and Control Systems branch (often presented as a model) were completely transferred; and the administrative links of this ministry--its chief administrations and the entire ministerial apparatus--began to be transferred as well. The goal was to give ministerial officials a direct stake in the economic results of the enterprises' work. Officially, the reform has also been "fully applied" to the Turbine- and Boiler-Building and Textiles branches.[45] In January 1969 3,000 enterprises were transferred, and at that time all the enterprises of four ministries were working according to the new pattern. Several territorial administrations of Gossnab (State Committee for Supply), including the Moscow one, were moving to the new arrangement at the same time. The economic reform had reached a "qualitative new stage."[46] From July 1968 to July 1970, 27,000 enterprises (more than half the total number) went over to the reform, making a total of 40,000 transferred.[47] By September 1970, 85 percent of all enterprises had been transferred; they account for more than 92 percent of the total volume of production and 95 percent of all profits. Since the number of industrial enterprises reportedly had increased to "almost 50,000" in 1970, this means that approximately 42,000 were working in accordance with the new system to some degree.[48] According to the directives for the Ninth Plan (1971-75), the new arrangement is to be implemented in all enterprises that operate on khozraschet by the end of 1975.[49]

However, formal transference does not mean complete conversion to the principles and procedures specified by the reform. The complete implementation of even the "Kosygin model" reform in an enterprise probably requires at least a few years and in many cases more, while in some it is not realizable for any of several reasons. As Soviet economists told me repeatedly, implementation of the reform is not a process of which all aspects can be achieved at any one time. (The reform is not an odnovremennyi akt, "simultaneous process").[50]

Despite the reform's progress, the rate of industrial growth slipped. Indeed, according to Soviet data, the average annual rate of output growth for 1966-70 (the period of initial implementation of the reform)--8.4 percent--was less than that for 1961-65--8.6 percent.[51] This seems to be a part of the slowing of the Soviet GNP that began in the 1950s. Herbert Levine, using Soviet figures, gives the following rates of growth for the periods indicated: 1950-58, 10.9 percent; 1958-67, 7.2 percent; and 1967-73, 6.6 percent.[52]

As has been shown, the reform did not progress without encountering difficulties, some serious. Before we begin to discuss them, it is best to clarify exactly what the Soviet political leadership's intent for the reforms was in 1965.

INTENDED GOALS OF THE ECONOMIC REFORM

We turn now to the official goals concerning behavior in the four major relationships of Soviet managers.

The Manager-Superior Relationship

The manager was to be freed from arbitrary interference by superior agencies.

Ministries

The most significant aspect of the manager-superior relationship is the manager-ministry nexus. The immediate superior of an enterprise is a chief administration (<u>glavnoe upravlenie</u> or <u>glavk</u>) or one of the three types of production association (<u>promyshlennoe obedinenie</u>). The fundamental statement of official policy on the manager-superior relationship and the other relationships is Kosygin's saying of the managers that "they themselves, together with the production collectives, will have to decide upon matters that previously were often decided for them from above."[53] This shift in responsibilities and in the locale of some decision-making was the essence of the intended reform.

A basic change in the organizational structure of industry was also announced. The sovnarkhozy were dissolved and the industrial ministries reestablished. But the recentralization was not to be a mechanical return to the system that existed prior to 1957. The reform was to set up a "more perfectly organized management"; and the ministries were "to work in a new way, on the basis of new principles of planning and evaluation of the economic activity of enterprises," to study the "economic laws of socialism, to occupy themselves more with technology and the organization of production on a scientific basis."[54] Kosygin strongly affirmed this when he said:

> It is necessary to abandon the customary notions that in the relations between the guiding economic agencies and the enterprises, the former have only rights and the latter only obligations. The [reform] . . . requires the establishment of mutual rights and obligations. . . .[55]

Soviet commentary on Kosygin's report emphasized that the ministries' reestablishment was not to "entail a swelling . . . of the [ministerial] apparatus. On the contrary, this apparatus should be whittled down."[56] In short, the ministries were expected to constitute a new type of organization operating in a transformed context. However, although the manager was to have some additional leeway in achieving his goals, these goals, fewer and in some ways new, were still to be set for him, partly by the ministries.

It is obvious that no radical reinterpretation of the enterprise's function had taken place, although it is evident (and significant) that some responsible persons now considered the enterprise to have new rights vis-a-vis its superiors. One commentator called the enterprise an "independent economic subject on the internal socialist market."[57] A Soviet lawyer even said that "the administrative guidance of agencies of economic management and the day-to-day economic functioning of the enterprises must be rigorously separated."[58]

Despite these calls for still greater change in the relationship between manager and superiors, independence of each economic unit was not the official goal. What was desired was coherent, planned, scientifically based development using all necessary resources.[59] In other words, the central or superior organs were not to give up powers but to exercise them differently. Nevertheless, it was widely asserted that the reform required "serious shifts of a psychological nature" for both bureaucrats and managers. One statement noted that

> The workers of enterprises will be freed from the
> habit of waiting on or requiring instructions from
> higher authority on that range of questions which
> is now within the limits of their competence. The
> workers of industrial management organizations
> will be freed from the prejudice that without their
> sanction . . . not one question of the life of en-
> terprises can be decided.[60]

What, then, were the duties of the new ministries to be? Various suggestions were made.[61] One proposal was that the new ministries would operate "on the initiative" of plants and factories, making the ministries servants of the enterprises, a most unlikely outcome. A more specific, but still limiting, suggestion was that the ministries would determine proportions for the development of their branches and the long-term volume of capital investment for them, and would also "facilitate" the establishment of credit relations between enterprises and Gosbank. A rather concrete suggestion was that two major tasks of the ministries would be supervising design, planning, and research institutions (areas in which the sovnarkhozy had been deficient), and providing new enterprises with technical assistance and information, skilled cadres, and the "economic and organizational control" for attaining capacity. A new, limited ministerial role was propounded by the chairman of the Council of Ministers of the Latvian SSR, who said the ministries' job should be "to summarize the work experience under new conditions and to help the enterprises in selecting the most expedient solutions of the problems which they encounter. . . ."[62]

Despite the general agreement that a greater division of functions between ministries and enterprises ought to exist, no consensus emerged on how this somewhat detached relationship was to work.

Nonministerial Superiors

Central Planning Agencies. The economic rights and powers of enterprises were said to be insufficient and constricted, but a stronger role for the central planning agencies was proposed nevertheless. The continuing existence of several centrally set indices necessitated this. Central planning was to have a "leading role," since its discard "would inevitably lead to the loss of the advantages of a planned socialist economy"--a view clearly indicating the continued viability of the ideology and the power of established bureaucratic interests.[63] It is in the planners' interests to retain as much to plan, or pretend to plan, as possible.

In his report Kosygin, again revealing his rationalizing bent, stressed the need for long-lasting, stable plans based upon rational calculations. He proposed a new major success index for the future: the index of volume of output sold (sales), which would cause enterprises to emphasize quality more than they had previously. But he did not suggest a basic alteration in the planning situation, although he announced the reduction of centrally set or confirmed indices from thirty-odd to eight or nine--including the volume of output sold and the wage fund--and specified that "the other indices of economic activity will be planned by the enterprises independently."[64] Four of these nine seem to be the most important: "the plan for output of the main commodities, the overall wage fund, total value of sales, and profit. The latter two replace the targets for cost reduction and for the ill-famed gross value of output. . . ."[65]

The post-reform Soviet commentary on the subject of planning is unavoidably dualistic. Although fewer things were now to be planned for enterprises, the principle of centralized planning continued unquestioned, at least openly. Liberman's creative interpretation of planning, involving direct contract ties and enterprise participation in planning, was definitely not the prevailing one.[66] A wide gap existed between the model of the planning situation generally accepted by higher-level bureaucrats and Party secretaries and that desired by "marketeers" among economists and enterprise directors. Nevertheless, enterprises could now independently use a "portion" of depreciation deductions and the enterprise fund, derived from a "portion of profits." Superior organs were "not permitted" to withdraw and redistribute the resources in these funds, and were prohibited from changing enterprise plans at will.

What was being given fell far short of what some managerial personnel wanted. The head of the planning department of a large automobile plant requested--almost demanded--plans of a half-year or a year's duration, asserting that none shorter would do. In addition, he specified that the planning organizations give the plan to the enterprise not less than two months prior to the beginning of the year and added that when the plan is not received by that time, the director "must" have the right to establish a new plan for the first quarter in accordance with the indices of the fourth quarter of the preceding year, a procedure that would forestall the application of the annoying "ratchet."[67]

Despite some degree of meaningful change in planning arrangements, a clear distinction between the planning powers of enterprises and their superiors remained to be worked out. Thus, the goal in this respect was unclear and unstable.

Gosbank. Although Kosygin said nothing specific about the role of Gosbank, with its nearly 8,000 offices, he did call for a shift from the outright granting of funds for capital construction to long-term credits, a change necessarily involving Gosbank and probably enhancing its role. The introduction of an interest charge paid out of profits for the use of capital would do the same.

The politically relevant question was how much supervision and control the bank was to exercise. Supposedly, its checking of enterprise activities was to be limited to two instances: consideration of a loan application and supervision of its use and repayment. But overseeing "use" is not consistent with an actual limitation upon the bank's examining powers. In fact, some bank officials wanted increased powers for the bank's local offices to "counter" the increased rights of the enterprise managers.[68] This pattern of wanting additional powers appears in the writings of officials of other organizations, and is an important and recurring theme, and not in keeping either with the spirit of reform or with its provisions. The implementation of the reform was thus jeopardized by a surge of lower-level bureaucratic self-interest. In addition, no high-level decision was made on the details of the bank's operation and its power.

Ministry of Finance

This ministry has long possessed a powerful complex of controls over enterprises' personnel, finances, and organizational structures. These powers gave it a role analogous to that of the Office of Management and Budget in the United States and the Treasury in the United Kingdom. The ministry's powers extended into the policy-making sphere, because a body that controls expenditures and personnel levels is able to suggest or even make policy. Indeed, a "budget need not be merely a device for economical administration . . . a budget is also a program."[69]

In his report to the plenum, Kosygin was limiting the ministry's role when he said: "The enterprises will establish their structures and staffs, and also the estimates of administrative-managerial expenditures, independently, without registration in the financial agencies."[70] The logical result of this new requirement would have been the withdrawal of the Ministry of Finance from its former supervisory role in the administration of industry. However, the powers of the Ministry over enterprises may have been implicitly upheld because reduction in staff could not be rationally and continuously effected except through its supervision. Nevertheless, new rights of the enterprise manager vis-a-vis the ministry were affirmed elsewhere. For example, K. T. Mazurov, First Deputy Chairman of the Council of Ministers, stated that "enterprise managers are granted the right . . . to establish independently the composition and size of the enterprise's staff and administrative-management expenses." A clear-cut statement of the same intent was made by the USSR Minister of Finance, who said: "The compulsory registration of estimates of administrative and management expenditures with the financial agencies has been abolished."[71]

However, nothing was said that explained what such statements mean in practice. In fact, the Ministry's functionaries assumed they were to exercise close supervision over the enterprises.[72] Therefore, the manager-superior relationship, as far as the Ministry of Finance is concerned, was still in a transitional state in 1965-67, the main normatives neither understood nor accepted by ministerial bureaucrats.

The Interstices

Republic Organs. The reform preserves an administrative role for the republics. In a new departure, several branches of industry--coal, petroleum, and light industry--were placed under new union-republic ministries,[73] indicating that a completely centralized control structure was neither "feasible" nor desired, and suggesting that the less centralized sovnarkhoz arrangement had some natural bases (including a political one) for existence. The republics were to have "more rights" in planning, capital construction, financing, labor, and wages. For example, "all products manufactured by . . . [local] enterprises out of local raw materials and by-products will remain at the disposal of the republics and oblasts."[74] This is a formalization of an aspect of mestnichestvo. Also, the territorial supply agencies were to remain.

Obedineniia. An institution of growing significance is the new Soviet-style "holding company" or "corporation" that may exist between the ministry and the enterprise.[75] "The reformists probably favored the merger form of industrial organization, which is considered to be a form facilitating direct ties and greatly expanded enterprise rights."[76] However, the development of obedineniia may actually be a negation of the "rights of enterprises," since their creation often means the end of the semi-autonomous position of the constituent enterprises. Nevertheless, these new organizations do present the ministries with a challenge. Just as they will take power away from the enterprises, they will also erode that of the ministries.

A controversy arose over the significance and worth of these amalgamations. Some writers argued conservatively that it would be desirable to avoid the concentration of the two different functions of cost accounting and planning within a single agency.[77] Others criticized the concentration of production in large, inefficient factories and innovatively advocated the establishment of smaller enterprises that would be cooperatives in which the workers would share in profits and losses. One proposal that such factories would employ up to 50 people suggests the laws on factory size of the NEP period.[78]

An important question remains--are the new obedineniia a form of survival of the sovnarkhozy? An attempt was being made to eliminate the problems brought about by the former sovnarkhozy without giving up some of the advantages. In summary, an attempt was begun, through use of the obedineniia, to combine organizational recentralization with decentralization or deconcentration in lower-level decision-making.

Soviets. Little significant change was to take place in this aspect of the relationship, at least for a time. (Neither Kosygin's report nor the statute contains a reference to the Soviets or their executive committees.) Since local industry (which was under the Soviets' jurisdiction) formerly produced only about 11 percent of the USSR's total industrial output, this is not a sphere in which changes could have had a great effect upon the management of Soviet industry.

Implications

In the new manager-superior relationship, as seen by the top leadership, fewer orders and standards were to be authoritatively presented to enterprise managers by central agencies. It was officially desired, somewhat unrealistically, that this would be more than repaid by a higher general responsibility on the part of managers and greater success by their enterprises in meeting the fewer, and hopefully more economically meaningful, goals set for them. The enterprise manager was to have greater responsibility for, and powers of, decision-making and to exercise them in a new, more flexible way for the realization of profits and the production of higher-quality products. However, operationally the reform came to have a more restricted meaning. For example, although the role of profits was strengthened, it was not to become the "all-embracing, decisive and generalizing index of Soviet production. The value of profits . . . cannot be detached from the social content of profits." Profit was said to be the "decisive" regulator of the economy only under capitalism. Under socialism, profit was not to regulate priority in the production of any item; instead, it was to serve as a "criterion of comparative efficiency of labor input" and as a means of "adjusting" the operation of the economy, making its use definitely a "subordinate" one.[79] This kind of attempt to limit the change to be brought about by the reform came up against statements of more liberal and innovative intent.[80] Thus, the reform contains built-in contradictions.

Certainly the elements of the reform were not carefully delineated. Many officials in industrial management, no matter what their position in the chain of command, were uncertain as to what the reforms were to mean in organizational terms. This made it easier for many bureaucrats to interpret elements of the reform in their own interest. One reason for the juxtaposition of incompatible views is that the reform had been made somewhat attractive to enterprise managers in an attempt to gain their rapid acceptance, but it contained no inducements for the middle-range bureaucrats of the ministries. Many of these individuals had moved back to Moscow from the headquarters of the sovnarkhozy, where they had been ensconced during the past several years. There is no reason to assume their attitudes had changed. Perhaps a tacit alliance now exists between the top Party leadership and progressive enterprise directors, but there is no such alliance between the rationalizing Party leadership and the bureaucratic personnel of agencies superior to the enterprises. The latter exhibit limited acquiescence in and limited understanding of the goals of the reform. A divided industrial leadership cannot successfully encourage managers to act in a new way. Accordingly, implementation would not be easy.

The Manager-Party Relationship

The Soviet industrial system has long functioned with active involvement by enterprise Party organizations. In this way the Party maintained its preeminent political position while keeping industry in operation. However, there was a constant strain between efforts to maximize efficiency and to perpetuate the Party's political position. Although Party intervention in industry is at times functional from the efficiency standpoint, because the Party is the only element with coordinative power to solve pressing problems, the frequent exercise of this power inhibits and hinders the people and agencies specifically charged with functions of management in industry from developing and applying nonpolitical, regularized procedures for the solution of difficulties. It has had a "chilling effect" upon the exercise of initiative by those formally charged with operational functions in industry. If the Party were to withdraw from direct and authoritative involvement in industrial management, a modification of the Soviet political system might occur. The reform somewhat alters the model of earlier Party involvement, mainly in terms of priority of aspects of intervention, but leaves the extent and functional role of this intervention ambiguous.

Official Goals

Since the new ranking of Party functions is not the same as that for behavior in the manager-Party relationship prior to the introduction of the reform (see Table 1.1), change in the relationship was intended. The differences between the pre- and post-reform lists of functions are to be noted. Cadres' work was still to be first in importance; it is crucial to the maintenance of the Party's power position. Enforcement was moved up to second from fourth place, probably due to the Party's big role in implementing the reform. But positioning this function here may be incorrect, because the secondary function formerly paired with it--reporting--was no longer stressed in Soviet discussions. Concern with actual enterprise operations was ranked higher than previously. Its position in third place is probably due to the present practice of Party organizations' becoming involved in the implementation of the reform. Ideological and organizational work ("agitation and propaganda") was also increased in importance. The reason is that the Party was to implement the reform through use of its powers and abilities in these spheres. The question of whether it can reduce such activities is pertinent. The determination of goals and priorities fell from third to fifth place. This seems consistent with the manager's new powers in this area. Interestingly, the Party's role in the solution of supply problems was no longer mentioned, again probably because of the creation of a new central supply agency (Gossnab) and an increase in managerial rights and capabilities. Arbitration and mediation were placed last because so little is said about them. It is possible, however, that they were to have a more important place in actual behavior.

TABLE 1.1

Party Functions in Industry
(in order of importance)

Pre-Reform Actual Behavior*	Officially Desired Post-Reform Behavior
1. Cadre and personnel "selection assignment, and training"	Remains same
2. Arbitration and mediation of conflicting interests	Enforcement (but not reporting)
3. Determination of goals and priorities, and solution of supply problems	Intervention in operational matters
4. Enforcement of discipline, legality, and plan fulfillment, and reporting of problems in these and other spheres to higher Party and state organs	Ideological and organizational work
5. Intervention in operational matters	Determination of goals and priorities (but not solution of supply problems)
6. Ideological and organizational work (through agitation and propaganda)	Arbitration and mediation

*Each function is fully stated in this column only.

Source: See Jerry F. Hough, "The Role of the Local Party Organs in Soviet Industrial Decision-making" (unpublished Ph.D. diss., Department of Government, Harvard University, 1961), pp. 121, 123; and Z. Nuriev, "Rukovodit' ekonomikoi, ne podmeniaia khoziaistvennye organy," Kommunist 16 (November 1965): 61-62.

The Party Organization and the Director

The central question here is the dominant interpretation of the concept of <u>edinonachalie</u> after the beginning of the reform. Managers have not been made safe from possible Party interference. A post-reform article on Party work in industry says that "how . . . policy is carried out at the enterprise, how the director uses the rights granted to him, how skillfully he operates--all this depends to a large extent on checkups from above and below."[81] The <u>Spravochnik partiinogo rabotnika</u> cites the standard formulation of Lenin on the need to subordinate the will of thousands to the will of one and mentions edinonachalie and its basic meaning, but adds that the <u>rukovoditel'</u> is a "fiduciary of the party" (<u>doverennoe litso partii</u>) and, therefore, must actively implement Party and state directives. It is similarly argued that Party <u>kontrol'</u> only gives edinonachalie a "new content," since "Soviet edinonachalie" operates through the <u>aktiv</u> and the masses.[82]

The Party Organizations in the Ministries

In October 1965 <u>Pravda</u> said that Party organizations in ministries were obligated to ensure that the "old ills"--"bureaucratism, red tape, and overcautiousness"--did not reappear. More specifically, the top Party Secretary of Moscow said that "militant Party organizations" must be created in the new ministries in order that "from the very first days they [the ministries] will direct their main attention to the education of workers in the spirit of the requirements of the CC CPSU."[83] This was a new step in Party control. It was carried further in 1971, at the Twenty-Fourth Party Congress. These Party committees engage in activities that duplicate the functions of the ministry's own organs, for example, examining how the ministry's correspondence is handled.[84] The Ministry of Communications houses a "shadow" apparatus of formidable size: 33 Party organizations of departments, 11 shop organizations, and 150 Party groups.

The new ranking in Table 1.1 shows that a definite change in the mutual behavior of enterprise managers and enterprise Party secretaries was envisioned. If the desires of the top Party leadership alone were the basis of this ranking, an even greater attempt at changing norms would be evident. However, the published views of middle-level Party officials were also considered in making a new model of the managerial-Party relationship because they were to have an important part in implementing it. It is obvious that at the enterprise level the Party was still organizationally well-situated to cope with several varieties of problems.

The Manager-Subordinate Relationship

The manager's relationship with his employees has many implications. Since a large number of those employed work in industry (31.5 million of 90 million in the late 1960s),[85] any significant changes in the authority and other patterns under which these people work will also have an effect upon the social structure and upon politics, although indirectly. The industrial managers will be instrumental in whatever occurs.

Edinonachalie

The concept of edinonachalie has always served to indicate that routine, "within policy" decisions are to be made by the director independently; that though managerial decisions are subject to influence by various groupings (particularly Party agencies), they must be implemented by the person or state agency formally and legally charged with their execution; and that any order or instruction issued by an agency must be obeyed by those subordinated to it. Jerry Hough concludes that "the strengthening of edinonachalie can mean little more than the strengthening of labor discipline."[86] In the context of "company unions," a command economy, and an administered society, this means, in effect, the strengthening of a manager's personal powers over the workers in his enterprise.

Some idealistic statements of possibilities for change in edinonachalie surfaced in 1966. One, for example, was reminiscent of Lenin's work of momentary optimism, State and Revolution, saying that as Communism is approached, the "foundations" of management will become more democratic; one-man management will be limited to the "level necessary for efficient regulation of the enterprise"; the director will "probably be elected at general meetings of the collective"; and "enterprise councils" will make basic decisions "binding upon the director and the entire management of the enterprise." No one, however, said outright that the workers will become the management. Rather, "those organizational forms through which the members of the collective will manage the affairs of the enterprise (the general meeting, the enterprise council, and so on) will then constitute the agencies of management."[87]

However, the new enterprise statute's article 90 states the manager's powers strongly: he "organizes the entire work of the enterprise, . . . bears full responsibility for its conditions and activity," and "acts without express authorization on behalf of the enterprise." It is clear that the Soviet industrial manager was to remain the main decision-maker in the enterprise that he heads. Edinonachalie was to be as strong as ever, and the possible loosening of the manager's powers over personnel was not encouraged.

ORIGINS AND CONCEPT OF REFORM

The Manager and Personnel

The people working in the enterprise can be divided into three basic types by general functions: management personnel, ITR, and the workers (including foremen) on the production line. Since the reform predicates definite change in the manager's ties to his workers, these will be emphasized below.

<u>Managerial Personnel and ITR</u>. The main change between the manager and the other management personnel lies in the position of assistant to the director. "At many enterprises, the position of chief economist has been introduced as that of the deputy director of the enterprise."[88] This means a downgrading of the chief engineer, formerly almost always the director's chief assistant, and a new emphasis on economic knowledge and its uses. The chief economist is now to coordinate the work of the economic services and connect it with production, supply, and sales in order to improve the enterprise's indicators.

It is not clear, however, that a new general pattern has evolved. Admittedly, the new significance of the chief economist or even the new intent for his position cannot be stated exactly. Enterprise organization charts vary regarding top management.[89] Even people in Soviet management are unclear on these questions. Interviews with Soviet managerial personnel and writers on industrial questions revealed a general lack of clarity and some differences of opinion. For example, in 1968, at the editorial offices of one economics publication I was told that the chief engineer and chief economist of any one enterprise were now both assistants to the director. Interestingly, now the chief economist may succeed to the post of director more easily. However, I was also told, somewhat contradictorily, that the chief engineer is still the "first" assistant although the chief economist has become the "decisive figure" because of the new stress upon profits. It was added that the chief engineer effects the reform through modernization and the chief economist supports him. But at a major obedinenie producing large electrical equipment I was told that the chief engineer remains the second man in the enterprise while the chief economist is an assistant to the director for "commercial affairs," a label implying he is more concerned with the external relations of the enterprise than with relations and processes within it.

Clarity was reduced still further by the assertion made elsewhere that each enterprise is working out the relationship among these positions in its own way, thereby raising the possibility of a future lack of uniformity in the structure and operations of industrial management. Interestingly, this latter interview revealed that holders of the two positions are sometimes in conflict, causing some to speak of a way out through a new ideal chief engineer who has assimilated economic knowledge and become a new interdisciplinary functionary. In any case, a broad attempt is under way to make enterprise management more responsive to the demands of the reform and to change personnel, management "types," and management positions accordingly.

The relationship of the manager to his other assistants and immediate subordinates also is not clear. The traditional "triangle" of managerial personnel, Party secretary, and trade union functionaries is still discussed but is not reflected in texts and books on management. In the latter the number of assistants is limited to four or five posts that would be of management rank in the West: the chief economist, the chief engineer, the assistant for cadres, the assistant for administrative-economic questions, and the assistant for commercial affairs.[90]

A major change is the director's new right to determine the size, composition, and expenditures of the managerial staff (within limits) without the need to obtain the approval of the financial agencies. Thus, it is likely that the director now sets the salaries of managerial personnel, although he does not determine their bonuses. Another factor here is the new requirements facing management personnel: improvement in their training; perfection of their work in terms of organization, style, form, and methods; and the mechanization of managerial operations. The director also has the right to "make or break" his assistants since, according to the statute, they are "appointed to and relieved of their posts on the director's representation to the superior agency."

The Workers. The relationship of the manager to his workers is the area in which his powers have most noticeably and significantly increased. Three of the four labor indices formerly confirmed for the plant are now determined on the spot: labor productivity, number of workers, and average wages. Only the total wage fund is confirmed from above. The enterprise manager now clearly has the right to set the number of workers, the power to "hire and fire."[91] As a result, his disciplinary powers are enhanced. Penalties are to be imposed "directly after discovery of the act" provoking them, and not later than one month thereafter. There apparently is no provision for a trial or hearing, although the applicable decree states that prior to the penalty's imposition, "it is necessary to obtain an explanation from the violator." The director's powers over labor are now so great that punishment for absenteeism is determined "exclusively by the director of the enterprise."[92]

The logical outcome of the combination of strong powers over personnel in the director's hands and his need to make a profit is a reduction in work force. It is fairly certain that this is intended.

ORIGINS AND CONCEPT OF REFORM 43

As the chief economist of the Red October Plant in Volgograd adroitly put it: "Where it is necessary, we will increase the number of personnel. But the general tendency will be a maximum economy of labor."[93] In other words, unemployment in limited amounts is a prospect. Since Soviet enterprises have long been overstaffed, this is now unavoidable. The potential seriousness of this situation is indicated by calls for the creation of a state system for the "distribution, redistribution and requalifying of the work force,"[94] that is, labor exchanges.

On the other hand, the government still wants to assign a quota of workers to managers (the bronia), despite the contradiction between this and the principles of the reform. It is not clear how this desire can be implemented in the face of managers' new orders to rationalize operations. Conflict between managers and higher authorities is likely to arise over this question.

Incentives

Kosygin said that it is necessary to "intensify" economic incentives through the use of bonuses and profits. The reform initially gave the director wide-ranging powers in applying bonuses. The only limitation on these powers to determine bonuses and other incentives of workers is a formal requirement that the director at times consult with the trade union organization.[95] Similarly, "the powers of the factory management to determine the way in which it spends the total allocation for wages are greatly increased; the manager may divide up the total allocations as he wishes between classes of employee."[96] Clearly, the Soviet leadership was highly conscious of the need to improve the system of incentives so that they actually motivate the manager and his employees to promote profitable production of the high-quality items desired.

A solution to critical problems relating to human relations in Soviet industry was attempted by altering the relationship of the manager to the enterprise in such a way that he would have more freedom over its personnel as well as its processes. It is in this relationship that the manager has gained the most. The critical question is whether the workers' gains from the increase in bonuses, wages, and other incentives compensate them adequately for the strengthening of the manager's position over them. The workers cannot but find this to their disadvantage, and the political leaders must realize that they require at least the passive support of the workers in order to remain as dominant as before. The result may well be the reimposition of the derationalizing controls of the pre-reform period on the managers, for "nothing seems more threatening [to the workers] than untrammeled economic liberty for the managers without countervailing institutions for workers' self-defense. . . ."[97]

The Manager-Manager Relationship

Initially, the official assumptions tended to favor a broad and relatively unhindered extension of economic contacts among enterprises. Managers' roles in the exchange and sale of materials and equipment, the use of other enterprises' facilities and buildings (sometimes for rent payment), the making of contracts for supplies and products, and the determination of the details of quality and assortment of products all were to expand. Article 30 of the enterprise statute states: "An enterprise producing consumer goods organizes the output of these goods on the basis of orders from trade organizations and contracts concluded with them." This implies that the entire Soviet consumer goods industry now (1965) was to be placed on a supply-and-demand basis. The logic of the reform would extend this practice to the rest of industry. The same article of the statute also says that the enterprise is to "expand and strengthen in every way its direct economic ties with consumer enterprises and organizations."

However, the old doubts regarding enterprise performance surfaced early in the game. Kosygin requested enterprises to observe their delivery obligations strictly, and intimated that laxity or failure in this would be punished through the imposition of some sort of material deprivation. He also said that "payment discipline" must be strengthened, and emphasized the promptness of shipments and deliveries.

Contracts and Inter-Enterprise Ties

According to the statute, contracts for deliveries of equipment and raw materials may be concluded between enterprises. An enterprise also may transfer funded resources and equipment to other enterprises for the manufacture by contract of necessary products, and it may independently conclude sales contracts for output not distributed by a superior agency. The joint Party-state resolution of October 1965 adds that economic relations between enterprises are to be based on the principle of mutual material responsibility, manufacturing and consuming enterprises are to develop permanent direct ties, and economic contracts are to have a greater role.[98] Some foresaw systemic change: "The distribution of goods by means of allocations and orders should gradually give way to contractual relations between enterprises. Consequently, the contract will become the basis for the planning of production."[99] Liberman, speaking for the reformist "marketeers," also strongly supported direct ties between enterprises, writing: "Contract ties . . . bind with transverse, horizontal threads the system of longitudinal, vertical central planning. . . . Enterprises themselves are granted the right to build up a portfolio of orders on the basis of contract agreements with their buyers [customers]."[100]

But authoritative qualifications were made--for instance, the "development of direct relations must not be understood in a simplified manner, as a chaotic search by suppliers for buyers of their output." And the State Committee for Material and Technical Supply began "attaching" consumers to producers. Even "reformers" spoke of some limitations on inter-enterprise contacts.[101] But they did hold out the reformist hope that the amount of central planning would be reduced when economic ties and the system of contracts became well developed.

Thus, even in 1965-66 the prospect of inter-enterprise ties being formed independent of centralized controls was not authoritatively accepted. (To what extent the reformers were imposing caution upon themselves for reasons of self-protection is unclear.) One obstacle to its acceptance was the leadership's desire to maintain a nationwide network of state controls over supply. This made the future of the manager-manager relationship unclear.

Supply and the Manager-Manager Relationship

The State Committee for Supply (Gossnab) became the central organization operationally limiting inter-enterprise ties. It is both a central supply agency and a supervisory organ. Its function as a supervisory agency is especially indicated by its power to stop or curtail the production of "products not enjoying demand," which implies a power to establish a definition of sufficient demand. It also is charged with conducting work for the "further expansion of rational direct economic ties among enterprises."[102] Thus, like so much else in the USSR, inter-enterprise economic ties and contracts were to be "guided" by a control agency.

Gosarbitrazh

The system of state arbitration is a complex of commercial courts that enforces contracts between enterprises and has a role, as does Gossnab, in guiding inter-enterprise relations. Officials of Gosarbitrazh, lamenting what they considered to be their lack of enforcement powers, suggested further centralization and asked for more supervisory power for central arbitration organs over the subordinate ones, since the "significance of . . . state arbitration has grown immeasurably because of the growing role of contracts."[103] Gosarbitrazh was to "influence" suppliers to provide customers with an expanded assortment of products under penalty of sanctions significantly larger than before. It was also to secure the elimination of "deficiencies" it uncovered in its work.[104] The influence of the organizational interests of Gossnab and Gosarbitrazh is apparent.

Contradictions developed within the manager-manager relationship. The managers of enterprises did obtain more rights and chances to establish economic ties; and arguments were being published for legally stabilizing this reform, notably through the wider and more meaningful use of contracts. On the other hand, two key institutions, Gossnab and Gosarbitrazh, limited the rights of enterprises to deal with each other. As the result of this and a fear of "commercialism" stemming from the ideology, the manager-manager relationship received the least chance and impetus for development.

THE GOALS OF MANAGERIAL CHANGE

By 1965 it was apparent that if industry were to operate more efficiently and with a wider range of products, some significant change in industrial management, and even in the managers themselves, was called for.

The Challenge

By the early 1930s most of industry was operating at a loss, and profits were not an important consideration. The Stalinist approach, though successful in a narrow sense, had become incapable of directing the more sophisticated economy of the 1960s. Also, the professional qualifications of industrial executives, although they had risen greatly since the First Plan, dropped after the mid-1950s and deteriorated still further from 1961 to 1964 because of the loss of these persons to retirement, because of science, and because of reduction in staff.[105]

The reform was meant to lessen the rigors and irrationalities inherent in this situation by allowing the manager a much wider latitude of action and by granting him security from the threat of arbitrary acts by superior organizations. A pattern of highly centralized hierarchical industrial management similar to that instituted by the first Henry Ford was being replaced by a system similar to the decentralized one pioneered so profitably by Ford's rather successful arch-competitor, General Motors.[106]

ORIGINS AND CONCEPT OF REFORM 47

Problems directly related to the managers themselves also limited good management. Their previous experience had not prepared them for "such concepts as profit, profitability and the use of production assets."[107] Their formal education, usually in engineering, was not of much help in these matters. The new conditions, in order for management personnel to be productive, require that they have a good understanding of economics and industrial management, and abandon their "engineering . . . or technocratic approach toward human problems."[108] These problems could not continue to exist at their long-existing level if the reform was to take hold and have the effects intended for it.

The Official Response and Intent

In his report of September 1965, Kosygin singled out the specific need for the better training of managerial cadres in economics and added that the training of economists themselves is taking on paramount importance. Like other elements in the new situation, the new need to make a profit and the manager's new rights in regard to the wage fund require a better understanding of economics. The reform also demands that managers be more than merely engineers occupying managerial positions; they also must have broad administrative capabilities. This perspective was reinforced by the First Secretary of Azerbaidzhan, A. Akhundov, who asserted that two "types" of economic managers are leaving the scene: the "unthinking executor" of orders and the type that overcomes economic obstacles "high-handedly or with an onslaught" (nakhrapom ili natiskom). A new "type," he said, is coming to the fore--one able to "cogitate" and act in accordance with scientific data and advanced practices. "In the new conditions the one who reaches the finish line will be he who masters commercial nerve, he who is nimble, economically calculating and at the same time innovative."[109]

In general, a concern is shown for some of the qualities often attributed to businessmen operating in a competitive environment. Of course, the Soviet manager has always been calculating, but heretofore in mainly bureaucratic and political ways. The stress is now on economics, commercial ability, and innovation. Another major point authoritatively stressed since 1965 is that the Soviet manager must be a generalist able to oversee the enterprise's work and willing to delegate all actual operational tasks to others. As is to be expected, the manager's "political qualities" of high idealism and devotion to Communism are given their due, but only in passing.[110]

One reason that managerial and other industrial cadres must be "reprogrammed" is that the reform includes a renewed emphasis on a modernized "scientific organization of labor" (nauchnaia organizatsiia truda, or NOT) meaning the use of computerized systems to keep track of and to control production processes. "A decisive condition in the development of NOT is the preparation and repreparation of managerial cadres. They must have specialized knowledge concerning scientific organization of work." There also have been calls for the recognition of "organizational-managerial work" as a specialty because, "according to Lenin's judgment," it is "the most complex art."[111] Since it is noted that for the past decade abroad there has been a process of perfecting management (menedzhment), the implication is that the Soviet industrial manager should become like his Western counterpart in many ways. The managers of reformed enterprises are also to refrain as much as possible from tasks for which no specialized knowledge is necessary. As an apparatchik in Sverdlovsk put it: "Managerial cadres are the most qualified category of workers. Therefore, their incorrect use and improper assignment is a waste of social labor. This determines the necessity of the rational organization of the labor of the administrative apparatus of enterprises and above all of its managers."[112]

A new system of education for managers was also being mentioned and discussed. One writer, for example, asked that an "Institute of Technical Management . . . as there was in the 20's" be set up and that a group of scientific research institutes be assigned management as a separate field of study. In his report, Kosygin also raised the subject, saying that a former system for raising the qualifications of managerial personnel must be restored.

CONCLUSION

The economic reform, a long time in coming, necessarily has been directed at the Soviet industrial manager's attitudes, knowledge, work relationships, and patterns of work. Although he has gained some measure of professional autonomy from the reform, most notably in his powers vis-a-vis his labor force, he has at the same time been made vulnerable to new pressures to change as a managerial type. Against this he can muster the protection afforded him by his crucial role in the economy. Although wide-ranging change was authoritatively predicated and a real beginning made toward its application, the reform stopped short of changes that would have any significant, immediate political effect. The reform model was a systemic one, but in the sense of a change of the industrial management system, not of a change in the larger system. The goal is significant nevertheless, and even politically so if its long-term effects are considered. But, since no single or complete model that satisfied the major criteria or was agreed upon by the main interests existed, the reform was inherently unstable in terms of power relationships, although it would, nevertheless, have some economically favorable results.

NOTES

1. Alec Nove, The Soviet Economy (rev. ed.; New York: Praeger, 1969), p. 248.
2. Francis Seton, "Economic Planning in Communist Societies," in George Schopflin, ed., The Soviet Union and Eastern Europe (New York: Praeger, 1970), p. 282.
3. Joseph S. Berliner, "Innovation and Economic Structure in Soviet Industry," a paper presented at the joint session of the American Economic Association and the Association for Comparative Economics, "Innovation and Public Enterprise: East and West," New York, December 30, 1969, p. 3; and Stanley H. Cohn, Economic Development in the Soviet Union (Lexington, Mass.: Heath, 1970), p. 86.
4. A. N. Kosygin, "Ob uluchshenii upravleniia promyshlennost'iu, sovershenstvovanii planirovaniia i usilenii ekonomicheskogo stimulirovaniia promyshlennogo proizvodstva," Pravda, September 28, 1965, p. 2.
5. T. Khachaturov, "Ekonomicheskaia effektivnost' kapital'nykh vlozhenii," Kommunist 13 (September 1966): 64.
6. L. Leont'ev, "Plan i khoziaistvennaia initsiativa," Pravda, April 29, 1966, p. 2.
7. F. Lentrinskii, Ekonomika Sovetskoi Ukrainy (Kiev) 6 (June 1966); JPRS 38,276 (October 21, 1966): 19.
8. Henryk Olsienkiewicz, "The Dialectics of Soviet Economic Revisionism," Bulletin of the Institution for the Study of the USSR 12, no. 6 (August 1965): 19.
9. V. Kantorovich, "U istokov ekonomicheskoi reformy," Novyi mir 11 (1968): 276, citing V. G. Venzher et al., Proizvodstvo, nakoplenie, potreblenie (Moscow, 1965), p. 37.
10. Bandiera rossa (Rome), July 1965, p. 6; JPRS 31,814 (September 1, 1965): 16. For evaluation see Abraham Katz, The Politics of Economic Reform in the Soviet Union (New York: Praeger, 1972), p. 122.
11. Barry M. Richman, Soviet Management (Englewood Cliffs, N.J.: Prentice-Hall, 1965), p. 163.
12. Kosygin, op. cit., p. 3. See also O. Nekrasov, "Otraslevoi prinstip upravleniia . . .," Voprosy ekonomiki 11 (November 1965): 4; G. Kulagin, "Obedinenie, predpriiatii i ministerstvo," Kommunist 3 (February 1966): 82-83; "Vazhnyi etap v razvitii sotsialisticheskoi ekonomiki," Pravda, October 4, 1965, p. 1; and "Posledovatel'naia leninskaia politika partii . . .," Partiinaia zhizn' 15 (October 1965): 7.

13. L. Brezhnev, Tass English broadcast, September 29, 1965, 21:20.
14. V. Lisitsyn, "Problemy upravleniia sotsialisticheskim khoziaistvom," Planovoe khoziaistvo 4 (April 1965): 42. For Liberman's views see Ekonomika i matematicheskie metody 5 (September-October 1968); JPRS 46,891 (November 18, 1968): 7. See also Eugene Zaleski, Planning for Economic Growth in the Soviet Union, 1918-1932 (Chapel Hill: University of North Carolina Press, 1971), p. 295.
15. A. Aganbegian, JPRS 31,814 (September 1, 1965): 16-17.
16. Kosygin, op. cit., p. 2.
17. A. Birman, "Sut' reformy," Novyi mir 12 (December 1968): 191.
18. I. Schreiber, "Bankovskii kontrol' rublem," Den'gi i kredit 1 (January 1966): 39.
19. M. Kuzin, "Polozhenie o predpriiatii . . . ," Ekonomicheskaia gazeta 3 (January 1967): 20.
20. "Printsipial'nost'--vazhneishee kachestvo kommunista," Partiinaia zhizn' 10 (May 1965): 6. See also Peter R. Prifti, "Corruption in the Soviet System," Problems of Communism 21, no. 1 (January-February 1972): 40-47.
21. See Z. Nuriev, "Rukovodit' ekonomikoi, ne podmeniaia khoziaistvennye organy," Kommunist 16 (November 1965): 65.
22. Grey Hodnett, "The Obkom First Secretaries," Slavic Review 24, no. 4 (December 1965): 637, 651.
23. Kosygin, op. cit., p. 4.
24. I. Karpenko, "Chto takoe khorosho," Izvestiia, July 30, 1965, p. 3.
25. I. Malyshev, "Khoziaistvennaia reforma v deistvii," Partiinaia zhizn' 20 (October 1966): 18. Ironically, in mid-1969 this writer was told in Rostov-on-Don that he could not be shown through the Rostselmash plant because it was "the end of the month."
26. Iu. Artemov, "Povysit' stimuliruiushchuiu rol' sistemy planirovaniia," Planovoe khoziaistvo 9 (September 1965): 53.
27. R. Conquest, Power and Policy in the U.S.S.R. (New York: Macmillan, 1962), pp. 107-08. Also see Wolfgang Leonhard, The Kremlin Since Stalin (New York: Praeger, 1962), p. 177.
28. Leonhard, op. cit., p. 88.
29. Merle Fainsod, How Russia Is Ruled (rev. ed.; Cambridge, Mass.: Harvard University Press, 1963), p. 509.
30. Leonard Schapiro, The Communist Party of the Soviet Union (New York: Random House, 1960), p. 576.
31. N. S. Khrushchev, "O Programme Kommunisticheskoi Partii Sovetskogo Soiuza," Izvestiia, October 19, 1961, p. 6.
32. See Pravda, September 28, 1962; and Peter Reddaway, "The Fall of Khrushchev," Survey 56 (July 1965): 13, reprinted in

Sidney Ploss, ed., The Soviet Political Process (Waltham, Mass.: Ginn, 1970), pp. 241-64.

33. Alec Nove, "Revamping the Economy," Problems of Communism 12, no. 1 (January-February 1963): 13.

34. See Fainsod, op. cit., pp. 203, 395-98; Hodnett, op. cit.; J. W. Cleary, "The Parts of the Party," Problems of Communism 13, no. 4 (July-August 1964): 55-60; and Nove, "Revamping the Economy."

35. See U.S. Central Intelligence Agency, Directorate of Intelligence, Office of Research and Reports, An Evaluation of Experimental Economic Reforms in the Consumer Industries of the USSR (Washington, D.C.: Central Intelligence Agency, 1965).

36. V. A. Trapeznikov, Pravda, August 17, 1964, p. 4.

37. See: F. Burlatskii, Pravda, January 10, 1965, p. 4; Trud, July 8, 1965; David E. Powell and Paul Shoup, "The Emergence of Political Science in Communist Countries," American Political Science Review 64, no. 2 (June 1970): 572-80; an article by A. L. Lepeshkin in Sovetskoe gosudarstvo i pravo 2 (February 1965); and the speech of N. K. Arutynian, Chairman of the Presidium of the Supreme Soviet of Armenia, at the Armenian Party Congress in March 1966.

38. Pravda, October 1, 1965, pp. 1-2; "Polozhenie o sotsialisticheskom gosudarstvennom priozvodstvennom predpriiatii," Ekonomicheskaia gazeta 42 (October 20, 1965): 25-29; Izvestiia, January 30, 1966, p. 2; and "Metodicheskie ukazaniia po perevodu predpriiatii na novuiu sistemu planirovaniia i ekonomicheskogo stimulirovaniia," Ekonomicheskaia gazeta 7 (February 1966): 31-32.

39. See Theodore Frankel, "Economic Reforms: A Tentative Appraisal," Problems of Communism 16, no. 3 (May-June 1967): 29-30; and N. Zotov, "Novaia sistema v deistvii," Den'gi i kredit 9 (September 1966): 3.

40. See R. R. G. (R. Rockingham Gill), "Governmental Changes in USSR," Radio Free Europe Research Report (Munich, October 4, 1965), pp. 5, 7.

41. R. R. G., "New Enterprise Statute Extends Powers of Soviet Managers, Reduces Those of Moscow," ibid., October 29, 1965, p. 5. Emphasis in original. Also see V. F. Garbuzov, Pravda, December 8, 1965, p. 4.

42. N. Fedorenko, "Reforma v promyshlennosti . . .," Planovoe khoziaistvo 4 (April 1967): 6; and Keith Bush, "The First Year of the Industrial Reforms" (Munich: Radio Liberty Research Paper no. 13, 1967), p. 2.

43. Izvestiia, February 27, 1966, p. 2; March 20, 1966, p. 2; May 15, 1966, p. 2; May 22, 1966, p. 3.

44. N. Baibakov, "Vnedrenie khoziaistvennoi reformy--vazhneishaia zadacha," Pravda, November 4, 1966, p. 2.

45. B. Sukharevsky, Pravda, April 12, 1967, p. 2.
46. N. Zenchenko, Sovetskaia Rossiia, March 13, 1969, p. 2.
47. Radio Free Europe, "Mid-Year Economic Report," July 23, 1970, p. 2.
48. B. Sukharevskii, Pravda, December 3, 1970, pp. 2-3.
49. Pravda, April 11, 1971.
50. Interview at the editorial offices of Ekonomicheskaia gazeta in August 1968.
51. New York Times, October 23, 1971; and data calculated by Schroeder from figures in Pravda, February 4, 1971, and Narodnoe khoziaistvo SSSR v 1969 godu (Moscow: Nanka, 1970), p. 144. See Gertrude Schroeder, "Economic Reform at an Impasse," Problems of Communism 20, no. 4 (July-August 1971): 44.
52. These data are from a presentation before the meeting of the American Academy of Political and Social Science, Philadelphia, April 5, 1974.
53. Kosygin, op. cit., p. 4.
54. M. Sakov, Pravda, October 17, 1965, p. 2; and "Posledovatel'naia leninskaia politika partii . . .," Partiinaia zhizn' 15 (October 1965): 8.
55. Kosygin, loc. cit. Word in brackets added.
56. Tass English broadcast, September 27, 1965.
57. B. Sukharevskii, "Predpriiatie i material'noe stimulirovanie," Ekonomicheskaia gazeta 49 (December 1965): 12.
58. S. N. Bratus', "Sootnoshenie administrativnykh i ekonomicheskykh metodov v regulirovanii khoziaistvennykh otnoshenii," Sovetskoe gosudarstvo i pravo 3 (March 1966): 25. Bratus' is a civil lawyer associated with the All-Union Research Institute of Soviet Legislation.
59. A. Rumiantsev, "Ekonomicheskaia nauka i upravlenie narodnym khoziaistvom," Kommunist 1 (January 1966): 51. This may be A. F. Rumiantsev, chief of the Soviet Economy Department of the Higher Party School and editor of Ekonomicheskaia gazeta.
60. L. Leont'ev, Pravda, April 29, 1966, p. 3.
61. F. Loshchenkov, "Samostoiatel'nost', initsiativa, otvetstvennost'," Kommunist 15 (October 1965): 52; S. Protserov, "Prava i otvetstvennost' predpriiatii," Planovoe khoziaistvo 1 (January 1966): 62-63; and O. Nekrasov, op. cit.; see JPRS, 34,136 (February 15, 1966): 17, 20.
62. M. Raman, "Ekonomicheskaia rabota v novykh usloviiakh," Kommunist Sovetskoi Latvii (Riga) 5 (May 1967); JPRS 42,225 (August 15, 1967): 10.
63. Kosygin, op. cit., p. 2.
64. Ibid.
65. R. V. Greenslade, "The Soviet Economic System in Transition," in U.S. Congress, Joint Economic Committee, New Directions

in the Soviet Economy (Washington, D.C.: U.S. Government Printing Office, 1966), Pt. I, p. 13.

66. Ye. Liberman, "Plan, priamye sviazi i rentabel'nost'," Pravda, November 21, 1965, p. 2; and "The Soviet Economic Reform," Foreign Affairs 46, no. 1 (October 1967): 58.

67. Protserov, op. cit., p. 64.

68. I. Chernov, "Bank v novykh usloviakh," Kommunist 8 (May 1966): 97.

69. Emmette S. Redford et al., Politics and Government in the United States (national ed.; New York: Harcourt, Brace and World, 1965), pp. 325-26.

70. Kosygin, op. cit., p. 4.

71. K. T. Mazurov, Pravda, October 2, 1965, p. 2; and V. Garbuzov, "Finansy i ekonomicheskie stimuly," Ekonomicheskaia gazeta 41 (October 13, 1965): 4.

72. See, for example, "V kollegii Ministerstvo finansov SSSR," Finansy SSSR 3 (March 1967); JPRS 41,437 (June 16, 1967): 50-53.

73. John N. Hazard, "The Politics of Soviet Economic Reform," in A. Balinky, ed., Planning and the Market in the U.S.S.R. (New Brunswick, N.J.: Rutgers University Press, 1967), p. 75.

74. S. Kheifets, "Mestnaia promyshlennost' i kontrol' finorganov," Finansy SSSR 2 (February 1967); JPRS 40,434 (March 28, 1967): 22.

75. See G. Kolobashkin and Ia. Proshko, "Kombinat--vygodnaia forma upravleniia," Partiinaia zhizn' 23 (December 1965): 38; and K. A. Lapinskas, "Mesto proizvodstvennykh ob'eninenii v sisteme upravleniia promyshlennost'iu," Vestnik Moskovskogo Universiteta ser. XII (law), 3 (1966): 62-63.

76. Katz, op. cit., p. 120.

77. See, for example, Bratus', op. cit., p. 32.

78. See, for example, Ia. V. Kvasha, "Kontsentratsiia proizvodstva melkaia promyshlennost'," Voprosy ekonomiki 5 (May 1967): 26-31, discussed in New York Times, June 13, 1967, p. 9; and Radio Liberty, Po Sovetskomy soiuzu (New York, August 25, 1967), pp. 1-2.

79. B. Sukharevsky, "Predpriiatie i material'noe stimulirovanie," Ekonomicheskaia gazeta 49 (December 1965): 13.

80. See "Trudom slaven chelovek," Pravda, August 22, 1965, p. 1; and "Polozhenie o predpriiatii," Ekonomicheskaia gazeta 24 (June 1966): 19.

81. A. Zaitsev and I. Pronin, "Kommissii po kontroliu . . .," Partiinaia zhizn' 14 (July 1967): 30.

82. Spravochnik partiinogo rabotnika (Moscow: Politicheskaia literatura, 1967), pp. 22-23, 30.

83. N. Yegorychev, Pravda, October 4, 1965, p. 2.

84. V. Shepetovskii and V. Pavlovskii, "Vospitanie rabotnikov apparata ministerstva," Partiinaia zhizn' 4 (February 1966): 44.

85. See Narodnoe khoziaistvo SSSR v 1969 godu (Moscow, 1970), p. 510.

86. See Joseph S. Berliner, Factory and Manager in the USSR (Cambridge, Mass.: Harvard University Press, 1957), p. 15, and Jerry F. Hough, The Soviet Prefects (Cambridge, Mass.: Harvard University Press, 1969), pp. 80-86.

87. B. M. Lazerev, "Gosudarstvennoe proizvodstvennoe predpriiatie i ego administratsiia," Sovetskoe gosudarstvo i pravo 5 (May 1966): 20.

88. Ekonomicheskaia gazeta 24 (June 1967): 30; Berliner, Factory and Manager in the USSR, pp. 13-15; and B. Zakharov, "Voprosy povysheniia urovnia ekonomicheskoi raboty na predpriiatii," Planovoe khoziaistvo 10 (October 1965): 35.

89. See B. V. Grigor'ev, Upravlenie gosudarstvennym promyshlennym predpriiatiem v SSSR (Moscow: Moskovskogo Universiteta, 1966), p. 25.

90. See V. Mazyrin, "Organizatsiia truda rukovoditelei predpriiatii," Planovoe khoziaistvo 2 (February 1966): 59 and, for example, B. V. Grigor'ev; V. B. Belkin and G. N. Kholodnaia, Osynovy organizatsii i ekonomiki promyshlennogo proizvodstvo (Moscow, 1964); and B. I. Zaitsev and I. E. Sonin, Glavnyi inzhener zavoda (Moscow: "Ekonomika," 1967), table between pp. 24 and 25.

91. K. Aver'ianov, "The Rights and Duties of a Socialist Enterprise," Kommunist (Yerevan), November 24, 1965, p. 2 (JPRS 33,600 [January 5, 1966]: 78); and A. G. Karpov et al., Khozraschet pronikaet vsiudu (Moscow: "Ekonomika," 1966), pp. 6-7.

92. "Decree of the State Committee of the Council of Ministers USSR on Problems of Labor and Wages and the All-Union Central Council of Trade Unions," November 9, 1966, no. 595/P-28, Biulleten' gosudarstvennogo komiteta soveta ministrov SSSR po voprosam truda i zarabotnoi platy, no. 1, 1967 (JPRS, 40,866 [May 2, 1967]: 15-16); P. Emel'ianov, "Luchshe ispol'zovat' prava," Trud, March 22, 1967, p. 2 (JPRS, 40,806 [May 1, 1967]: 1-2).

93. A. Karpov, Pravda, February 11, 1966, p. 2. For statistics on the number of workers displaced by the reform in certain Moscow enterprises, see I. Goberman, Pravda, October 1, 1965, p. 3.

94. L. Gatovskii, "Edinstvo plana i khoziaistvennogo rascheta," Kommunist 15 (October 1965): 43.

95. See A. S. Budaev, "Stimuli for Efficient Management," Stroitel'naia gazeta, March 22, 1967, pp. 3-4 (JPRS, 41, 087 [May 19, 1967]: 15-21); and "For the Enterprise Workers--on the Practice of Converting to the New System of Planning and Economic Incentive," Sotsialisticheskii trud 5 (May 1967): 147-53 (JPRS, 41,681 [July 5, 1967]: 39).

96. R. W. Davies, "Planning a Mature Economy in the USSR," Economics of Planning 6, no. 2 (1966): 148.

97. Zygmunt Bauman, "Twenty Years After," Problems of Communism 20, no. 6 (November–December 1971): 52-53.

98. "V tsentral'nom komitete KPSS i Sovieta Ministrov SSSR," Pravda, October 10, 1965, p. 1.

99. Sh. Sverdlik, "Enterprise Sales Services Under the New Conditions of the Economic Reform," Material'no-tekhnicheskoi snabzhenie 5, May 1967 (JPRS 41,811 [July 13, 1967]: 4); and N. I. Klein, "Rol' khoziaistvennogo dogovora . . .," Sovetskoe gosudarstvo i pravo 6 (June 1966): 38.

100. Liberman, Ekonomika, p. 9.

101. Sverdlik, op. cit., p. 1.

102. Material'no-tekhnicheskoe snabzhenie 3, March 1967 (JPRS 41,340 [June 9, 1967]: 2-3.)

103. I. T. Gavrilenko and I. G. Pobirchenko, "Struktura gosudarstvennogo arbitrazha . . .," Sovetskoe gosudarstvo i pravo 6 (June 1966): 47.

104. Iu. Ia. L'vovich, "Povysit' dogovornuiu distsiplinu . . .," Sovetskoe gosudarstvo i pravo 4 (April 1966): 80; and N. G. Egorov, "Boriba s nedostatkami . . .," Sovetskoe gosudarstvo i pravo 12 (December 1965): 92.

105. D. G. Kurakov, Voprosy filosofii no. 3 (March 1970): 75-85, translated in Current Abstracts of the Soviet Press 11, no. 6 (June 1970): 16.

106. See Alfred Chandler, Jr., Giant Enterprise: Ford, General Motors, and the Automobile Industry (New York and Burlingame, Ind.: Harcourt, Brace and World, 1964).

107. M. Vasil'ev, Izvestiia, May 14, 1967, p. 5.

108. John A. Armstrong, "Sources of Administrative Behavior: Some Soviet and Western European Comparisons," American Political Science Review 59, no. 3 (September 1965): 654, emphasis in original; and Jeremy R. Azrael, Managerial Power and Soviet Politics (Cambridge, Mass.: Harvard University Press, 1966), p. 153.

109. A. Akhundov, "Sovetskii khoziaistvennik," Kommunist 17 (November 1965): 22-25.

110. A. A. Godunov, Vvedenie v teoriui upravleniia (Moscow: "Ekonomika," 1967), p. 64. This book draws upon D. M. Gvishiani, Sotsiologiia bisnesa (Moscow: Sotsial'no Ekonomicheskoi literatury, 1962), pp. 98-99. Gvishiani is a son-in-law of Premier Kosygin and a Deputy Chairman of the State Committee on Science and Technology.

111. I. Slepov, "Voprosy nauchnoi organizatsii truda," Planovoe khoziaistvo 12 (December 1965): 13. A basic book on NOT is T. K. Fedorov, Pamiatka po nauchnoi organizatsii truda i proizvodstva (Moscow: "Ekonomika," 1966).

112. Mazyrin, op. cit., p. 58.

CHAPTER 2

MANAGERS AND MINISTERIAL SUPERIORS

ISSUES

It has been said that it is not the countries where scientific discoveries are made that will lead in exploiting the production process, but those that can best organize its utilization.[1] This is prompting great concern in the Soviet Union, a country that has never been a leader in either sense. Since the industrial revolution began, only a relatively few countries stand out as good organizers of the utilization of technological discoveries. Many in the USSR favor joining this group.

The ministry is clearly one of the most important agencies in the implementation of the economic reform, in which its supervision is an essential feature. The reconstitution of the ministries seemed a justifiable course in 1965. Certainly Brezhnev then gave some plausible reasons for the act, including the defects of the former sovnarkhozy. His arguments at the time seemed to focus upon the advantages of industry's division into branches for technological development. He expressed hopes that "branch management" would make possible a unification of technological and economic management, a more rational distribution of workers and ITR, and an increase in "state discipline." Kosygin's major speech on the reform, given at almost the same time, also emphasized the contributions to technological progress expected of the new ministries.[2]

The industrial ministries constitute the administrative foundation of the Soviet production process. They make policy definite, issue directives, specify major enterprise targets by establishing the centrally set success indicators, and exercise controls over many of the materials and some of the personnel of industrial enterprises. Soviet sources sometimes refer to the ministries as the "headquarters" (shtab) directing the enterprises. They form the lower level of the elite that, said Gaetano Mosca, is more important to the functioning of a political system than the "few dozen persons who control the state machine."[3] Any change in the operation of the production process in the enterprises requires a corresponding and consequential change within the industrial ministries, some 22 of which were established out of the sovnarkhozy in 1965. By 1968 there were approximately 18 industrial ministries of all-Union or USSR rank, and some three of Union-republic rank.[4] This is not the first time the ministerial structure or its equivalent has been reshuffled and reshaped, nor in all likelihood is it the last. Despite this pattern of change, much was unchanging. For example, some rules valid for the new ministry-enterprise relationship in 1965 dated back decades.[5]

The ministries and similar agencies employ the key persons of the more than 10 million working "directly in the . . . administration of the national economy."[6] One issue related to the ministries discussed here is their political influence and power in relation not only to the reform and the enterprises but also to the political process in general and the Communist Party in particular. Does a significant degree of "institutional pluralism" exist in the USSR and, if it does, what role do the administrators of industry play in it? It is unlikely to be a minor role. As Abraham Katz correctly notes, although the return to the ministerial system was a logical step to assure macroeconomic control in a somewhat more rational fashion, it created a conflict between the reform's top politician supporters and their goals and the officials charged with implementation.[7] In other words, the bugbear of a bureaucracy pursuing its own interests arose as an "unintended consequence" of the reform. The result was an irregular, self-propelled, and divisive interrelationship of economic, political, and bureaucratic needs and forces.

The "model" of decentralized or regionalized administration of industry introduced by Khrushchev in 1957 is not completely defunct, despite a temporary appearance to the contrary. This is proved by the creation of regional obedineniia in 1973.[8] At present there are definite limits to decentralization. The requirements for it lie outside the realm of political possibility. According to Francis Seton, "Decentralization requires for its permanent success a system of depersonalized signals like market prices, interest rates and freely disposable profits which can push and pull individual managers in the desired direction without a constant string of detailed orders from the centre."[9] Regionalism continues to exist to a noticeable degree in, for example, the comparatively large number of Union-republic ministries now in existence; the movement for the creation of obedineniia; and the tendency, however restricted, of managers to make more economic connections with other enterprises on their own. It is not fully safe, however, for voices have been raised against it.[10]

Another related issue is whether the ministries are to give detailed instructions for the planning process and to use sanctions against enterprise noncompliance (the oft-cited <u>administirovanie</u>), or to provide general guidance and supervision and so some of the research and overall planning that is beyond the capability of individual enterprises (though perhaps partly within the capability of the new obedineniia). And will the ministries use their new computer capabilities as an aid to the enterprises or as a means to fasten a new iron net of controls--effective ones this time, it will be argued--over the enterprises? Cybernetics may be made to counteract competition in favor of a new centralization, and will the ministries yield power even to the obedinenie?

Another question is the ability of the ministry's personnel to think and operate in new ways. Khrushchev's successors staffed the "new" ministries with many of the functionaries of the pre-1957 ministries, and returned to them the power of active direction of the <u>predpriiatiia</u> (enterprises) with only a vague exhortation not to wield their powers in the high-handed and even capricious manner they had before. The seemingly concrete limitation on the reduction of centrally determined indices was not firmly binding. Despite many Western claims that "Libermanism" had been accepted and its implementation had been begun, Liberman's proposals were not being applied in toto. He then wanted even fewer centrally set indices and a sort of "market" situation to determine enterprises' production goals. By 1970 Liberman had modified his position so much that some spoke of a "recantation." For example, he now states that profit is important only insofar as it aids centralized planning and that the pre-1965 economy was effective.[11] As the rejection of full-scale "Libermanism" suggests, a major question is the number of centrally set success indicators that the enterprise manager will have to attain. Will the ministries increase them further? Will the enterprise be allowed to use the profits it earns?

Often the Soviet press vaguely suggests a simplification of administrative structure and the elimination of some of the staff. Specifically, can the hierarchical chain be shortened to only two or three links: ministry-obedinenie-enterprise, or even just the first two? In addition, will the large-scale use of computers and data-processing result in a more rationally run or a still more cumbersome and erratically operating economic system? (The addition of machinery cannot in itself solve problems of human organization.) The size and importance of the ministries make the results here of wide-ranging significance. The ministries' new relationships with the Party apparatus, with the trade union network, and with one another also raise questions. In the Stalinist economy every unit had its place; but when the system was altered, the interrelationships and roles of its constituent units were less clearly defined. Each unit of the economy was to take the same action, but independently. However, the units reacted differently under the new "rules of the game."

The outcome was not a foregone conclusion in 1965, and still is not today. Although the Soviet political leadership wields great and diverse powers over a state bureaucracy that it interpenetrates, that bureaucracy has the capability to resist the leaders' policies and alter them. Bureaucrats are "permanent politicians" who exercise a "negative power" to act or not act in order to protect and further their own interests.[12] All bureaucracies have this ability by virtue of their knowledge, organizational cohesion, and the capacity to turn implementation (the "rule application" stage) into the remaking of policy. This is particularly true of the Soviet bureaucracy, and is due partly to the lack of free-flowing and well-organized oppositional currents in Soviet society. An independent and effective union movement can do far more than government in limiting the power of industrial administrators. As a result, the Soviet industrial bureaucracy, to which industrial managers belong, is capable of serious resistance to and change of the economic reform. "Not only may the operating entity be inappropriately organized for the transformation task, the vested interest and the habits ingrained in the operating entity will often provide the major source of resistance and the bitterest opposition to transformation."[13]

T. H. Rigby says that in Soviet policy-making, "the upward pressure of opinion of particular interests" is more important than "the twist that particular interests . . . give to policies in the course of implementing them."[14] In Soviet politics a grouping opposed to a policy tends not to oppose it until it comes into its hands for implementation, at which time it can disembowel it. Under the dead weight of Lenin's codified exhortations for "democratic centralism," outright disagreement with policy is risky if not perilous, as P. Shelest's abrupt demotion from the Politburo in 1972 shows. In addition, there is no easy outlet for open disagreement, no organized political opposition exists, and political resignation is not a feasible alternative because no significant centers of power exist outside the Party and state machines. Resignation renders one ineffectual, and penniless besides. As a result, effective disagreement with policy tends to exist within established structures and is expressed as resistance to, and even sabotage of, policy in its implemental stage.

Beside the issue of resistance looms the major, but necessarily vague, question of inefficiency. As two Soviet economists point out, if the organization of production is not genuinely "scientific" and consequential, economic reform cannot operate to achieve the desired effect. Any such "scientific" system necessarily would involve a top-to-bottom restructuring of ministries and a rethinking of both their operations and their functionaries' attitudes, a tall order. This would require, as Soviet writers have noted, that the ministries be put on <u>khozraschet,</u> as are the enterprises. This "tying" of the "main administrative apparatus to material production in order that . . . the bonus be paid for a specific personal contribution to production" has been called the "most difficult problem."[15]

This issue relates, of course, to the question of Soviet industry's organizational structure. Even enterprises with fewer than 200 workers often have relatively large, and therefore costly, administrative staffs. The reform has not solved the problem. The cost of industrial administration rose faster than industrial output between 1966 and 1968 (25-30 percent, compared with 15 to 20 percent).[16] One reason is that small enterprises model themselves upon larger ones, a tendency aggravated by the Russian tradition of a bureaucracy staffed by "a silent majority" of Gogolian clerks. Certainly, Russian society has long shown a propensity for the replacement of socio-economic units and relationships by state organizations. Making administration efficient is difficult everywhere. Peter Drucker notes that whereas large businesses in the United States have added "layer upon layer" to management for twenty-odd years, the outcome in terms of productivity is not clear. He adds, "We learned, some seventy years ago, how to define, how to measure, and how to raise the productivity of manual work. But we have yet to learn what productivity really means in any other kind of work."[17]

THE MINISTRIES: PERSONNEL, POWERS, STRUCTURE, AND THE CHALLENGE OF CHANGE

Personnel

Although the ministries now in existence are presented in most Soviet discussions as being totally new, they are in fact the pre-1957 ministries reconstituted. Despite the fact that ministries are now operating within a context that renders illegitimate actions carried out in the old manner, they have been able to prevent the application of the new rules of the game. The fundamental continuity of personnel in the ministerial-sovnarkhoz structure is a well-documented fact. Two Soviet authorities write:

> In most cases sovnarkhoz workers and employees of old ministries which existed in the 1950's entered the new ministries and [their] departments.
> Some of them, frankly speaking, are completely unable to divorce themselves from the old,

> out-dated methods of administration. As heretofore, some of them consider their unreasoned, impulsive decisions as infallible.[18]

The collective attitudes and actions of the multitude of holdovers from the sovnarkhozy and pre-1957 ministries who filled the new control agencies without any change constitute a fundamental limitation on the possibility of developing the manager-superior relationship in accordance with the official intentions. Using the old personnel was an understandable act, but perhaps not an unavoidable one. Of course, even the introduction of a new generation of industrial bureaucrats would not have solved the whole problem. New men "would soon develop the habits and interests of their predecessors, just as happened before."[19] Certainly, organizations do have the power to remold the thinking of their members, something consciously attempted by American corporations in training programs.

The continuity of directing personnel bridging the eight-year gap has been stated in numerical terms by Jerry Hough, who notes:

> ... the new ministers were chosen from the same type of engineer-manager who had dominated the ministries for over two decades.
>
> In fact, to a considerable extent, the new ministers were the very men who had held top posts in the ministries a decade earlier. Of the thirty-three USSR industrial and construction ministers appointed in the Fall of 1965 (and without exception still in their post in February 1968), twelve had been USSR ministers in 1957. Another ten had risen to the level of deputy minister by that time, four had become glavk heads, and one was the RSFSR minister for his branch of industry.[20]

The return of the former ministers to Moscow was not sudden. By 1963 many of them were already there as members of state committees, a proto-ministerial organizational form. "Of twenty-six chairmen of state-committees in the industrial and construction fields, eight had been USSR deputy ministers, and another six had risen to a post above that of plan manager (prior to 1957)."[21] Top-level personnel such as these would not take easily to more flexible and less authoritarian methods of management. The very fact that they were again ensconced in Moscow must have boosted their senses of assurance and importance, and consequently reduced their willingness to change their outlook and behavior. Tibor Szamuely mentions nine ministers who have held their posts for many years, some for 30 years or more, and notes:

> One is fully justified in speaking of an incredible amount of stability in the top governmental offices of the USSR . . . the same men remain in the top jobs. Even the British Civil Service seems ephemeral by comparison.
>
> . . . . . .
>
> The Soviet elite has finally achieved the personal security it so sorely lacked under Stalin. Hence its vastly increased political weight.[22]

In addition to the gap between the ministers and the official image of the reform, a similar gap may well have existed between ministers and enterprise managers. There are not many former managers in ministerial positions; few may want to move into the ministerial structure because they are content with and enjoy their present duties and powers as managers.[23] What we may have here are two different life styles and a conflict between them, usually referred to by the imagery of frogs, fish, and ponds.

Unfortunately, no actual study of the ministerial grouping is known, a surprising fact in light of the existence of interest group analyses of almost every other important grouping in Soviet society.[24] As a result of this serious lacuna in scholarship, we are confronted with a mass of generalities. The impression derived from them is that the ministries are cohesive, entrenched bureaucratic formations exhibiting a determined though muted effort to preserve and enhance their positions through their abilities in policy implementation and behind-the-scenes politicking. On the other hand, differing views can be found, for example, in Alec Nove's statement that "both the Minister and the Deputy-Minister must be seen essentially as senior business executives or civil servants, not as politicians. . . . They are technical executants, not policy-makers."[25] We shall see whether this definitional remark holds up in the face of ministerial behavior (some of which is provided by Nove). David Lane is probably nearer the mark when he says that "the ministries, and other committees . . . are the effective government of the country."[26]

One indicator of ministerial influence and power, although not conclusive in itself, is the rate of turnover of top ministerial personnel, which has been decreasing since 1956 and became, as ascertained by Hough, "unbelievably low" between 1966 and 1971, a part of the reform period. He discovered that "not one of the 11 first deputy or deputy chairmen of the USSR Council of Ministers was replaced between the last two congresses [23rd and 24th], and only four of the 57 ministers and state committee chairmen that sat on the Council of Ministers were removed in the same period. . . ." The turnover rate of members of the USSR Council of Ministers was

67 percent in 1956-61, 45 percent in 1961-71, but only 10 percent in 1966-71.[27]

The high cohesiveness of the ministerial bureaucrats is shown by the relatively small number who have also served in the Party apparatus. The "dual executive" or person with a mix of economic and political experience exists mainly at the republic and lower levels of the state bureaucracy. (A notable example was D. S. Korotchenko, twice Chairman of the Ukrainian Council of Ministers, who "alternated between work in . . . Party line posts and positions in the state bureaucracy.")[28] Although George Fischer has shown that a large percentage of top Soviet party executives had an "overlap" of specialized and organizational work in their careers, it must be recognized that Fischer chose Party executives (Party secretaries) for his sample. He did not test his "dual executive" thesis by comparing his sample with top executives in the state apparatus.[29] John Armstrong states emphatically: "Certainly it is well established that industrial ministerial staffs in Moscow rarely interchanged top personnel with either state or party organizations. . . ."[30] He adds that "even the sovnarkhoz episode . . . did not overcome this career-line isolation" and suggests that this correlates with differing views on policy and even hostility among groups in different career lines, a hostility with political implications. Some confirmation of "career-line isolation" among state bureaucrats is provided by Robert Donaldson's study of the 1971 Central Committee. He found that "none of the incumbent full members who had held state jobs in 1966 had . . . shifted into party positions by 1971."[31] The isolation is not total; some occupants of positions in the state bureaucracy have worked in the Party bureaucracy. This continues. After 1965 some of the new deputy ministers were former Party apparatchiki. This is in line with Brezhnev's continuing attempt, clarified and formalized somewhat at the 24th Party Congress in 1971 and expressed again in 1974, to use the Party organizations in the state bureaucracy to supervise the latter's work more closely. This attempt indicates the ministries' power all the more strongly. If the power had not existed, there would have been no reason to limit it.

The issue of where loyalty primarily lies cannot be settled with finality. However, Rigby, discussing conflict among the Party's leaders in the 1950s, says that "the role of the leaders in these conflicts seems to have depended not on their past career-patterns, but on their current jurisdictions."[32] The same general point of view is upheld by Derek Scott, who sees the state bureaucracy holding great powers apart from the party apparatus and states:

> The preponderance, for most of the period since the revolution, of ministries concerned with the management of particular industries, and the indispensable

> requirement of specialised skills in the technology and economics of those industries, has regularly brought into membership of the formal government men whose careers have been cast in as narrow a field of activities as those of industrialists of the western world. Though party members, as most successful men in the Soviet Union become, they probably give their first loyalties to their industries.[33]

This means to the organizations representing their industries. We also have some other knowledge concerning top Soviet bureaucrats: they have not been military officers for lengthy periods, they have not had a general education or legal training but technological training, and they have been "socialized" primarily in the organizations in which they have worked, not earlier in schools or their families.[34] In-service socialization would tend to increase a grouping's cohesiveness, technological training would give it the capability to act decisively, and a lack of legal training could increase its inclination to act in its own interests. These bureaucrats may be a bit older than the Party apparatchiki in their areas, and "older Central Committee members are more likely to be associated with the government than with the party apparatus."[35]

The ministers certainly head a large bureaucracy, with employment in state administration having risen to approximately 1,874,000, an increase of 516,000 (38 percent) in the period 1964-70, a period of "reform."[36] The actual figure may be much larger. Two Soviet writers state that "more than 10 million persons are occupied directly in . . . the administration of the national economy. . . ." W. Keizer cites the figure of 12 million, given by N. P. Fedorenko in 1965, and notes that Peter Wiles and Leon Smolinski estimate that the grouping increased by 50 percent between 1955 and 1962.[37] Although it is now policy to reduce the size of the bureaucracy, results are less than desired despite the efforts of the People's Control Committee. For example, in late 1971 it charged that at least one ministry allowed most of its 14 glavki to exceed their maximum allocations for the maintenance of the administrative apparatus.[38] In the country as a whole, although the percentage of administrative and managerial personnel reportedly dropped from 17 to 9 percent during the period 1940-66, during 1965-68 it increased.[39] The reasons for this growth are various: the operation of "Parkinson's Law," the understandable desire of those with higher education for white-collar positions, and the creation or retention of unnecessary administrative positions in order to maintain the budgets of agencies and the influence of their leaders.

Significantly, those who in their work emphasize the power of the Party apparatus have said that the state bureaucracy is superior in some instances, particularly in technical questions and matters of detail. As Hough puts it:

> Whatever devolution of authority to the leading regional officials has occurred, it is clear that the Soviet Union remains a country in which the vertical administrative units--the ministries and state committees . . . are on the whole much stronger than the horizontal or regional ones.[40]

The bureaucracy's power relationship with the Party apparatus is in a kind of general balance that fluctuates to some degree on each specific issue but that survives the tension generally intact.

The Foundations of Influence and Power

One of the main sources of the state economic bureaucracy's power in policy concerning industry lies in its superior knowledge of the complexity of industrial matters. The closest to official recognition of the fact that the Party apparatus is limited by the state bureaucracy is Khrushchev's statement in 1963 that the most formidable opposition to his policies was the Council of Ministers.[41] Rigby has likened the Presidium of the Council of Ministers, as well as the Secretariat, to standing committees of the Politburo, which are masters of routine.[42] In 1965 Brezhnev admitted that policy in agriculture was being frustrated by the state bureaucracy when he said, "It must be stressed that, at certain levels of our State apparatus, at Gosplan, in the ministries and various administrations, there is to this day a tendency to alter this or that point, juggle with figures . . ., and slight the interests of the kolkhozes and sovkhozes."[43] Brezhnev was served by the Minister of Agriculture that Khrushchev had removed, V. Matskevich, until the poor harvest of 1972 allowed or necessitated his removal once again.

The grouping gaining the largest number (17) of new seats (46) in the Central Committee of 1971 was the central state bureaucracy, an indication of an increase in its political stature. Christian Duevel notes the "good showing made by the central government bureaucracy . . . as against that of the central Party apparat. . . ." The central state bureaucracy increased its representation on the new Central Committee from 73 to 85, whereas the representation of the Party apparat increased only from 44 to 47 during the same period.[44] A study of the 1971 Central Committee found that "the proportion of full member seats on the Central Committee occupied by the apparatchiki had decreased slightly since 1966, while the proportion occupied by members of the state bureaucracy had increased somewhat [and] . . . the balance between party and state positions on the Central Committee as a whole remained relatively stable."[45] Even the increase of the Party apparat's representation on the Central Committee may be less a successful power grab by the apparatchiki than a determined and perhaps desperate attempt by them to retain overall political dominance in the face of a general trend in Soviet society toward greater importance and representation of specialists and particular interests.

The significance of these statistics becomes clear when it is noted that 9 of the 28 Central Committee members promoted from alternate to full membership were ministerial personnel (almost all ministers and deputy ministers). These figures do not mean that the bureaucracy is beginning to overtake the Party apparat in representation on the Central Committee, only that the bureaucracy continues to get a notable share of the increase in seats. However, although the corresponding figure for Party apparatchiki is 17, almost all of these (15) are persons based in the provinces. Persons in or near the "head office" of an organization tend to have greater information and access to decision-makers and to policy-making than do those at the periphery. (A generally accepted case in point is the informal but effective joint policy-making carried on in London by members of formally separate governmental and nongovernmental organizations.) Perhaps because of these developments Hough can say: "Rather than the regional political leaders, it seems to be the leading specialized establishments which have been the main beneficiaries of the diffusion of power from the top party leadership."[46] The entire question becomes even more significant if Scott's suggestion is correct: ". . . the Council of Ministers--and the corresponding bodies at the lower levels of administration, with the departmental apparatus answering to them, may . . . exercise some of the functions of an opposition."[47]

The way in which this may occur is suggested by R. H. S. Crossman, who held two ministerial positions in Harold Wilson's cabinet. He notes that a minister unavoidably acquires a "departmental view" after three years in his job. (Soviet ministers may have ten times this period in one job, hence the dilution of any partiinost' they may once have had.) Crossman says:

> The greatest danger of a Labour Cabinet is that its members will be corrupted from being a team of Socialists carrying out a collective Cabinet Strategy into a collection of individual departmental Ministers.

> ......
> That's one danger. .... The other danger we face
> is that the Departments get together and dictate to
> the politicians behind the scenes in Whitehall.
>
> ......
> If Whitehall gangs up on you it is very difficult to
> get your policy through, or even to get a fair hearing for a new idea.[48]

Having illustrated the nature of the foundations of the power wielded by the state industrial bureaucracy, particularly the ministries, the latter's new structure and internal operation, as well as the new overall administrative arrangement, can be briefly sketched out.

Ministerial Structure and Process

Bywords concerning the goals of Soviet administrative structures in industry are simplicity, efficiency, and computerization.

The Structure of Industrial Administration

The overall structure of industrial administration is supposed to change in several important particulars. One change desired is the shortening of the "chain of command" between the ministry and the individual enterprise. In some cases the implementation of this process means elimination of the enterprise as a separate organization. The key word and institution here is the obedinenie. The approach basically involves the replacement of the glavk (chief administration) by the obedinenie, which is itself made up of enterprises. The hierarchical scheme of a branch generally is to become a ministry-obedinenie, except that the largest and the most geographically isolated enterprises are retained at the bottom of the ministries' organization charts. Interestingly, although this policy is now in its particular form, as claimed, the result intended bears some similarity to a past attempt at administrative rationalization, thus revealing another instance of the operation of a Soviet "tradition." During the 1930s there was "considerable progress in rationalizing the administrative structure . . . the so-called two- or three-link system was adopted as a model scaler pattern for the organization of a commissariat"[49] (renamed ministries in March 1946). The rationalization of that period lacked the element of the obedinenie, which is new. The term "three-link" is again used.

Some progress has been made. In certain branches, notably petroleum and coal mining, the number of major levels of administration has been reduced from five to three, partly through the replacement of glavki by obedineniia.[50] The former mnogostupenchatyi ("multi-stage system") had been one of ministry-combine-trust-mine. During 1970, 85 mines in the Ukraine were combined into 41 mine administrations (skakhtoupravleniia) and 26 trusts were abolished. Eleven combines remain with 13-30 mines under each. (One combine, Donetsugol', has 27 mines, 168 sections, and 260 brigades.) By these and other means the administrative apparatus (below the ministerial level, presumably, though this is not made clear) was reduced by 9,000 persons and its cost by 18 million rubles per year. In at least one instance a two-link system (ministry-enterprises) has been established. The apparatus of the Estonian Food Industry Ministry has taken on the functions of a territorial-branch obedinenie without changing structurally. Its enterprises are directly subordinated to it. In addition, all the operating expenses of the ministerial apparatus are now covered by the profits of its enterprises.[51] The process of change is not considered complete, for information flows have yet to be simplified.

The elimination of levels of administrative structure, while no panacea for the problems of Soviet industrial administration, is likely to have a rationalizing effect by shortening lines of communication and clarifying responsibility. This may, however, increase the power of the ministries over the enterprises and even over the obedineniia that absorb the enterprises.

The Cybernetic Chimera

An important reason for the current emphasis upon the application of computer technology to the administration of industry in the Soviet Union is ideological and political. "In a grand effort to salvage the system of central economic management, rationalization of that system through cybernetics has been proposed."[52] Many Soviet economists and political figures consider central planning to be an essential and desirable difference between the Soviet and "bourgeois" systems. Accordingly, the wide-scale adoption of computers is founded upon a hope that the present philosophy and organizational structure of the economy can thereby be retained. Since "cybernetics is the science of control and communication directed toward funding off increasing entropy, or disorder,"[53] it has been pressed into service with an enthusiasm and political support reminiscent of such seeming panaceas of the past as GOELRO (electrification of the country), Taylorism, and Lysenkoism-Michurinism. As Loren Graham puts it, cybernetics

> . . . restored faith in overall planning by presenting clear analogies for the combination of decentralization with overriding central purposes.
>
> Cybernetics revitalized at least temporarily, the Soviet leaders' confidence that the Soviet system could control the economy rationally.[54]

This confidence continues unabated and is well exemplified by the plan, announced in 1966, for an integrated nationwide network of computing centers (SNCC) linking ministries, planning and supply agencies, and enterprises. The network is being built not only out of confidence. "The inconsistencies of the partially decentralized system" tempted the planners to reestablish the controls they almost gave up. "Central physical allocation [even if incomplete--K.R.] carries an inherent tendency towards higher degrees of centralization" because the "tauter" the plans, the better it works. Computerization would seem to facilitate taut plans. However, "progress currently is being severely crippled by administrative confusion and by a debate between two top government agencies over the structure and control of the network."[55] The inter-bureaucratic power conflict is raging between two would-be controllers of the proposed computing system, the Central Statistical Administration (Tsentral'noe Statisticheskoe Upravlenie, or TsSU) and Gosplan. Gosplan's scheme, sophisticated and flexible, would have enterprises passing on data to their ministries and to regional Gosplans--and only then to central agencies, such as the USSR Gosplan and TsSU. Gosplan advocates decentralizing data collection, computing, and minor decision-making, thus allowing the computing process to be close to production. TsSU, on the other hand, would have ministries getting their data only from it, making it a quite powerful central agency and the computing system one of some rigidity and subject, perhaps, to the magnification of whatever errors are fed in.[56] "Junk in, junk out" has been called the first rule of computer use.

The problem is more than one of conflict alone; paradoxically, the system "is being built before any design for it has been agreed upon."[57] The number of TsSU computing centers is increasing, as are those of ministries and their departments. "All ministries are developing their own automated control system designs. . . ."[58] Obviously, the ministries fear "to surrender their control over information flows to a 'super' computing agency [and instead] they would each organize their own computer centers, serving only their own functional areas" and "[are] opposed [to] the proposal for a hierarchy of computer centers."[59] Problems include conflict and lack of coordination among different agencies and levels of industry, limitations of Soviet computers, and some lack of compatibility between different computers. For example, all the automated control systems of 15 plants of the USSR Ministry of Heavy Power and Transport Machine Building have different capacities and, more important, "informationally they are all incompatible."[60] Even the several dozen new systems to be created by 1975 will not be compatible. And, to compound this ludicrous but serious problem, none of these systems meshes with the systems of the planning agencies. The perverse Soviet talent for autarky is limiting the development of a national computing system.

As a result, a dilemma of sorts exists: a deficient but growing "system" into which new installations are to be fitted, but only with more and more difficulty. Although the future course and exact form of the network are not clear, it probably will grow until a corrective effort is unavoidable. That effort, if it is begun, necessarily will have to be a Herculean one involving the massive addition of foreign computers.

The problems of the network derive from various factors: the rejection of cybernetics during the Stalinist period, the later emphasis upon computers mainly for scientific uses, the lack of enough standardized data, a lag in the development of "software," a pronounced shortage of programmers, a lack of managerial familiarity with computers, and the existence of an economic system that operates through involved procedures impossible to change merely by the introduction of machinery.[61] Several specialist Soviet participants have said that computerization can be a real help to the economy only if it is preceded by basic reorganization. G. Popov, a prominent economist, forthrightly stated:

> Mathematical methods and computers are among the tools for the rationalization of management and must be regarded as part of the overall system of work in improving management. When these tools are used in isolation from other sectors or are unjustifiably put into use before their time, they do not yield the proper gain.[62]

The American economist Herbert Levine pointed to a specific problem when he noted:

> New ways of reporting data must be devised before the data can be handled by computers. If there is to be a unified computer network, the data classifications must be standardized for all reporting data. Such standardization requires a complete overhaul of all existing accounting systems. . . .[63]

A major problem for Soviet planners will be the integration of the reform of management with the introduction of computer technology, while they are trying to close the widening technological gap with other countries, particularly the United States. At present third-"generation" computers are on the scene, though hardly in sufficient numbers, and the influential Academician A. Glushkov speaks of the arrival of a fourth "generation" that will bring a national automated system of management "significantly nearer . . . something that is possible only in a socialist society."[64] Fourth-"generation" computers may be rendered superfluous by new minicomputers.[65] Glushkov optimistically promises computers with fantastic increases in calculating speed and storage capacity. These, however, are as yet phantom computers of a phantom network. Academician V. A. Trapeznikov is more realistic when he notes that "we are in reality only starting our work" in controlling extensive complexes and "big systems."[66] Nevertheless, movement is taking place. Since the early 1970s hundreds of Soviet enterprises have introduced automated systems of organization and planning of production each year.

Despite this progress, it is difficult to acquire from Soviet sources a sense of the specific accomplishments attained in production through the use of computers. We can find names of management computer systems (such as the M-1000, made in Georgia, and the Pyta-110, made in Lithuania) and some general or vague claims for their capabilities, but little concerning their specific industrial accomplishments and defects. It is significant that only one-seventh of the computers in seven East European countries are Soviet-made, whereas more than half have been imported from non-Communist states (about 30 percent of these from the United States). This procurement pattern probably "reflects the generally poor performance of Soviet computers, the difficulty of obtaining service and spare parts, the low reliability, particularly of peripheral equipment, and the inadequate library of standard programs for Soviet machines and no doubt also reflects a desire to maintain a real degree of independence of the USSR in a key sphere."[67] An associated project is a nationwide system aimed at controlling the information explosion. Its purpose is to provide users with systematized information on research completed and in progress. Its components are almost 200 territorial centers and about 9,000 information departments at major enterprises, research institutes, and design bureaus, which reportedly cover 75-80 percent of the scientific research conducted in the country.[68]

Since cybernetics is based on the control of actual, rather than projected, performance, the Soviet government will not be able to rationalize the economy by relying on a centralized national network of computers stuffed with data on industry. As Loren Graham points out:

> It is a mistake to believe that cybernetics makes it
> possible to control the most complex processes by
> collecting in a central location enormous amounts
> of information. Indeed, cybernetics holds that
> barriers to information matter as much for control
> of processes as do free-flowing avenues of information.[69]

The Soviet leaders will not be able to merge cybernetics and industrial management in a way that aids in producing the desired material results until they make the organizational, economic, and personnel changes that ensure that computers are connected with a rational, efficient industry. Fitting cybernetics into the prevailing ideology and scheme of industrial administration is no substitute for increased, overall rationality.

Ministerial Structure and Operations

Although the overall environment of Soviet industrial administration has undergone a real change, only a few of the ministries themselves seem to have changed either their structures or their methods substantively. Although it is difficult to say what changes in their structure and internal workings have been brought about by the reform, general structural changes have been authoritatively suggested. In 1965 Brezhnev called for the simplification of ministerial structures through reducing the number of levels within them, in order to make their administration "capable of settling all problems of the operation of enterprises promptly, efficiently and in a competent manner."[70] This demanding, perhaps too unrealistic, wish has not been realized in any general sense, although some ministries, notably one presented as a "model" ministry, may have made some movement in the direction outlined. The Ministry of Instrument-Making, Automation and Control Systems is often held up as a paragon of the "new" or "reformed" ministry. Its minister grants interviews, and its innovational acts are widely publicized in the press. Supposedly, "planning power has been delegated to the department-chief level. Every department forms an industrial unit with the enterprises under its control to work out detailed production planning jointly--and the ministry has no veto power over the decisions."[71] "Part" of the same ministry's reserves and of several funds, such as those for circulating capital and wages, were put at the disposal of its glavki and, in addition, Councils of Directors were established within the glavki in order to permit closer contacts and greater exchange of information among the ministry's units.[72] However, the organization chart of a republic ministry (Moldavian Food Industry) shows that "organization, forms, methods and style of the branch administrations [glavki and so on] of the ministry have changed little in comparison with the branch administrations of the sovnarkhoz."[73] It seems that few innovations have been introduced.

If the functions of the ministries are no longer to include the direction of actual enterprise operations but are to be long-range planning, coordination, study of demand, determination of the requirements of production, and the locating of supplies, then the roles of their economic and financial services will have to increase. The resulting ministerial role will bear a certain similarity to that of a central corporation in the United States. The structural goal has been stated to be the welding together of the enterprise and the ministry into a "single economic organism, a production economic complex" in which the salaries of ministerial workers will depend directly upon the results of the enterprise's work. In the Moldavian example just cited there seems to be a plan to eliminate the glavki and create obedineniia instead. If widely introduced, this new arrangement will represent a systemic change in the structure of Soviet industrial administration.

The idea of placing the ministry "on khozraschet" or making it directly affected by the relative success of its enterprises is motivated by the desire to make ministerial officials feel the effects of their actions and to change those actions from purely bureaucratic to more economically based ones.

> It is entirely improper . . . [that] the work of the enterprises . . . and the work of the production control agencies . . . are built on different economic principles: cost accounting in the former case and the state budget in the latter case.[74]

The change would make ministerial functionaries financially dependent upon the success of enterprises within their branch; for instance, they would be paid bonuses only when enterprises fulfilled the main success indicators, sales and profits. In certain Latvian ministries, bonuses are connected with "additional conditions" for success in ministerial administrative work.

The ministries, then, are being given an unenviable task: that of remaking their enterprises in a fundamental way while remaking themselves. It is difficult enough to make others change; to alter oneself is the most difficult and demanding task of all. Perhaps too many opposites have to be balanced. As an article in *Izvestiia* put it, it is necessary for the ministries "to harmonize a single state plan with the complete cost accounting of enterprises, centralized guidance with broad local initiative, the principle of one-man management and responsibility with the enhanced role of production groups."[75] The extent of success in this difficult labor of self-reform is not at all clear; the task may be Sisyphean. Although we can, as usual, find statements that the "model" Ministry of Instrument-Making has stormed this height of the reform, it is not clear exactly what this statement means for it, much less for other ministries, particularly when the Minister for Domestic Services of the Georgian Republic said in 1971 that his ministry was the only one in the republic on khozraschet.[76] Although some commentators seem to believe that a new system of rewards for functionaries in the industrial apparat can be introduced that is so precise that the personal contribution to production of each functionary can be ascertained, success is an unrealistic prospect.

Certainly, the reform is being implemented in a narrow or limited way (nekompleksno) within the ministries, their research, design, and construction institutes, and their other constituent organs. Even the highly touted Ministry of Instrument-Making is deficient in this regard. Although it was formally "reformed," its research, design, and construction organizations were not. The lowest levels, the enterprises, have been most affected by the reform, but the middle and higher levels have been left almost untouched.[77]

One way to try to effect change conducive to reform within the ministries is to provide them with the means and requisite personnel to facilitate the performance of their functions more efficiently. Adjuncts of the administrative process have been relatively scarce. Clerical facilities are "extremely poor" and

> office space is limited and poorly arranged, with file cases crowding the corridors. . . . Relatively simple items . . . such as typewriters and carbon paper, are in short supply and poor in quality . . . the ratio of secretaries, typists and file clerks to administrators is very low.[78]

Alec Nove calculated the number of stenographers and typists in the entire USSR as only 130,000 in 1960, compared with 559,000 in the United Kingdom in 1951. The situation cannot have changed greatly, although in 1973 a campaign was begun to give some prestige to the office secretary and to train more. The USSR has only seven secretarial schools.

Of course, although this is a limiting factor, it has not been so in an absolute sense. Soviet industry has had great successes, relying upon high inputs of labor, materials, and technology in a context of massive political pressure. In the present stage of development of the Soviet economy, when some definite change in hitherto neglected areas could go a long way toward providing the impetus for putting the USSR into a qualitatively new stage, a rationalization of ancillary administrative services holds some promise.

In recent years there has been a decided publicizing and organizational effort to blunt the extreme nature of the problem and to provide Soviet industrial management personnel, from the ministry down to the enterprise, with the secretarial, mechanical, and electronic means for dealing more effectively with the essential administrative issues. However, the provision of up-to-date office equipment and computers has not reduced the managerial apparatus, but has increased it.[79] Introduction of office machinery cannot in itself bring about a reduction in staffs unless carefully utilized along with a general rationalization of administrative structures and relationships. Perhaps what we are seeing is several processes, now out of phase, that will yield results in the future.

The introduction of computers is proceeding within the ministries, and not solely as part of the national network. By 1975, according to the Deputy Chairman of the politically influential State Committee for Science and Technology, all all-Union ministries dealing with productive processes (and about one-fifth of the republic-level ministries) are to have begun to introduce computerized control systems in branches. Foreign computers are snapped up whenever possible. When IBM exhibited a 360/50 in the USSR for the first time, the system was bought on the spot by the Ministry of the Chemical Industry.[80] Since then large Control Data Corporation computers also have become favored.

The retraining of ministerial personnel in an attempt to make them capable of working more effectively in the new context of industrial administration is also an important process. This involves an imparting of some knowledge and consciousness of economic concepts, issues and methods of organization and management, questions of finance, and the fundamentals of psychology and sociology. The general goal is to impart what might be called "profits-people" thinking and to eliminate "rules-materials" thinking among functionaries of industrial management. The degree of success will depend on the extent to which the overarching rules of the economic game are changed. Two general processes are involved: the retraining of personnel now in the administrative apparatus and the creation of a new or quite changed system of education for students who may become industrial administrators.

Associated with retraining is an assessment of the qualifications of the personnel currently in administration; for example, the USSR Ministry of Industrial Construction Materials established a certification program, presumably in 1969, that supposedly was almost completed by 1973. Approximately 130,000 persons in the ministry had been processed by May 1972. The certification program had two goals: the placing of each administrator in the position in which he or she will produce the most, and the creation of a reserve cadre or corps of persons suitable for promotion. The process is carried out by special commissions and takes the form partly of oral encounters dubbed "businesslike conversations." During the four-year period, 7,995 cadres were selected as fit for promotion; of these, 300 were named enterprise directors and 600 chief engineers or first assistants to directors. Approximately 2,000 were found unfit. Of these latter "some" were demoted, while "others" were allowed to face a new examination within one year. One goal of the certification program seems to be the creation of a "shakeup" atmosphere that may spark people to perform better. Only polling would indicate to what extent morale and performance were lowered by the process. Other ministries have also been assaying their administrative cadres' qualifications.[81]

An example of a retraining program for administrative personnel is that of the Ministry of Machine Building for Construction, which established a branch Institute for Upgrading the Qualifications of Supervisory Personnel and Specialists at Ivanteyevka, a Moscow suburb. Every shop or department head and every chief engineer or director now has to complete a course there of from ten days to one month every three years. The institute has three departments: equipment, machine-building technology, and production economics and organization, the last of which is concerned with changes in administrative behavior. Most of the instructors have the <u>Kandidat</u> degree. Growing pains exist: The institute "lacks even the simplest of instructional aids and textbooks" (a general problem in Soviet management training), the instructors' teaching load is too heavy, and they lack possibilities for doing industry-related research.[82]

Retraining has begun at the level of the ministries as well. In February 1971 the Institute for Management of the National Economy, designed for teaching ministerial personnel, was opened in Moscow. The two members of the Politburo present at the opening of this training school, established by the State Committee for Science and Technology, were Kosygin and A. P. Kirilenko (who, Michel Tatu says, is "closely allied" with Brezhnev). Kosygin spoke, alluding to the "great importance of enabling leading cadres to refresh their knowledge in connection with the greater tasks facing the country's economy. . . ." Almost predictably, the first lecture, on the automation of management, was delivered by that prophet of cybernetics Academician Glushkov, thus artificially surrounding the endeavor with an atmosphere of science somewhat reminiscent of the Lysenko affair. V. Kirillin, a Deputy Chairman of the State Committee on Science and Technology, also spoke:

> The scientific technical revolution, the development of economic and social relations in our society, the expansion of the network of enterprises and associations, the growth of the flow of information--all this has made the process of control considerably more complicated. Therefore, a knowledge of the scientific foundations of the production organization and of the methods and techniques of control are today necessary for the leaders of the national economy.[83]

The institute has chairs of social and economic sciences, mathematical planning, management and forecasting, automated control systems, and social and psychological aspects of management. Laboratories for operations research and the psychology of work are being set up. The period of training is up to three months, with the "students" on paid leave from their places of employment. They are to attend a similar course every three to five years. The teachers are, according to Kirillin, the "country's greatest scientists" and Gosplan and ministry officials.[84] But, despite the intent of the new retraining program, the actual effect will be to strengthen the hand of the ministerial bureaucracy. It is no wonder that since the 24th Party Congress an attempt has been under way to build a system of "countervailing power" by enlarging the purview of the Party organizations within the ministries (see Chapter 5).

BEHAVIOR

As suggested above, the effects of the reform upon the industrial ministries are best revealed by their actions toward the enterprises. Ministerial actions indicate attitudes of political significance as well as limitations affecting the process of reform. They also show the present extent of ministerial powers over enterprises and tell us quite a bit about what is probably the most important of the enterprise manager's relationships with outside bodies. Prior to 1965, the Soviet industrial manager confronted "the most extensive and costly managerial control apparatus in the world."[85] Had it become any less powerful by 1975? Nove says that in 1965, "The ministries did acquire virtually all the powers of control over their enterprises which they possessed before 1957, with the single exception of supply-disposal functions. . . ." Abraham Katz says, "There is a constant tension between the ministries and the enterprise directors. . . ." As a result, a problem of fundamental importance arose out of the reestablishment of the ministries: "How can rights to autonomy, even if established in an official set of regulations, be protected against the right of a superior to give orders to an inferior?"[86] Although several component ideas of the reform were departures from traditional Soviet assumptions and practices, the decision to use the ministerial form was very much in the Soviet and, of course, the Russian tradition. It is as if the paradoxical idea that structured centralistic forces were to bring about decentralized initiative in the Soviet economy was the guiding conception of the political leadership in 1965. That leadership continues its unimaginative long-term policy, broken partially but for only a few years by Khrushchev, of working through conventional bureaucratized forms.

Preparation and Transfer

The first test of the ministries lay in their preparation and transfer of enterprises to the changed conditions and rules of operation called for by the reform. Many individual enterprises that were transferred were not in outstanding operational order. This elicited a rash of charges in the press that ministries were not preparing enterprises properly. Even the Deputy Chairman of the RSFSR Gosplan so complained. One prominent economist, P. Bunich, wrote of the "insufficiently consistent and systematic introduction" of the reform. Apparently, too, ministries often allowed enterprises to carry with them the special understandings they had been granted under the old conditions. The same economist criticized an "individualization" of criteria of evaluation, saying that "as a rule, the index that is most advantageous and convenient to the enterprise becomes [its] chief index."[87]

The problem of "individualization" seems to have been a real one. No less a personage than V. Zhigalin, the USSR Minister of Heavy, Power, and Transport Machine Building, noted that individual norms were set for all sections of the ministry's enterprises at the time of transfer. This practice is not in the spirit of the reform, since it encourages central direction and stifles development of the enterprises. The same minister suggested "several quite mandatory conditions" to be observed in transferring plants: self-sufficiency; stability in planning, supply, and sales; certainty of improving indicators; and clarity of future technical development and sales.[88] The house organ of the Ministry of Finance noted: "Individual ministries solve the problems of the transfer of subordinate enterprises to the new system of planning and economic incentives in a formal manner. . . ."[89]

The transfers took some time and were accompanied by definite delays. For example, the USSR Council of Ministers established a model transfer schedule by decree only on August 10, 1967, and the Kazakh Council of Ministers issued transfer schedules only that December.[90] But by March 1969 a member of the RSFSR Gosplan said, "The economic reform has now reached a qualitatively new stage."[91] By that date all the enterprises of several USSR ministries, including Nonferrous Metallurgy and Construction Materials, had been transferred.

At some time between June and October 1970, more than 40,000 enterprises (85 percent of the total number), producing 92 percent of gross industrial output and 95 percent of the profits, had been transferred, with the reform having begun in construction, trade, public catering, everyday services, communal facilities, and material-technical supply. This did not mean that completion was imminent. As late as the 24th Party Congress in 1971, completion was forecast only for the end of 1975--a target date several years later than the ones tossed about so confidently in 1965. Actual economic results are unclear; and any figures are to be regarded with the utmost caution, if not skepticism. Schroeder therefore concludes that gains have been "modest at best."

TABLE 2.1

Transfer of Industrial Enterprises, 1966-70

By the End of	Number Converted	Accounting for Percent of			
		Total Enterprises	Output	Employees	Profits
1966	704	1	8	8	16
1967	7,248	15	37	32	50
1968	26,850	54	72	71	81
1969	36,049	72	84	81	91
1970	44,300	90	92	--	95

Source: Gertrude Schroeder, "Soviet Economic Reform at an Impasse," Problems of Communism 20, no. 4 (July-August 1971): 38.

Transfer does not mean conversion, of course. It was emphasized to me in the Soviet Union more than once that full conversion to the reform was not an odnovremenyi akt; time was required for actual change to occur.[92] It is still to be seen whether actual conversion is complete even by 1976.

The Bases of Active Ministerial Control

The ministries began, even during the early stages of the implementational period, to act toward enterprises as they had prior to 1957. This activity took many forms. Besides changing plans frequently--a serious violation of the new spirit--they exerted direct, authoritarian control continuously if not daily, applying the old "ratchet principle" to enterprise plans,[93] breaking the law when it suited them, and in general interfering in the enterprises' fields of activity. The much-advertised "economic methods" often went by the board, and the ministries "diligently set about the task" of violating the new rules and resurrecting the "established routine" of the old days of autarkic ministerial dominance.

The holdovers from the old ministries used the institutional bases of power recently returned to them to regain a position of active and wide-ranging dominance over "their" enterprises. The increase in agencies solely to find "suitable" positions for functionaries from the defunct sovnarkhozy did not help matters.[94] No clear distinction between the rights of the ministries and the managers has evolved. Contributing to this failure in the reform model is the fact that ministries do not yet bear legal and financial responsibility for rulings and acts that bring economic harm to enterprises. Industrial managers view this as a grave problem.[95] Soviet lawyers have pointed out repeatedly that certain ministerial actions, notably the arbitrary changing of enterprise plans, constitute violation of the law. Even the "model" Bolshevichka obedinenie ran into serious difficulties due to arbitrary decisions by its glavk.[96]

One reason for the reimposition of elements of the old pattern is its acceptance by some managers. According to Katz, who has interviewed several Soviet managers, "most enterprise managers would prefer to deal with their 'own' [rodnoi] ministry than with either another central or a regional organ."[97] A way for pinning failures on "higher authority" is welcomed everywhere. Ironically, the Party apparatus itself encourages some ministerial pressure upon enterprises when it publicly pressures ministries to make enterprises act in certain ways. For example, Pravda discusses Party "instructions to [a ministry to] intensify supervision over and verification of fulfillment." Pressure for more and stronger ministerial supervision also comes from the People's Control Committee (KNK), which often asserts that ministries' inspections of enterprises are pro forma and that some sort of conspiracy of silence tends to exist between the ministry and the enterprises associated with it. The solution proposed by KNK--elimination of branch inspection and enlargement of the inspection functions of the Ministry of Finance--

sounds sensible but might, if implemented, be only an exchange of watchdogs.[98] This sort of publicity, however justified, creates "waves" that ultimately must break upon the enterprise.

Apart from the problem of causal relationships, it is clear that ministries engage in several activities that, under the new rules or model, constitute nothing other than gross interference in the work of the enterprise. For example, although reductions of staff are no longer to be dictated to enterprises, ministries continue to do so-- and in quite specific terms, sometimes even appending their orders to the legitimate index of the wage fund. Ministries also try to limit the size of production development funds, and even use them for the financing of investment for the entire branch. In short, enterprises often are not allowed by the ministries to use means granted them by the reform. These problems exist because a mixture of ignorance, authoritarianism, and absence of concern prevails in the ministries, their departments, and the glavki.[99] Soviet economists have said that the problem is essentially that the ministry and the glavk have "no direct economic interest in the success of their own work."[100]

A quite serious impediment to the development of the new system introduced by the ministries early in the reform is the "additional conditions" (dopolnitel'nye usloviia) defining enterprise success. These are, in effect, new main indices, clearly anti-reform in spirit and effect, added to the eight or nine remaining after the beginning of the reform in 1965. If these indices are not fulfilled, along with the authorized main indices of profitability and sales, bonuses either are not paid (to managerial personnel) or are cut by half (for workers).[101] Among these new indices are product quality, targets for the reduction of fuel and materials use, and the maintenance of growth in labor productivity over growth in average earnings. In commenting on the meaning of these new indices, which may have improvement as a goal, Schroeder says that "the bureaucracy is stronger than ever."[102] Ironically, Bolshevichka now faces more than ten success indices, including gross output in 1967 prices, a target that seems a sort of resurrected VAL.[103] Another indication of the ministries' opposition to the reform is their tendency to increase the number of centrally planned and approved indices, for example, "especially important tasks" in producing new products and installing new technology.[104] This indicates the existence of informalist bureaucratic activity, differences and even conflict between the Party apparat and figures high in the state bureaucracy, and the power of ministries to take anti-reform measures. As a result, the official ideal in this aspect of the manager-superior relationship has not been realized. The new ministries have tightened their control of enterprises.

Ministries and the Enterprise Plan

An act of the ministries that undermines the reform has been their forceful and frequent injection of changes into enterprises' plans. This common pattern need not be a problem if enterprises are given sufficient advance notice of impending plan changes and an exact statement of their content or if they are adequately compensated or reimbursed for the expenses caused by changes. Fifty-eight different plan changes were made for five customers of the Kolomna textile-machine building plant. This sort of activity obviously is common, since mention of it appears throughout the press.[105] A fabric plant in Moscow had its profits plan changed seven times during one year. A plant's trade union committee chairman complains that although his plant has been on the reform for four years, the ministry "often" alters the plan, an activity that he recognizes "is clearly opposed to the spirit and the letter of the economic reform." As a result, he adds, "Today you do not know what you will be doing tomorrow." This is decided, apparently, by urgent telegrams from the ministry or its glavki.[106]

Despite the widespread nature of the problem, the reasons for its existence are not completely clear. Certainly the ministries change enterprises' plans frequently, abruptly, and in some detail. The ministries issue what are in effect false plans and then correct them throughout the year whenever they can. Gosplan must be heavily at fault in this matter also. Nove, citing Liberman, emphasizes the sheer complexity of the planning problem and the need to correct for "disequilibria discovered after the plans have been approved." The task "overwhelms the apparatus," he says, and then adds, almost getting into the metaphor of the unraveling skein:

> Unbalances, when discovered, must be put right. The plan must then be altered in the course of the year or even the quarter. New instructions must be issued to produce or to deliver. They then become "internally inconsistent," because of incomplete amendment and because they are formulated by different planning organs bit by bit.[107]

The problem is recognized in the USSR. For example, a trade union official states unequivocally: "No matter how scientific the planning level may be, the prediction of the forthcoming production processes with all of their factors and consequences can never be complete."[108] One basis for the changing of plans is the pattern of excessive communications between ministries and enterprises. (This general feature of Soviet administration seems a part of the Russian administrative tradition.) John Armstrong notes that "in comparison with Western European administrative systems, vertical communication channels are overloaded in Soviet administration" and that "formal communication is relatively inefficient" and "grossly inadequate." He adds, agreeing with Nove, that "reliance on oral communication and neglect of correspondence is traditional in Russia. . . ."[109] My own experience bears this out. When I visited the showplace Elektrosila obedinenie in Leningrad, the director, his assistants, and the Party secretary were all at the ministry in Moscow on one of their periodic and frequent trips there for consultations. The problem continues to exist, as shown by a Pravda article criticizing the high number of komandirovki ("business trips") enterprise personnel must make to ministerial and glavk headquarters to solve supply and other problems.[110]

Soviet economists complain that a great deal of bureaucracy and attempts at excessive supervision remain. For example, "higher organizations" "vetoed" the application of Articles 2 and 4 of the new statute on enterprises in the case of some enterprises in Tomsk. In addition, the ministries continue to demand frequent reports, even telephoning daily.[111] Perhaps communications between enterprises and ministries are greater than before. The Red October plant in Volgograd is required to communicate to the minister daily a "great deal of information about the production not only of basic types of products (steel, rolled products), but also of articles of consumption and their assortment (knives, forks)."[112] This "petty tutelage" is a great obstacle to carrying out the reform.

This pattern produces the injection of a great many minor indicators into the enterprises' plans. For example, the Rostsel'mash plant still has planned for it the production of liquid steel, processed wood, bricks, and other items processed within the plant, and for the Elektroinstrument plant production is planned, as before: volume of goods produced, cost, consumption per ruble of goods production, and a cost reduction assignment. A widening circle of minor indicators is being brought to bear on enterprises, thereby rendering ineffective any economic stimulus to fulfill the plan.[113] For example, one plant received more sets of instructions "from above" in 1970 than it ever had in a year prior to the reform.

Since ministries often change the plans for the amount of goods produced, the financial plans have to be changed as often. One writer comments, "Under these conditions it is difficult to establish credit relations with enterprises." The balance of revenues and expenditures also is changed unnecessarily often. In one case, Gosbank had to warn a ministry of the impending cancellation of credit for one of its plants because of ministerial action.[114]

Although all the reasons for this kind of ministerial behavior cannot be given, Soviet commentary emphasizes that as long as economic decision-makers are bureaucrats first, administrative methods will predominate. In the Soviet context,

> In comparison with economic methods, the administrative ones are simplest and impress many officials.
>
> . . . . . .
>
> The development of democracy in planning will always depend upon the nature and degree of personal dependency for the individual planning levels. No matter how well the enterprise regulations are worked out, if the director . . . is completely dependent upon the leadership of the glavk, then centralism and thus administrative methods will be given broad scope.[115]

As a result of this continuing petty tutelage, managers remain cautious and secretive. As before, they try to adopt easy plans. Planning is, it has been said, "as before . . . based on the 'achieved.'" As a commentary on the attempt to apply the Shchekino experiment elsewhere notes: "Can one expect a director to lay all his reserves on the table? He is unaware of what planned surprises await him tomorrow or in the next quarter." Another discussion says that directors lack faith in the future of their enterprises.[116]

Besides the refusal to allow managers the rights in supply matters granted by the model, the ministries are attempting to retain their powers in this area as against those of the State Committee on Material and Technical Supply (Gossnab). Although it cannot be said definitely that a rivalry or conflict exists between the two types of state agencies, a high-level coordinating (and arbitrating?) body in matters of supply nevertheless has been formed, and ministries attempt to fulfill functions that logically belong to it. Accordingly, Gossnab has not fully succeeded in controlling supplies. Although it was intended that a single state supply system exist, ministries have supply offices, too, in violation of a decree of January 27, 1967. As one Soviet source trenchantly puts it: "In Leningrad, as in other cities, two supply systems operate in parallel. One is legal--it belongs to Gossnab. The other, semi-legal, was established by ministries and agencies."[117]

Some ministries even created new supply offices, the number in Leningrad alone growing from three in 1966 to 17 in 1967. Similar situations exist elsewhere. The new ministries not only resist the full implementation of the reform but also pursue traditional autarkic policies. Thus, the supply aspect of the manager-superior relationship remains imprecisely defined.

Ministries Versus Ministries

Ministries engage in more than one type of inter-bureaucratic conflict. They are also in conflict with one another. The old tradition of rigidly dividing the economy among themselves into autarkic "duchies" or "narrow, departmental corridors" and not engaging in any cooperative ventures dies hard.[118] As for the reasons, one analyst says: "The proven undependability of outside suppliers, together with great pressures to meet planned output targets, have led Soviet industrial ministries, as well as individual plants, to try to keep as much of the manufacturing process as possible within the organization."[119] This undercuts the task of effecting inter-branch cooperation in planning, research, production, and distribution. What economic ties exist between branches are mainly at the ministry level, far removed from actual production and its problems. Cooperation even at this level is still low. For example, technological processes, equipment, and methods discovered or developed in one branch often are not transferred to another. Pravda vainly urges ministries "to strive for fundamental improvement in the utilization of the scientific and technical advances brought forth by related industries."[120] Bonuses are now awarded for passing on a discovery to another branch. Their effect is still unclear.

The tendency of ministries that are large bureaucratized entities to keep their distance, and when in contact to be in conflict, is quite normal. In the (quasi-) capitalist West, "corporations compete as keenly as states" and have internal political dynamics similar to those of states even though they are public corporations. In Britain, for example, "the three great nationalized boards that run coal, gas, and electricity are in constant and vicious competition with each other. . . ."[121] Inter-bureaucratic conflict of this sort also has long been common in the United States, that between the Navy and the Air Force after World War II being a glaring example. More recent instances include the "intense internecine struggle" among the Federal Water Quality Administration, the U.S. Army Corps of Engineers, and the Council on Environmental Quality concerning responsibility for issuing dumping permits, and the difference in views on expanding Soviet-American trade among the Departments of Commerce, Defense, and State, and the President's adviser on national security. In addition to the rivalry between TsSU and Gosplan for control of a national computer network, already noted, the various ministries rushed into implementation of their own particular computer systems as soon as the national network was proposed. Obviously, they felt threatened.

Other examples are common. A particularly ludicrous one is the unwillingness of two ministries to determine, even after seven years of the intervention of national agencies and the writing of "mountains of paper," which of them was to have formal custody of the slings to be used in "packeting" timber shipped by rail.[122] This sort of problem is now of great importance because the economy has reached a degree of complexity requiring close inter-branch cooperation in order to maintain growth. There are numerous examples of production of the wrong types of products or of poor-quality products because of a lack of cooperation among enterprises in different branches. This is actually encouraged by Gosplan's practice of considering for incentive purposes only the enterprise that produces the end product as the producer of "consumer goods."

Although inter-branch cooperation is not completely lacking, a deputy chairman of the Lithuanian Council of Ministers notes that ". . . we are faced once again with the tendency to 'create one's own preserve' . . ., we still suffer from a fear of non-delivery. . . ." and that "under conditions of the economic reform, enterprises which are not able to obtain interbranch articles from other areas of industry prefer to enlarge their own production in those lines, or begin producing such items by making use [read 'misuse'] of the production development fund."[123] He informs us that the 28 enterprises and shops in Lithuania that produce iron castings are subject to 19 uncoordinated ministries and departments. Gosplan seems unable to encourage and enforce cooperation and specialization. Further, Pravda has vainly editorialized on the lack of coordination among Gosplan, Gossnab, and various ministries, and the discrepancies between plans and production thus produced. The result is the continuation of the "closed production cycle." Ministries sometimes even sabotage interbranch production links--for instance, take equipment intended for the enterprises of other branches for their "own" enterprises.[124]

The Climate of Ministerial Operations

Ministerial actions necessarily derive from the attitudes of their functionaries. These, in turn, are affected by the prevailing tendencies in the administrative climate. Especially important are attitudes on methods and style of administration and enterprise profits. These attitudes cannot be stated precisely; ministerial personnel, except for the minister and his deputies, do not speak frequently on major issues. Most of my sources are outside the ministries and may be hostile. Nevertheless, it appears that ministerial decision-makers often act in a near vacuum, conduct themselves and their organization with some aloofness if not haughtiness, handle issues apart from the overall situation in the branch and the economy, and tend not to work nearly as fast as they could to increase the supply of consumer goods.[125] The ministries have ideological allies among economists who favor centralization and denounce opposing points of view. One cannot know whether the volume and stridency of this pro-centralist "conservative" argument is merited by the size and vigor of the opposition, for the latter is not allowed to speak.

An example or two will set the tone. D. Allakhverdian, a prominent economist, charges in Pravda that unnamed "right opportunist theoreticians" are trying to give an "absolute value" to relative operational and economic independence of socialist enterprises, viewing them from positions of market socialism and competition. He also charges that these theoreticians counterpose the law of value to centralized principles of planning as the "main regulator of the socialist economy." He concludes by referring to the reform and asserting that "the intensification of economic methods of management in no way means the renunciation of administrative forms of control," though he softens his stand by adding that these "forms" ought to be based upon "a strictly scientific foundation" that, however, he does not describe.[126] This sort of argument against invisible idealists who want administrative relationships eliminated in favor of commodity-monetary relationships suffuses loyal economists' discussions of the reform even into 1974.[127]

Ministries can derive encouragement for their resistance from this widely and authoritatively circulated point of view. Although their attempts to protect their own position have even been idealized by high-sounding formulations such as "representative of the branch and of society before the enterprise,"[128] their motivations must derive from their fears of what the reform promises to do for their power position. Fear of losing status would tend to increase their "bureaupathic" behavior toward subordinates. Bureaucrats fearing a loss of their status are likely to react by asserting their rights in the system, notably in decision-making. This leads to increased friction between them and professional managers, and to an atmosphere not conducive to efficiency and productivity. For example, Polish bureaucrats generally have responded negatively to strategies of separating "economy" and "state," since these strategies would strip them of some of their power in favor of a managerial class. "Even where they have . . . been forced by economic pressures to make partial concessions to the principal of managerial autonomy under programs of economic reform they have usually tried to the best of their ability to sabotage the implementation of these concessions. . . ." In the USSR "the industrial bureaucracy tenaciously holds onto its old ways and opposes any change in essentials."[129]

Two conceptions of the role of profit are in conflict. Although profit has always been a goal, the reform required an increase in its importance. A professor of economics attempted to make it ideologically more respectable by saying:

> Profit is a category of commodity production. It appeared before capitalism and represents not a technical instrument with an unaltered nature but rather an economic category, i.e., an expression of the production relationships predominant in a society like the other categories of commodity production. . . . For this reason, profit in the U.S.S.R. differs from profit in capitalist nations to the same degree that the economic relationships of socialism differ from the economic relationships of capitalism.[130]

In contrast, a refrain now heard is the charge that under the new arrangement, enterprises are disregarding the needs of society in their quest for profit-yielding products. There must be some foundation to the charge. Even the eminent V. Nemchinov has pointed out that, given the irrational prices in effect, the commodities in greatest demand are also often the least profitable, whereas those yielding the enterprise the most profit may find no demand.[131] Other opposition seems, however, to be more ideologically based, although the frequency of the charge that some managers increase production of their most profitable goods and violate the assortment plan lends it objective credibility.[132] The argument tends to become one for increased emphasis upon the nomenklatura or some other less economically based indicator.

The recent Czech experiment is rejected, as are the "absurd" "petty bourgeois slogans" of "certain Marxists"--"shift to balanced market prices," "more freedom, less planning," "eliminate the bureaucracy of centralized management," "ensure the autonomy of enterprises in practice"--indicating that these ideas are having some currency and effect in the Soviet Union.[133] The ideological position is staked out by a kandidat of economics, who states:

> The economic reform must bring about the fullest realization of the socialist principle: what is advantageous for society should also be advantageous for the enterprise and its individual workers. . . . A different relationship--the subordination of the national interests to the interests of the individual enterprises--would contradict the objective economic patterns of socialism, and would lead to a loss of the advantages of its economy, an inseparable feature of which is centralized planning.[134]

This position also tends to be found in conjunction with the view that enterprises, though they ought to make a profit, ought not to keep it but instead give it (or, more exactly, the "free profit balance") to the state budget, for society. This view in its fullest form goes against a major point of the reform--that enterprises begin to retain at least a definite and significant portion of their profits for incentives, modernization, and other purposes. Some writers do not go so far as to deny enterprises the use of profits, but want enterprise interests to correspond to national interests in this matter. This shows how far the USSR is from a "socialist market economy" like Yugoslavia.

Suggested Solutions

Naturally, the difficulties that have been presented in this chapter are not all suffered in silence. Many suggestions have been made for either elimination or alleviation of the burdens that ministries impose upon enterprises and the obstacles they place in the way of the reform's implementation. Most of them seem to relate to making the ministry, through changes in the law, financially liable for losses incurred by enterprises as a result of its actions, particularly in changing enterprises' plans. Suggestions also relate to making the pay of ministerial functionaries depend upon the production achievements of enterprises and facilitating cooperation between ministries.

The general idea of giving functionaries a material stake in the work of enterprises has been forcefully expressed in Pravda by a USSR minister:

> As is known, workers in the ministerial apparatus now receive a definite wage from the budget, whose size has virtually nothing to do with whether any given person has been working well over the previous month, quarter, or year. If, however, the main administration [glavk] transferred to financial autonomy, then every worker will know that any "breakdown," . . . will make the indicators at the main administration less good, disrupt the plan for further development, create extra difficulties and problems, lead to smaller amounts being paid into the incentive fund of the management apparatus and have an adverse effect on his personal wages.[135]

Various specific proposals designed to lessen the pattern of ministerial autarky and increase inter-ministerial cooperation stand out. These include the establishment of a new Union-republic ministry "for the guidance of interbranch production," and the increase of information between branches, partly by granting obedineniia powers to enter into production relationships across ministerial boundaries, thus creating a "most important means for resolving the task of the reform."[136]

Much has been written of late on using the force of law to restrict the powers of ministries over enterprises. However, there is no doubt that the law has had little meaning for Russian public administration, whether under the tsars or since. The USSR Minister of Justice, V. Terebilov, has noted that "there are substantial shortcomings in the work of the legal services of the ministries . . . whose primary function is to ensure legal regulation and to promote the observance of legality in the national economy." Of course, if part of an agency in charge of an operation is responsible for ensuring legality within it, there unavoidably will exist, as he notes, "frequent instances of the outright underestimation of legal work."[137] An administrative agency tends to be much more interested in getting work done than in doing it legally. One strong suggestion is for a law that would provide automatic financial liability for an agency that causes an enterprise losses, the indemnity or compensation being significant and paid on the basis of the enterprise's accounting data, with any disagreement being ironed out by the state arbitration system (gosarbitrazh). At present only small fines are involved in such cases. An enterprise faces what is euphemistically called a "psychological barrier" in lodging claims against its ministry. The promise inherent in the general suggestion is great; enterprise directors would not have to conceal reserves and the ministries would not have to "squeeze them out."[138]

By 1971 the call for greater regulation of the ministry-enterprise relationship had resulted in a joint Central Committee and Council of Ministers resolution that obliged ministries to "put in order" their legal work and provide enterprises with "appropriate legal services."[139] The resolution fell far short, however, of the strict specification of mutual rights and obligations that had been widely called for. It was further weakened by its emphasis upon "guidance" of enterprises to fulfill their agreements. This is a problem, of course, but the emphasis upon it shows that the ministries seem to have been able, temporarily if not for the long term, to appropriate the call for increased legality to the maintenance, if not the strengthening, of their own position.

Others, also concerned about ministries' tendency to create a nonplanned life for the enterprise, have raised the shadow of the now defunct sovnarkhozy by suggesting that territorial and local planning organs be given greater responsibility for shaping the national economic plan. One writer even says that "the planning commission of a USSR economic region should be imbued with full rights as a territorial economic planning organ of the USSR Gosplan, implementing . . . the coordination of branch and territorial organs' plans and the formulation of proposals for the complete development of the national economy of the economic region."[140] Since one of Khrushchev's purposes in instituting the sovnarkhozy was to give greater power to the regional Party apparatus, it is likely that some of the latter's members feel aggrieved by the present centralized arrangements. Writers raising the idea of institutionalizing a new regionalism in economic planning never mention the former sovnarkhozy but cannot avoid, in effect, suggesting that they had a real role to play that should be played again. This may well be their intent. (The section titled "Interstices" in the next chapter examines the issue of the "new regionalism," given institutional form in the spring of 1973.)

There have been no suggestions made in the Soviet press that the economic reform was fundamentally misconceived in relation to the enterprise-ministry relationship, much less any hint that the Soviet system requires fundamental or significant change for a real solution to the economy's problems. Nevertheless, the specialists concerned with economic and industrial matters are both thinking actively and trying to make an impression upon policy, which indicates that the specialist intelligentsia still has faith in the Soviet system if only elements in it are altered. The ministries, it is thought, can be remade into institutions of a new type that would actually aid Soviet enterprises in meeting the tasks of producing goods of higher quality and a large amount of consumer goods. Such active and resourceful "moderate" thought is a reservoir of strength for the Soviet polity. Will it remain, increase, and prosper, or will it sour and decline, and perhaps turn into active dissatisfaction or even disaffection and opposition if the changes suggested are not implemented? Many of the critical statements made concerning ministries early in the reform period continue to apply, albeit perhaps with less agreement.

How long the ministries will apply bureaucratic inertia was still unclear in 1974, an indication of their staying power. Rush Greenslade's statement of 1966 is still appropriate: "When the leadership initiates more activities than it can control and manage, management and control drift inexorably into the hands of an amorphous bureaucracy."[141] Schroeder, another analyst for the U.S. government, writing in 1971, maintained that "the [ministerial] bureaucracy is stronger than ever," having come "to administer in ever greater detail the new 'economic levers' which were supposed to have operated automatically" as a response to whatever diversity the reform initially inspired. Nothing presented above vitiates these concerns. As for reasons, although ministries continue to have the same success indicator as of old--the seemingly eternal VAL--a more fundamental reason is their use of the powers of long-standing bureaucracy.

Where does this leave us? In midstream, without doubt. How is Soviet industrial administration to move to the other shore and up the bank? This is quite unclear at present. Only a general crisis can make an entire politico-economic system change its course and gain momentum. A crisis of such magnitude is not yet clearly in sight, despite the dire forecasts made by dissidents like A. Amalrik. The advantages of the present unclear compromise will have to run out before further movement is probable. It can, however, be suggested what the land beyond the stream might look like in an administrative sense. In a post-industrial society the only way effectively to obtain actions that further systemic goals without generating stresses and strains weakening the system is to discard a subsystem of stifling traditional bureaucratic controls and to operate on the basis of a decentralized network of institutions of optimal size with goals of their own that further the entire system's goals. Could this be called "limited participatory bureaucracy"? "The locus (or primary institution) of the society is the industrial enterprise and the axis . . . is the social hierarchy which derives from the organization of labor around machine production."[142]

Improving this situation necessitates a prior establishment of general agreement upon goals and the methods for attaining them--a new belief system or ideology. The recrudescence of traditional ministerial activity in Soviet industrial management has a chilling effect upon the idea, however poorly developed it was, of enterprises serving the general goals by pursuing, at least within definitely circumscribed parameters of activity, their own best economic interests. (This is not an unrealistic call for a classical liberal state in the USSR, but only for a more imaginative and responsive administrative arrangement in Soviet industry based upon some serious political rethinking.) The reform has not lived up to its limited promise in the enterprise-ministry dimension. It does, however, constitute a modest but definite step away from the economic form of Stalinism that the ministries in their old guise represented. Other steps will be taken, but not until pressure builds up sufficiently to prompt a desire and need for the political leaders to move on, and an ideological rationale under whose cover they can safely do so.

NOTES

1. Attributed to Academician M. Keldysh by N. Obolenskii, First Deputy Minister, USSR Ministry of the Electrotechnical Industry, Ekonomicheskaia gazeta 46 (November 1969): 5.
2. L. I. Brezhnev, speech at the Central Committee plenum, Tass English broadcast, September 29, 1965, and A. N. Kosygin, Pravda, September 28, 1965, p. 3.
3. Geraint Parry, Political Elites (London: Allen & Unwin, 1969).

4. L. G. Churchward, Contemporary Soviet Government (New York: American Elsevier, 1968), p. 170; and Constitution of the USSR, Arts. 77 and 78, reprinted in John N. Hazard, The Soviet System of Government (4th ed., rev.; Chicago: University of Chicago Press, 1968), pp. 231-32.

5. S. M. Korneev, Imushchestvennaia samostoiatel'nost' predpriiatii v usloviiakh ekonomicheskoi reformy (Moscow: Suridicheskaia literatura, 1969), abstracted in ABSEES no. 4 (April 1971): 65.

6. I. S. Shkorupeev and G. N. Singur, Khoziaistvennaia reforma i ministerstvo (Moscow: "Ekonomika," 1968), p. 47.

7. Abraham Katz, The Politics of Economic Reform in the Soviet Union (New York: Praeger, 1972), pp. 158-61.

8. See Leon Smolinski, "Towards a Socialist Corporation," Survey 20, no. 1 (Winter 1974): 24-35.

9. Francis Seton, "Economic Planning in Communist Societies," in George Schopflin, ed., The Soviet Union and Eastern Europe (New York: Praeger, 1970), p. 285.

10. F. Kotov, "Sovremennaia organizatsiia planirovaniia i puti ee sovershenstvovaniia," Planovoe khoziaistvo 10 (October 1968): 3-18; JPRS 46,984 (December 2, 1968): 25-44.

11. See Ye. Liberman, Ekonomicheskie metody povysheniia effektivnosti obshchestvennogo proizvodstva (Moscow: "Ekonomika," 1970), pp. 5-6.

12. See Peter Woll, American Bureaucracy (New York: Norton, 1963), p. 161.

13. Robert Solo, Economic Organizations and Social Systems (Indianapolis, Ind.: Bobbs-Merrill, 1967), p. 109.

14. T. H. Rigby, Communist Party Membership in the USSR, 1917-1967 (Princeton, N.J.: Princeton University Press, 1968), p. 41.

15. D. Allakhverdian and E. Slastenko, "Khoziaistvennaia reforma i nekotorye problemy upravleniia promyshlennost'iu," Voprosy ekonomiki 3 (March 1968): 16, 23.

16. Voprosy ekonomiki 11 (November 1970): 75-78; cited in ABSEES, April 1971, p. 94.

17. Peter F. Drucker, "The Surprising Seventies," Harper's Magazine, July 1971, p. 39.

18. G. Mantsurov, T. Selivanova, "Effekt budetnarastat'," Ekonomicheskaia gazeta 15 (April 1967): 10.

19. Robert Conquest, Power and Policy in the U.S.S.R. (London and New York: Macmillan and St. Martin's, 1962), p. 305.

20. Jerry F. Hough, The Soviet Prefects (Cambridge, Mass.: Harvard, 1969), p. 75; also see Gwendolyn M. Carter, The Government of the Soviet Union (3rd ed.; New York: Harcourt Brace Jovanovich, 1972), p. 68.

21. Hough, op. cit., p. 57.
22. Tibor Szamuely, Survey no. 72 (Summer 1969): 61-62;
23. Interview with Professor David Granick of the Economics Department, University of Wisconsin, at the Russian Institute, Columbia University, August 22, 1967. See also Benjamin Ward, The Socialist Economy (New York: Random House, 1967), p. 130.
24. See, for example, H. Gordon Skilling and Franklyn Griffiths, eds., Interest Groups in Soviet Politics (Princeton, N.J.: Princeton University Press, 1971).
25. Alec Nove, The Soviet Economy (2nd rev. ed.; New York: Praeger, 1969), p. 70.
26. David Lane, Politics and Society in the USSR (New York: Random House, 1971), p. 149.
27. Jerry F. Hough, "The Soviet System: Petrification or Pluralism?" Problems of Communism 21, no. 2 (March-April 1972): 32.
28. See John A. Armstrong, The Soviet Bureaucratic Elite (New York: Praeger, 1959), p. 54.
29. See, for example, George Fischer, The Soviet System and Modern Society (New York: Atherton, 1968), Tables 1.1 and 1.2, p. 27, and Table 5.1, p. 108.
30. John A. Armstrong, "Tsarist and Soviet Elite Administrators," Slavic Review 31, no. 1 (March 1972): 24.
31. See Robert H. Donaldson, "The 1971 Soviet Central Committee," World Politics 24, no. 3 (April 1972): 403, 408.
32. T. H. Rigby, "Crypto-Politics," Survey no. 50 (January 1964): 191. This finding is confirmed by Allen H. Barton et al., eds., Opinion-Making Elites in Yugoslavia (New York: Praeger, 1973).
33. D. J. R. Scott, "Resistance and Opposition," Survey no. 64 (July 1967): 43.
34. Armstrong, "Tsarist and Soviet Elite Administrators," pp. 18-19, 26-27.
35. See Donaldson, op. cit., p. 397, Table 6.
36. Gertrude E. Schroeder, "Soviet Economic Reform at an Impasse," Problems of Communism 20, no. 4 (July-August 1971): 37.
37. Shkorupeev and Singur, op. cit., p. 47; W. Keizer, The Soviet Quest for Economic Rationality (Rotterdam: University of Rotterdam Press, 1971), pp. 231-32.
38. On October 13, 1969, a joint Central Committee-Council of Ministers resolution was promulgated: "On Measures for Improving the Staffs and Reducing the Costs of Management," Pravda and Izvestiia, October 24, 1969, p. 1 (translated in CDSP 21, no. 43 [November 19, 1969]: 8), and Pravda, December 9, 1971, p. 3 (translated in CDSP 23, no. 49 [January 4, 1972]: 42).

39. V. Batysheva and K. Grishin, "Leninskie printsipy khoziaistvennogo rukovodstva," Planovoe khoziaistvo 1 (January 1970): 11.
40. Hough, "The Soviet System," p. 34.
41. Norman Cousins, "Notes on a 1963 Visit with Khrushchev," Saturday Review 47, no. 45 (November 7, 1964): 16-21, 58-60.
42. T. H. Rigby, "The Soviet Leadership," Soviet Studies 22, no. 2 (October 1970): 176.
43. Pravda, September 30, 1965. Quoted in Tatu, op. cit., p. 431.
44. Christian Duevel, "The Central Committee and Central Auditing Commission Elected by the 24th CPSU Congress," Radio Liberty Research Paper no. 46 (1972): 27-28.
45. Donaldson, op. cit., pp. 8-9 and 401.
46. Hough, "The Soviet System," p. 34.
47. Scott, op. cit., p. 43.
48. R. H. S. Crossman, The Myths of Cabinet Government (Cambridge, Mass.: Harvard, 1972), pp. 63-65.
49. Merle Fainsod, How Russia Is Ruled (rev. ed.; Cambridge, Mass.: Harvard University Press, 1963), p. 391.
50. A. Zhdanov, Pravda, September 24, 1970, p. 2; (translated in CDSP 21, no. 39 [October 27, 1970]: 5, 7).
51. Sotsialisticheskaia industriia, May 20, 1971, p. 1 (an interview with Ia. Tepandi, Minister of the Food Industry of Estonia).
52. Richard W. Judy, "Information, Control and Soviet Economic Management," in John P. Hardt et al., eds., Mathematics and Computers in Soviet Economic Planning (New Haven: Yale University Press, 1967), p. 45.
53. Loren R. Graham, "Cybernetics," in George Fischer, ed., Science and Ideology in Soviet Society (New York: Atherton, 1967), p. 88.
54. Loren Graham, Science and Philosophy in the Soviet Union (New York: Knopf, 1972), p. 329.
55. Richard D. Portes, "The Tactics and Strategy of Economic Decentralization," Soviet Studies 23, no. 4 (April 1972): 629-58; and Kathryn Bartol, "Soviet Computer Centres," Soviet Studies 23, no. 4 (April 1972): 608.
56. For the two agencies' schemes see Pravda, July 17, 1969, p. 2; and Planovoe khoziaistvo 7 (July 1967): 19-20.
57. Bartol, op. cit., p. 614.
58. F. Goldin and S. Skorik, "Edinyi iazik sistemy," Moskovskaia pravda, September 9, 1970, p. 2; translated in Soviet Cybernetics Review 1, no. 1 (January 1971): 47.
59. "Commentary," Soviet Cybernetics Review 1, no. 2 (February 1971): 30-31.

60. S. Gurenko, Izvestiia, July 10, 1970, p. 3. The writer is a director of a plant of the ministry.

61. See K. W. Ryavec, "Soviet Industrial Management: Challenge and Response, 1965-1970," Canadian Slavic Studies 5, no. 2 (Summer 1971): esp. 171-73.

62. G. Popov, Pravda, February 28, 1970, p. 2; partially translated in CDSP 22, no. 9 (March 31, 1970): 6. Popov is head of the Management Problems Laboratory at Moscow State University.

63. Herbert S. Levine, "Economics," in George Fischer, ed., Science and Ideology in Soviet Society (New York: Atherton, 1967), p. 124.

64. A. Glushkov, Izvestiia, September 17, 1970, p. 5; translated in CDSP 22, no. 37 (October 13, 1970): 20. Glushkov is head of the Institute of Cybernetics of the Ukrainian Academy of Sciences.

65. See Gene Bylinsky, "The Computer's Little Helpers Create a Brawling Business," Fortune, June 1970, pp. 85-87, 140, 144, 146.

66. V. A. Trapeznikov, Nauka i zhizn' 1 (January 1969): 10-20; translated in JPRS 47,681 (March 19, 1969): 48. Trapeznikov is Director of the Institute of Automation and Telemechanics.

67. Robert L. LeBoeuf, "Production and Use of Computers in the Communist Countries of Eastern Europe," in Joint Economic Committee, U.S. Congress, Economic Developments in the Countries of Eastern Europe (Washington, D.C.: U.S. Government Printing Office, 1970), pp. 331-32; and B. O. Szuprowicz, "East Europe: The Search for Computers," East Europe 21, no. 4 (April 1972): 2-6.

68. See M. Korolov, Pravda, November 20, 1971, p. 3; partly translated in CDSP 23, no. 47 (December 21, 1971): 4-5.

69. Graham, "Cybernetics," p. 89. Also see the series in New York Times, December 12-14, 1973.

70. Tass English broadcast, September 29, 1965.

71. Jerrold L. Shechter, "Report from Moscow," Fortune, May 1970, p. 106.

72. Izvestiia, April 12, 1969, p. 3.

73. See Shkorupeev and Singur, op. cit., Table 1, pp. 9-11.

74. Allakhverdian and Slastenko, op. cit., p. 23.

75. Izvestiia, April 3, 1969, p. 1.

76. Sotsialisticheskaia industriia, June 6, 1971, p. 2 (an interview with F. Dumbadze, the minister).

77. M. Demchenko, Sotsialisticheskaia industriia, June 11, 1971, p. 2. Demchenko is a professor at Moscow's Ordzhonikidze Engineering-Economics Institute.

78. See John A. Armstrong, "Sources of Administrative Behavior: Some Soviet and West European Comparisons," American Political Science Review 59, no. 3 (September 1965): 647; Alec Nove, Economic Rationality and Soviet Politics (New York: Praeger, 1964), p. 276; and New York Times, March 25, 1973.

79. Batysheva and Grishin, op. cit., p. 12.
80. D. Zhimerin, Pravda, June 5, 1971, p. 3; C. Olgin, Bulletin of the Institute for the Study of the USSR 17, no. 1 (January 1970): 28, 30; and Szuporowicz, op. cit., p. 2.
81. P. Voronin, Pravda, May 15, 1972, p. 2. (Voronin is Assistant to the USSR Minister of Industrial Construction Materials.) See also Sotsialisticheskaia industriia, May 20, 1971, p. 1.
82. N. Petrov, Pravda, April 16, 1971; partially translated in CDSP 23, no. 15 (May 11, 1971): 47.
83. Tass Russian broadcast, February 2, 1971.
84. Pravda, February 2, 1971, p. 3.
85. Barry M. Richman, Soviet Management (Englewood Cliffs, N.J.: Prentice-Hall, 1965), p. 216. Also see A. Nove, The Soviet Economy (rev. ed.; New York: Praeger, 1966), pp. 73-74.
86. Nove, The Soviet Economy, pp. 83, 84; and Katz, "The Politics of Economic Reform in the Soviet Union" (1967), p. 268.
87. See "A More Business-like Approach: More Responsibility," Narodnoe khoziaistvo Kazakhstana (Alma-Ata) 10 (October 1966) (JPRS 39,487 [January 11, 1967]: 3); Ia. Chadaev, "Reforma v deistvii," Planovoe khoziaistvo 6 (June 1967): 48-49; and Pravda, September 17, 1970, p. 2 (translated in CDSP 22, no. 37 [October 13, 1970]: 1-3).
88. Pravda, May 8, 1969, p. 2.
89. V. Kulinanova, Den'gi i kredit 10 (October 1966): 31-37; JPRS 39,193 (December 21, 1966): 52.
90. T. Smagalov, "The Stride of the Economic Reform," Narodnoe khoziaistvo Kazakhstava (Alma-Ata) 6 (June 1968): 3-5; JPRS 46,391 (September 10, 1968): 3.
91. See N. Zenchenko, Sovetskaia Rossiia, March 13, 1969; Ekonomicheskaia gazeta 15 (April 1969): 1; Sotsialisticheskaia industriia, September 26, 1970, p. 2; Radio Free Europe, "Mid-Year Economic Report," July 23, 1970, p. 2; and Gertrude E. Schroeder, "Soviet Economic Reform at an Impasse," Problems of Communism 20, no. 4 (July-August 1971): 44-45.
92. Interview with Professor Anchishkin, an economist with the Scientific Research Institute of the USSR. Gosplan, Moscow, August 1968. The point was also made during a visit to Elektrosila, a large obedinenie in Leningrad.
93. See C. Olgin, "Cybernetics in the Soviet Economy--II: Organization," Bulletin of the Institute for the Study of the USSR 16, no. 10 (October 1969): 13.
94. Schroeder, op. cit., p. 40; and Pravda, May 19, 1970, p. 2.
95. See I. Malyshev, "Khoziaistvennaia reforma v deistvii," Partiinaia zhizn' 20 (October 1966): 20; G. Kulagin, "Obedinenie predpriiatii i ministerstvo," Kommunist 3 (February 1966): 83;

and G. Kulagin, Pravda, August 9, 1967, p. 2. Kulagin is the director of a machine-building obedinenie.

96. See S. Bratus', N. Klein, and E. Polonsky, Izvestiia, July 31, 1966, p. 5 (JPRS 37,783 [September 23, 1966]: 4-7); and Izvestiia, August 10, 1972, p. 2.

97. Katz, "The Politics of Economic Reform in the Soviet Union" (1967), p. 269.

98. Pravda, August 18, 1970; February 4, 1972; October 20, 1970.

99. Ekonomicheskaia gazeta 6 (February 6, 1968): 30 (translated in CASP 1, no. 2 [May 1968]: 8-9); Ekonomicheskaia gazeta 16 (1968): 4; Planovoe khoziaistvo 1 (1968): 21; and Promyshlennost' Belorussii 3 (1968): 3 (all cited in Keith Bush, The Implementation of The Soviet Economic Reform, Radio Liberty Research Paper no. 36 [Munich, 1970], p. 15); and N. Rodionov, "Partiinie komitety i sblizhenie nauki s proizvodstvom," Kommunist 9 (June 1970): 20 (written by the First Secretary of the Chelyabinsk obkom).

100. Komsomolskaia pravda, April 3, 1969, p. 2; (translated in FBIS, Daily Report [Soviet Union], April 15, 1969, p. C3).

101. I. Edinovich, "Ekonomicheskaia reforma i khoziaistvennyi raschet," Den'gi i kredit 12 (December 1966): 48-49.

102. Schroeder, op. cit., p. 46; and Bush, op. cit., p. 20.

103. Izvestiia, August 10, 1972, p. 2; (partially translated in CDSP 24, no. 32 [September 6, 1972]: 9-10).

104. F. Lentrinskii, Ekonomika Sovetskoi Ukrainy (Kiev) 6 (June 1966): 1-12; JPRS 38,276 (October 21, 1966): 18-28.

105. See Trud, March 14, 1969, p. 2; Ekonomicheskaia gazeta 50 (December 1968): 20; and Sovetskaia Belorossiia, March 7, 1969, p. 1.

106. Pravda, June 12, 1971, p. 3.

107. Nove, The Soviet Economy, pp. 223-24.

108. M. Breyev, "Sistema metodov planirovaniia," Planovoe khoziaistvo 10 (October 1968); JPRS, December 2, 1968, p. 56.

109. See Armstrong, "Sources of Administrative Behavior," pp. 646-47. Emphasis in original.

110. Pravda, September 16, 1972, p. 2.

111. Ekonomicheskaia gazeta 24 (1966); and Kulagin, "Obedinenie, predpriiatii i ministerstvo," loc cit.

112. A. Karpov et al., Khozraschet pronikaet vsiudu (Moscow: "Ekonomika," 1966), p. 57.

113. P. Rivnii, Ekonomicheskaia gazeta 15 (April 1967): 16.

114. O. Korzimov, "About Shortcomings in Planning," Den'gi i kredit 9 (September 1968); JPRS 46,956 (November 26, 1968): 32-33.

115. Breyev, op. cit., p. 57.

116. Ekonomicheskaia gazeta 50 (December 1968): 20; V. Moev, "Forward in Reverse," Literaturnaia gazeta 46 (November 12, 1969): 10 (translated in FBIS, Daily Report [Soviet Union], November 20, 1969, p. C2); and Pravda, April 6, 1969, p. 2.

117. A. Nikitin and V. Seliunin, "Pis'ma ob upravlenii: II," Ekonomicheskaia gazeta 12 (March 1967): 18. See also Nove, The Soviet Economy, p. 224.

118. E. Liberman, "Mysly posle plenuma," Novyi mir 12 (December 1965): 209.

119. A. J. Alexander, R & D in Soviet Aviation (Santa Monica: RAND, 1970), p. 9.

120. Robert W. Campbell, "Management Spillovers from Soviet Space and Military Programmes," Soviet Studies 23, no. 4 (April 1972): 586-607; and Pravda, October 9, 1971, p. 1 (partially translated in CDSP 23, no. 41 [November 9, 1971]: 30).

121. Antony Jay, Management and Machiavelli (New York: Holt, Rinehart & Winston, 1967), pp. 12, 37; and New York Times, November 18, 1970, and January 20, 1972.

122. Sotstialisticheskaia industriia, October 20, 1970, p. 2.

123. P. Kul'vets, "Mezhotrazhlevye proizvodstvennye sviazi promyshlennosti," Kommunist (Vil'nius) 3 (March 1969): 21-27; JPRS 47,931 (April 28, 1969): 48-49.

124. Pravda, September 4, 1970, p. 1 (translated in CDSP 22, no. 36 [October 6, 1970]: 16-17); and Ekonomicheskaia gazeta 35 (August 1969): 3.

125. See Rabochaia gazeta, October 21, 1970, p. 3; Sovetskaia Latviia, June 17, 1971, p. 2; and Ekonomicheskaia gazeta 1 (January 1971): 3.

126. D. Allakhverdian, Pravda, September 26, 1969, p. 2.

127. G. Popov, "Problemy sovershenstvovaniia metodov upravleniia sotsialisticheskoi ekonomiki," Kommunist 2 (January 1974): 68-69.

128. Anchishkin interview.

129. Zygmunt Bauman, "Twenty Years After: The Crisis of Soviet-Type Systems," Problems of Communism 20, no. 6 (November-December 1971): 52; and Werner Klatt, "The Politics of Economic Reforms," Survey no. 70/71 (Winter/Spring 1969): 164.

130. I. Zlobin, Finansy SSSR, November 1968, pp. 24-37 (JPRS 47,666 [March 18, 1969]: 44); and I. Bunich, Izvestiia, September 29, 1968, p. 2.

131. Leon Smolinski, "The Soviet Economy: In Search of a Pattern," Survey no. 66 (April 1966): 98-99.

132. See, for example, Finansy SSSR 2 (February 1969): 66-68 (JPRS 47,819 [April 10, 1969]: 45). The authors are officials of the Ministry of Finance.

133. "Economic Theory and Economic Practice," Planovoe khoziaistvo 11 (November 1968); JPRS 47,130 (December 24, 1968): 10.

134. Finansy SSSR 10 (October 1968); JPRS 47,031 (December 9, 1968): 29.

135. See Pravda, May 8, 1969, p. 2.

136. Kul'vets, op. cit. (English version), pp. 46, 53; Izvestiia, September 26, 1970, p. 3; and Komsomolskaia pravda, April 3, 1969, p. 2.

137. Izvestiia, January 30, 1971, pp. 1-2; partially translated in CDSP 23, no. 5 (March 2, 1971): 9.

138. Izvestiia, August 8, 1970, p. 3; CDSP 22, no. 32 (September 8, 1970), pp. 8-9, and Moev, op. cit. (English version), p. C4.

139. Pravda and Izvestiia, January 27, 1971; CDSP 23, no. 5 (March 2, 1971): 8-9.

140. N. Nikolaev, Ekonomicheskaia gazeta 35 (August 1969): 3; FBIS, Daily Report (Soviet Union), September 12, 1969, p. C7. Nikolaev is a secretary of Khabarovsk kraikom (territorial Party committee).

141. Rush V. Greenslade, "The Soviet Economic System in Transition," in U.S. Congress, Joint Economic Committee, New Directions in the Soviet Economy, Pt. I (Washington, D.C.: U.S. Government Printing Office, 1966), p. 7; and Schroeder, op. cit., pp. 37, 46. See also Keith Bush, "An Appraisal of the Soviet Economic Reform," in U.S. Congress, Joint Economic Committee, Soviet Economic Performance: 1966-67 (Washington, D.C.: U.S. Government Printing Office, 1968), p. 142.

142. Daniel Bell, The Coming of Post-Industrial Society (New York: Basic Books, 1973), pp. 75, 153.

CHAPTER

3

THE ROLE OF NONMINISTERIAL AGENCIES IN THE IMPLEMENTATION PROCESS

GOSPLAN

The industrial enterprise, besides contending with the ministry, works within a complex and even confused web of relationships with other regulatory and directive agencies, including the Communist Party. One of these agencies is the State Planning Commission, or Gosplan, which, like all state agencies, is overseen by the Party. Nevertheless, it is a large bureaucratic structure of long standing that exerts a degree of direction over enterprises by wielding many of the powers inherent in a system of centralized authoritative or administrative planning. Gosplan is next in importance to the USSR Council of Ministers in the general supervision of the reform. It works out "directions for further improving the new system"[1] and is high in the political-bureaucratic hierarchy. Its chairman, usually also one of the several Deputy Chairmen of the Council of Ministers, is presently N. K. Baibakov, a full member of the Central Committee since the Nineteenth Congress in 1952 (with the exception of 1961-66) who has been in his post since 1962 and on the Council of Ministers since October 1965, the time of the formal beginning of the reform. (Gosplan's former chairman, P. F. Lomako, is also a member of the Council as Minister of Nonferrous Metallurgy, a Union-republic ministry, and has been a full member of the Central Committee since the Twenty-Second Congress in 1961.)

The reforms of 1965 initially had an ambiguous meaning for Gosplan. Although the principal texts on the reforms indicated definite movement toward a system of flexible planning, Gosplan itself was given a greater role and freed from supervision by the Supreme Council of the National Economy (VSNKh), which was abolished. (The appointment of Baibakov may also have increased the agency's stature, since his tenure as a Central Committee member is longer than that of his predecessor.) The core of Gosplan's power lies in the reimposition of centralized planning; it has the say on specifics. It also serves as a sort of "motor" of the reform by housing a major committee for planning its further development (the Inter-Departmental Committee on Economic Reform). Its power also rests on its ability to issue planning directives and thus make the reform fit its institutional needs. The power of Gosplan is illustrated by the sharp public criticism of two ministers in 1971 by a member of Gosplan's Board.[2] This aggressive stance is not new. Gosplan had begun to take on a more activist role vis-a-vis the industrial system prior to the reform. By the early 1960s, in addition to its original task of drawing up plans, Gosplan had begun to check upon their execution, with more and more use of field inspections, and also had begun to allocate more products. This hindered the movement toward a system of flexible planning.[3]

Soviet planning was "a vast bureaucratic phalanx" with a vested interest in "targetry." A Soviet economist notes: "At one time it could not have been simpler for the head of a chief administration to set a factory's plan. He took last year's level, tacked on a growth percentage, argued a bit with the plant's officials--and that settled the matter!"[4]

Despite the absurdities rampant under the former rigid and unimaginative system of planning, the reform has not seen any decisive change. Planning remains as stolid, pyramidal, and bureaucratic as ever. Its existence is an institutional testimonial to the continued resolve to plan administratively and in detail from the center, although detailed long-term planning from a distance is an impossibility. The central planners do not, and cannot, have all the requisite information because it is being discovered in the production and planning processes themselves. No one has all this information at any one time. What actually occurs in economic planning is an unavoidable process of bargaining and attempting corrective action--that is, a process akin to the political.[5]

The idea of a national computerized planning network has had a role in limiting the earlier possibilities for decentralization. This does not mean that individual changes, significant in themselves, have not occurred. For example, enterprises now are supposed to have their five-year plans broken down by years and stabilized as well.[6] Another change is the reduction in the number of "most important types" of products centrally planned from 1,250 in 1966 to 615 by 1968, and fewer now. Also, Gosplan is no longer to issue material expenditure norms (up to 20,000) for certain products but instead to issue only general assignments that enterprises are to refine into actual standards. In addition, in the 1971-75 (ninth) plan, the list of industrial goods centrally planned was reduced from 886 to 536. However, the plans for approximately 40,000 different types of industrial products are still adopted centrally. The problem is compounded by the ministries. For example, the "model" Ministry of Instrument Making is planning more items now than previously.[7]

The call for improvement in planning is an unending litany of the Soviet media. Some of its high notes can be found in the lengthy directives of the ninth plan, which call again for an improvement in planning but provide few specific means or suggestions.[8] A continuous accompanying theme is the claim that the plan charts out a continuing course that moves ever closer toward the personal needs of the individual. Some of this signifies a creeping movement toward adoption of optimal planning, "the application of the techniques and approach of operations research to the national economy as a whole."[9] The optimal planners or "moderate marketeers" want to introduce three significant departures from the old system of planning: a market-price mechanism, a real devolution of decision-making, and a recognition that the object of economic activity is consumption. Naturally, given the relationship of political forces in the USSR, the exponents of optimality would have a very difficult time getting their entire program or even its core accepted by the powers that be. For one thing, the present economic and planning officials would not accept their own retirement (for that is what the conscious pursuit of optimality implies). Many economists, particularly political economists, also have hostile attitudes toward optimal planning. The result of this situation is an interesting compromise, but one weighted far toward conventional Soviet thinking.

The National Computerized Planning Network Program

The political leadership (or at least its dominant grouping) and some among the conventional economists and planning officials have favored an element, but only one, of the optimalists' program--a national computer network for planning. Its alleged purpose and its justification are not, however, optimality, but the politically safe and perhaps politically necessary improvement of the existing system of planning by giving it a more efficient means for coping with the enormous amount of information and the many decisions involved. Also involved is the provision of means allowing wide-scale, long-range forecasting of economic requirements and possibilities. K. T. Mazurov, a Politburo member, has spoken of the economic reform as a technocratic device that will allow better economic and political controls because of the use of computers.[10] The full threat of the optimalists' assumptions and proposals is thereby avoided and their intent perverted, at least until the limitations of the new computational chimera become widely apparent. But the threat of failure remains, even if submerged or shunted to one side. As Michael Ellman notes: "The emergence of the theory of optimal planning is largely a reflection of the fact that the Soviet Union clearly needs a science which will provide useful ideas for improving the functioning of the economic system and [Communist--KR] political economy is not such a science." The Twenty-Fourth Party Congress called for the "wide employment of mathematical economics methods and the utilization of electronic-computer and organizational technology and means of communication."[11]

The fundamental reason for the present emphasis upon the use of computers and operations analysis is to enable the present organizational structure and philosophy of the economy to continue in existence. The significance of the attempt is heavily ideological; many in the Soviet political elite consider central planning to be the essential difference between the Soviet and "bourgeois" systems. But a centralized national network of computers from Gosplan to enterprises, even if efficient in itself, will not be sufficient for the rationalization of the entire economy or even of its industrial sectors. (The possible implications of computerization for the rationalization of new totalitarian controls is an interesting topic but outside the scope of this study.)[12] Cybernetics allows the control of actualities, not plans. To make the merger of computers with economic planning fulfill the hopes of the centralists would require the end of centralism and the prior creation of an efficient, rational industry.

Several forceful exponents of optimal planning point out that "it is obvious that it is necessary to combine the introduction of computer technology with simultaneous improvements in the organization of management based on the methods of optimal planning and regulation."[13] A strong attack on overcentralization and the overestimation of computer technology has been made by V. G. Afanasev of the editorial board of Voprosy filosofii, who argues that "one cannot expect correct decisions for all of life's problems from one center--however great or competent it may be." He concludes his politically colored criticism of the technocratic grouping by asserting: "The main role in the solution of the theoretical problems of management belongs to the social sciences, since the management of society, like that of its individual links, is above all an economic, sociopolitical, ideological problem, and not one of cybernetics, natural sciences, [or] technology. . . ."[14]

At present the network remains a dream whose possible realization is lodged in an imbroglio between the two top-level government agencies, Gosplan and the Central Statistical Administration (TsTU), over the precise shape the project is to take. A. Glushkov has called for a "special state agency"--other than Gosplan, TsSU, or the

Ministry of Communications--to run the planned nationwide computerized control system for economic planning, presumably with himself as its director.[15] Viewing the situation realistically, however, the Soviets are still engaged in the necessarily confusing and contradictory task of attempting to give substantiation to a vague vision. One Soviet scholar has noted that "there is no precise notion of how such a network would perform its functions."[16] This attempt at substantiation is not wholly impractical; the national network might be built if the technical and interagency conflicts can be solved. No one in the United States ever doubted, for example, that the proposed national data "bank" could be built. Its opponents were quite convinced of its feasibility in the technical sense. The real question facing the project for a Soviet computerized planning network is whether it can, when completed (perhaps by 1980), actually allow the continued use of centralized, administrative national planning at its current level of application. Academician N. K. Fedorenko has demonstrated that a fully computerized model for industry alone would have to cope with 10^{18} (10 million million million) operations. This would take a current Soviet computer, with a capacity of about one million bits a second, about 30,000 years.[17]

If one backs off from the vision of the completed network, a number of problems are apparent. In the first place, there are neither enough computers nor enough cadres "professing" (ispoveduiu-shchie) the new principles of administration. This means that most cadres in industry either are not in favor of or are actively opposed to the new principles. In addition, the proliferation of different types of computers goes on, magnifying the problem of incompatibility and making it ever more difficult to come to grips with it. Rapid "mass standardization" of computers and software becomes an urgent though unheeded necessity. The quality and characteristics of the computers and their peripheral equipment also are criticized, as are their insufficient numbers.[18] Still another problem, again involving the ministries' old tendency to adopt autarkic policies, is the uncoordinated compilation of classifiers, the ten-digit numbers used to code materials and products in the computers' memories. The full size of the all-Union output classifier exceeds 50 volumes. Since no classifier can be established in an immutable version, but must be changeable in order to take account of modifications and new industrial items (100,000 annually), the unsystematic compilation by ministries "for themselves" is creating a serious hindrance to any computerized national planning system. It is even possible that the number of centrally required forms is increasing and becoming more detailed. The suggestion has been made that "uniform information standards" having the "force of state law" be introduced.[19]

Suggestions for getting on with the job are numerous, such as the implementation of "junctional" tasks allowing the linkage of computers in different agencies and at various levels. This will require considerable politicking and some imaginative technical solutions. The ministries are maintaining their autarkic practices even with space-age computers. This would be very intelligent for their own inter-bureaucratic political interests. If ministries were tied into a general computer grid or system, they would no longer have what M. Weber called the "files"; their data would be knowable by the agency controlling the grid. This agency would be very close to the Politburo.

The outcome of the discussion concerning the dream of a nationwide computerized planning system is unclear because it has begun only recently, and "attainment" would require years of prodigious and detailed efforts. The project probably will be dropped at some point after the use of computers is an accepted and meaningful part of the industrial management scene in the USSR. By then, or soon thereafter, the realization of what computers can and cannot do will sink into the consciousness of the technical intelligentsia, and current romantic theorizing about them will fade away. At that point facing up to the possibility of market socialism in some degree will be unavoidable (unless another seeming panacea is accepted instead by the Party leaders).

The Present Planning Environment

By 1967 a counterattack was mounted against new ideas of planning. One economist asserted that the strengthening of khozraschet at all levels "in no way reduces the role and significance of centralized planning in the development of the socialist economy."[20] Attitudes such as this tended to support overcentralized planning. Gregory Grossman asserts that the steady and meaningful general introduction of innovation ("routinization of innovation") could be achieved in the Soviet economy only through "deroutinizing" certain aspects of planning, such as production and supply.[21] But present "atmospherics" make any degree of decentralization difficult. Whereas in 1965 the devolution of planning powers seemed to have a chance of making some headway, by now centralized planning has regained its effective strength. As a result, a number of planning decisions resulting in irrationalities and inconsistencies at the enterprise level are evident.

Another factor contributing to the failure to make planning effective has been the lack of any systematic price reform since 1955-57. The 1967 reform was inconsistent and lacking "any set of principles at all" on price determination. Besides, the "statistical consequences" of the prices of 1926-27 "are still with us (growth indices, for instance) . . . ."[22] The problem was stated forthrightly by Academician N. K. Fedorenko, who wrote:

> After the September [1965] plenum of the CPSU Central Committee, the number of centrally set indicators expressed in physical terms was reduced. . . . But as for the setting of prices, the old system was preserved almost in toto. . . . A paradoxical situation is created. It has been recognized that it is impossible to have central planning of everything down to the tiniest nail. . . yet it seems that the price of the nail can be set from the center.[23]

Fedorenko's suggestion that the "center" no longer plan for all the entities subordinate to it, "as was formerly the case," but only for "links which are in directly subordinate subordination," conflicts with the stark fact of plans commonly being changed by organs, sometimes referred to as "planning organs," which the context of reports implies are rather high in the chain of command. In any event, a kandidat of economic sciences points out that "the most important problems [pertaining to] changes of centralized planning under conditions of the economic reform are almost unmentioned by the press."[24]

Planning: Action and Nonaction

The essence of Gosplan's failure to institutionalize a new pattern of less centralized and detailed planning is its inability or unwillingness to prevent either ministries or its republic-level equivalents from changing enterprises' plans frequently. Its power cannot be applied because of the fundamental failure of the political leadership to push forcefully for a clear and simple resolution of the planning problem and the consequent absence of an impetus for such change at lower or operational levels of the economy. For example, the Chairman of the Latvian Gosplan writes: "It has not yet proved possible to eliminate numerous inconsistencies between the production plans and the supply of materials and machinery." In addition, the general director of the Sverdlov lathe-building obedinenie in Leningrad complains that planning is still determined by the amounts of production attained previously and that the "ineradicable 'VAL' appears in disguise."[25]

The obverse side of the planning picture is Gosplan's failure to make other agencies comply with the reform model. Pravda has criticized "branch departments" of Gosplan for being slow in alleviating shortages of consumer goods with high demand and for allowing a ludicrous old problem to reappear--the increase in the production of heavy items. The result is the same as before: "The plan is being fulfilled in total tonnage, but there is an insufficient amount of essential items." The government's response is typical-- a new rule is promulgated: "It is now forbidden [for enterprises] to discontinue or reduce the production of everyday goods or household items without the approval of the U.S.S.R. Ministry of Trade and the governments of the union republics."[26] One of the current tactics for increasing the production of goods for mass consumption is utilizing the capacity of "group A" enterprises, to some degree living up to the rationalization that Marxist economists have long given for heavy industry: it could someday produce consumer goods. But, says Pravda, there is still some strange devotion to the "purity" of the heavy-industry production line, an understandable commitment in the light of almost 40 years' forceful and sometimes single-minded emphasis.[27]

Some of this criticism has a liberal connotation, criticizing the continued rigidity of Soviet planning and indicating that there is some support at higher political levels for further decentralization. For example, Ekonomicheskaia gazeta has noted that "planning has still not been totally redesigned in terms of the reform program requirements. . . ." Gosplan also has been criticized by ministerial functionaries for not taking into account the fact that an enterprise's adoption of new technology temporarily lowers its attainment of goals.[28]

Criticism of a centralist persuasion also exists. Gosplan is attacked because in some branches the reduction in the amount of products planned centrally supposedly has not been in the public interest.[29] Criticism of the reform and the current system of planning for being too "liberal" is quite common, and indicates that a considerable number of people fear and oppose further decentralization of planning.

It seems, then, that the "planning organs," including Gosplan, are operating somewhere between Stalinist hyper-centralism and the reformist vision of 1965. The resultant course is erratic, and is criticized from various sides.

Solutions: Discussion and Attempt

A major part of the managers' suggestions for an improvement in planning is understandably the placing of a limitation upon the ability of agencies superior to the enterprise to change its plan. This point is made again and again in various ways. A straightforward set of suggestions for establishing, in effect, a protected area of noninterference was made early in the reform at the Economics Institute of the USSR Academy of Sciences: "A change in the plan of an enterprise . . . should be permitted only in exceptional cases, after discussing the changes with the enterprise. If the plan is changed, corresponding adjustments must be made in the entire system of indicators reflecting the interrelations with the state budget."[30]

Although this suggestion has not been implemented, an attempt at amelioration seems to have been promised, and perhaps even begun, during the ninth five-year plan period (1971-75). In 1970 Kosygin promised that during 1971 each enterprise was to receive its tasks for the five years. "If we succeed in this it will, in fact, probably be the first time a 5-year plan was presented to the enterprises in a concrete form."[31] This is an extraordinarily frank admission of a problem of long standing, and a seemingly serious attempt to correct it. Other, more specific suggestions have been made (some presented in Chapter 2). A step toward providing a significant new basis of knowledge for planning was the establishment in 1972 of an all-Union market research agency called the Inter-Departmental Council for the Study of Demand, lodged in the USSR Ministry of Trade. Its creation was a belated response to the decade-old problem of unsold consumer goods, this time in the form of 2 million obsolete and unsold washing machines. Its existence may aid in making planning somewhat more realistic and stable.

Some writers dealing with planning have advocated a market situation. For example, one stated that some problems cannot be eliminated by a central plan and that "local production and consumption conditions" must be taken into account to avoid "serious miscalculations." The "market" is almost unveiled when he argues for increased freedom between suppliers and customers, including the right to sell and buy using (interestingly) "contractual prices"-- prices that "may deviate somewhat both upwards and downwards from the average level set by the state, performing the function of a sort of 'barometer' of the economic situation."[32]

Although few others have so strongly advocated fundamental change, many economists have indicated varying degrees of dissatisfaction with Soviet planning. Some have said that "combining centralized planning on an overall public scale with enterprises' operational and economic independence" is both possible and sufficient. Others have called for strict observance of the present rules and procedures, saying that if the regulations regarding the socialist enterprise are really observed, there will be no need for a director to conceal reserves and the planners will not have to worry about "squeezing them out."[33] Liberman himself has pointed out the limitations of the present planning system by noting that "no amount of success in the theoretical development of planning, no matter how important, can 'compensate' for a lack of practical development of an effective system of [economic] stimulation of [enterprises]" and that "planning in itself certainly does not guarantee the mechanical homogeneity of . . . interests. . . ."[34]

The publishing of such views did not make traditional statements any less plentiful. The idea of a market is vigorously denounced, especially now. It has been charged that "market socialism" would lead to disproportions and inflation, violate the Soviet pattern of payment for labor, and slow the tempo of development. The idea obviously goes against some of the central ideas of the Soviet ideology, one that, although Marxist in terminology, is statist in much of its actual content. It is this centralist inclination that remains dominant and has even increased its presence. The movement for a decentralization and transformation of the planning process, though possessing a certain vitality in the early stages of the reform, has again been submerged in Soviet orthodoxy.

Conclusion: Planning in Midstream

The position that has emerged victorious, for a historical moment at least, is not the old Stalinist one. It is a new centralist predisposition structured in major institutions and processes that is buttressed and refined by the leaders of a new top-level Soviet movement for efficiency in planning. The main division in views of planning is no longer between upholders of unimaginative and inefficient centralized planning and proponents of a free market, though both of these still exist; it is now between the proponents of central planning with the aid of computers and the supporters of increased managerial autonomy and some decentralization.[35] Nevertheless, the old rigidities and inanities remain as a sop to those holding Stalinist views and as a source of future problems (and, hence, of future change). The whole situation, then, is more complex than it was prior to the mid-1960s. Nevertheless, a modified central planning system is being used to attain goals not dissimilar to those set for the Soviet economy in the past. It does not seem farfetched to suppose that the Soviet economy is permanently wedded to some degree of central planning. Since "Western" economies are tending in the same direction, perhaps the most change possible will be increased rationalization.

THE STATE BANK

Like the ministries and central supply and planning organs, Gosbank has been conducting a fairly successful "holding operation" against the realization of the intentions for the reform and for the enlargement of its powers. Its work in industry relates primarily to its economic control powers over industrial enterprises.[36] Gosbank is their only supplier of short-term credits and also keeps their accounts, audits their finances, and pays out all but their smallest bills. These control powers, under the rubric of kontrol' rublem, are implemented by its 8,000 branch offices. The bank may take over an enterprise if it is a financial failure, although a ministry or glavk usually will step in and take drastic reorganizational action before that point is reached.

In practice, the bank's operations have often been accomplished poorly, and occasionally not at all. Since its offices lack a direct economic interest in enterprise operations and act only upon the basis of formal regulations, its supervision is of an aggregate and after-the-fact nature that is hindered still further by the mass of paper work within the banking system itself. For example, in one year only 0.3 percent of the amounts handled by the bank generated one-third of its paper work.[37]

The reform strongly implied that Gosbank would have a new role vis-a-vis the enterprise, one less narrow and supervisory and at the same time more helpful and economically based. Enterprises were to have greater flexibility in their use of resources, and the bank was to use its "economic judgment to a greater extent, instead of acting as a mixture of financial policeman and a 'conduit for budgetary investment funds'. . . ."[38] Since the reform prescribed the eventual end of free economic grants from the state, the role of investment credit, paid for by the enterprises through interest payments derived from their profits, was intended to be central in expanding and modernizing industry.

These goals were not radical in terms of the role of bank financing in Yugoslavia, where, for example, the establishment of a free market for socialist capital exists. Such a point of view may appear in the USSR only when all the benefits generated by the reform have been realized and more are demanded. At present Soviet writers sharply differentiate the bank and its role from "capitalist" institutions and practices, stressing the planned and "nonfictitious" character of "socialist credit."[39]

The result of the changing of the relationship between the state and the bank, generated by the atmosphere of the beginning of the reform, has been to set loose a drive within Gosbank for an increase and broadening of its powers vis-a-vis industrial enterprises. Times of change often allow greater movement than anticipated at their inception. Interestingly, Gosplan is engaged in a "self-strengthening" movement even though its head is no longer a major political figure (which suggests the powers of organizations in the Soviet state).

Bank officials claim that a "significant broadening in the boundaries of credit" has occurred through increasing the number of purposes for which enterprises may receive credit and through lengthening the terms of loans. Loans are important for organizing the production of new items and increasing assortment, both stressed at present. An interest rate for bank loans was instituted and then increased, in hopes of establishing "a direct relationship between interest and the operational indices of enterprises--profit and the level of profitability."

Approximately 90 percent of Gosbank's loans now go into enterprises' working capital, but of course they still represent a minor share of their operating funds. An increased share of the bank's short-term loans goes for technical improvements and increasing the supply of consumer goods, both objects of the reform.[40] By the beginning of 1971 in the Russian Republic alone, Gosbank credits to the economy had grown by more than 50 percent during the eighth plan and totaled 63 billion rubles. One example of the expansion of consumer goods thus furthered was the production of enameled iron articles by a casting plant in Kalushnaia oblast. The bank had loaned the plant 415,000 rubles in order for it to begin production. Bank officials claim that its credits are "quite effective" in making enterprises operate more profitably and at greater volume, since the credits must be repaid in a set time and with interest.[41]

Since this increase in the role of bank credit might justify some corresponding increase in the powers of the bank (not even a Soviet bank lends money without looking into its uses), it is no surprise to find officials of Gosbank pressing for a greater role for their organization vis-a-vis the central headquarters of Gosbank as well as enterprises. Bank officials ask for even more: the withdrawal of all credit funds from the ministries and their concentration in the bank.[42] Some Gosbank economists want the rights of the bank's divisions and agencies broadened so that they may have a stronger influence, through the selective use of credit, on enterprises and their operations. Supposedly, "the time has come also to give local state bank institutions themselves the right to apply all credit and accounting measures of influence."[43] At present, higher-level offices of Gosbank or the collegium itself must grant permission for the application of sanctions of this nature. It has been argued that this arrangement does not allow effective influence on enterprises that violate the principles of economic accountability. Some even suggest that the bank's local agencies should be able to change interest rates as a function of the results of enterprises. One writer calls for a system of "organizational and control functions" for the bank, thus going beyond the limit of economic influence to the realm of administrative actions.[44] This is not in agreement with the spirit of the reform.

Although a minority have said that "agencies of the bank must structure their relations with enterprises on a new basis, fully eliminate petty tutelage over the economic-financial activity of the enterprise, [and] concentrate their attention upon the improvement of economic methods of influence,"[45] actions of the bank have a different impact. It began meting out sanctions to enterprises to such an extent that "excesses" in bank supervision have been mentioned. Several other issues exist. For example, two writers complain that "a real 'barrier' has . . . not disappeared--the index of Gosbank connected with the wages fund."[46] Another difficulty is that the representatives of Gosbank and of enterprises tell different versions of the availability and terms of bank credit, indicating that a disagreement, perhaps a conflict, exists between them. Also, although the bank will grant credit to a producing enterprise while a shipment is on its way to a consumer, it will immediately withdraw the loan if the consumer cannot pay as soon as he receives the goods, thus causing real problems. One enterprise manager in Kiev says: "It is easier to obtain bird milk in its natural form than a bank loan."[47] And this is the manager of a plant that has been transferred to the reform, a seeming indication of efficient operation.

It is clear that the relations between Gosbank and enterprises are not considered satisfactory by either side, each of which blames the other for the difficulties. The situation is not one conducive to the cordial relations envisioned by the model. Even bribery of bank officials, the use of false documents, and collusion between project managers and inspectors have been mentioned.[48] The Council of Ministers has ladled out some general criticism to Gosplan: "A number of USSR Gosbank establishments did not take the proper measures for finding additional commodity resources and extending the range of financial services offered to the population."[49]

Despite these difficulties, the relationship between the bank and enterprises may have become less bureaucratic in a few ways--for instance, it is now easier to borrow funds for the preparation of design-estimate documentation and for capital investments. But Gosbank maintains that this must not be interpreted as a weakening of repayment discipline. Rather, its purpose is only to ensure that enterprises continue to operate and that construction is kept going.

Although there is evidence that in some respects enterprises have a greater degree of independence in their relationship with Gosbank, bank officials are striving to effect and maintain a direct and sometimes strict supervision over their activities, which is to some degree a bureaucratically based supervisory power. Of course, the granting of credit only to profitable enterprises might be consistent with the goals, and might even stimulate conformity to them on the part of enterprises. However, the desire of local officials of the bank for increased powers of active supervision tends toward petty tutelage (and toward inefficiency, since the bank's offices at the raion level lack personnel with the requisite skills for working under the new conditions). There is as yet no denouement in this struggle for power between Gosbank and enterprise managers. The result can only be further disagreement and inter-bureaucratic maneuvers necessitating another attempt, at higher levels, to formulate a workable arrangement conducive to the efficiency of enterprise operations.

THE MINISTRY OF FINANCE

The major change intended for the relationship between the USSR Ministry of Finance (including its republic counterpart ministries) and enterprises was the end of the requirement that staffs be registered with the ministry's Central Establishment Administration, a goal with important implications. This change would lessen the ministry's tendency to exercise detailed supervision over the operational policies of enterprise managers, including their personnel policy. The reform implies that managerial personnel will increase in number, so that enterprises will be able to take on the new tasks now required of them and to operate more flexibly. It will be remembered that the Ministry of Finance has had a powerful hold upon enterprises' personnel, finances, and organizational structures. For example, its local inspectors audited enterprises' accounts in order to limit falsification of financial records. Realistically speaking, the Ministry's former powers vis-a-vis enterprises still exist, although official intention favored change in those powers.

The Minister of Finance in Moscow is V. G. Garbuzov, who has held the post since 1960. He does not have much political importance, although he is a member of the CPSU Central Committee (since at least the Twenty-Second Congress in 1961). Everyone at the Ministry's top level has been in his position since 1964 or earlier (1956 in two of the 20 cases, and 1955 in one case). Its structure is somewhat larger than that of the State Bank but not as large as that of Gosplan. Like most other state agencies, the Ministry was caught unprepared for operating under the reform, and was given a role in the implemental process that it seems not to have performed well, according to admissions in its own "house organ," Finansy SSSR. Although it naturally has not allowed criticism of itself to appear in print there, it has tolerated critical statements of republic ministries of finance and lower-level offices, including the financial services of enterprises. The counterpart ministries of finance have been criticized for not exerting a rationalizing influence upon operational ministries when they were transferring their enterprises to the new conditions. A fear was expressed that the reform allowed a greater possibility of embezzlement of state funds.[50]

Once the reform was under way, the Finance Ministry began, as did other agencies, to try to carve out a greater role for itself. Like Gosbank, it argued for the maintenance of financial indicators from above. In general, the Ministry wants to maintain its active role in overseeing the operations of enterprises and even of industrial ministries. For example, its journal notes that "finance agencies must make a more thorough study of the economics and finances of enterprises and . . . branches. They must work more actively to reveal and mobilize internal reserves, draining additional income into the [state] budget."[51]

The Ministry adopts other positions that are anti-reform, at least by implication. For example, one of its Deputy Ministers has labeled the "suggestion" that enterprises retain the "unused remainder of profit" as an "incorrect" view. He argues that "budget receipts of the unused remainder of profit are . . . a necessary condition for balancing the centralized financial resources of the state." Of course, the USSR is a socialist state in its economic arrangements, albeit of a very particular variety. What is significant is the conservative nature of the argument. It is by nature anti-reform and at least neo-Stalinist in content, if not in intent, since it emphasizes central controls, bureaucratic instrumentalities, and the sanctity of the central state budget as against decentralized profit-seeking and self-strengthening by industrial enterprises.

The Ministry "obliged" the republic ministries of finance "to institute systematic control over the fulfillment of the profit plan by the enterprises which have converted to the new procedure . . ., considering the additional obligations [of the enterprises]."[52] The bureaucratic grip, once rigidified, does not relax easily. This is a foot in the door of the new arrangement and another limitation upon it. For the Ministry it is a move from institutional attitude to institutional action. It bases its claims partly upon legislative actions. An article in <u>Finansy SSSR</u> states: "The conclusions of the permanent commissions [of the USSR Supreme Soviet] . . . recommend that the Ministry of Finance USSR strengthen control over the financial and economic activity of enterprises and economic organizations. . . ."[53] High Ministry officials assume a rather strict supervision of certain enterprise activities. The Ministry is also to "establish control" over certain activities of other ministries and soviets. The reform supposedly has "expanded the sphere of financial control, including in its orbit problems of the efficient utilization of fixed productive and circulating capital, uncovering resources for the growth of profitability, and so on."[54] It is assumed that "independence" for enterprises in this work will redound to the advantage of their ministries because of their influence over enterprises' financial services.

The Ministry of Finance often is highly suspicious of the accounts of enterprises and their managements' intentions--for example, when they make out reports on sales. Its inspectors look into more than 20 items connected with the sales reports of enterprises. The examination procedure is very complex. Enterprises are under as close a scrutiny as they were prior to the reform. The only difference is the objects of the controls. "An important sector in financial control under the new conditions of management is verification of the correctness of report figures on sales and plan fulfillment."[55] A market and a rational price situation would obviate the need for much of this "financial control."

The Ministry of Finance retains several functions that might serve as a basis of petty tutelage: "to simplify and reduce the costs of the management apparatus" and to control the fulfillment of "corresponding tasks." These are not specified, but they include the former duty of determining the natures and sizes of staffs. Certainly, this power is often a concomitant of powers over costs. These powers seem very close to those long held by the Ministry in its earlier incarnation. Regional financial organs have fined enterprises for not submitting reports on the fulfillment of the plan for the supposedly defunct VAL.[56] As is the case with ministerial officials, the personnel of the Ministry of Finance are, in general, not capable of operating effectively in the new conditions. Few of the "cadres" and specialists have a knowledge of economics.[57] In addition, Ministry personnel who deal with the staffs of enterprises do not have any knowledge of personnel relations or organization theory.

It is clear that grounds for the possible continuation of the supervisory activities of the past still exist, and that this aspect of the model has not been fully realized.

THE INTERSTICES: OBEDINENIIA

Issues and Developments

One authority noted as early as 1965 that the obedinenie or firm "may eventually become the dominant form of enterprise organization in Soviet industry." The economist Leon Smolinski has called firms the "first major organizational innovation on the enterprise level in thirty years." This organizational form is the latest example of the long-term Soviet effort to find an ideal compromise in the centralization-decentralization continuum in industry, an effort common in complex organizations. (A similar process of concentration and specialization is occurring in Soviet agriculture, spurred by Brezhnev himself).[58] Herbert Simon poses the general question succinctly:

> . . . how much of the decision making should be done by the executives of the larger units, and

> how much should be delegated to lower levels. But centralizing and decentralizing are not genuine alternatives. . . . The question is not whether we shall decentralize, but how far we shall decentralize. What we seek . . . is . . . to find the proper level in the organization hierarchy--neither too high nor too low--for each important class of decisions.[59]

Simon astutely points out that decentralization and specialization in American companies were accompanied by many crosscurrents of centralization. It appears that Soviet practice will not be qualitatively different.

The ever more numerous species of production association or amalgamation, a Soviet-style industrial corporation or "merged multiplant concern,"[60] is closely related to other important issues: the future role of ministries and especially of the thousand-odd glavki, the amount of economic decision-making to be devolved to the production unit, and the level and size of the main production unit. These specific questions are related to the general issues of concentration-deconcentration, centralization-decentralization, and centralism-regionalism. For example, although the sovnarkhozy were disbanded in 1965, after having suffered excoriating and justified criticism for encouraging "localism," there obviously remains a widespread feeling that some sort and degree of economic-production organization cutting across territorial lines should continue to exist. In April 1973 this attitude became manifest institutionally with the creation of seven large planning regions covering the entire Soviet Union and the authorization of new all-Union industrial associations (promyshlennye obedineniia) just under the ministries.[61] Besides appearing to focus on the development of the Soviet East, and promising to weaken the republics and the entire concept of ethnically based administrative subdivisions, it also may presage the end of the enterprise as the fundamental industrial unit.

There is a need for the coordinated organization of production based upon khozraschet in a form larger than the enterprise. The small enterprise or predpriiatie cannot fulfill this requirement, nor can the glavk, which is an administrative, not a productive organization. Put differently, an attempt is being made to eliminate the problems connected with the former control of enterprises by sovnarkhozy without giving up some of the advantages associated with middle-level territorial organization. This attitude operationalizes itself in increased roles for Union-republic ministries, the soviets, and notably the obedineniia themselves, including the new all-Union and republic obedineniia. The obedineniia constitute one way of combining the principles of organizational recentralization, a conservative reaction to some of Khrushchev's "hare-brained scheming," with decentralization and downward devolution of micro decision-making.

The proliferation of obedineniia poses a threat to the "rights of enterprises," since it brings the lowest level of production organization closer to the higher level.[62] What is crucial for the maintenance of the principles of the reform is the degree to which these new organizations can operate without petty tutelage from the ministries and the Party. "It appears that the associations will gain at the expense of both enterprises and ministries."[63] A complex of several enterprises as a "production association" (proizvodstvennoe obedinenie) will have greater political weight than individual enterprises without "horizontal" connections. This is implicitly recognized by the statement of one top Gosplan functionary that obedineniia can make far better use of the "wide rights" in the existing enterprise statute than individual enterprises can. In the economic sense, obedineniia have greater bargaining power with suppliers.[64]

The obedinenie, although quite an innovation in terms of the scale of its present development, has precedents both in the USSR and in the "family" of Leninist Party-states, despite a tendency in some American accounts to consider the obedinenie as modeled on the American corporate structure. Romania has "industrial centrals" and the German Democratic Republic VVBs (Vereinigungen Volkseigener Betriebe). The Romanian centrals were to take over some of the prerogatives of the ministries but still to be "controlled" and "coordinated" by them. Their functions include the drawing up of proposals for annual and long-term production plans, the working out of research plans and surveys, and the modernization of production. These are strikingly similar to the tasks proposed for ministries in the USSR: studying demand, planning technical progress, and determining the course of the branches' development.[65] The Romanian Ministry of Machine Building controls at least five centrals, including electronics and automation and trucks and tractors, the latter a grouping of 12 enterprises. These and other examples indicate that the Romanian industrial centrals are of a larger scale than most Soviet obedineniia.

The highly paid and efficient director of a German VVB makes many key decisions on his own: hiring and firing the labor force, allocating investment capital from earnings, dealing directly with domestic and foreign suppliers and customers. The main limitation upon his operations is the requirement that he submit his production plan to one of the industrial ministries, which also exercises financial control, though only in a distant and ultimate sense. As one director told an American correspondent, "If your plants make profits, you don't see the planning people for long stretches. They don't come around here very often, I can assure you." Again, the VVB is a larger-scale organization than the Soviet obedinenie although the changes announced in the spring of 1973 may lead to "super-obedineniia." "The eighty-odd V.V.B.'s turn out some 70 percent of East Germany's industrial production and account for all major industries."[66] These "conglomerates," as Nicolas Spulber calls them, have cut down on papierflut. The East Germans have vested decisive executive powers in the management of the VVBs' leading enterprises, have improved market connections among them, and have developed a national computer network based upon them. Spulber maintains that the East Germans have been emulated in some of these respects by the Soviets, the Bulgarians, and the Romanians. This suggests that the GDR is an important source of innovation for the other East European economies and the USSR as well. Another possible source of inspiration for the proliferation of obedineniia in the USSR is the recent Bulgarian emphasis upon industrial associations within a pattern of increasing centralization of economic administration and planning. This may be part of a backlash against the "Prague Spring."[67]

A major and significant difference between the Soviet obedineniia and the more developed and more nearly autonomous Romanian and East German variants is the latter's necessary and major orientation toward the export market. A German VVB, for example, has to export 40 percent or more of its output, almost half of it to "capitalist" countries. As a consequence, as the VVB director quoted above says, "So we have to be competitive." Since the Soviet economy is still semi-autarkic, with no signs, despite the recent upsurge in trade with the United States and other non-Communist states, that it is entering the mainstream of world trade, the Soviet obedinenie still suffers from the hindrances imposed by the administrative pattern long dominant in the Soviet economy. Foreign competition provides the East Europeans with a challenge and stimulus to efficient development that is largely absent in the USSR. The Romanian and German developments do show that it is possible within the framework of a latter-day Leninist Party-state to modify the administrative pattern underlying industrial production significantly, specifically by limiting the ministries to a key advisory and support role.

The obedinenie is not totally new in the USSR, in either name or content. Lenin established the first public corporations in 1923 and directed them to compete with private enterprises in the market environment of the NEP. Since they were created in a period of loose central planning, their renewed prominence may mean that planning will again be less centralized. During the 1920s glavki were for a long time known as obedineniia, and groups of enterprises producing similar commodities existed for some years but were known as trusts (tresty). These were eliminated during the 1930s, except for some in the extractive branches.[68] Then, beginning in 1962, a number of small footwear plants in Lvov were joined together by the local sovnarkhoz, with the grouping called a firma. The "new" organizational form was publicized and duplicated widely; but this was sharply curtailed in 1965 by the restored ministries, to which it probably represented a threat. The actual numbers of firmy set up by 1965 is unclear, although the figure of approximately 500 has been given by three scholars.[69] The terms firma and obedinenie often are used interchangeably, even though the latter dates from 1964 and often contains enterprises scattered over a large area, not only those in one general locality. The present obedineniia, despite their respectable size and their superficial similarity to Western corporations, are not really similar to them, since they are not operationally independent of the governmental structure. (The combines [kombinaty] set up in 1919 between glavki and tresty seemed analogous to public corporations for a time.)[70]

The idea of corporation and amalgamation among industrial enterprises producing similar products is a permanent part of Soviet economic history that periodically receives institutional form, although of differing kinds. The kombinat is an example of vertical integration, while the obedinenie is the most recent example of horizontal integration.

Reasons

Political and Administrative Reasons

The political basis of the creation of obedinenie, though unclear, involves both a conservative distrust of small, individual enterprises operating semi-independently and the chief political figures' desire to limit the ability of the ministerial bureaucrats to make policy through implemental activities. The fact that "individual" ministries and glavki have eliminated obedineniia indicates that ministerial officials perceived a threat to their power and tried to deal with it forcefully. At least 240 obedineniia were eliminated between 1965 and 1969.[71] Brezhnev came out decisively for the obedineniia in 1971 when he said that "they must become the basic self-supporting [khozraschetnyi] links of social production." This was publicized in a Pravda editorial touting the new form, that also explicitly criticized a USSR ministry (Machine Tool Building) for impeding the formation of obedineniia among its enterprises in the Belorussian republic. Significantly, one economist says that "since the 24th C.P.S.U. Congress no one has to be persuaded of the advantages of the new forms of uniting science and production."[72] The anti-bureaucratic and pro-efficiency slant of the leadership's position is exemplified by its concurrent warning against the new organization becoming an "additional administrative link." Many commentators have called for moving ministries and glavki from an administrative to a productive basis, making a "unified economic complex."[73]

Another important part of the causal matrix is the continuing salience of the idea that regionalism ought to play a meaningful role in industrial planning and management. This interrelates with the attempt to limit the new ministries' powers. It has been argued convincingly that planning on the basis of a single branch of industry does not permit the solution of problems related to the activities of several branches operating in the same area, such as construction and transportation, and cultural, educational, and health services. As a solution one economist advocates an "economically based territorial cross section of the national economic plan in which there would be a correct reflection of territorial proportions and an integrated development of the economies of an oblast, economic region and union-republic."[74] This is in line with what has developed organizationally since 1973. Similar suggestions have been made by other writers. In general, the effects of the "narrowly bureaucratic interests" of ministries upon inter-branch cooperation and enterprise specialization are decried.

Some interesting concessions to regionalism or territorialism in planning have been made in recent years that have presaged the creation of regional industrial bodies. Their connection with the pervasive "national question" cannot be stated. In December 1970 a "scientific council" to deal with the development and distribution of the productive forces of the Transcaucasus was set up at a meeting in Tbilisi held under the auspices of USSR Gosplan. An economist who heads a research institute of the Azerbaidzhan Gosplan stated: "There are no great differences in natural resources in the Transcaucasus economic region. Their rational exploitation is becoming more and more difficult without a mutual agreement among the republics on the potentials and the needs of the economy in the light of the prospects of further development."[75] Other regional planning areas with councils exist. Significantly, in late 1972 a proposal was made in Voprosy ekonomiki that the borders of republics be altered to place economically similar areas in the same administrative subdivision of the state structure.[76]

Besides this reinstitution of regionalism there has been some talk of supra-ministerial and inter-ministerial combinations, such as joining all the ministries dealing with fuel and power, metallurgy, or consumer goods.[77] This scheme is reminiscent of the VSNKh (Supreme Council of the National Economy) of the 1920s. The interbranch organization in various forms has not avoided ministerial opposition. One writer says that a ministry adapts a plant to its "own" needs alone, asks "How is the appetite of the agencies to be curbed?," and suggests that all inter-branch enterprises be placed under the planning commission of an economic region.[78] This is a plain argument for regionalism and against organizing industry purely by branch. There is a growing body of opinion saying, as does the Deputy Chairman of the Ukrainian Gosplan, that "the practice of branch planning . . . while ensuring maximum utilization of production capacities and correct technical policy, . . . does not adequately resolve the problems concerning the most comprehensive and rational utilization of all the potential resources of the territories."[79] A number of subjects that extend beyond the framework of individual enterprises and branches, and that necessitate a "territorial interrelationship" between indices of the national plan, are said to exist. These include utilization of manpower and natural resources, development of transportation, cooperation and specialization, and supply.

This call for a meaningful role for territorial organizations is consistent with the model, although its present degree and form of development are innovational. In his report of September 1965, Kosygin intimated that territorial organizational structures have a place under the reform.

"Industrial centers," each comprising a group of closely located enterprises "regardless of their departmental allegiance and the nature of their production," also have appeared. One such "center" exists in Brest and is comprised of seven enterprises of several ministries. Others are at Kirov and Kulindorov, and plans have been drawn up for more. Many problems connected with them have yet to be solved, including the question of their relationship to ministries.[80]

It is clear that the structure of Soviet industrial management is still not completely established, that some fluidity is present, and that the regional pattern of organization is reappearing.

Economic and Administrative Reasons

There are several substantive reasons for accelerating the widespread development of obedineniia. First, however, one must recognize that these "reasons" have existed for a long time, perhaps decades. The general political, social, and economic climate that has allowed the reasons to be openly recognized and derivative action to be taken was discussed in the Introduction.

In a nutshell, the reason (and presumed benefit) most often cited for the introduction of obedineniia is increased efficiency. This carries its usual connotation of reduced cost per unit of output but also includes the additional desiderata of reduced complexity of planning, increased product specialization, reduced administrative personnel and labor force, heightened knowledge by management of both production functions and the market, more efficient use of capital, more rapid introduction of scientific discovery, fewer small enterprises, combination of production and research in single organizations, the centralization and rationalization of managerial functions, the creation of new subunits such as computer centers and their attachment to production activity, and even reduced inventories.[81]

Such a multi-purpose economic unit may be more a planner's dream than a realistic short-term organizational goal. One Soviet newspaper invokes the ideology and idealistically presents the obedinenie as a means of realizing Marx's old hope of eliminating the differences between town and country by suggesting that large enterprises set up filialy or branches in areas of poor industrial development.[82] The main watchword or slogan for the obedineniia seems to be specialization and cooperation (with emphasis upon the conjunction). At times, definitional statements of some singularity or even originality are made. Two Soviet jurists have argued that the central function of obedineniia is performing the managerial tasks of enterprises "and enabling them to concentrate on their basic work of production."[83] This point of view seems to have triumphed in 1973. They go on to make the questionable idealistic assertion that the performance of these functions by the obedineniia is not administrative activity of the usual kind (over "subordinate enterprises") but instead is the provision of "economic services" to members of a small economic community.

One source for the move toward obedineniia that is particularly emphasized is the pattern of small-scale productive activity common in the USSR (despite the image of "gigantomania" commonly associated with Soviet industry) and the possible corrective effect of the creation of obedineniia. As a Deputy Chairman of Gosplan says, "The reform has worked best in large enterprises and combines, and the policy must now be to merge the many small enterprises with larger units so that they can work on the new system with advantage too."[84] In 1964 there were "more than 130,000 small enterprises," apparently meaning plants and factories with fewer than 200 workers. In any case, in 1965, 55.9 percent of the enterprises in the USSR had fewer than 200 workers and 76.6 percent had fewer than 500. Labor productivity and profitability are low and production is comparatively expensive. In addition, the administrative apparatus is relatively large and expensive, since it has often been unimaginatively copied from that of large enterprises.[85] Naturally, the directors of some small plants want as complete an administrative structure and as many staff members as possible. Even enterprises with 500 or so workers, twice the size of those under discussion, "are unable to maintain serious research-and-development operations."

Labor productivity at plants of fewer than 200 workers is said to be "between one-fourth and one-third the level at large enterprises, and production costs are two to two-and-a-half times as high as at the large plants." It also has been noted that only a complex of enterprises will be large enough to have some knowledge of the market for its products, and that organizing industry on the basis of obedineniia might allow a reduction in the size of the supply apparat and the elimination of wasteful duplication and unnecessary competition between products.[86] Another kind of advantage was suggested to me by a Soviet engineer who, noting that factories producing an item such as a tractor often are unwilling to repair it, surmised that when the same plant became part of an obedinenie, there might be a special repair enterprise that would provide service and spare parts. A goal, then, is to create and benefit from economies of scale by a greater utilization of equipment, managerial talent, and specialization.[87]

One of the other major reasons for initiating obedineniia is the more rapid introduction of new technology into production. Applied scientific ideas have been called "the most valuable, and at the same time the most perishable, form of production 'raw material'" which cannot be handed on from one organization to another as if they were "relay batons in a race." Many directors of Soviet enterprises have complained that, despite the existence of research institutes and laboratories within their branches, new discoveries find their way into production slowly, if at all. Even the supposedly exemplary Ministry of Instrument Making produces some low-quality products partly because its glavk, Soiuzglavnauchpribor, has only small enterprises.[88] Large-scale research and development activity seems to be a function of large organizations. For example, in 1959, 86 percent of the total industrial research and development work in the United States was performed by companies with more than 5,000 employees. Daniel Bell notes that "something substantially new about technology has been introduced into economic and social history . . . the systematic development of research and the creation of new science based industries." These lessons have probably been learned in the USSR. One Soviet writer says that obedineniia "have emerged as a result of accelerating the process of socializing production under the conditions of the scientific and technical revolution."[89]

It seems inevitable, then, that some Soviet enterprise managers will be called upon to direct larger organizations as a consequence of the present development of associations. As it has been put in Soviet terminology, "theory and practice . . . confirm that, at a certain stage of development, production concentration inevitably goes beyond the limits of the individual enterprise, no matter how large it is."[90] It is not at all clear, however, that reductions in managerial and other staff will result automatically from the creation of obedineniia. "Parkinson's Law" will tend to operate to some degree, although an assumption seems to be widely held that "reduction [of the 'managerial apparatus'] is inevitable, for there are extensive and numerous parallel services" in industrial enterprises. It is clear that there is now a decided emphasis upon concentrating industrial management at a level above that of the single enterprise, establishing specialization of production without static autarky, and deepening the effects of capital.

The possible functions of obedineniia are indicated by an example drawn from an existing one, the Sigma obedinenie in Lithuania, which manufactures electronic instruments and control systems, all important for the reform. It is discussed as a model that is to be widely copied. Its major functions are as follows:

1. Preparation of long-range and annual development plans, the approval of planning assignments for subordinate enterprises, and the control of plan fulfillment
2. Approval of norms of profit taxes for groups of enterprises or separate enterprises, and of the norms for payment for capital
3. Organization and provision of material and technical supply of the enterprises, and the distribution of capital among them
4. Approval of the norms for the expenditure of raw and other materials, fuel, and electric power, and of the norms of production reserves
5. Approval of the wage fund
6. Financing of subordinate enterprises and the establishment of the norms of working capital for them.[91]

This list of the Sigma obedinenie functions shows that it has taken over many of the tasks of both a ministry and a glavk.

The reasons for and sources of this process of organizational change on the production front have been presented. It is now time to discuss the structural forms that the new manner of organizing production has assumed.

The Forms and Definitions of Obedineniia

A new species of organization does not appear exactly the same in all places, even in a country as noted for standardization as the Soviet Union. It is nevertheless possible to define an obedinenie generally as a complex of structurally separate, but mutually supporting, units of industrial production, most of which are producing the same or very similar items. The units are organizationally united, and often include such nonproduction units as research laboratories, under a common director and managerial staff. The shortest Soviet definition is "enterprises with subsidiaries," although the term "affiliates" also is used. The present trend is for each obedinenie to have a single technical, financial, and output plan (tekhpromfinplan), a single budget and bank account, and the same economic incentive fund.[92] Although this may be taken as a working definition, the usage of the term obedinenie is so broad at present that it is also applied to associations that have no material output but concentrate upon the provision of a service to producing enterprises. These are called "associations for scientific services to enterprises." Accordingly, an obedinenie can be some form of "research-and-production and scientific-technical complexes." There are seven types of obedineniia, in accordance with the number of phases of the "research-to-production" process:

1. Scientific and technical, such as a design bureau
2. Educational, scientific, and technical (includes a higher educational institution)
3. Research and production
4. Technical
5. Production and technical (an interesting example noted is an amalgamation of production enterprises, research and development institutes, and construction units)
6. Production and scientific
7. Scientific services to enterprises.[93]

This kind of categorization does not reveal the major forms an obedinenie can take in terms of internal power relationships. Its main emphasis is upon the assimilation of research and development. If obedineniia are categorized on the basis of internal relationships, essentially three forms are discerned. The first is the formal association of enterprises that remain independent in terms of staffs, work forces, budgets, and so on; here, cooperation pure and simple is the effect of association. In the second the affiliates have lost the right of a judicial entity but preserve a partial accounting independence. In this case some amalgamation has occurred. The third form is the "more progressive" and favored association comprising a head enterprise with affiliates that now have, in effect, the status of shops. Here a single tekhpromfinplan exists and a new organizational entity has been created, "head enterprises with subsidiaries having the rights of shops" (golovnye predpriiatiia s filialami na pravakh tsekhov).

The effects upon the size and structure of management vary.[94] The third form naturally is favored at present, since it is the only one to allow, at least potentially, the implementation in production and management of a new approach that includes the widespread use of recent scientific discoveries, a knowledge of the obedinenie's "market" sufficient to ensure sales, and an easy internal maneuverability in terms of manpower, materials, and structures. Some try to label the first two types with the old terms of "trust" and "combine" (a vertically integrated multi-plant complex), reserving the term "firm" for the third form. [95] The decision of which to establish supposedly is determined by the characteristics of the branch of industry and the natures, sizes, and territorial location of enterprises.

It is clear that the obedinenie has not yet been institutionalized in one definite form. The number of enterprises in a firm can vary from 2 to 22 but 3 to 5 is common, with most within a single oblast and with an average distance of 50 to 60 miles between the head enterprise and the affiliates. Additional variations appear, some only for brief periods. As one writer says, referring to the matter of form, "You cannot give a single recipe here."[96] This discussion, then, proceeds in an atmosphere of continuing development and change. Despite the air of flux, a consensus nevertheless seems to exist on the general structural pattern that most of industry should have at some point in the near future. This is often referred to as the "three-link system"; that is, the model hierarchical scheme of a branch is to be enterprise-obedinenie-ministry (with the number of enterprises being very few, probably restricted to the largest ones, those quite isolated from others territorially, or those quite distinctive in terms of technology or production). The concept of powerful obedineniia organized over very large areas, implemented in 1973, was under discussion in 1970 if not earlier. [97]

The oil and gas extraction ministries have eliminated a few lower levels of organization. Reportedly, all petroleum-extracting brigades and sectors are being abolished as independent entities and combined into larger units. Some 500 enterprises of 27 subbranch industries of the Ukrainian Ministry of Light Industry now operate in accordance with the three-link system. More than 4,500 persons have been let go from the administrative apparatus and 4.7 million rubles saved. To do this, the Ministry's nine trusts were abolished and its main administrations (glavki) were transformed into republic-level production obedineniia. [98] This example shows that some potentially significant developments are taking place. The transformed glavki are said to be in charge of the operational administration of enterprises and to have freed the Ministry for the solution of "important strategic questions," such as the formation of the branch's long-term plans. To be meaningful, of course, this process will have to rest upon opening up the glavki to the operation of khozraschet, something that cannot yet have occurred in all cases. As two Izvestiia correspondents explain the change:

> In the first place, a superfluous level of administration . . . is eliminated . . . the firm does not need what the chief administration can provide, while the chief administration cannot, as a rule, provide what the firm does need.
>
> . . . . . .
>
> The main thing is that the production unit has directly taken over the administrative functions that are most important for it . . . planning, production, supply and sales, which encompass the entire sphere of business management.[99]

This development is viewed as an inevitable development for the future, as a prototype of a new kind of flexible and simple administrative structure.

Besides beginning to make a significant change in the relationship between enterprises and ministries, the obedinenie is having at least two other important effects upon the power relations in industrial management. The old style of authoritarian one-man directorship is being altered in the direction of collegiality, and the structure and operation of the Communist Party at the level of the industrial plant is being modified. (The nature of the latter modification is taken up in Chapter 4. Suffice it to say at this point that the Party is striving to maintain its usual degree of control but that this is not easily possible if an obedinenie's units exist within the territories of different Party organizations, thus involving such issues as span of control.)

Naturally an obedinenie with dispersed units cannot afford the edinonachalie of old. It would not be feasible on two counts. No totalistic direction from the "top" is possible because of the variety of conditions and operations in the different units, and that kind of direction within the units themselves would work against the cooperative effort and meshing of operations demanded by the very concept of the obedinenie. Accordingly, an association is governed by a council of directors (sovet direktorov). This new management institution has been mentioned several times, the first time noticed by this writer being in mid-1969, although it probably existed earlier. Authoritative political approval no doubt was required before the press could carry discussion of it. Not every association has such a council. In some the general director enjoys the power and privilege of edinonachalie, as at Positron in Leningrad, where general'nyi direktor iavliaetsia edinonachal'nikom, while in other obedineniia, such as the one named for Sverdlov, it is necessary to gain the concurrence of individual directors by "persuasion."[100]

The primary advantage of the council of directors has been given as the combination of "one-man management with board management,"[101] and it may be an imitation of a capitalist board of directors. Although procedures vary from one association to another, this variation is accepted as a necessary consequence of differences in size, structure, and production. But some general working procedure does exist. An agenda is drawn up two to three weeks prior to meetings, and copies of reports and decisions in draft form are submitted to members of a council about ten days prior to a meeting, usually held at the "head enterprise." The decisions taken by a council are assumed to be reached jointly and are to be put into effect as orders. Membership varies but, including the Party secretaries, the chief legal advisor, and various technical advisors, some become so large that excessive complexity in managerial structure and delay in decision-making may result. Another weakness may be the retention or "reinvention" of a large, unwieldy, and costly management apparatus. Nevertheless, the council seems to allow greater participation by specialists, that is, by staff people. It is an example of managerial decentralization within a structural centralization, and was probably an unavoidable step. A larger, more diversified organization cannot be ruled; it must be coordinated and managed. "Convergence" may or may not be involved. There have been some clashes between the councils and glavki. To cope with this, a procedure exists whereby the head of a glavk must inform the ministry when he is acting in disagreement with a council and request it to resolve the differences. This means the ministries have arbitrational powers.

In early April 1973 a codification of the obedineniia and a formal expansion of them occurred. In effect, a second and higher level was created, the nationwide industrial association of all enterprises making a particular type of product. The official and legal notice of this step was a joint resolution of the Party Central Committee and USSR Council of Ministers issued on April 3, 1973, and blandly entitled "On Certain Measures for the Further Improvement of Industrial Management."[102] A reading of the resolution suggests that the higher-level or "super" obedineniia are to become, in effect, ministries. It is not clear what functions are definitely to remain with the old ministries, although Theodore Shabad asserts that these super associations "will . . . take over many ministry functions, such as industrial research and development and some export-import decisions [with] the role of ministries . . . [being] long-term planning, investment policy and technological innovation."[103] We shall see whether the new exile of ministerial bureaucrats to the provinces (which is implied) will last as long as that of 1957. Other questions are also open; for instance, who are to be the nachal'niki of the all-Union or republic obedineniia, former deputy ministers or department heads of ministries? (The heads of the lower-level "production" obedineniia are to be called rukovoditeli, not nachal'niki. Significantly, the glavki are slated for almost total elimination and are to become, in effect, operational units of the new obedineniia. The change no doubt will provide some economies of scale and the usual advantages of specialization, but cannot eliminate fundamental problems.

One of the defects of industrial concentration in socialist economies is old-fashioned monopolistic behavior that "tends to eliminate competition and to strengthen monopolistic elements." Possibly "in Socialist countries . . . industrial integration has [already] gone too far." Additional bureaucratization also has occurred, notably in Poland and Hungary, where a trend of restoring the powers of enterprises now exists.[104] But Soviet enterprises are to lose their independence. "The Statute on the Socialist State Production Enterprise shall not be applied to the production units comprising the production association [combine]," although the same statute will operate as the guiding document for the associations until a new statute is issued for them.

Such a logical and seemingly value-free emphasis on improving administration may eventually exacerbate the Soviet nationalities question. The ultimate goal of the merging of 50,000 individual industrial enterprises into a few thousand obedineniia under the control of the large, coordinating regional obedineniia that overarch republic or other lower-level ethnic administrative boundaries might lead to the elimination of the old internal boundaries by a new Constitution. After all, what "productive" purpose would ethnic subdivisions then serve?

Development: Accomplishments and Difficulties

All the figures found on total numbers of associations are in general agreement. It seems reasonable to estimate that by 1973 there were approximately 1,000 industrial associations in the USSR containing about 3,700 enterprises. It is possible they account for 12 percent of industrial output and about 9 percent of the enterprises.[105] The new form is most common in light industry and in certain areas, such as the Ukraine. By late 1970 the Ukraine had 50 or so production associations in light industry, comprising 273 enterprises and branches employing about 250,000 workers and producing 40 percent of the output of Ukrainian light industry. The rise in their volume of production during 1966-70 reportedly was 66 percent, compared with an increase of 57.5 percent for enterprises not in associations. The indices for labor productivity and profits rose comparably. It is even asserted that associations in the Ukraine have always fulfilled their plans in terms of basic indicators.

Similar figures for the Belorussian republic and Leningrad oblast exist.[106] Statistics on other results are rarer. A smattering exists, however, and it does seem that the creation of an association results in the release of workers. After the Grozny Petrochemical Association had applied the "Shchekino experience" for three years, "more than 1,200" people in the work force had been released and labor productivity had climbed by 23 percent during the period (instead of the 17.5 percent planned).[107]

Some Advantages and Some Difficulties

First, the question of what might be called "formalism," artificiality, or even phoniness arises. The amalgamation of enterprises into obedineniia is often a "mechanical" process. One economist derisively stated: "What has really changed by giving the appellation of associations to the chief administrations of the Ministry of Light Industry in the Ukraine? Essentially nothing." Another said that "unfortunately, the creation of the new obedineniia . . . delays [the solution] of certain unresolved questions."[108] In addition, some firms have been established mainly to employ administrative personnel of the former sovnarkhozy. For example, under questioning by a Pravda reporter, the Ukrainian Minister of the Meat and Dairy Industry admitted: "We call them association-administrations now. It's all in the hyphen. You understand, don't you? . . . It's to maintain high salaries there."[109] This seems to confirm what may be a law of administrative change: responsible personnel who are fired in a reorganization often move horizontally at the same level and wind up in positions much like their previous ones, but in different organizations. (Examples of this occurring between American universities and within the U.S. aerospace industry are common.)

Besides dissatisfaction, the obedineniia have met resistance of various kinds. The actions taken by ministries against associations since 1966 have already been mentioned. They have created obedineniia only "unwillingly, reluctantly, and apprehensively." Interestingly, some ministries disbanded associations as late as 1970.[110] The chief administrations in particular have exhibited opposition to the associations, fearing that they will lose all reason for existence. Other sources of resistance also exist. Many directors of the enterprises slated for amalgamation are not enthusiastic about the possible results. A type of petty mestnichestvo seems to operate. "The administrators of particular plants and factories are afraid to lose [their] independence. . . ." Managerial staff also fear for their "material blessings" and even their posts, since one goal of the new units is to reduce administrative personnel and expenses.[111] Two writers lament: "Unfortunately, one encounters people who do not accept innovation. One also encounters persons who have allowed their hurt feelings to get the better of them: Watch out, they say; if you surrender any of your rights to others, the next thing you know, you'll be losing your title."[112] Managerial personnel probably try to instill "backbone" into their ministerial superiors and invent reasons why amalgamation will not work or will create difficulties.

Some opposition to the formation of associations has welled up from local-level Party organizations as well, since the creation of an association entails delegation of decision-making and of financial control to higher echelons of both the government and the Party. One analysis says that "Brezhnev's warning [at the 24th Congress] that administrative boundaries must not stand in the way of improvement of economic management was prompted mainly by this problem."[113] Some economists and commentators on economic topics also express skepticism or even opposition to the associations. One asserts flatly that "a conglomerate of 'autonomous' enterprises which are entirely and fully independent of the state [and] which build relations between themselves strictly on the basis of market conditions would represent a base for the occurrence of anarchosyndicalist relations in the economy. . . ."[114] Some of the critical remarks made concerning associations present an authoritarian view of the new entity. The obedinenie must have cohesion and a unified policy to be meaningful. Yet in the Soviet context the dominant organizational tendency is the automatic imposition of excessive centralization.

One position appears only in statements made by critics. A general director of an obedinenie argues against an opposition or "liberal" position, saying that "a certain segment" of economists and lawyers (note the groups mentioned) argues that the administrative organ of an obedinenie cannot function simultaneously as the management organ of the leading enterprise, since this situation prevents the administrative organ from carrying out principles of cost accounting within the entire obedinenie.[115]

A structural difficulty that causes some dismay and even consternation among all who write about the associations is the continuing lack of a "statute" or polozhenie that would establish their rights and obligations and normative acts governing the merger of enterprises. The general rules set forth in the Statute on Enterprises are considered "clearly inadequate." A new statute would have to regulate the rights, structures, and pay involved, and "much else." The Party-state joint resolution of 1973 does not say enough.[116]

Advantages of the new firms are several, at least in theory. They allow the consolidation of supply and sales departments, the lowering of the costs of administration and planning, the increase of managers' confidence in their powers, and, thus, the reduction of that old bugbear, the concealment of reserves through hoarding. In addition, market research and technical progress should be easier and closer to production.[117]

The Party

Although lower-level Party organizations have on occasion opposed the establishment of obedineniia, it appears on balance that the Party as a whole has favored the policy and has taken the initiative in promoting it. "As a rule it is the Party committees that are the initiators in the founding of firms."[118] This, of course, fits well with both the general assumption that the main source of power in the USSR is the Party apparatus as "super-coordinator" and with the less widely held view that the Party is the main force for change and the most progressive organization in Soviet society. Certainly, large-scale structured change such as this can be effectuated at this time by no other grouping. The Party has made the establishment of a large number of associations an element of policy. At times, of course, since the Party apparatus operates by campaigns (po kampanski), the Party organs have been exhorted to engage in "more serious involvement" in the process of setting up associations. Instances of Party intervention on the side of the obedinenie can be documented. For example, G. V. Romanov, the Second Secretary of the Leningrad oblast Party Committee and now also a candidate member of the Politburo, castigated glavki and ministries for holding back the development of obedineniia.[119] The Party apparatus is favoring the obedinenie because its leading strata are efficiency-minded and because they think they have solved the problem of control, the methods for which are discussed in Chapter 4.

Implications for the Reform

A new organizational form has been born amid the fumes of late Soviet industrialization. Its ultimate results in terms of the efficiency sought so eagerly by the technocratic political elite are not clearly visible now. Claims of success, though rife, are still premature. It is not clear, of course, that the economy is in fact helped by the obedineniia in the long run. Even if they are on khozraschet, they either may be as given to administirovanie as ministries have been, or as given to obfuscation and informalism as enterprises long have been. The words of Peter Drucker may apply:

> Large businesses, these past twenty years, have added layer upon layer of management and all kinds of specialized staffs, from market research

to personnel and from cost analysis to long-range planning. Whether there has been any corresponding increase in productivity and performance of management is, however, by no means proved.[120]

In addition, obedineniia may not be able to operate on khozraschet. Some maintain that "the latter [obedineniia and glavki] as administrative organs, cannot carry out production and economic functions and, consequently, cannot operate on the basis of khozraschet." Others do not support this view and say instead that obedineniia "are not administrative organs but production and economic systems consisting of enterprises and their managerial staff."[121] Strong arguments supporting the creation of obedineniia operating on khozraschet are made. For example: "It is completely apparent that there can be no full-scale khozraschet without the creation of production associations.... The creation of cost accounting associations of enterprises is the most important element for the further development of the economic reform...."[122]

This desire for intermediate industrial organizations operating on khozraschet is an important outgrowth of the reform, although it may go against the model's spirit because it presupposes the elimination of the small enterprise. In some types of production, however, smallness of size allows a high degree of efficiency. It remains to be seen whether the large obedineniia can have the advantages of both large-scale and small, specialized industrial units. A major tendency of Soviet industry, however, has been a drive for autarky, one of the things the reform was to reduce. The director of an obedinenie in Sverdlovsk argues against this possibility, saying that obedineniia allow more intra-firm specialization and the liquidation of petty parallel services and shops and, therefore, greater economy.[123]

The divergent views indicate that different persons are trying to lead the same development in opposite directions, another example of bureaucratic maneuvering under the cover of the rationalization of Soviet industrial management.

A danger to the reform is that obedineniia, being much closer to the activity of enterprises, may be able to reestablish the old type of control over them. Obedineniia began early to change the planned indicators for sales and profit of enterprises,[124] a serious and blatant form of interference in enterprise operations. The Bulgarian experience may portend the Soviet future. The creation of 44 regional state industrial associations in early 1971 stripped the enterprise, which had enjoyed some independence, of most of their capability to make economic decisions. As Stephen Larrabee points out:

"The extent to which the powers of individual enterprises are accumulated upward to the associations under the 1971 reorganization suggests that the end result is an increased rather than decreased centralization of management in the Bulgarian economy."[125]

Although the Bulgarian NEM (New Economic Model) of late 1965 provided for some degree of meaningful decentralization, since 1968 a process similar to that now operating in the USSR has been at work. Whether the Bulgarian or the Soviet shift in emphasis came first is open to examination. Several possibilities suggest themselves. Perhaps a dialectic of sorts is at work. Although the process involves the transfer of industrial power upward, it may also enhance the political significance of the industrial managers as a class because the organizations they now run are much larger and richer. At the least, it is "clear that the ministerial system recreated in 1965 did not meet the expectations."[126]

CONCLUSION

In summary, it appears that either the manager-superior relationship has in practice not lived up to the model of the reform or has developed considerably beyond it. Ministries and ministry-level organizations--as well as such intermediate-level administrative organs as trusts, glavki, and obedineniia--are either not always allowing enterprises to operate completely in accordance with the model or are attempting to exercise their former or new rights and prerogatives over the enterprises and obedineniia. "So far, . . . ministries . . . remain administrative agencies."[127] Also still in question within the relationship between enterprises and their superiors is whether the profit motive, which has been approved, supported, and glorified by the Soviet leadership and all its communications media, can be made the vital and effective operating force at the working level of Soviet industrial management--the predpriiatie or enterprise, be it a separate entity or a part of an obedinenie. The reform is making demands that overtax the understanding, abilities, and self-interest of industrial bureaucrats and tempt them into previous patterns of action.

Under the guise of implementing the reform, each bureaucracy is contending for the most advantageous position it can obtain. This may result in a "reform" implemented not in accordance with the model but in conformity with the final balance of forces among the bureaucracies involved. In this the enterprise and obedinenie are likely to come off less than second-best. Brian Chapman's dictum, "The way the question of controlling public administration is approached reflects both a philosophy of the state and a national social psychology," is not fully applicable in a particular situation.[128] However, there is no doubt that the Stalinist tendency to detailed supervision still has numerous supporters in the state bureaucracy and that orders of the political leadership are distorted or not understood by that same bureaucracy. The latter problem is endemic to all political systems, although rarely present to as great a degree as in Russia. The professional bureaucrats of the state machinery are concerned that their positions not be adversely affected during the implementation of the reform, and certain bureaucratic groups are trying to emerge with improved positions.

It is too early to tell whether the leadership's attempt to create a new class of super-managers in the super-enterprises of the obedineniia will be able to head off this creeping bureaucratic paralysis. The reform's implementation is being hampered not only by a stikhiinyi ("spontaneous") process caused by normal bureaucratic caution and difficulty of adjusting to the new requirements but also by a soznatel'nyi ("conscious") process of bureaucratic struggle for improved power positions. It is a moot question which complex of attitudes and actions is limiting the implementation of the model more. Nevertheless, it is evident that the model of the manager-superior relationship has not been institutionalized.

NOTES

1. Izvestiia, July 19, 1969, p. 2, and April 12, 1969, p. 3.
2. Pravda, May 10, 1971.
3. Merle Fainsod, How Russia Is Ruled (rev. ed.; Cambridge, Mass.: Harvard University Press, 1963), pp. 406-07; and Eugene Zaleski, Planning Reforms in the Soviet Union: 1962-1966 (Chapel Hill: University of North Carolina Press, 1967), pp. 104-05, 182-83.
4. L. Velikanova, "Demand for Prognosis," Ekonomicheskaia gazeta 50 (December 10, 1969): 11 (CASP 2, no. 3 [March 1970]: 31). Also see Francis Seton, "Economic Planning in Communist Systems," in George Schopflin, ed., The Soviet Union and Eastern Europe (New York: Praeger, 1970), p. 284.
5. Suggested by a lecture on Polish planning by Witold Trzeciakowski, the Deputy Head of the Polish Institute of Foreign Trade, at the Russian Research Center, Harvard University, on April 29, 1971.
6. G. Sotnikov, Pravda, January 4, 1972, p. 2; excerpted in CDSP 22, no. 1 (February 2, 1972): 23.
7. F. Kotov, "Sovremennaia organizatsiia planirovaniia i puti ee sovershenstvovaniia," Planovoe khoziaistvo 10 (October 1968): 7; P. Krylov and M. Chistiakov, "Questions Concerning Perfection of

Industrial Planning Methods," Planovoe khoziaistvo 3 (March 1966): 11-23 (JPRS 45,218 [May 2, 1968]: 53-54, 67); and A. Kurskii and E. Slastenko, Voprosy ekonomiki 10 (October 1966) (JPRS 39,334 [December 30, 1966]: 48).

8. See Pravda, April 11, 1971, pp. 1-7; (completely translated in CDSP 23, nos. 18 and 19 [June 1 and June 8, 1971]: 9-19 and and 15-26).

9. Michael Ellman, Economic Reform in the Soviet Union (London: Political and Economic Planning, 1969), p. 330.

10. Christian Science Monitor, November 16, 1972.

11. Ellman, op. cit., p. 331; and Pravda, April 11, 1971 (fully translated in CDSP 23, no. 19 [June 8, 1971]: 25). Emphasis in original.

12. See Victor Zorza, "Kremlin Prepares for a Computerized 1984," Washington Post, July 25, 1971; and Kommunist Sovetskoi Latvii 6 (June 1972): 40.

13. Pravda, October 12, 1971, p. 3; (partially translated in CDSP 23, no. 41 [November 9, 1971]: 15).

14. Quoted and discussed in "'Problems of Philosophy' Versus the Computer Lobby," Radio Free Europe Research Report, December 12, 1971, pp. 3-4.

15. Pravda, October 28, 1971. Discussed in R.R.G., "A 'Special State Agency' for Computer Controls?," Radio Free Europe Research Report, November 15, 1971.

16. B. Del Rio, Pravda, January 5, 1971, p. 2; (partially translated in CDSP 23, no. 1 [February 2, 1971]: 8). The author holds a candidate's degree in technology.

17. Rabochii klass i sovremennii mir 5-6 (1971): 23-24; cited in Keith Bush, "The TsSU Report for 1971," Radio Liberty Dispatch, January 25, 1972.

18. Pravda, November 28, 1970, p. 2; and D. Zhimerin, Pravda, June 5, 1971, p. 3 (partially translated in CDSP 23, no. 23 [July 6, 1971]: 13). (Zhimerin is Vice-Chairman of the State Committee for Science and Technology.) Also see Pravda, January 21, 1972.

19. See E. Panfilov, Izvestiia, February 19, 1971, p. 3 (fully translated in CDSP 23, no. 7 [March 16, 1971]: 19); and N. Vasilkova, Pravda, September 24, 1971 (partially translated in CDSP 23, no. 38 [October 19, 1971]: 10-11). Panfilov is director of a coding institute of Gosstandart.

20. A. Kurskii, "Itogi khoziaistvennoi reformy . . . ," Voprosy ekonomiki 4 (April 1967): 28.

21. Gregory Grossman, "Innovation and Information in the Soviet Economy," American Economic Review 56, no. 2 (May 1966): 128-29. See also Peter F. Drucker, Management (New York: (Harper & Row, 1974), pp. 785-88.

22. Alec Nove, The Soviet Economy (2nd rev. ed.; New York: Praeger, 1969), pp. 144-50.
23. N. K. Fedorenko, "Reforma v promyshlennosti . . .," Planovoe khoziaistvo 4 (April 1967): 10-11.
24. S. Miskin, "Rychagi i tormoza," Literaturnaia gazeta 12 (March 22, 1967): 10. Emphasis in original.
25. M. Raman, "Ekonomicheskaia rabota v novykh usloviiakh," Kommunist Sovetskoi Latvii (Riga) 5 (May 1967): 42-48 (JPRS 42,225 [August 15, 1967]: 5); and G. Kulagin, "Reservy reformy," Pravda, August 9, 1967, p. 2.
26. Pravda, September 15, 1970, p. 1; (partially translated in CDSP 22, no. 37 [October 13, 1970]: 17).
27. See, for example, Maurice Dobb, Soviet Economic Development Since 1917 (New York: International Publishers, 1948), pp. 23, 378, 406, and passim; and Pravda, June 30, 1970.
28. Ekonomicheskaia gazeta 50 (December 1968): 20 (JPRS 47,291 [January 22, 1969]: 21); and Sovetskaia Belorussia, December 18, 1970, p. 2.
29. Sotsialisticheskaia industriia, June 11, 1971, p. 2.
30. A. Kurskii and E. Slastenko, "Nekotorye itogi perevoda gruppy predpriiatii na novuiu sistemu," Voprosy ekonomiki 10 (October 1966): 16.
31. A. N. Kosygin, Moscow domestic service, November 25, 1970; FBIS III, November 27, 1970, p. B2.
32. S. Anufrienko, "Khoziaistvennaia reforma i initsiativa predpriiatii," Voprosy ekonomiki 12 (December 1968): 26-27, 33.
33. V. Kamankin, Ekonomicheskaia gazeta 11 (March 1969): 19; and V. Moev, Literaturnaia gazeta 46 (November 12, 1969): 10. Kamankin is a professor at the Central Committee's Academy of Social Sciences.
34. E. G. Liberman, Ekonomika i matematicheskie metody 5 (September-October 1968); JPRS 46,891 (November 18, 1968): 5-6.
35. For a similar view see Richard Lowenthal, "Development Versus Utopia in Communist Policy," Survey 74/75 (Winter-Spring 1970): 25.
36. See Nove, op. cit., pp. 106, 127-30; Barry Richman, Soviet Management (Englewood Cliffs, N.J.: Prentice-Hall, 1965), pp. 226-27; David Granick, The Red Executive (Garden City, N.Y.: Doubleday, 1961), pp. 203-04; Fainsod, op. cit., pp. 318, 410; and James E. Connor, "The Soviet State Bank: A Study in the Development of an Instrument of Control" (unpublished Ph.D. dissertation, Faculty of Political Science, Columbia University, 1968).
37. V. K. Vorob'ev, Den'gi i kredit 7 (July 1968): 3-15; JPRS 46,597 (October 4, 1968): 17. Vorob'ev is Deputy Chairman of the Board of Gosbank. Also see Granick, op. cit., p. 204.

38. G. Garvy, Money, Banking and Credit in Eastern Europe (New York: Federal Reserve Bank of New York, 1966), quoted in Nove, op. cit., pp. 129-30; and Zaleski, op. cit., p. 147.
39. I. Levchuk and A. Cheblokov, Den'gi i kredit 2 (February 1968); JPRS 45,230 (May 2, 1969): 23.
40. Den'gi i kredit 7 (July 1968); JPRS 46,597 (October 4, 1968): 82-83.
41. M. Zotov, Pravda, July 31, 1971, p. 2 (partially translated in CDSP 23, no. 31 [August 31, 1971]: 27; and Den'gi i kredit 2 (February 1968); (JPRS 45,230 [May 2, 1968]: 5). The author is manager of the Russian Republic office of Gosbank.
42. I. Chernov, "Bank v novykh usloviiakh," Kommunist 8 (May 1966): 97, 98.
43. V. Chelnokov and V. Rybin, "Partner predpriiatii," Izvestiia, February 5, 1967, p. 2.
44. V. Batyrev, Den'gi i kredit 12 (December 1968); JPRS 47,562 (March 4, 1969): 14. Batyrev holds a doctorate in economics.
45. M. Rabinovits, "Bank i predpriiatie," Den'gi i kredit 12 (December 1965): 26.
46. S. Gal'perin and A. Shabanov, "Zakonomernost' i problemy," Sovetskaia Belorussia, May 25, 1967, p. 2.
47. O. Kuznetsov, "U nas v banke pol'nyi poriadok!" Trud, August 27, 1966, p. 2; JPRS 38,068 (October 10, 1966): 32.
48. N. Rodionov, "Partiinie komitety i sblizhenie nauki s proizvodstvom," Kommunist 9 (June 1970): 20. Rodionov is the First Secretary of the important Chelyabinsk obkom. See also Literaturniia gazeta, November 11, 1970, pp. 10-11 (cited in ABSEES, April 1971, p. 108); and Den'gi i kredit 7 (July 1968): 85.
49. Izvestiia, September 6, 1969, p. 3.
50. See, for example, Finansy SSSR 11 (November 1968): 94-96; JPRS 47,666 (March 18, 1969): 72, 75, 78.
51. Ekonomicheskaia gazeta 48 (November 1970): 17 (ABSEES, April 1971, p. 108); and Finansy SSSR 3 (March 1969): 92-95 (JPRS 47,972 [May 5, 1969]: 66).
52. Finansy SSSR 11 (November 1968): 73, 77.
53. Finansy SSSR 3 (March 1967): 94.
54. V. Shatilo, Ekonomicheskaia gazeta 36 (September 1968): 11; JPRS 46,642 (October 11, 1968): 58-59.
55. I. Belobzhetskii, "Finance Organ Realization and Control Index," Finansy SSSR 3 (March 1969); JPRS 47,971 (May 5, 1969): 48.
56. M. Kuzin, "Voprosy shatnoi raboty," Finansy SSSR 9 (September 1965) (JPRS 34,122 [February 14, 1966]: 8-9); and Abraham Katz, The Politics of Economic Reform in the Soviet Union, unpublished draft. Mimeographed, Cambridge, Mass. Center for International Affairs, Harvard University, May 1967, pp. 557-58.

57. Finansy SSSR 8 (August 1965); JPRS 32,606 (October 28, 1965): 46.

58. Richman, op. cit., p. 248; Leon Smolinski, "The Soviet Economy: In Search of a Pattern," Survey 66 (April 1966): 99; and Pravda, December 16, 1973.

59. Herbert A. Simon, The Shape of Automation (New York: Harper & Row, 1965), pp. 102-03.

60. Alice C. Gorlin, "The Soviet Economic Associations," Soviet Studies 26, no. 1 (January 1974): 3.

61. See New York Times, May 4, 1973, p. 2; and Leon Smolinski, "Towards a Socialist Corporation," Survey 20, no. 1 (Winter 1974): 27-28.

62. See Michael Kaser, "Planned Economies Under Reform," in G. Schopflin, ed., The Soviet Union and Eastern Europe (New York: Praeger, 1970), p. 298. For criticisms of the process, see S. N. Bratus', "Sootnoshenie administrativnykh i ekonomicheskykh metodov," Sovetskoe gosudarstvo i pravo 3 (March 1966): 32; and particularly Ia. V. Kvasha, "Kontsentratsiia proizvodstva i melkaia promyshlennost'," Voprosy ekonomiki 5 (May 1967): 26-31.

63. Gorlin, op. cit., p. 5.

64. Pravda, August 25, 1970 (condensed in CDSP 22, no. 35 [September 29, 1970]: 9); and Richman, loc. cit.

65. See Kaser, op. cit., pp. 293, 298; and Smolinski, "Towards a Socialist Corporation," p. 29.

66. See Radio Free Europe, Romanian Press Surveys no. 728, December 20, 1967, and no. 794, April 22, 1969; and Situation Report Romania/36, April 11, 1969. See also Welles Hangen, The Muted Revolution: East Germany's Challenge to Russia and the West (New York: Knopf, 1966), pp. 86, 88.

67. Nicolas Spulber, Socialist Management and Planning (Bloomington: Indiana University Press, 1971), p. 14; Zvi Y. Gitelman, The Diffusion of Political Innovation: From Eastern Europe to the Soviet Union (Beverly Hills, Calif.: Sage, 1972); and F. Stephen Larrabee, "Bulgaria's Politics of Conformity," Problems of Communism 21, no. 4 (July-August 1972): 48-49.

68. John N. Hazard, Communists and Their Law (Chicago: University of Chicago Press, 1969), p. 353, citing First Decree on Trusts, 10 April 1923 [1923] 29 Sob. Uzak. R.S.F.S.R. Pt. I, item 336; Nove, op. cit., p. 68; and David Granick, Management of the Industrial Firm in the USSR (New York: Columbia University Press, 1954), p. 18.

69. See Smolinski, "The Soviet Economy," p. 100; Zaleski, op. cit., p. 157; and Gorlin, op. cit., p. 9.

70. See Gregory Bienstock et al., Management in Russian Industry and Agriculture (Ithaca and New York: Cornell University Press, 1948), pp. 7, 185.

71. A. Kurskii, Voprosy ekonomiki 4 (April 1967): 32. Also see Gorlin, op. cit., and Smolinski, "Towards a Socialist Corporation," p. 34.
72. Pravda, May 24, 1971, p. 1. Also Pravda, December 1, 1971, p. 3, translated in CDSP 23, no. 48 (December 28, 1971): 1.
73. G. L. Bulgakov, Promyshlennost' Belorussii, October 1968; JPRS 45,956 (November 26, 1968): 76.
74. A. Kachanov, Ekonomicheskaia gazeta 48 (November 1968); (JPRS 47,098 [December 17, 1968]: 1).
75. Bakinskii rabochii, December 12, 1970, p. 3; and Moscow Domestic, March 14, 1971 (FBIS, March 16, 1971).
76. New York Times, January 3, 1973.
77. F. Kotov, Planovoe khoziaistvo 10 (October 1968); JPRS 44,984 (December 2, 1968): 43.
78. V. Seliunin, Economicheskaia gazeta, September 10, 1968; (JPRS 46,519 [September 25, 1968]: 46-47); and J. Shechter, "Report from Moscow," Fortune, May 1970, 105-06.
79. S. Ostrovskii, "On the Combination of Centralized Branch Management with Territorial Planning," Ekonomika Sovetskoi Ukraini (Kiev) 12 (December 1966); JPRS 46,221 (March 10, 1967): 1-2, 7.
80. V. Zamaraev, Sotsialisticheskaia industriia, November 20, 1969, p. 2.
81. The benefits claimed are the link between science and production, Pravda, December 1, 1971, p. 3, and Ekonomicheskaia gazeta 46 (November 1969): 5; reduction in the managerial apparatus, Izvestiia, June 15, 1971, p. 3; centralization of functions, Planovoe khoziaistvo 11 (November 1970): 36-46 (condensed in CDSP 23, no. 4 [February 23, 1971]: 7); creation of new subunits and services, Ekonomicheskaia gazeta, January 1969, p. 11; easing the planning task, N. E. Drogichinskii, Organizatsiia upravleniia promyshlenostiu . . . (Moscow: "Ekonomika," 1965), pp. 19-24 (cited in Smolinski, "Towards a Socialist Corporation," p. 25).
82. Sovetskaia Belorussiia, November 10, 1970, p. 2.
83. S. Bratus' and V. Rakhmilovich, Izvestiia, August 7,
84. A. Bachurin, Ekonomicheskaia gazeta 16 (1970): 16. Quoted in ABSEES 2 (October 1970): 106.
85. D. Allakhverdian and E. Slastenko, "Khoziaistvennaia reforma . . .," Voprosy ekonomiki 3 (March 1968): 11-12 (JPRS 45,234 [May 3, 1968]: 1-13); Sovetskaia Belorussiia, November 10, 1970, p. 2; and N. Borisenko, Pravda, January 17, 1969, p. 4 (translated in JPRS 47,472 [February 17, 1969]: 57). Borisenko is the First Secretary of Chernigov oblast.
86. A. S. Aganbegian, Komsomolskaia Pravda, July 30, 1970, p. 2 (quoted in CASP 2, no. 7 [September 1970]: 7); V. Boldyrev, Pravda, June 3, 1971, p. 3 (partially translated in CDSP 23, no. 22

[June 29, 1971]: 12); and interview with Professor Anchishkin of the Scientific Research Institute, USSR Gosplan, Moscow, August 1968.

87. J. Wilczynski, Socialist Economic Development and Reforms (New York: Praeger, 1972), p. 198.

88. Pravda, December 1, 1971, p. 3; Z. Poliakov, Sotsialisticheskaia industriia, June 4, 1971, p. 2 (Poliakov is general director of a plastics obedinenie); and a draft of a study on Soviet science policy by Dr. Herbert Sawyer of Bentley College.

89. Robert A. Solo, Economic Organizations and Social Systems (Indianapolis: Bobbs-Merrill, 1967), p. 129; Daniel Bell, The Coming of Post-Industrial Society (New York: Basic Books, 1973), p. 196, emphasis in original; Pravda, October 30, 1970, p. 3; and V. Boldyrev, Pravda, June 3, 1971, p. 3.

90. Boldyrev, op. cit., p. 12, emphasis in original; and N. Lisovenko, Izvestiia, June 15, 1971, p. 3 (partially translated in CDSP 23, no. 24 [July 13, 1971]: 16. Lisovenko is a staff correspondent of Izvestiia.

91. A. Kurskii, "Itogi khoziaistvennoi reformy za 1966 g. ...," Voprosy ekonomiki 4 (April 1967): 32-33.

92. I. Shifrin, Izvestiia, June 2, 1971, p. 3; (partially translated in CDSP 23, no. 22 [June 29, 1971]: 11). Shifrin holds a candidate's degree in economics.

93. A. Khandros, Rabochaia gazeta, December 15, 1970, p. 3; Pravda, March 12, 1973, p. 1; Izvestiia, April 14, 1973, p. 2 (condensed in CDSP 25, no. 15 [May 9, 1973]: 14); and Pravda, December 1, 1971, pp. 1-2.

94. Khandros, op. cit.; Ekonomicheskaia gazeta 10 (March 1969): 10 (JPRS 47,819 [April 10, 1969]: 139); and N. Fedorenko and P. Bunich, Pravda, February 9, 1970, p. 2 (translated in CDSP 22, no. 6 [March 10, 1970]: 8, 10).

95. S. Balbekov, Pravda, February 12, 1969, p. 2 (JPRS 47,681 [March 19, 1969]: 79-80); and Sovetskaia Belorussiia, November 10, 1970, p. 2, where the first type is called a "scientific production obedinenie."

96. Gorlin, op. cit., p. 9; also see Khandros, op. cit.

97. See N. Drogochinsky, Sotsialisticheskaia gazeta, September 26, 1970, p. 2; A. Dumachev and E. Gailish, Pravda, August 15, 1971, p. 2 (partially translated in CDSP 23, no. 33 [September 14, 1971]: 4). Drogochinsky is head of USSR Gosplan section for the introduction of new planning and incentive methods, Dumachev is a head of a department of the Leningrad oblast Party committee, and Gailish is the First Assistant General Director of the Positron obedinenie.

98. See A. Zhdanov, Pravda, September 24, 1970, p. 2 (translated in CDSP 22, no. 39 [October 27, 1970]: 5, 7); V. Fadeev,

Rabochaia gazeta, October 20, 1970, p. 3 (Fadeev is the head of the planning-production administration of the Ukrainian Ministry of Light Industry); and S. Saratikiants, Rabochaia gazeta, October 15, 1970, p. 3.

99. I. Karpenko and V. Nevelskii, Izvestiia, July 28, 1970; (partially translated in CDSP 22, no. 31 [September 1, 1970]: 6).

100. For early discussion see Zhdanov, op. cit.; A. Babash, Rabochaia gazeta, October 20, 1970, p. 3; and Sovetskaia Rossiia, October 29, 1970, summarized in "The Council of Directors--A New Managerial Device," a Radio Free Europe Research Report, January 11, 1971. Also see Pravda, July 18, 1969, p. 2.

101. Sovetskaia Rossiia, October 29, 1970.

102. Pravda, April 3, 1973, pp. 1-2; Izvestiia, April 3, 1973, p. 1 (translated in CDSP 25, no. 14 [May 2, 1973]: 1-4).

103. New York Times, April 4, 1973, p. 57; also April 3 and 8, 1973.

104. See Wilczynski, op. cit., pp. 199-201; Gorlin, op. cit., pp. 24-25; Smolinski, "Towards a Socialist Corporation," p. 33; and Pravda, April 3, 1973.

105. Voprosy ekonomiki 11 (November 1970): 63-74, 75-78 (cited in ABSEES, April 1971, pp. 93, 107); Pravda, March 3, 1973, p. 3; Gorlin, op. cit., p. 3; and Smolinski, "Towards a Socialist Corporation," p. 27.

106. Pravda, May 24, 1971, p. 1; V. Fadeev; Sovetskaia Belorussiia, November 10, 1970, p. 2; Leningradskaia pravda, January 5, 1971, p. 1; Pravda, May 24, 1971, p. 1; and Sovetskaia Rossiia, February 25, 1970.

107. Pravda, March 24, 1972, p. 3; (partially translated in CDSP 24, no. 12 [April 19, 1972]: 14).

108. Drogochinsky, op. cit. Also see Lisovenko, op. cit., which cites an association in Kramatorsk which "exists and operates almost in theory only"; Shifrin, op. cit.

109. Pravda, May 19, 1970, p. 2.

110. See Ekonomicheskaia gazeta 48 (November 1970): 6 (abstracted in ABSEES, April 1971, p. 94); Komsomolskaia pravda, April 3, 1969, p. 2; Lisovenko, op. cit.; and Pravda, August 13, 1970, p. 2 (translated in CDSP 22, no. 32 [September 8, 1970]: 9).

111. Sovetskaia Belorussiia, November 10, 1970, p. 2; Pravda, August 13, 1970, p. 31; and Sovetskaia Rossiia, February 25, 1970.

112. V. Vukovich and V. Nevelsky, Izvestiia, August 12, 1970; (translated in CDSP 22, no. 32 [September 8, 1970]: 9).

113. "Assessment of 24th Communist Party Congress," U.S. Congressional Record, 94th Congress, 2nd Session, January 18, 1972, p. E68.

114. "Ekonomicheskaia teoriia i khoziaistvennaia praktika," Planovoe khoziaistvo 11 (November 1968): 9.

115. A. Khovin, Ekonomicheskaia gazeta 11 (March 1969): 10; JPRS 47,880 (April 18, 1969): 43. For an overview of the resistance see Smolinski, "Towards a Socialist Corporation," pp. 34-35.

116. See I. Shifrin, Izvestiia, May 13, 1970, p. 3 (abstracted in ABSEES 2 [October 1970]: 86); and A. Orlov, Sotsialisticheskaia industriia, May 20, 1971, p. 2. Orlov is General Director of the Soiuzsteklomash obedinenie.

117. Gorlin, op. cit., pp. 15-20; Smolinski, "Towards a Socialist Corporation," p. 32; and V. Seliunin, Ekonomicheskaia gazęta 34 (August 1968): 18 (JPRS 46,622 [October 8, 1968]: 19.

118. Pravda, August 13, 1970; see the editorial in Pravda, May 24, 1971, p. 1; and Sovetskaia Belorussiia, November 10, 1970, p. 2.

119. "Glavk or 'Firm'?" Radio Free Europe Background Report, August 26, 1970, p. 3. Romanov has been in this position since December 1964. Also see S. Balbekov, Pravda, February 12, 1969.

120. Peter F. Drucker, "The Surprising Seventies," Harper's Magazine 243, no. 1454 (July 1971): 39.

121. V. Grigor'ev, "Problemy nauchnoi organizatsii upravleniia . . .," Voprosy ekonomiki 8 (August 1966): 150. This may be V. E. Grigor'ev, a member of the Leningrad Oblast Party Committee.

122. A. Kurskii, "Itogi khoziaistvennoi reformy . . .," Voprosy ekonomiki 4 (April 1967): 32.

123. G. Kulagin, "Obedinenie predpriiatii i ministerstvo," Kommunist 3 (February 1966): 87.

124. A. Mochalova, "Nedostatki eshche ne izzhity," Den'gi i kredit 12 (December 1966): 45-46.

125. Larrabee, op. cit., p. 49.

126. Smolinski, "Towards a Socialist Corporation," p. 28.

127. Pravda, March 27, 1972, p. 2; condensed in CDSP 24, no. 13 (April 26, 1972): 30.

128. Brian Chapman, The Profession of Government (London: Allen & Unwin, 1959), p. 182.

CHAPTER 4

THE COMMUNIST PARTY AND INDUSTRIAL MANAGEMENT

INTRODUCTION

The issue that all writing on Soviet industrial management touches is the conflictive relationship between the Party apparatus and the state bureaucracy (here, the industrial management bureaucracy in ministries and the corps of industrial managers and the managerial personnel associated with them). Several false corollaries of this conflict can be rejected out of hand. For example, Jeremy Azrael has shown convincingly that Soviet industrial managers are not proponents of a new political order, much less democrats, no matter how small the "d" is written.[1] Another fantasy meriting quick rejection is the idea that the managerial bureaucracy could become politically dominant. Enterprise directors are not politicians who just happen to be industrial managers as well. In addition, this group of managers does not want to be supreme politically; and even if they did, they could not displace the entrenched super-coordinator, the Party apparatus. A third myth holds that the Party apparatchiki are "irrational" while the managers are "rational." Ernst Kux upholds it by saying that "the attempt to base the rule of a totalitarian party on the only powerful foundation in modern times, a highly industrial economy, must necessarily lead to a conflict between the irrational ideology of communism and rational economics. . . ."[2] But if there is no clear way to specify the referrents of these terms or meanings, such statements are of little use for scholarly inquiry. A tension does exist between some aspects of Soviet ideology and economic policy, but within a stable relationship, not from the starkly opposite poles of a long continuum.

Surprisingly, we can also find the incorrect view that there is no difference between industrial managers and enterprise Party secretaries. For example, David Granick states:

> There seems to be no sound basis for differentiating between a "management class" and a class of "full-time Communist Party officials.
>
> . . . . . .
>
> The Party official, after all, is also primarily an administrator. . . .[3]

This view ignores the fact that the Party secretary is an administrator of a type different from the industrial manager. The essential difference is brought out by John Armstrong's statement:

> A Party line official is responsible for the successful operation of economic enterprises in his area, but he has no formally defined authority over most of them. His . . . role is to aid, to stimulate, to observe, and to check economic enterprises, but not to take over their management.[4]

The Party secretary is a local politician or political administrator who, though working within an enterprise alongside its director or nearby at the same level, is in a different hierarchy--that of the Communist Party--and who derives his influence from that organization's national power, its organizing capabilities among the Communists and activists within the enterprise, and its network of communications and influence with the other important groupings in the area. Interestingly, John Armstrong found that industrial managers in the Ukraine were "conspicuously absent" from the [Ukrainian] Central Committee's considerations of "the most important questions."[5] P. D. Stewart's study of Stalingrad (now Volgograd) produced similar findings for the period 1954-62. Certainly, any group of potential politicians would have to enjoy a better political position than this.

We cannot, however, deny some degree of political importance to Soviet industrial managers. To do so would be to fail to recognize that Soviet politics is one of bureaucratized elites, each in a hierarchy separate from the Party's apparatus but still inter-penetrated and guided by it. Any real independence by the managers, even in the area of their own expertise, limits the Party dictatorship and thus qualitatively changes the political system--without, of course, overtly giving a political justification for a new system.

What we are trying to find out, then, is whether the Party has been able, under the changed "rules of the game," to exert in industrial management the same degree of influence and, when necessary, power as it did previously. That is, does the manager have a freer hand over his work qua manager than he did prior to 1965? The same question applies to the top people in the ministries. Some observers have seen the Party's quest for the continuation of its privileged position as negating the progress of the reform. A. Amalrik charges: "The so-called 'economic reform' . . . is being sabotaged in practice by the Party apparat, since, if such a reform were pursued to its logical end, it would directly threaten the apparat."[6]

Although it is no doubt true that the Party will allow change only insofar as it is able to control it, this in itself does not mean that the Party is opposed to the implementation of the reform to some meaningful degree. The question should be whether that degree is sufficient. And, even if Amalrik and others are correct, does the apparat realize it? Politicians often are overly confident that they can make things work to their own advantage. Restraint does not necessarily mean sabotage. We look closely at areas of activity where the Party has long taken control: the selection and assignment of managerial cadres, the arbitration and mediation of conflicts within enterprises and between them and other agencies, the determination of the context in which "discipline" operates, the maintenance in "ideological work" of a basis for mass (worker) mobilization, and even the retention of a capability to intervene decisively in operational matters.

A question of fundamental political importance is closely bound up with the role of the Party in the development of the economic reform. If the idea of spheres of professional expertise existing relatively free from political ideology, organization, and diktat were to become legitimate in industrial management, a modification of the Soviet political system would no doubt be in the offing. Whether Soviet industrial management would thereby become more rational and efficient is a moot question. But Premier Kosygin's bleak report in late 1972 that the Soviet economy would grow by only about 4 percent during 1972 and that several primary industries would not meet their targets indicates most powerfully that the goals of increased rationality and efficiency are now even more important than formerly.[7]

The old Menshevik Boris Nikolaevsky (one of the very few of that breed who understood questions of power) summarized the essence of the relationship between the Party apparatus and the industrial managers thus:

> This struggle for power need by no means at each moment be a struggle for the overthrow of the government or removal of the Central Committee first secretary. Such "maximalist" goals always are fixed at the end of a long road of development which is marked by heightening animosities. On this road are always many intermediary phases, when the contending groups see "limited objectives." . . .[8]

A Soviet expert on Party organization who accepts inner Party conflict writes, "Insofar as the party is an animate political organism, there will always be clashes of different viewpoints." Despite what has been said above, we "should not assume <u>a priori</u> that conflict is either necessary or endemic between party secretary and director, any more than it is between managing director and shareholder in western firms. Both manager and party secretary have a common interest and stake in the success of the enterprise."[9]

But what happens when "success" is not being attained or when differing conceptions of it are held? And, even in the best of times, "Tensions often arise <u>where there are personnel appointed under two or more different systems of employment within the same organization</u>." The Kremlinologist-poet Robert Conquest says the same thing: "Yet as long as two apparatuses exist there are bound to be areas of conflict."[10] The economist Robert Campbell strongly links the implementation of economic reform to political tensions and political change, noting:

> Economic reform cannot help but be an active reagent in the process of political change. Interim steps in the reform . . . are less the result of moving toward a design the leaders know . . . than <u>ad hoc</u> reactions to pressures and difficulties that grow out of preceding steps, and this situation offers a continuing chance for aggrandizement on the part of various groups. Traditional power relationships are being disturbed. Politically or socially determined status is to be challenged by the cash nexus. In short, things that count are up for grabs, and this probably includes the really fundamental thing: political power.[11]

Frederick Mosher says that "tensions [between hierarchies or groupings within an organization] . . . become especially significant factors in reorganization. . . . Reorganizations tend to reinforce and reignite some of them. . . . Reorganizations also give rise to new tensions. . . ."[12]

Explicit official recognition that the new "looseness" has had some political effect has been made many times. For example, a <u>Pravda</u> editorial states: "It is no secret . . . that individual economic leaders have an incorrect understanding of the role of party control under the new conditions. At times they regard it as an infringement of their rights, or as substitution or guardianship." Earlier, <u>Pravda</u> had said (as it has so many times) that many Party organizations are

INDUSTRIAL MANAGEMENT

not under the close supervision of the raikom and that "it is no secret that individual economic managers sometimes try to ignore the opinion of the party organization and its secretary [and] do not consult with them."[13]

The existence of actions objectively against Party directives and control indicates that complementary subjective attitudes are present as well. Several writers on the Party have long emphasized the independent power of the industrial bureaucracy vis-a-vis the enterprise Party secretary, which power rests both upon the industrial managers' specialized knowledge and often upon their greater political influence. Enterprise directors are sometimes bureau members of raion, city, or oblast party committees or deputies of soviets at some level. Jerry Hough notes that "top Soviet industrial officials remain men with great technical authority, and they remain very formidable opponents in bureaucratic struggles on planning and technical questions." He adds that "the party organs have clear-cut legal authority but not a great deal of influence with respect to technical policy and several other 'intra-industry' questions."[14]

Taking a comparative perspective, those with formal power are limited everywhere in their attempt to apply it within operating specialized or bureaucratized enclaves. John Kenneth Galbraith states as a general principle, though perhaps with slight exaggeration:

> It seems likely that the Soviet resolution of the problem of authority in the industrial enterprise is not so different from that in the West. Like that of the shareholder in the United States or Britain, the authority of the people and party is celebrated in public ritual. . . . But in practice, as with us, extensive and increasing power of final decision is vested in the enterprise.[15]

But the Party drives on despite its limitations, striving for as strong a hand in industrial matters as possible, consonant with the many other claims upon its time and energy and the "convention" (to use a British political term) long defining its role in industrial management. The Party leadership holds firm to its position that "it cannot retire from leadership of the economy" and that a factory director not heading the Party organization is not fulfilling his responsibilities as a manager.[16]

Hough argues that area coordination by the local Party organs is vital for effective development administration, since economic development and the expansion of industrial capacity and production are nonroutinized processes in which the values of precision, predictability, legality, and orderliness are outweighed by those of "creativity, initiative, and discretion." Hough continues the theme elsewhere, saying, "No large institution undertaking nonroutinized tasks can function effectively without the existence of formal or informal control instruments which destroy the neatness of the real organization chart."[17] It is likely, however, that "control" negates the very qualities desired. As Robert A. Solo says:

> Probably every economic system requires some form of mobile economic power detached from operations and able to deliver an innovationary thrust that will disrupt and dismember the existing organization or processes . . . but able radically to reorganize the form of operations.[18]

The words are strongly suggestive of the kind of power a ruling Communist Party disposes. The problem in the Soviet Union lies in the fact that the Party's powers to "dismember," a political capability, are so great that they threaten the optimal performance of economic management functions by the specialists. Does even the most effective functioning of industry require the regulation of industrial life by a single organization that monopolizes the political power of the system? If it ever did, the time is past. Gaetano Mosca has noted that "the upper stratum of political decision-makers is insufficient . . . to perform the great range and variety of leadership functions necessary in a society."[19] Economic progress requires the balanced interaction of two processes, the political and the economic. Their optimal progress requires quite different abilities, skills, and organizations, as well as mutual forbearance in good measure.

The ideologists of the CPSU have long recognized and extolled the Party's interventionist powers. <u>Kommunist</u> comments:

> The decisive intervention of Party organizations is needed . . . to clear a path for all that is advanced and progressive, where the elements of conservatism and inertness are still strong and the new is having difficulty in smashing through bureaucratic obstructions.[20]

A reason specific to Soviet conditions for this interventionist capability is the strong concern of the Party leaders, in an environment of inflation and suppressed buying power, that increasss in production not result solely from monetary incentives but derive

INDUSTRIAL MANAGEMENT 151

heavily from "moral stimuli" and mass mobilizational efforts engendered and led by the Party. As a secretary of a plant's Party committee said, "The Party organization of our plant considers its special concern [to be] the development of moral stimuli."[21]

The Party strives for economic direction and intervention in operations; and many of its most senior and powerful members have engineering training and administrative experience in the economy, a process that began in the 1930s. George Fischer, in his study of 306 top Party executives, points out that this is essential in the Soviet "monist" society, where

> All or most of the power is state power [and where] ... the leaders who hold that power must either yield some of it or keep it by using it knowingly in basic realms of activity [and] because the economic realm tends to be central in any modern society it is economic skills that political leaders of a monist system must increasingly possess.

This seems almost like an attempt to disprove Mosca.

Fischer's data appear to reveal a "quite recent" trend toward "Dual Executives"; that is, top Party members with a "special mix of past economic and political work" who did "extensive work of two kinds within the economy, technical work and party work, prior to getting a top party post."[22] T. H. Rigby, viewing the composition of the present CPSU Politburo, comes to similar conclusions. He cites "the great increase in the proportion of members with experience in industrial management" as "one of the most important changes in the Politburo over the past 20 years"; notes that "this striking extension of managerial experience should make for more sophisticated perceptions of problems of administering the economy and more realistic decision-making in this area"; and concludes by saying that "the careers of most current Politburo members have been highly specialized in . . . organizational activity aimed at maximizing economic production. . . ."[23]

It is apparent, then, that the struggle of the Party to remain the "super-coordinator" of industry has continued since the reform's beginning. An examination of the relationship between Party organizations and industrial management since 1965 will reveal some of the particulars of this struggle. This will be followed by a discussion of the Party's relationship with the industrial ministries and a section that brings developments in the Party's work in industry up to date.

THE PARTY, INDUSTRIAL MANAGEMENT, AND THE ECONOMIC REFORM: THE FIRST TWO YEARS

Emphasis here is upon the extent ot which the Party-manager role relationship or pattern of expectations and interactions had changed by 1968 in accordance with the new goals of 1965. The official, or at least publicly stated, intent in this regard was to give managers more rights and powers in their work than they had enjoyed previously. This unavoidably involved, if it was to be carried through, a limitation upon the prerogatives of Party organizations in regard to the operations and internal life of industrial enterprises. Political tensions and activity arose out of the desire of the Party organizations that the managers' gain not be so great as to reduce their own powers in the industrial sphere.

The Official Goals

The list of what the Party's functions in industry and their relative priorities in the reform is as follows: cadres' work; enforcement (but not the associated function of reporting); intervention in operations; ideological and organizational work; determination of goals and priorities (but not the related function of solution of supply problems); and arbitration and mediation.

This ranking is not the same as that for behavior in the manager-party relationship prior to the introduction of the reform (see Table 4.1). Therefore, change in the relationship was called for. But carried out by whom, to what extent, and toward what ends?

The Reality: Post-Reform Behavior of the Party in the Manager-Party Relationship

Many of the attitudes expressed by Party apparatchiki prompted them to resist the officially sponsored changes at the enterprise level. The goals of the reform were watered down in implementation and thus, in effect, changed. Despite this overall outcome, the relative priority of the Party's functions did change. Two sets of functions (determination of goals and priorities and the solution of supply problems, and arbitration and mediation) were not mentioned by mid-1967. As a result, the headings for activities of party organizations in industry became fewer.

TABLE 4.1

Lists of Party Functions in Industry
(in order of importance)

Pre-Reform Actual Behavior[a]	Officially Desired Post-Reform Behavior	Post-Reform Actual Behavior (as reported during 1965-67)
1. Cadre and personnel "selection, assignment, and training"	1. Cadres' work	1. Cadres' work
2. Arbitration and mediation of conflicting interests	2. Enforcement (but not reporting)	2. Enforcement (but not reporting)
3. Determination of goals and priorities, and solution of supply problems	3. Intervention in operations	3. Intervention in operations
4. Enforcement of discipline, legality, and plan fulfillment, and reporting of problems in these and other spheres to higher Party and state organs	4. Ideological and organizational work	4. Ideological and organizational[b] work
5. Intervention in operational matters	5. Determination of goals and priorities (but not solution of supply problems)	
6. Carrying out of agitation and propaganda ("ideological work") for the purpose of mobilizing individuals and groups ("organizational work")		

[a]Each function is fully listed in this column only.

[b]Although two former functions are not listed, they may continue to exist.

Sources: The rank orders in the first two columns were derived partly from Jerry F. Hough, "The Role of the Local Party Organs in Soviet Industrial Decision-Making" (unpublished doctoral dissertation, Department of Government, Harvard University, 1961), Ch. IV; and Z. Nuriev, "Rukovodit' ekonomikoi, ne podmeniaia khoziaistvennye organy," Kommunist 16 (November 1965): 59-67.

Cadres' Work

This was still the most important task of the Party organizations, and it has long been primary. For example, the first secretary of the Yaroslavl obkom cited the example of the Rybinsky machine-building plant, where, before an engineer is promoted, the Party committee and the plant's directing body together examine his work, both in his collective and in his Party organization. At these gatherings the candidate and others speak, telling what is "positive" in the style and methods of his work and what not. In some cases organizations and collectives do not agree with the proposals of the plant's directing body and "the former groupings participate[d] in the final selection." Individual organizations even replaced managerial cadres on insufficient grounds.[24]

Another sphere of cadres' work in which Party organizations were actively involved is training. The Party had a key role in training managerial and other industrial personnel to work under the new conditions. For example, the Party organizations in the Altai area organized a special faculty on "public principles" at the Altai Polytechnic Institute, with four divisions in other cities and four correspondence courses. "The student body consists of secretaries of Party committees at large enterprises, plant directors, trust managers, chief engineers, directors of economic services--350 persons in all." Interestingly, "not everyone" readily accepted the order to return to school, but "an order is an order." The goal of the course was to "mold economically literate production managers, people who think on a broad scale."[25]

The work of the Party with cadres involved the continued presence of its capabilities for rukovodstvo and kontrol', a willingness to use them if its interests demanded it, the sponsorship of retraining programs that it compelled personnel to attend, and the checking of the progress of the participants in these courses of study. By fostering and controlling a key element in the implemental process, the training of cadres, the Party apparat began to ensure their continued ultimate dominance in industry.

Enforcement

Party organizations still engage in an enforcement role. The Party workers' guide enunciates the principle when it states:

> The knotty problems of production are always under the supervision of Party organizations: the fulfillment of particularly important orders and . . . deliveries; the quality and cost of

INDUSTRIAL MANAGEMENT 155

production; the implementation of the plan for
the introduction of new technology; the mechanization and automation of production processes.[26]

The list meanders on, turning into a lengthy catalog of matters to be watched. Enterprise and other local Party organizations were to concern themselves with the enforcement of all orders of the Party and state. The result cannot be completely satisfactory because there is too much to do for most of it to be done well.

One example of such supervision developed from an undue consumption of electricity at Moscow's Hammer and Sickle plant. The plant's Party committee established a subcommittee of seven Party members, headed by an engineer, to correct this difficulty. The group conducted checkups (in shops and departments) and submitted corrective proposals. The data discovered and the proposals based on them were transmitted to the enterprise Party committee, which examined them and worked out "recommendations" that, when adopted by the management, are supposed to have led to a significant drop in power consumption. The group still "follows the course of fulfillment of the adopted plan of technical-organizational measures to save electric power and submits its proposals." In addition, the group's members wrote on these questions in the plant newspaper and commented on them on the plant's broadcasts. The same plant also had Party committees for checking the quality of output, the safety of valuable materials, and the fulfillment of the capital construction plan.[27]

Operations

Intervention in operational matters by Party organizations also exists. For example, a Party Secretariat functionary says that at the plenums and sessions of bureaus of municipal and raion Party committees, a "detailed examination" of economic subjects at enterprises took place--for instance, improved utilization of equipment and better use of working time. In Yangiyul, Uzbekistan, functionaries of the city Party committee "intervened" (vmeshalis') to solve a series of problems. "They helped decide questions of material and technical supply, . . . provided the construction project with transportation . . . and cleared up the existing lack of coordination with design organizations, the State Construction Bank and the clients."[28] Party control committees also "warned" heads of shops and other managerial personnel that if they did not change their attitudes and actions toward certain questions, such as the introduction of new machinery, "the committee would place the question before the [full] Party committee." It was laconically added that "this produces an effect." These groups often operated at the lowest levels of the enterprise, even dealing with the drafting of blueprints. They at times became <u>tolkachi</u> ("pushers" or "middlemen"), although this was not officially desired.[29] An example of the Party's concern with purely technical questions was its controlling role in the perfection of a new production line at the Chelyabinsk tractor plant.[30] The Party may be even more involved in operational matters than previously, as a result of the separation of the Party and state control networks in December 1965.

Ideological and Organizational Work

The fourth function of Party organizations--ideological and organizational work--is still important as a basis of their ability to act in industrial matters. A Party journal notes that "work as creativity must be in the center of the attention of Party organizations." This concern is not to be restricted to the enterprise. Party organizations, through their activist formations, are "to probe deeply into everything that is connected with a person outside of production." For example:

> It is characteristic . . . that now the leader of a group conducts work not only with the family of one or another worker, but even with the school where his children study, with the local territorial Party organization, with housewives, . . . with councils of pensioners, with hospitals. And how can it be otherwise if it is necessary to help someone or influence someone?[31]

This process, part of the Party's normal work of agitation, was carried out through "Councils of Aid to Communist Education" of nine or so persons, each council directing more than 80 "groups" that "exercise their influence" at the places of residence of almost all the 1,500 persons working in a shop. The councils and groups were supposed to have exercised a "noticeable influence" on the reduction of the number of workers quitting, of instances of violation of labor discipline, and on the improvement of the ability of children and adults to do well in schools and training programs. "There have also been instances when they helped to establish peace in families." Examples of such activities more closely related to production are also common. At many plants and factories, Party organizations led mass competitions for saving raw materials and for the production of additional items. However, some Party organizations pursued economies only during campaigns. Some of the types of "Party-economic activist groups" (and their numbers just in Gorky oblast) that were

INDUSTRIAL MANAGEMENT 157

being used extensively to "supplement" the production and economic services of enterprises are the following: economic analysis bureaus (more than 900), norm-setting bureaus (300), and design and production bureaus (600). Supposedly "they provided scope for the technical and economic creativity of the masses."

Some Party spokesmen want the capability to intervene in production to be as strong as it was under Khrushchev, who favored this sphere of activity for Party organizations. However, other Party secretaries and enterprise managers do not want Party control committees, arguing that comparable groups organized on public principles, with many Communists as members, already exist and that parallelism and duplication are to be avoided. In any case, the organizational network available to the Party for the performance of its several functions is a formidable one in terms of size, diversity of forms, membership, and levels and points where its efforts can be applied.[32]

Determination of Goals and Priorities, Solution of Supply Problems, Arbitration and Mediation

In all probability the Party has not divested itself of its rights and capabilities in these activities even though their exercise (or at least, discussion of them) may be temporarily in abeyance. As to the determination of goals and priorities, Hough, writing of the sovnarkhoz period, states: "It is clear that the local Party organs played an extremely important role in the setting of day-to-day priorities for industrial production." And, in regard to supply problems, Party organizations have long served as collective tolkachi, intervening effectively in the procurement of supplies and in the settlement of departmental disputes within enterprises[33] (the arbitration-mediation function). Given the attitudes and experience of Party functionaries and their present capabilities and actions in other respects, it must be assumed that present practices have not changed greatly.

Summary

The "model" of the reform in its manager-Communist Party aspect seems, at first glance, to have been partly realized. There is no explicit evidence that the fifth and sixth functions in the list of desired behavior (goals, priorities, and supplies, and arbitration and mediation) were still being performed. As a result, the overall picture of apparent Party operations is one in which the local Party organizations have withdrawn from activities that the model puts in a subordinate position. This is a change in the Party's role; but the all-pervasive Party supervision, backed by consequential action servant organizations, remains.

THE PARTY AND THE MINISTRIES: AN UNCOMPLETED ATTEMPT AT CHANGE

Fundamental Issues

The essentials of the Party apparatus' relationship to the personnel of the industrial ministries in recent years can be sketched out briefly. The ministries' key role in the reform's implementation requires, for the process to proceed as originally planned, that they not revert to the authoritarian style and content of their work prior to 1957. Their role therefore was to be reworked in agreement with the intent of the economic reform. Specifically, the directive and operational functions of ministries were to be reduced and transferred to the enterprises and obedineniia, and the ministries were to operate less by administrative means and more by the use of information and economic levers, and by giving aid to the enterprises' efforts to become more productive. The watchfulness and activity of the Party were required in order to realize this change and prevent a complete backsliding on the part of the ministries to "unnecessary, excessively centralized leadership,"[34] a path upon which they embarked easily and with some negative effect on the reform.

Party organizations also have been called upon by Pravda to "resolutely oppose manifestations of inertia, paper-shuffling and red tape," common examples of "bureaupathology." Party secretaries of various oblasty and boroughs have joined in this criticism of ministries, particularly after the Twenty-Fourth Party Congress in 1971.[35] In addition, and perhaps most important, a question of relative power was involved. The leaders of the Party apparatus had to try to break out of the anomalous situation of having responsibility but also having to serve as "broker politicians" for specialized, more knowledgeable ministerial officials protected by the bureaucratic routine and structure.

In order for the Party apparatus to get the additional leverage on the ministries necessary to try to make them act in a "reformed" manner, a serious campaign (still in progress in 1974) was mounted for an increased role of the Party organizations within ministries, research institutes, and several other state and "public" agencies. The Party apparatus' long-term goal, periodically pursued, is a definite margin of superiority over other institutions that is somehow legitimized and definitely represented in the symbolism of the ideology and its expressions in the media. In particular, Soviet politics periodically sees attempts to get past the political problems posed for the Party by its main rival, the "high State administration."[36] In order to stay where it is politically, the Party apparatus must now and again strive to obtain a definitely higher position--which, of course, it never achieves for long, for its obtaining this position permanently would bring all economic and administrative work to a grinding and wasteful halt reminiscent of that during the Chinese Cultural Revolution of the mid-1960s. This is an outcome that the "dual executives" of the Party apparatus seek to avoid. In order for this particular campaign to be seen with some clarity, it must be put in recent historical perspective and its development charted, at least in outline.

The Anti-Bureaucratic Campaign: Past and Present

Khrushchev's period offers several examples of the campaign against state bureaucrats (ostensibly directed at "bureaucratism"). Leonard Schapiro says that the industrial reorganization of 1957, already discussed, "had the effect of strengthening . . . the system of party control." More than this was attempted, however. Z. K. Brzezinski notes that Khrushchev was "stimulating increased activity by the agitprop and . . . assigning greater responsibility to the apparat, thus compensating for the necessarily greater importance of the experts. . . ."[37] In other words, the goal was to effect the political corrective action already alluded to. It is even possible that, considering the enthusiasm and virulence of this anti-bureaucratic campaign, Khrushchev's aim was a systemic change not dissimilar to Mao's goal in loosing the Cultural Revolution. (Many of Khrushchev's political initiatives, such as the comrades' courts, reflect a populistic and anti-structural vision not unlike Maoism but without any Chinese influence.)

A Party "crackdown" on managers may have begun between 1955 and 1957, and Khrushchev's "increase in authority during the first four years after the death of Stalin was accompanied by an ever-rising emphasis on the role of the Party apparatus in industrial management."[38] During 1961 and 1962, Khrushchev waged a general campaign against several kinds of bureaucratic behavior, from informalism and alleged haughtiness of attitude to outright corruption. Although one notable feature of the campaign was an intensification of legal penalties and legalistic means used (such as execution by a firing squad as a penalty for "economic crimes"), the style resembled a populistic Party-led assault against state economic institutions and their cadres (witness the emphasis upon a Khrushchevian variant of the Maoist "mass-line" utilizing the people's militia, the comrades' courts, and the "all-people's" Party and state).

All this may well have been a ploy whereby Khrushchev hoped to eliminate the "anti-Party group" from the Party and then make them liable to trials that would result in their complete elimination from politics. This would have been a telling symbolic blow against the state bureaucracy as a whole, since the members of the "anti-Party group," particularly Georgi Malenkov, M. Pervukhin, and M. Saburov, were entrenched mainly in the government and were on record as favoring a greater role for it. They also favored the "retention of the ministerial system . . . and reliance on a strong ministerial coordinating group to give coherence and direction to the economy," and were determined to prevent Khrushchev from utilizing his strength in the Party apparatus to extend his control over the national economy. It was later charged that some in the opposition to Khrushchev even went so far as to attempt to "substantiate the primacy of state agencies over party agencies."[39] Khrushchev's statement to Norman Cousins on the opposition emanating from the Council of Ministers (already cited) lends some substance to the problem (and this was said after the "anti-Party group" was well out of the way).

Even with the victory over the cabal in 1957, Khrushchev had not achieved any solution to the Party-state problem. The campaign against "bureaucratism" that ran riot in 1961-62 testifies to this. This "noisy campaign" was an unsuccessful "quasi-terrorist tactic to 'Khrushchevize' the bureaucracy."[40] After Khrushchev's removal in October 1964, a balance of sorts between Party and state leaders came into existence with even a promise, as the beginning of the reform in 1965 indicates, that the reconstituted state apparatus, supposedly somehow transformed by its years in the wilderness and the new ideals for it splashed throughout the press in 1965, would have new responsibilities and powers, giving it a role coordinate to the Party apparatus in the administration of industry. In mid-November 1964, however, Pravda came out against "incompetent interference" of the Party in the work of the economic organs.[41]

The new equality did not last, though it is difficult to pinpoint a time when a decisive shift occurred. Some analysts see signs of the shift as early as 1965; others, such as Sidney Ploss, see it in late 1969, when the theses for the Lenin centenary said that the Party "accomplishes its tasks both directly and through the soviets, state bodies and public organizations." The 1967 theses on the revolution had said only that the Party works "through the system of state and public organizations."[42] In April 1970 two "veteran" regional Party officials were named to key posts in Gosplan and the State Committee for Science and Technology. Pravda affirmed that although the Party organization of the State Committee of the USSR Council of Ministers for Science and Technology lacked the right of administrative supervision, "it nevertheless has broad capabilities to influence the administrative apparatus. . . ." It also criticized ministries' work for being haphazard and, significantly, called for more inter-ministerial contacts and meetings in which Party organizations would play a broker-like role.[43] This was, it turned out, the shape of things to come, with grave implications for the state bureaucracy. An attempt was under way to drive living wedges of the political bureaucracy both horizontally and vertically into the state apparatus. This clever strategy undermined one of the key bases of bureaucratic strength, the clear and undisturbed hierarchical chain of command.

By early 1970 a new anti-management and anti-bureaucratic campaign existed. Pravda reported that leaders of some ministries, enterprises, and other institutions were engaging in "excesses" in furnishing their private offices; referred to criticism of "ministries and [government] agencies" at the Central Committee plenum in December 1969; spoke of a "blunting [prituplenie] of the feeling of responsibility in some economic leaders"; and concluded that "such facts require intervention by party organizations."[44] The other shoe was finally dropped, but not without having been preceded by additional warnings, at the Twenty-Fourth Party Congress, which met from March 30 to April 9, 1971. There the Party organizations of ministries were formally awarded the "right of supervision" (pravo kontrolia) of their administrative apparatuses through a change in the Party statutes or rules.

Goals, Methods, Means, and Actions

The decision announced at the Twenty-Fourth Congress had no doubt been made earlier. A stream of criticisms of the state administration and calls for just such action had appeared in the press during the preceding two years. One such criticism of ministries concluded with the laconic statement:

> future improvement of the administration of the
> branches depends in many ways also upon the
> Party committees of ministries. Their task
> is to come forward as the standard bearer of
> the Leninist style in the work of the state administration [and] educate cadres in the spirit
> of complete responsibility for assigned work.

This was a clear warning to the ministries to get cracking on the implementation of the reform or face a take-over bid by the Party.

Later another newspaper said a ministry's Party committee must be a "militant staff, . . . actively helping the ministry's personnel fulfill the tasks set . . . by the Party and state. . . ."[45] There may have been some attempt by the state apparatus to defend itself and even to counterattack. One article of 1970 claimed that "one still sees attempts by some persons to avoid the solution of questions entrusted to them, shifting the blame for shortcomings onto other organs."[46] In one place even the local Party organization may have formed an ethnically based "family circle" with the state bureaucracy.[47] The disclosure of evidence of effects of Georgian nationalism, retirement of the Georgian Party leader V. P. Mzhavanadze, and the reorganization of the Party in Georgia during 1972 and 1973 indicate that the anti-bureaucratic campaign may have been necessary in some areas. As a result of the Twenty-Fourth Congress:

> Party organizations within ministries and comparable state agencies have been given the right to . . . oversee the observance of Party as well as State discipline by all employees of the agency. Heretofore, ministerial-type Party organizations were specifically forbidden exercise of such rights; now they are only prohibited from directly interfering in the activities of enterprises and institutions subordinate to the ministry, which are, of course, already monitored by local Party organs.[48]

The change was incorporated as an amendment to Article 60 of the Party statutes. Its still-limited nature indicates that Brezhnev and the Party apparatus could not ask for full control of the state administration. However, the elimination from the statutes of the explicit statement that Party organizations of ministries do not supervise administration, and the addition of "Party discipline" as an enforced guideline for the ministries, shows that the Party apparatus did win a victory that had been long in the making. Brezhnev personally emphasized the change in his report to the Congress.[49]

Formalities aside, what, if anything, has actually changed? Here intent is clearer than accomplishment. The tasks and goals set for ministerial Party organizations, though lacking absolute clarity, can be stated in outline. They "must persistently strive for: the improvement of the style and methods of the work of administrations and departments, the introduction of a rational organization of labor, the scientific processing and analysis of information, [and] the elaboration of sound decisions in order that the apparatus may secure an <u>effective</u> and <u>flexible</u> administration of the branch." (Emphasis

INDUSTRIAL MANAGEMENT

supplied.) The same source says the "chief goal" of the ministerial Party organization is "to perfect the work of the [ministerial] apparatus, raising the level of its guidance of the branch," but that this is not a goal in itself; the final result is to be an improvement of the work of the enterprises in its branch and particularly an increase in their "national economic return." Perhaps the Party committees in the ministries will achieve no more than a greater access to the "files."[50]

An interesting justification is made for the Party's new role. A ministry's functions are given as "administration of the branch" and "leadership of a state agency" (rukovodstvo gosudarstvennym uchrezhdeniem), and a Party committee has the right to place before its leaders questions directly connected with various aspects of the work of the ministerial apparatus. "The Party committee put such questions even before, but now they are acquiring a still greater scale and sweep" (masshtabnost' i razmakh). (The term razmakh recalls Stalin's usage in his formulation "Bolshevik revolutionary sweep.") The means to be used to accomplish this are the primary Party organizations in the ministries. For example, in the USSR Ministry of Construction, Road-Building and Civil-Engineering Machinery, there are 409 Communists in the ministerial apparatus serving in 24 primary Party organizations (i.e., about 17 members in an organization, on the average), and with 14 Communists in the Party committee of the ministry. Party organizations in units of ministries, such as glavki and departments, occasionally act jointly with the Party organizations of industrial enterprises.[51] This is a significant organizational change if it becomes regularized. Enterprise primary Party organizations have often done this, in effect acting as collective tolkachi or "expediters," but in a different atmosphere and of course at a much lower level.

The new "sweep" of the work of ministerial Party organizations clearly is not acceptable to all involved. Even Pravda has on occasion stated that "Party organizations of ministries . . . cannot directly influence the work of the enterprises and institutions under the jurisdiction of these ministries." As a result, some attempts at clarifying functions are being made, although it is also said that "no standard recipes can be drawn up."[52] It is specifically said that the Party is not to be either an "inspector general" (revizor) or an inspector (kontroler). It appears that such a disclaimer is necessary, because after the Twenty-Fourth Congress some Party members said derisively, "Now we'll show the administration! . . ."[53] Some functions of the ministerial primary Party organizations are enlistment of all Party members in supervision; improving the selection and assignment of ministerial personnel; forming committees of supervision, both standing and ad hoc; and the issuance of guidance and advice to the administration. One of the matters in which ministries' Party organizations have become quite involved is the introduction of computer systems and automation into the ministries,[54] again indicating the Party's modernizing bent.

Claims are of course made for beneficial results alleged to have flowed from the new arrangement. However, the renewed stress on "Party style of work" in the government administration reveals that dissatisfaction with the state bureaucracy is still a severe irritant within the higher reaches of the Party. The controversy over the idea of eliminating edinonachalie in favor of a new kind of collegial rule within the ministries shows that Party pressure for reorganization mounts. The "trial balloon" of amalgamating ministries into larger agencies may be one harbinger of a major reorganization. The question of whether significant changes of this magnitude can be made without splitting the Politburo unavoidably arises.[55] Politics aside, it is important that some of the Party leaders recognize that the top ministerial personnel represent the corporate "establishment."

Summary

The actual changes in bureaucratic relationships, personnel, and the operations of ministries probably are quite slight. What has evolved is more a new emphasis and atmosphere than a definite change in the Party-ministerial relationship. The overt attempt at ideological conformity so apparent in the Party's new supervisory position in research and educational institutions, with its overtones of charges of disloyalty, is lacking in the Party's stance regarding the ministries. The issue here is more one of relative power and shadings of viewpoint, and in implementing a generally agreed-upon policy.

In its efforts to achieve additional control in the ministries, the Party apparatus is to some degree a rational, modernizing influence of the typical Western sort. This is shown by the stress, quite at variance with the populistic ideas on administration presented by Lenin in his State and Revolution, in the balmy summer of 1917. Lenin is quoted as asking: "How do you think you can administer . . . without complete knowledge, without knowledge of the science of administration?" (Emphasis supplied.)[56]

The combination of this kind of emphasis, including the wide introduction of computers and automation, with a parallel emphasis upon "productive" ideas and ideological conformity, may not seem like modernization but it is, by and large, the way Russia has always partaken of what is loosely called progress--that is, selectively, and in harness. The Party apparatus has achieved some sort of victory, although no doubt only a temporary one, against forces striving for a greater gap between themselves and the grasp and viewpoints of the Party apparatus. The ministerial bureaucracy was moving in this direction without, it would seem, any ideological framework peculiarly its own while other groupings seem to have been evolving specific intellectual and political positions. In the case of the ministries, as in those of the research and educational institutes, problems remain. For example, the exhortation of Party members to supervise administration more closely may tend to defeat the avowed purpose of strengthening Party control over the ministries. The further heavy involvement of the members of Party organizations in administrative work may result in their being molded into persons with an even more "ministerial" viewpoint than they possessed previously, for there is no clear line at which the primary Party organizations can stop. Confusion at best, and assimilation at most, may result.

What is fascinating to note is the continuity between Khrushchev and Brezhnev that this policy reveals. Of course, Brezhnev had clearly been a "client" of Khrushchev, not an "ally." But the causes lie in more than this. Obviously the Party apparatus is facing some of the same problems with the state bureaucracy that it did ten and more years ago. Put most generally and at the lowest level of significance, the question is one of expediting the implementation of policy through the minimization of bureaucratic resistance. But problems more serious than this may be involved as well. And the implications are that the apparat will still face these problems ten years hence. Soviet state administrators are likely to continue to display that "certain agility" in counteracting the pressures from above for which they have long been noted.[57]

THE PARTY AND THE MANAGER: RECENT DEVELOPMENTS

Introduction

The post-1968 period has been one of the consolidation of Brezhnev's personal power (but only to a point), the renewal of Soviet confidence and movement in international affairs, and the reassertion of the Party apparatus in the main currents of Soviet domestic affairs. In industry, for example, the First Secretary of the Rostov obkom proclaimed the view that the economic reform necessitated a more active role for enterprise Party organizations. He reasoned that since the enterprise as a production entity had been granted a greater role in the production process, the role of the Party organization had also increased.[58] Not long thereafter an article in <u>Kommunist</u> affirmed:

> There has never been any support in our Party for the views of those who hold that the role of the Party as the guiding and leading force of society and as the political leader of the workers gradually diminishes with the development of socialist society. On the contrary, life has confirmed and continues to confirm that with the extended scale of communist construction and with the growth in complexity of socioeconomic, political, and ideological tasks facing society, this role constantly increases. . . .[59]

In the months preceding the convocation of the Twenty-Fourth Party Congress, an attempt was being made by the Party apparatus to legitimize the important place in the reform's implementation that it had begun to assume. In December 1970, A. Snechkus, the Party First Secretary in Lithuania, indicated that the rights granted to directors by the reform are to belong to enterprise Party committees too. He said that "Party and trade union committees must make fuller use of the wider independence accorded to production collectives by the economic reform in deciding economic and social questions of the development of enterprises." Less specific but equally pertinent, the Party's main theoretical journal declared at the same time that "the party's role in leading all the processes of sociopolitical life is increasing." This firm and demanding stance had also been expressed by the change in the slogan on the Party listed among the October slogans for 1970. Whereas in 1969 the slogan had read "Long live the CPSU, which is confidently leading the Soviet people along the Leninist road toward the victory of communism!," the 1970 slogan became "Long live the CPSU--the militant vanguard of the working class, of all toilers, the <u>political leader and organizer</u> of the Soviet people in the struggle for communism!" (Emphasis supplied.) The new tone for Party supervision was buttressed by the 1972 statement that the Party's task "is not the registration of deficiencies, but to be an effective means for eliminating and preventing them."[60]

The reasons for this stronger stance include not only a desire to curb liberal currents in Soviet society but also to produce more good consumer goods and to introduce into Soviet industry the achievements of the "modern scientific and technological revolution." Authoritative complaints of poor-quality consumer goods, often remaining unsold, are common. "Losses from substandard output amounted to 35,000,000 rubles during the [8th] five-year plan."[61] The Party apparatus is now firmly committed to a substantial improvement of Soviet citizens' economic situation, perhaps because Soviet citizens hold a definite expectation that they will have more consumer goods and enjoy a generally better economic situation year by year, and that if the system does not provide this, the Party leadership is failing in its duty. The effects of blocking these expectations cannot be foreseen, but would constitute a crisis of political confidence. Though Russians might not react the way Czechs and Poles reacted to their economic difficulties of 1967 and 1970, the political effects in the USSR would still be severe and the results, given a nontotalitarian atmosphere, unpredictable. Thus, the pressure upon the Soviet leaders to make the economy highly productive of the material elements of a "brighter tomorrow" is great if not overriding.

By June 1971, after the Twenty-Fourth Congress, enterprise Party organizations were taking a direct and authoritative role in certain broad processes in industry, notably the introduction of automation, the placement and training of managerial personnel, the increasing of labor productivity, and the rationalization of administrative processes. This fits in with the emphases Brezhnev had enunciated more than once. Whereas Kosygin had spoken of rationalization and modernization, implying some carefully and finely wrought development guided by the Party, Brezhnev introduced a more politicized atmosphere of rapid movement forced onward by Party "muscle." He also seems to want to do more with less. For example, in his speech to the workers of the Kharkov tractor plant in April 1970, he warned that future increases in production would have to depend mainly upon economies and better use of existing facilities. One wonders who benefits from the economies. He also mentioned "subjective" weaknesses in the economy, such as slowness and a lack of discipline and responsibility, areas in which the Party has always claimed a special role.[62]

This drive by the Party apparatus for a stronger and more wide-ranging role for itself in industry did not take place without a hitch or two. In Rostov oblast, for example, "certain Party organizations . . . judged the results of their activity solely on the basis of external indicators of plan fulfillment." Some directors, despite their Party membership, "from time to time . . . are oversensitive about the Party committee's right to oversee their work and consider that such supervision virtually undermines management's authority." And there has been sharp criticism of those who try to shatter the Party's unity in industry while speaking of democratizing it.[63]

Resistance by directors to the Party policy of pushing the introduction of additional technology is almost unavoidable, since it would reduce their sphere of activity. The pressure became greater after the Twenty-Fourth Congress, with Pravda often urging enterprise Party organizations to exercise their pravo kontrolia over management. In June 1971 the First Secretary of the Tbilisi gorkom (city Party committee) noted that additional apparatchiki of raikomy and the gorkom had been assigned to industrial plants and various agencies to decide "many" current questions on the spot. In addition, the gorkom took under its own "special supervision" the implementation of the Shchekino experience in Tbilisi's enterprises. The very next day Pravda printed two articles, one an editorial, on the relative powers of the enterprise Party organization and the director, pointedly warning that "leading positions among us are not permanently secure for anyone. . . . It is necessary to suppress decisively and in good time any manifestations of a narrow-minded approach, of presumptuous conceit, of suppression of criticism, and of bureaucratic ways from whomever they originate."[64] The same issue of Pravda discusses an ultimately unsuccessful attempt by a factory manager to silence and discredit a worker who had criticized him for mismanagement. The plant's Party bureau is severely criticized for "not finding in itself the required principle to judge the mistakes of the director" and was told firmly to exercise its right to supervise the plant's administration.

In order for the Party to exercise its authority more firmly, in more detail, and with greater effect, there was some recognition that its structure had to undergo changes that would allow it to act in the way now desired. One suggestion, made by P. Shelest, then the First Secretary in the Ukraine, was that Party organizations engage in long-range planning of their own operations. This, if practicable, would be a decisive shift away from the scandalous and seemingly most common practice of operating po kampanski. He also called for Party organizations "to make fuller use of their right of supervision over the management's economic activity." (Emphasis supplied.)[65] This emphasis may be connected with the current experiment of the "enlarged Party committee" (partkom rasshirennogo sostava) introduced, for example, into the most important industrial enterprises of Nizhny Tagil, in the Urals not far from Sverdlovsk, which may give the apparatus a greater "reach" and power in the enterprise.

In general, then, the years since 1968 have seen an attempt, undoubtedly prompted by a grouping or faction high in the Party apparatus and probably including the General Secretary, to obtain a more active and detailed role for the Party organizations in industry. One aim of this initiative was, as for many similar initiatives taken by the apparatus in the past, the modernization and greater effectiveness of industrial administration and productive processes in industry. This drive may also be a conventional political response to old bottlenecks and new scarcities in the economy.

Cadres' Work

This sphere of the "selection, assignment and training" of industrial administrators and key workers remains the main concern of the Party's activity. It has a nomenklatura, or appointive power, over enterprise personnel akin to that which it has over approximately 400,000 local and 200,000 central and republican government positions.[66] Although Party organizations are not to get bogged down in "petty supervision" of economic management personnel or to take on "questions which could and must be decided by those charged with them," they are supposed to have a decisive role in the hiring and firing of administrative personnel and key workmen. At present the Party is emphasizing the promotion of former workers. In stepping in and replacing administrative personnel, the Party's goal often is to make certain that "each executive is imbued with the consciousness of responsibility before the Party and the people. . . ."[67] The aim seems to be the instilling of a stronger feeling in administrators that the Party is omnipresent, ever watchful, and always ready and able to act decisively. This may approach a fear-mongering campaign with the word "responsibility" actually denoting "fear" or "concern." In fact, in one Pravda editorial administrative responsibility is equated with discipline through a curious use of words: "One of the important features of the reform is the specific connection between initiative and responsibility and between democracy and discipline in all links of production management."[68]

The nonpolitical aspect of the goals for change in management executives includes upgrading technical qualifications, accordingly raising the matters of training and retraining and the Party's attitude toward them. The Party's role here is to see that "management cadres master scientific methods of production management, all-round analysis of the results of economic activity, and skill in managing a labor collective. . . ."[69] As earlier in the reform, the Party continues to organize retraining sessions for managerial and leading Party and soviet personnel. The work of enterprise Party organizations at present also includes dealing with what might be called the psychological "restructuring" (perestroika) of managerial personnel to deal with the effects of introduction of automation and management using computers. The secretary of an electrical plant's Party committee says that it is necessary for the Party organizations in industry "to struggle for strengthening trust in new technology."[70] The Party has brought Soviet managers face to face with post-industrial society, no doubt a disturbing prospect.

Enforcement

A new element in the Party's enforcement function is the enforcement of the implementation of the reform. As before, general supervision and checking on execution are said to be a "most important part" of any Party organization's activity.[71] One way this is carried out is through committees or commissions "in charge of supervising management work." At one Siberian plant, six were set up to deal with technical progress, economic questions, output quality, safety, production of consumer goods, and construction of cultural and social projects, each headed by "highly qualified specialists." Supposedly, in an electrical plant in Riga, half the Party members participate in examinations of "production reserves," the sources of materials and labor that Party apparatchiki seem to think are always understated. The commissions are to bring up the "most urgent and important problems" at sessions of the plant Party committees and then oversee the fulfillment of their decisions. But "not everything runs smoothly." The commissions encounter "difficult situations and conflicting points of view," most probably circumlocutions for managerial opposition.[72] Another problem may be in the making: What might the use of specialized commissions headed by specialists ultimately mean for the Party as an organization of general ideological guidance?

Operations

If enforcement fails, the Party takes a more direct and active hand. "Intervention" is still called for,[73] an exhortation having more weight in the heavier atmosphere laid down by the Twenty-Fourth Congress. Operational work--actually doing something--is not difficult for a Party organization to get into. A secretary of the Ivanovo obkom says, "Practice shows that enterprise executives invariably turn to local Party bodies if any operational question is not solved by the appropriate glavk or ministry." He adds that Party committees cannot ignore such inquiries because the plan's outcome might be at stake, but does note that this tends to make the Party deal with questions that properly belong to state agencies.[74] Another problem is that the Party organs often are contacted only when failure is imminent, a bit late for any fine corrective action to be taken. As a result, massive "intervention" is unavoidable.

In Dagestan in 1971, the Party committee in an inefficient armature shop set up a commission to study the situation "in detail." Notably, an engineer who headed an experimental shop and who was a Party member was co-opted into the Party committee and sent to the

INDUSTRIAL MANAGEMENT

shop to solve its difficulties. Obviously, here we see a contrived and purposeful combination of political power and technological expertise. The engineer, it is said, operated on the basis of the Party organization throughout his work in the backward shop and used the Party's "own paths" toward the solution of economic problems.[75]

This inclination toward direct involvement extends to the application of science in industry, and not without effect. The Party may be "the key force in promoting discontinuous jumps in technology." Its involvement does not originate with the top of the political ladder or even with the local Party organizations, but with specialists who make representations for action and direct them to the Party organizations and higher echelons.[76] Of course, these specialists are likely to desire greater participation in decision-making.

The Party has even been instrumental in establishing quasi-entrepreneurial research and development agencies, such as Fakel in Novosibirsk and Lennauchtekhsnab in Leningrad.[77] Another organizational means of the Party's intervention is the "people's control" (narodnyi kontrol' or NK) apparatus, an adjunct to the primary Party organizations and to their other enforcement and operational agencies. The NK groups usually have been subordinated to some more or less nationally structured and centralized organization, such as the State Control Commission or the Party Control Commission (merged by Khrushchev in 1962 and made separate again in 1965). The NK system provides a "bureaucratic" means either to offset or to complement the "public" (or voluntary, nonpaid, Party-led) means of exercising Party supervision.[78] The NK organs at present seem not to be so much subordinated to agencies above them in any NK structure as to be affiliates of local-level Party organizations. They do work very similar to that of the Party commissions just discussed and may overlap with them in membership as well as function.

Almost all the NK people are in the Party network, and the introduction of new technology and the completion of scientific projects is one of their present major concerns. The solution of supply questions is also a function. The usual "raids" (reidy) and "checkups" (proverki) of the effectiveness of execution of Party and state policies continue. Deficiencies are reported to the gorkom or raikom, which decides whether to punish the guilty Party members and to make recommendations to the appropriate state administrators.[79] These recommendations may have the force of orders or directives.

Ideological and Organizational Work

This activity lies at the base of Party thought and action. Through agitation and propaganda, the Party engages in the personalized imparting of policy directives and, more generally, political socialization, and in the acquisition of political intelligence and the gauging of public opinion or mass moods. A direct outgrowth of this work is mobilizational activity directed toward actual policy implementation. This category includes a wide range of activities from old-fashioned "agitprop," however it may have been redefined, to the new "Party sociology" (the germ of which always existed in agitational work). Although in recent years some attempt has been made (but without clear results) to replace the network of agitators, whose often dry and formalistic expositions were said to be having less and less effect upon an increasingly better-educated and better-informed public, with more knowledgeable and specialized "political informers," much agitation has always been directed toward motivating workers to produce more and better products by "showing them the relation of their work to the greater economic development of society as a whole."[80] Although the launching of the economic reform may show by its increase of monetary incentives and stress upon profits that the old agitation had definite limits in economic effectiveness, the process of agitation continues much as before on the factory floor, and may have received new emphasis since late 1969. It is just possible that agitation may have more effect in a context in which the worker's personal economic situation is improving.

The "ideologues" in the Party must realize that if the reform were to develop on the basis of material incentives alone, they would lose a real degree of their political influence and value to the rest of the political elite, and as a result would face the loss of their jobs. This is, of course, an unacceptable prospect. Accordingly, the First Party Secretary in Lithuania argued, citing Mikhail Suslov, that "the task which confronts us now is how best to throw light on the ideological aspects of the economic reform." He went on to say that "it is incorrect to reduce everything to material incentives. . . . This can give rise to individualism. . . ." The First Secretary of the Rostov obkom made similar assertions. A logical extension of this view is a concern for more "labor discipline" by Party functionaries.[81] Some apparatchiki have a more positive but an equally committed view.

Here stands revealed a major reason and aim of the Party's ideological and organizational-mobilizational work: welding the workers into a force on its terms, thus helping management fulfill both its own goals and those of the Party, but also limiting the power of management in the enterprise. The Party always stops far short of creating workers' councils or allowing the workers to have an organizational base of their own. (This is discussed in Chapter 5.) Evidence of this sort of thinking among the Party apparatus is not hard to find. Prominent apparatchiki argue, for example, that "economic

INDUSTRIAL MANAGEMENT 173

leadership achieves its purpose precisely when one-man rule is rationally combined with the creative activity of the collective," activity engineered by the Party organization in the plant as a means of leverage and pressure against the managers and the ministerial apparatus above them. [82]

In late 1969 <u>Pravda</u> implied the institutionalization of additional leverage against managers by calling for more "production conferences, workers' assemblies, people's control, and other forms of direct participation by the working people in running the enterprises" and noted that "it is this combination [of state and party organs and activities] which produces a genuinely business-like and creative climate in present-day production."[83] The introduction of labor-saving machinery and processes, one of the Party's main goals now, necessitates the release of workers from their jobs. The prospect of a socialist form of unemployment, even if temporary, must be difficult to wash away with words. The emphasis in economic agitprop seems heavily technological, as is understandable, given the aims at present. Specialists and scientists are given a real role in the process. In addition to "lecture groups" of Party committees, the "Knowledge" (<u>Znanie</u>) Society and the trade unions engage in this work. In terms of its intelligence-gathering function, agitprop has been supplemented by the new "Party sociology" (sociological research carried out by Party organizations).[84]

Determination of Goals and Priorities, Solution of Supply Problems, and Arbitration and Mediation

These functions are not, as noted in the discussion of the 1965-68 period, performed as much or with as much determination as the four others. Nevertheless, they have not been dropped from the Party's armory of organizational weapons. Party organizations have never made major goals for industrial enterprises; but they do sharpen, refine, or give them greater specificity. One example will suffice: the pressure that Party organizations currently put upon managers to adopt the Shchekino experience, a means of increasing output by reducing the work force. (The essence of the matter seems to be paying more to workers who can master two or three jobs and firing those who will not or cannot do this. The result is a smaller work force performing more tasks.)[85]

Supply is still a problem despite the creation of a new nationwide supply agency (Gossnab), and Party mediation often is necessary. The Party organization becomes a collective tolkach when "its" enterprise lacks something essential. The task can be time-consuming. As a secretary of the Ivanovo obkom said: "The secretary of the obkom, department heads and other Party staff personnel frequently have to begin their workday--and sometimes finish it up as well--writing various telegrams and letters to ministries and their administrations and supply and sales offices. . . ."[86]

Though not much attention is given to this work in print, it is still carried out. Perhaps the reform and the Party's concurrent emphasis on improving technology have given the first four functions greater importance and urgency, and hence greater space in the press. The latter two functions are being left mainly to the formal state industrial structure.

OBEDINENIIA AND THE PARTY

The challenge to the Party control system of several enterprises in different locations that are joined organizationally has been mentioned. The fostering of obedinenie cannot be approached by the Party apparatus, either as a whole or as a primary-level organization, without concern that its ultimate control be endangered. This is the decisive question for the Party apparatus, not considerations of economics or management. These larger and richer industrial organizations, each containing several former enterprise directors, are bound to acquire great weight vis-a-vis the Party (as well as the ministerial) apparatus. (Interestingly, the recent aborted formation in agriculture of kolkhoz "associations and unions" may show that elements high in the apparatus fear the political effects of amalgamations.)

A major problem for establishing meaningful Party control of the new forms was coping organizationally with the elements' dispersion over areas encompassing the territories of different Party organizations. To deal with this the Party statutes were changed to grant intermediate-level committees the right to form primary Party organizations within the units of an obedinenie (former enterprises) even when these are located in different administrative-territorial divisions of the state structure. The Communists in an obedinenie entirely within one city are registered with the raikom or a Party committee na pravakh raikoma at the place in which the head enterprise is located. If some of the enterprises are outside a city, the Party organization of the obedinenie is separate from but subordinate to the appropriate raikom. One analysis concludes that though this represents a departure from the usual paralleling of Party and state divisions, "It does, however, constitute an improvement over the muddled structure obtaining during the sovnarkhoz period when Party officials within a given sovnarkhoz frequently reported through different channels."[87] Lately the Party seems to have cautiously

INDUSTRIAL MANAGEMENT 175

restricted an obedinenie's units to enterprises within a single raion. Another means for entree of Party wishes into the management of obedineniia is the limiting of edinonachalie in some of them by creating "councils of directors" that may allow the Party organization a greater say in decision-making. The necessary control reestablished or at hand, the Party can favor the obedinenie and also appear as the exponent of progress and efficiency.

CONCLUSION

The Party apparat has been able to merge into the new situation with its powers over industry unimpaired and perhaps even enhanced. The ministries and the dissident specialists pose a limitation upon the Party, of course, as do, to a greater degree, the Party's own commitments to an ever larger stream of consumer goods and to the widespread adoption of automation that creates labor problems. Despite these limitations, the Party apparat has both launched the reform and maintained itself as the active predominant organization. This shows that the Party is still a vital force in the Soviet economy, but difficulties can be discerned. The party could have done better; it could have implemented the reform more rapidly and more fully.

The lack of a firm guiding hand from the start of the reform made it inevitable that all agencies, even the control agencies, would follow the path of least resistance and continue to do what they had been "programmed" to do under Stalin. In other words, the CPSU gave in to "bureaucratism," a failure to lead that would have horrified Lenin, Trotsky, Stalin, and Khrushchev and that is a serious limitation on the Party's will and ability to act, despite its maintenance of its position in industry. As a result, no decisive change in the Party's relationship with industrial enterprises and their management occurred, although the Party did try for greater kontrol'.

The Party's seeming abstention from active involvement was only apparent and temporary. As it reasserted its powers by actively intervening in operational matters, it emerged with a role in industry similar to the one it has long had. Since the political system was not fundamentally changed by the reform, such an outcome was almost inevitable. One wonders when it will choose to reenter the fields of goals, priorities, and supply, and arbitration and mediation, with a will.

Although change in the roles of enterprise directors and Party secretaries has been desired, the manager-Party relationship, without an open conflict arising between the goal and reality, has not been greatly changed. Few changes in accord with the official goals have occurred. The relative priorities of aspects of Party intervention have changed, but the extent and function of this change are not clear. If the Party is to remain the unquestioned leader of the Soviet economy and political system, the local Party organization must exercise powers of ultimate control or of final determination in setting goals and priorities. Similarly, they must direct to key points the supplies necessary for the fulfillment of production tasks. In other words, the reform's goal will have to be subverted and made to fit the continuing reality of Party controls in active operation or, less probably, the actuality will have to be basically altered.

During the progress of the reform, the former process has been much more in evidence than the latter. Party organizations are still engaged in the delicate and never fully successful balancing of their needs for kontrol' against the modern economy's requirement of rational, consequential acts not heavily dependent upon political considerations. The Party's involvement in economic and administrative matters is necessitated by the fundamental fact that the system's goals are set by the Party. The continuation of this role of the Party often destroys efficiency.[88] The Party also must resolve conflicts within and between bureaucracies, groups, and individuals in industry, since it is the "supercoordinator" of all significant processes in the USSR. If any group were to replace it in this role (particularly in industrial management), the Party would lose a key basis of its political supremacy.

Two broad but important issues arise. What is the real economic effect of Party involvement in the enterprises? Is it in the last analysis more productive and creative than limiting and typically bureaucratic? Can the Party presence, however it is defined, continue without encountering some strong hindrance or reaching some definite limit? If the answer is yes, what is this as yet shadowy obstruction? Milovan Djilas has taken up the question of the role and effect of a Leninist party upon the reform of a Stalinist economy. As he puts it, "People were putting no effort into making a success of the reform, and they could not do so because the old political and administrative structure was still there and the ownership structure was unchanged; i.e., the same monopoly of party bureaucracy was guardian and controller."[89] Of course, Yugoslavia was temporarily able to make an end run almost around the problem by allowing some degree of administrative and economic, though not political, decentralization and allowing some foreign investment. But the USSR remains an "ideological economy." Djilas probably goes too far, or is premature in relation to the Soviet case, in regarding the "Party bureaucracy's privileges in the government and the economy" as akin to the former "feudal lords'" acting as "brakes on modern transport, modern management, and modern technology, and even on the socially owned property that has developed under Communism."

The Party is a major force in introducing modern processes. The question can still honestly exist, however, whether this "modernization" is being accomplished slowly, artificially, and poorly because of the Party's decision to intertwine it with its power needs. Joseph Berliner has suggested that the Soviet Union will engage in large-scale, continued modernization but at a pace that allows the continuation of the present political system, and therefore at a pace that will keep it technologically behind several other systems. The Party's present stress on modernization is no assurance it can handle the resulting social "spin-offs": unemployment, a need for large-scale retraining, a larger class of unideological technicians and scientists, a semi-leisured class of workers.[90] Of course, the Party can remain a dictator, but not of the same sort of system, and therefore not the same dictator. Even some apparatchiki seem to think operational acts by the Party can go too far. As one Party secretary complained in 1972:

> The upshot of all this is that ultimately the local Party bodies, busy solving operational and administrative questions, get bogged down with day-to-day matters and are diverted from the business with which they should be dealing, and at the same time, willingly or unwillingly relieve managerial personnel of the responsibility for the state of affairs at a given enterprise. Incorrect decisions are not ruled out in such an atmosphere. . . .[91]

Lack of a "socialist market" or some objectively operating regulator of product quality requires that the Party, an engine of "ideology and organization,"[92] try to fulfill the duties of the economic regulator. The Party is, among other things, a poor organizational and political substitute for a system of economic regulation. This is not to deny that, as Hough has said, all modern economies have governmental regulation. This can be fruitful when the essentials of individual liberties and creative economic and social forces exist and are operative, but it has deleterious effects on the possibilities of such liberties and forces when the economic regulator is also a general, unlimited political regulator and able to bury its mistakes.

There have been two trends in writings on the Party's economic role in recent years, a brief discussion of which may elucidate the second issue mentioned above--that of possible limits to this role. While there has been much said in the Soviet press on the Party's work on innovation, rationalization, and the widespread implementation of the practical discoveries of modern science, there is at the same time a renewed stress on the role of the Party in increasing work discipline, controlling economic executives at all levels, manipulating workers, and propagating the ideology. Suslov has used the term "moral factor," and Brezhnev has spoken of "socialist law and order." A basic process at work in industry, then, is the interaction of considerations of political power and efficient, highly productive operation without a definite or satisfactory resolution of either. The Party justifies its position and activities not only on ideological grounds but also on the grounds of efficiency itself, actually saying that its <u>vmeshatel'tsvo</u> ("intervention, interference") makes the productive process occur. Since a primary goal of the Soviet system is the increase in production somewhat independently of other considerations,[93] such an emphasis strengthens the Party and the political system to a point but challenges them as well.

How might this contradiction be resolved? There is the inevitable desire and demand for participation, influence, and even power by the professionals brought into organizations because of the need for their new knowledge. This applies both to the Party organization and to Soviet industrial management, in both of which the number of technically trained specialists has increased greatly in recent years and in which it continues to increase.[94] Of course, Party controls, particularly over cadres (now strengthened) and recruitment policies for apparatchiki can mitigate effects of this process somewhat and allow the partial channeling of these new pressures, but not completely nor with any certainty of success. There is just a chance that a "brave new world" of effective centralized social control can be achieved. However, instead we will probably witness the sight of a changing Party apparatus holding on to its prerogatives in industry until, as a result of some serious failure or accidental circumstance, it retires to being mainly an ideological guide indulging in ideologized goading. (But the recent reassertion of its old role by the League of Communists in Yugoslavia indicates that the process will not occur smoothly or be uncontested.)

In conclusion, with the full reemergence of the Party's former pattern of behavior, the Soviet industrial manager will again face the enterprise Party organization in its combined role of ally and policeman, the official goals of the reform will have been rendered obsolete, and the reform will have to be reformed in order for further changes to be made along the lines originally indicated. The discussion of the reform in the Soviet press since the early months of 1970, including Brezhnev's speeches of December 1969 and April 1970,[95] strongly indicate that new deficiencies have been recognized but that no realistic corrective policy has been implemented. Instead, the Party leadership and many state bureaucrats have opted for a quasi-Stalinist stress on "discipline" and additional central controls. This outcome clearly reveals that the relationships of the Soviet industrial manager with the Party organization, although altered to a degree, have not been qualitatively changed by the present economic reform.

NOTES

1. For example, see Jeremy R. Azrael, Managerial Power and Soviet Politics (Cambridge, Mass.: Harvard University Press, 1966), p. 170.
2. Ernst Kux, "Technicians of Power Versus Managers of Technique," in S. Ploss, ed., The Soviet Political Process (Waltham, Mass.: Ginn, 1971), pp. 172-73.
3. David Granick, The Red Executive (Garden City, N.Y: Doubleday Anchor, 1961), pp. 276-77.
4. John Armstrong, The Soviet Bureaucratic Elite (New York: Praeger, 1959), p. 60. He utilizes L. Slepov, Mestnye partiinye organy (Moscow: Vyshaia Partiinaia Shkola pri TsK kPSS, 1954), p. 41.
5. See Armstrong, op. cit., p. 67; and Philip D. Stewart, Political Power in the Soviet Union (Indianapolis: Bobbs-Merrill, 1968), pp. 73-74, 208-09, 211-12.
6. A. Amalrik, "Will the USSR Survive Until 1984?" Survey 73 (Autumn 1969): 60 infra (footnote 25).
7. Kosygin said national income had risen by 10 percent over the first two years of the ninth plan. Since the growth rate was 6 percent in 1971, it had to be acout 4 percent in 1972. See A. N. Kosygin, "Sotsial'no-ekonomicheskoe razvitie sovetskogo mnogo-natsial'nogo gosudarstva," Kommunist 17 (November 1972): 15-41. Discussed in New York Times, December 14, 1972.
8. Boris Nikolaevsky, Sotsialisticheskii vestnik no. 3/4 (763-64) (March-April 1962): 46. Quoted in Sidney I. Ploss, Conflict and Decision-Making in Soviet Russia (Princeton, N.J.: Princeton University Press, 1965), pp. 284-85.
9. G. Shitarev, Kommunist 5 (1957): 33, quoted in Ploss, Conflict and Decision-Making, p. 7; and David Lane, Politics and Society in the USSR (New York: Random House, 1971), p. 319.
10. Frederick C. Mosher, ed., Governmental Reorganizations (Indianapolis: Bobbs-Merrill, 1967), p. 490 (emphasis in original); and Robert Conquest, Power and Policy in the U.S.S.R. (London: Macmillan, 1962), p. 304.
11. Robert W. Campbell, "Economic Reform in the U.S.S.R.," American Economic Review 58, no. 2 (May 1968): 557.
12. Mosher, op. cit., p. 492.
13. Pravda, July 4, 1969, and September 30, 1968. For a similar case see Pravda, December 9, 1967, p. 2.
14. Jerry F. Hough, The Soviet Prefects (Cambridge, Mass.: Harvard University Press, 1969), pp. 78-79; and "The Soviet System: Petrification or Pluralism?" Problems of Communism 21, no. 2 (March-April 1972): 34 infra. See also P. D. Stewart, "Power

in the Provinces," Problems of Communism 20, no. 3 (May-June 1971): 76-78. Also see K. W. Ryavec, American Political Science Review 64, no. 1 (March 1970): 204-05.

15. J. K. Galbraith, The New Industrial State (Boston: Houghton-Mifflin, 1967), p. 107.

16. See Jerry F. Hough, "The Soviet Concept of the Relationship Between the Lower Party Organs and the State Administration," Slavic Review 24, no. 2 (June 1965): 215-40; Sel'skaia zhizn', January 10, 1971; and Pravda, December 12, 1970.

17. Hough, The Soviet Prefects, p. 296; and his "The Prerequisites of Areal Deconcentration: The Soviet Experience," in James J. Heaphey, ed., Spatial Dimensions of Development Administration (Durham: University of North Carolina Press, 1971), p. 162.

18. Robert A. Solo, Economic Organizations and Social Systems (Indianapolis: Bobbs-Merrill, 1967), pp. 109-10.

19. Gaetano Mosca, The Ruling Class (New York: McGraw-Hill, 1939), p. 404.

20. Kommunist 17 (1959): 3-21; quoted in Ploss, Conflict and Decision-Making, p. 166.

21. G. Alekseev, "Partiinaia organizatsiia promyshlennogo predpriiatiia," Kommunist 13 (September 1972): 65.

22. George Fischer, The Soviet System and Modern Society (New York: Atherton, 1968), pp. 13, 39, 47, 56.

23. T. H. Rigby, "The Soviet Politburo," Soviet Studies 24, no. 1 (July 1972): 20-22. See also Z. K. Brzezinski and S. H. Huntington, Political Power: USA/USSR (New York: Viking, 1964), p. 411.

24. F. Loshchenkov, "Samostoiatel'nost', initsiativa, otvetstvennost'," Kommunist 15 (October 1965): 45-57. (The pattern is still common.) Also see Pravda, November 10, 1969, p. 1; and Joseph Novak (Jerzy Kosinski), No Third Path (Garden City, N.Y.: Doubleday, 1962).

25. M. Vasil'ev, "Direktor za partoi," Izvestiia, May 14, 1967, p. 5; also see V. Kutsevol, "Ekonomicheskii poisk," Kommunist 17 (November 1965): 39-40. Kutsevol is First Secretary of the Lvov obkom.

26. Communist Party of the Soviet Union, Spravochnik . . . (2nd ed.; Moscow: Politicheskoi Literatury, 1967), p. 24.

27. I. Zaitsev and I. Pronin, "Kommisii po kontroliu deiatel'nosti administratsii," Partiinaia zhizn' 14 (July 1967): 32-33.

28. G. Trifonov, "Rezhim ekonomii i partiinye organizatsii," Ekonomicheskaia gazeta 23 (June 1967): 19; and Pravda, August 23, 1967, p. 2.

29. N. S. Semigorelov, Metody partiinogo rukovodstvo khoziaistvom (Moscow: "Ekonomika," 1967), p. 28; and Zaitsev and Pronin, loc. cit.
30. Pravda, February 21, 1970, p. 2.
31. A. Masiagin, "Kommunisty zavoda," Kommunist 2 (January 1966): 20, 26.
32. See I. Naidis, "Zavodskoi kollektiv, partorganizatsiia, direktor," Kommunist 18 (December 1965): 46.
33. Hough, "The Role . . .," pp. 151, 153.
34. A. P. Alekhin et al., Pravovoe polozhenie ministerstv SSSR (Moscow: Iuridicheskaia Literatura, 1971), pp. 20, 21.
35. Pravda, February 3, 1972, translated in CDSP 24, no. 6 (March 8, 1972): 3; Sotsialisticheskaia industriia, June 15, 1971, p. 2; and Pravda, February 4, 1972, p. 3 (translated in CDSP 24, no. 5 [March 1, 1972]: 22).
36. Michel Tatu, Power in the Kremlin (New York: Viking, 1970), p. 428.
37. Leonard Schapiro, The Communist Party of the Soviet Union (New York: Random House, 1960), p. 579; and Z. K. Brzezinski, "The Nature of the Soviet System," in his Ideology and Power in Soviet Politics (New York: Praeger, 1962), p. 78 infra (originally in Slavic Review, October 1961).
38. Hough, "The Role . . .," pp. 74-77.
39. Carl Linden, Khrushchev and the Soviet Leadership (Baltimore: Johns Hopkins Press, 1966), p. 33; Merle Fainsod, How Russia Is Ruled (rev. ed.; Cambridge, Mass.: Harvard University Press, 1963), p. 394; and Kommunist 10 (October 1957): 5, quoted in Ploss, Conflict and Decision-Making in Soviet Russia, p. 22, infra.
40. Sidney Ploss, "Deadlock in the Party Presidium," in his The Soviet Political Process (Waltham, Mass.: Ginn, 1971), p. 218.
41. Pravda, November 18, 1964. Quoted in Christian Duevel, "Pravda Reinterprets Party Leadership of Soviets and Mass Organizations," Radio Liberty Dispatch, December 13, 1967, p. 5.
42. Sidney I. Ploss, "Politics in the Kremlin," Problems of Communism 19, no. 3 (May-June 1970): 13.
43. Pravda, November 26, 1967, p. 2.
44. Pravda, January 15, 1970. Quoted in Christian Duevel, "Brezhnev's Secret Report," Radio Liberty Dispatch, January 29, 1970, p. 10.
45. Pravda, April 2, 1969, p. 1; and Rabochaia gazeta, November 19, 1970, p. 3.
46. Partiianaia zhizn' 5 (March 1970): 5. See Christian Duevel, "'Partiinaia zhizn' Is Critical of Party and Government

Leadership of the Economy," Radio Liberty Dispatch, March 16, 1970, p. 4. The article in Rabochiia gazeta cited in note 45 commented favorably upon the same Central Committee decree.

47. Pravda, March 23, 1971, p. 2.

48. "Assessment of the 24th Communist Party Congress," U.S. Congressional Record, 94th Congress, 2nd Session, January 18, 1972, p. E65. See also Leonard Schapiro, "Keynote-Compromise," Problems of Communism 20, no. 4 (July-August 1971): 5.

49. Pravda, March 30, 1971, p. 10. See also Christian Duevel, "Proposed CPSU Statutes Changes Strengthen Authoritarian Rule," Radio Liberty Dispatch, April 6, 1971, pp. 7-9.

50. N. Petrov, "Partiinaia organizatsiia ministerstva," Kommunist 1 (January 1972): 45, 53. See also Robert J. Osborn, The Evolution of Soviet Politics (Homewood, Ill.: Dorsey, 1974), p. 319.

51. Petrov, op. cit., pp. 45, 53-54.

52. Pravda, August 25, 1971, p. 2; (translated in CDSP 23, no. 34 [September 21, 1971]: 1).

53. Pravda, May 22, 1972, p. 2.

54. Pravda, August 25, 1971, pp. 2-4. See also Pravda, July 12, 1971, p. 1 (condensed in CDSP 23, no. 28 [August 10, 1971]: 19-20), for an example drawn from the Ukraine; and Pravda, September 24, 1971, p. 3 (condensed in CDSP 23, no. 38 [October 19, 1971]: 37-38.

55. See, for example, the editorial in Izvestiia, February 14, 1974; the report on Brezhnev's talk at the Central Committee plenum of December 1973 in Pravda, January 27, 1974; the lead article by M. I. Piskotin in Sovetskoe gosudarstvo i pravo 10 (October 1973); and several Radio Liberty Dispatches written by C. Duevel, dated October 29, 1973; February 24, 1974; March 11, 1974; and March 22, 1974.

56. V. I. Lenin, Polnoe sobranie sochinenii, XL (Moscow: Gos.iyd-vo polit. lit-ry, 1958-65), p. 222. Quoted in Petrov, op. cit., p. 51.

57. Fainsod, op. cit., p. 418.

58. Ekonomicheskaia gazeta 34 (August 1968): 5-6; JPRS 46,622 (October 8, 1968): 37. This statement is by V. Vishniakov, First Secretary of the Rostov obkom.

59. A. Stepin, "Rukovodiashchii printsip zhizni i deiatel'nosti leninskoi partii," Kommunist 6 (April 1969): 42.

60. Sovetskaiia Litva, December 8, 1970 (FBIS 3 [January 5, 1971]: B23); Kommunist 18 (December 1970), p. 6 (editorial); Pravda, October 18, 1970. Discussed in C. Duevel, "Comparison of October Slogans--1969-1970," Radio Liberty Dispatch, October 21, 1970; and A. Alekseev, "Partiinaia organizatsiia promyshlennogo predpriiatiia," Kommunist 13 (September 1972): 68.

INDUSTRIAL MANAGEMENT   183

61. Kommunist 18 (December 1970): 7; and Pravda, February 2, 1971, p. 2.

62. Radio Moscow, April 13, 1970. For discussion see R.R.G., "Brezhnev Again on Economic Problems," Radio Free Europe Research Report, April 14, 1970.

63. Ekonomicheskaia gazeta 34 (August 1968): 39; and Pravda, August 12, 1972, p. 2 (condensed in CDSP 24, no. 32 [September 6, 1972]: 14). The director is head of the Siberian Farm Machinery Plant in Novosibirsk. See also Stepin, op. cit., pp. 46-47.

64. Pravda, June 15, 1971, p. 2, and June 16, 1971, pp. 1-2.

65. Pravda, August 20, 1971, pp. 2, 3 (condensed in CDSP 23, no. 3 [September 14, 1971]: 2-3); also see Pravda, October 22, 1970. Discussed in C. Duevel, "A Dubious Experiment: The 'Enlarged Party Committee,'" Radio Liberty Dispatch, November 3, 1970.

66. An estimate given by L. G. Churchward, "Bureaucracy in the USA-USSR," Coexistence 5 (April 1968): 205-06.

67. Pravda, June 7, 1972, p. 1; Pravda, March 3, 1972, p. 2 (condensed in CDSP 24, no. 9 [March 29, 1972]: 13); N. N. Rodionov, "Partiinye komitety i sblizhenie nauki s proizvodstvom," Kommunist 9 (June 1970): 21; and Pravda, April 15, 1972, p. 2 (excerpted in CDSP 24, no. 15 [May 10, 1972]: 19. The quotation on "consciousness" is from V. F. Dobrik, "Vospitanie khoziaistvennykh kadrov," Ekonomicheskaia gazeta 26 (June 1972): 3.

68. Pravda vostoka, February 26, 1971, p. 2. The author is head of a department at the Tashkent Higher Party School. See also Pravda, November 10, 1969, p. 1.

69. Pravda, November 10, 1969, p. 1.

70. A. Pershin, "Avtoritet rukovoditelia," Kommunist 1 (January 1971): 69-79; and Sotsialisticheskaia industriia, June 13, 1971.

71. Pravda, October 17, 1970, p. 2.

72. Pravda, August 12, 1972, p. 2; April 15, 1972, p. 2; October 23, 1970, p. 2; and August 12, 1972, p. 2.

73. For example, see Pravda, July 28, 1970, and October 16, 1970, p. 2.

74. Pravda, February 13, 1972, p. 2 (excerpted in CDSP 24, no. 6 [March 8, 1972]: 20; and Pravda, September 12, 1970, p. 2, in which the First Secretary of the Izhevsk gorkom speaks of using "one's own hands" when confronted by "serious problems." See also Pravda, January 28, 1972, p. 2, condensed in CDSP 24, no. 4 (February 23, 1972): 12.

75. Pravda, May 31, 1972, p. 2. The author, M. S. Umakhanov, is First Secretary of the Dagestan obkom.

76. See A. J. Alexander, R & D in Soviet Aviation (Santa Monica, Calif.: RAND, 1970), p. 27.

77. I am indebted for this information to Professor Herbert Sawyer of Bentley College and the Russian Research Center, Harvard University.

78. See Grey Hodnett, "Khrushchev and Party-State Control," in Alexander Dallin, ed., Politics in the Soviet Union (New York: Harcourt, Brace & World, 1966), pp. 113-64.

79. V. Dolgikh, "Partiinye komitety i organy narodnogo kontrolia," Kommunist 8 (May 1972): 79, 82-83, 86. The author is First Secretary of Krasnoyarsk kraikom. See also Pravda, October 15, 1970, p. 3, and July 3, 1969, p. 3.

80. Gayle D. Hollander, Soviet Political Indoctrination (New York: Praeger, 1972), pp. 154, 157, 167. See also A. G. Meyer, The Soviet Political System (New York: Random House, 1965), p. 115.

81. Sovetskaia Litva, December 8, 1970; Ekonomicheskaia gazeta 23 (June 1971): 5; and the remarks of O. Lolashvili, then the First Secretary of the Tbilisi gorkom in Pravda, June 15, 1971, p. 2.

82. V. Zaluzhnii, "Ideinost' khoziaistvennogo rukovoditelia," Kommunist 7 (May 1968): 85-95. See also C. Duevel, "Sharpening Conflict Between Soviet Industrial Management and Party Apparat," Radio Liberty Dispatch, June 6, 1968, p. 5. Zaluzhnii, a former Deputy Chairman of the Party-State Control Committee, may be "Shelepin's man," thus giving him a non-liberal political cast. See Hodnett, "Khrushchev and Party-State Control," p. 151.

83. Pravda, November 10, 1969, p. 1 (editorial).

84. Ekonomicheskaia gazeta 26 (June 1972): 9. The author is the head of the agitation department of the Sverdlovsk obkom. See also Ekonomicheskaia gazeta 34 (August 1968): 5-6 (JPRS 46,622 [October 8, 1968]: 40-41); and Zev Katz, "Sociology in the Soviet Union," Problems of Communism 20, no. 3 (May-June 1971): 22-40.

85. Pravda, January 4, 1971, p. 2. The author is a Moscow obkom secretary.

86. See Pravda, February 13, 1972, p. 2.

87. "Assessment of 24th Communist Party Congress," loc. cit.; and Sovetskaia Belorussiia, November 10, 1970, p. 2.

88. See New York Times, December 12, 1966, on J. K. Galbraith and his Reith Lectures for the BBC in 1966.

89. Milovan Djilas, The Unperfect Society (New York: Harcourt, Brace & World, 1969), pp. 142, 181, 192.

90. On post-industrial or "technetronic" society, see Zbigniew K. Brzezinski, Between Two Ages (New York: Viking, 1970), particularly pp. 150-76.

91. Pravda, February 2, 1972, p. 2; excerpted in CDSP 24, no. 6 (March 8, 1972): 20. The author is a Secretary of the Ivanovo obkom.

92. See Alexander Eckstein, "Economic Development and Political Change in Communist Systems," *World Politics* 22, no. 4 (July 1970): 479-95.

93. See Abram Bergson, "Development Under Two Systems," *World Politics* 23, no. 4 (July 1971): 605.

94. For similar conclusions based on empirical research, see Jerald Hage and Michael Aiken, *Social Change in Complex Organizations* (New York: Random House, 1970), p. 76.

95. See *Pravda*, January 13, 1970, and April 14, 1970.

CHAPTER

5

THE MANAGER AND INDUSTRIAL WORKERS: THE EFFECT OF THE REFORM ON LABOR

INTRODUCTION

Content and Significance

This chapter concentrates on three major considerations: the present power of Soviet managers over enterprise personnel, particularly the workers; problems of the Soviet labor force, such as the tight supply and "fluidity" (tekuchest') of workers, and their difficulties and dissatisfactions (especially of young workers); and the strikingly new phenomenon of unemployment produced by certain aspects of the reform. Neither the role of the trade unions nor the increase in wages the reform promises is dealt with here.[1] Concentration upon these three major problems, including current attempts to cope with them, stems from their connection with the implementation of the economic reform and certain political questions. The Party leadership faces major political problems in allowing managers to increase their powers over workers and in allowing unemployment, short-term as it generally is, to increase. The former pits efficiency against the power of the political elite, and unemployment raises both thorny ideological questions and the practical need to establish new institutions to cope with an enlarged, and thus new, problem.

It was noted in the previous chapter that the Party apparatus is trying to limit the managers' powers in industry. The Party organizations' tie to workers is one basis for doing this. But the Party faces a difficult task in attempting to maintain its leverage, since it also wants to give additional operational powers and responsibilities to the managerial experts in order to make them more effective in guiding the production process. At the same time it does not want to allow the Soviet proletariat to form or exert its will against the managers (and ultimately it) in any manner similar to that of unions in liberal-democratic societies, workers' councils of the Yugoslav type, or the workers' activities during the Cultural Revolution in China. This is a difficult course to steer in the absence of effective totalitarian controls, such as Stalinist labor legislation or "special" or secret police sections in the factories.

In the Soviet economy the still highly emphasized goal of increases in quantity of production, as well as the more recent emphasis upon higher-quality goods and more consumer goods, are heavily dependent on increasing labor productivity. This logically means, besides providing workers with better machinery, getting them to work better and more. Eighty percent of increases in output now are due to increases in labor productivity. The whole growth in the volume of industrial production planned for Moscow during the ninth plan (30 percent) was to be achieved solely by increasing labor productivity. Interestingly, according to Gertrude Schroeder, "the Plan Directives for 1971-75 target a 37- to 40-percent increase in national income, of which 80-85 percent is to be provided by increased labor productivity."

A Soviet economic report released in December 1972 revealed that the lag of labor productivity in industry had continued, with productivity through November in 1972 rising by 5.4 percent, as against a rate of 6.1 percent planned for all of 1972. It was only 5.2 percent for the entire year.[2] It seems, therefore, that earlier Soviet statements that the economic reform "has provided few incentives to increase labor productivity" are justified. Of course, Marxist-Leninist socialism has not increased labor productivity as much as in the Common Market countries or Japan. The problems rest, then, on structures and processes more fundamental than incentives--for instance, the continued stress on quantity of output, associated tautness of enterprise plans, and the failure to give managers sufficient discretionary powers.[3]

Any survey of the contents of the Soviet press and of economics and sociology journals during the past several years reveals a renewed concentration upon the worker, his situation, and his role in the economy. This is particularly apparent in articles on Party work in industry and industrial management, and parallels the recent emphasis upon the industrial worker elsewhere, notably the United Kingdom and the United States. There is still a problem of fitting the industrial worker into the society that his labors had a key role in creating. This is a new form of the problem seen by Marx and others more than a century ago. It has now come to affect developed "socialist" societies of the Marxist-Leninist type as well as older "capitalist" societies. Milovan Djilas, that fallen angel of Communism, discussing the problem's basis in Soviet-type systems, notes that although Communism has been able to transform a peasant economy, it "has plunged into difficulties . . . because it now has to pass out of the industrial stage, with the aid of electronics and massive education programs and the employment of skilled scientific workers, into . . . the age of automation and mass production and consumption" but without "any systematic development of ideas concerning the future political and ideological evolution of the Soviet system. . . ."[4]

In attempting to get the Soviet working class to work harder and produce more, the Soviet political elite is emphasizing the more efficient use of working time and workers' mastery of additional occupations. (This is exemplified by the "Shchekino experiment" discussed below.) In 1969 a new newspaper, Sotsialisticheskaia industriia, was introduced in midyear to focus new attention on the Soviet worker and his work situation. Its first editorial presented as its aims the encouragement and facilitation of the rapid introduction of scientific and technological developments into industry and the increase of labor productivity.[5]

Atmospherics

Soviet appeals to the energy of the working class have always referred to both material and "moral" (ideological) incentives. The predominance of one type of incentive over the other gives a special tone to labor policy in any period and indicates which set of policy preferences are in effect. The balance has been tipped in favor of "moral" incentives in recent years, at least since late 1969, as shown by ideological exhortations, increased Party interference in production, and the expansion of "socialist competition." Such a strategy can bring economic results. The Chinese experience may even offer proof. However, it cannot produce great results within a pattern of constrained opportunities, and avoids correcting some of the real difficulties: the maintenance of rigid centralistic planning, the devolution of too little real responsibility to operating units, and the lack of incentive to take risks. One reason for the increased stress on "moral" incentives is the insufficiency of the material incentives offered by the reform's bonus system. The increase in workers' premia or bonuses after 1965 was imperceptible.[6]

The atmosphere became more ideologically charged. The 1971 October slogans included a change in slogan number 6 from a vague call to fulfill the "tasks" (zadaniia) of the ninth plan to purposive exhortation to "broaden the scale of socialist competition. . . ." This continued a trend, since the October slogans of 1970 had included a new number 20, reading: "Workers of socialist industry! Make fuller use of existing possibilities for increasing the output of industrial production and goods for the population" (emphasis added). The very next slogan called upon the workers to "struggle for the fulfillment of the planned tasks with the least possible expenditure of labor and material resources. . . ."[7] A note on this is Brezhnev's favorable reference to Stakhanovism at the 24th Party Congress (1971) and the expansion of socialist competition ordered by a Central Committee resolution of September 1971 that went on to call for greater "mobilization of the working people" and greater attention to moral incentives, which, it added, "are increasingly becoming the main motive force of our progress." Other pertinent features include the drive for strengthening labor discipline called for by the 24th Party Congress and mentioned frequently afterward.[8]

The degree of emphasis to be given to moral incentives and Party controls is, of course, a question of political significance upon which the political leadership divided to some degree. Kosygin has presented a different view of the workers' role in achieving higher labor productivity than has Brezhnev. For example, in one speech he put "good organization of labor" first and, although he spoke of "discipline," he said it was the "true socialist discipline of awareness" in which workers and managers are to be "educated." Significantly, nowhere did he hint at somehow forcing workers to be more productive. Brezhnev, on the other hand, has spoken ominously on the subject, referring to the law and the comrades' courts, in addition to the Party, as important means for making workers become more productive.[9] This renewed emphasis upon the Soviet ideology is a political requirement for the Party. Any lapse in active use of ideological assumptions and precepts weakens the Soviet leadership by opening it even more to charges of "decadence" from both within and without.

Returning to the question of incentive policy, it is clear that a definite shift in emphasis to the nonmaterial has taken place and that this shift is inextricably intertwined with the political maneuverings within the Party verkhushka (apex of the leadership) and the Party apparatus as a whole. Brezhnev has "leaned to one side," that of the "ideologues" and hard-liners. Although initially the "Brezhnev center" supported the Kosyginists' pragmatism, it shifted to favor moral incentives. While it does not seem possible to pinpoint any reason for this shift, several processes that were at work can be cited, although no clear priority is apparent. At the general level, the exacerbation of the Vietnam situation after 1965 raised fears of a counterattacking United States and triggered both an ideological response and an increased defense expenditure. This reduced the economic resources available for material incentives. More specifically, the workers' bonuses under the reform were not large, although a new bonus had been introduced (an end-of-the-year bonus or "thirteenth wage"). This undermined the Kosyginists' position and encouraged the other view. Leonard Kirsch's findings generally confirm this.[10] As a result, the reform cannot inspire any strong supportive feelings among ordinary workers.

Another issue affecting the relationship of managers to workers involves the supply of labor and the seemingly paradoxical issue of a shortage of labor. Actually, this is more a problem of shortages of particular kinds of workers at particular places. Also seriously involved here are the severe planning problems caused by the mobility or "fluidity" (tekuchest') of the labor force, the large-scale free movement of workers from job to job. Still another related general issue is the combination of the social effects of automation, notably unemployment, and measures to cope with them. More specific problems involved include the wages and material incentives of workers, boredom and drunkenness, and young workers. Capping all this is the important issue of workers' rights and the powers of management, which brings up the role of the trade unions and the personnel powers of Soviet industrial managers.

MANAGERIAL POWER: EDINONACHALIE AND DISCIPLINE

We now concentrate upon the degree of independent authority vis-a-vis workers that managers now have, the means by which they exert it, and the rights and opportunities open to the workers to put forth their views and wants. This requires some reference to the present role of the trade unions. According to the 1965 official model of the reform, edinonachalie is as meaningful as ever, if not more so. A recent Soviet book on the theory of management states that the director of the enterprise still acts "on the basis of edinonachalie" and continues to bear the "full responsibility for the management of the given [production] cell." The very next sentence relates this activity to the leadership of people and their mobilization, stating:

> The chief task before the manager is, out of many working people, . . . to create a single productive collective which is not a simple sum of the workers comprising it but instead a social community [obshchnost'] which possesses a new quality and the capability of carrying out production and social tasks . . . beyond the power of each person in it.[11]

Thus, at present the concept of edinonachalie stands fundamentally unimpaired. This is attested to by A. M. Birman, who says that without edinonachalie, "the correct conduct of a centralized economic policy, and the maintenance of a state discipline, which are objectively necessary for the successful development of social production," would be "impossible."[12] He adds, significantly, that the new enterprise statute "broadens" the rights of economic managers, increases their ability to influence production operations, and allows them to apply both material incentives and sanctions to their workers "more effectively." The reform has fostered an increased emphasis on edinonachalie, mainly in matters of labor discipline, the question of incentives in general (and that of wages and granting of bonuses in particular), and the hiring and firing of workers. As a result, the argument that edinonachalie is a "very limited concept" meaning "little more than the strengthening of labor discipline," certainly does not hold.[13] It may never have, due to the weakness of labor unions and social groups.

This broadening of edinonachalie is supported by the authoritarian style common to Soviet plant managers, particularly those trained and tempered during the period of Stalin's rule, but may be countered to some degree by the current purging from management of rigid executors of orders who use the high-handed methods so common in the past. There is a strong feeling that social changes require this. For example, the head of the promotdel ("industrial department") of a Soviet city newspaper said that the old methods of plant management are now "out of the question," since part of the work force now has a secondary or even a higher education and accordingly has to be directed in a new way.[14] However, despite the demands of the reform and the times, attitudes of long standing, coupled with the managers' enlarged powers within the plant, have given managers an advantage. And this outcome is in effect justified by the new enterprise statute, which allows managers to apply sanctions to their workers "more effectively." The deputy director for personnel of the Lenin-Nevskii machine-building plant in Leningrad says that ". . . the new system has demanded an even greater strengthening of labor discipline and a steadfast observance of the standard factory regulations."[15]

There are other reasons why the managers' authority has risen. While the scope of application of patently Stalinist instrumentalities of rule has been reduced, the political leadership now relies much more on various relatively satisfied and well-placed institutionalized groupings in the population for mass mobilization and control. This indicates a shift from the populistic or "mass" means used by Khrushchev for these same ends. The present leaders have, it appears, felt safer with more conventional and "respectable" instruments. A key grouping in this strategy is the industrial managers, who are in charge of a good part of the work force during much of its productive hours and, through the network of enterprise-controlled apartments and vacation spots, have some influence during much of its time off the job as well. As a result of this relative shift in loci of control points, the potential importance of institutionalized interest groups such as the industrial managers has increased.

A rise in actual political significance awaits, of course, the problematical increase in these groups' consciousness of their new importance and the even more problematical increase in their desire, willingness, and ability to have political effect. A decrease of workers' rights vis-a-vis management in general is apparent from a look at Soviet statements on managerial authority over workers,[16] on recent Soviet labor legislation, and some of the actions of managers toward workers. A Party journal states that "in accordance with the principle of one-man leadership the right to appoint, shift or dismiss a worker belongs exclusively to the economic manager, whether he is a member of the Party or not. . . ." And the powers of managers were magnified by the new Fundamentals of Labor Legislation put into effect in 1970.[17]

The main spheres of action in which managers' initiative has been enlarged are release from work (firing) and the application of punishments, including reduction in material incentives. The degree of freedom that managers have in this sphere shows the relative weights assigned in the political system to the goals of production and and to workers' rights and concepts such as "state of the whole people."

Reductions in Force

Most non-Soviet commentators agree that Soviet industrial managers have received a definite degree of freedom in determining the sizes of their work forces. Katz says that "perhaps the greatest freedom granted the enterprise director under the reform schema was in regard to labor," and sums up by noting that the right to fire definitely existed after 1965 but that it was not to be referred to much.[18]

The number of workers employed in the enterprises converted to the new system declines in almost all cases. Izvestiia predicted: "The economic reforms . . . will lead in a number of works to a reduction in the number of personnel." An economist warned of unemployment by noting that "as the reform develops, surpluses of manpower will increase."[19] Terms such as "surpluses of manpower" and "excess labor reserves," Soviet euphemisms for unemployment, are being used more. Layoffs began to occur as early as 1966. Theodore Frankel writes:

> Reports of fairly drastic lay-offs by the [first] 43 enterprises have been common; thus the Uglich Watch Plant released 200 employees . . .; at the

Moscow Automobile depot about 7 percent of the personnel were dismissed in quick order, and elsewhere figures went even higher.[20]

The reform has quickened and broadened this process, as indicated by the statement of a Soviet factory director who raises the question of "numbers of personnel," then says, "The success of production will be attained not by numbers, but by skill." Perhaps it is the manager's new right to fire more easily than formerly that he means when he says, "The plenum . . . has untied our hands."[21] Unequivocal Soviet statements that the reform has reduced the number of workers employed in enterprises are common. For example, N. P. Fedorenko (probably the Academician-Secretary of the Economics Department of the USSR Academy of Sciences) says that the reform has brought about an "improvement" in the use of labor, and adds:

> For the first time in many years . . . the number of industrial personnel at enterprises operating in the new way was 0.8% below the planned figure. At some enterprises the absolute number of workers declined, even though up to 1966 it had risen steadily. . . . As more enterprises are transferred to the new system, the release of manpower will increase in scale. . . .[22]

A specific example of the release of workers as a result of application of the reform is that of the Svetlana obedinenie in Leningrad, where 4,400 positions were eliminated. Three analysts ask what will happen to these displaced workers, but answer only that "further improved and more thorough social planning must provide an answer." In 1971-73 the number of workers in the Kusbass (Kuynetsk coal basin) engaged in manual and heavy physical labor was reduced by 20-30 percent, and certain types of workers in the mines by 50 percent. A definite drive for increased productivity is a major cause. For example, the Moscow railroad system fulfilled an increased volume of operations during 1965-70 while reducing the number of workers employed.[23]

Actions such as these must put a strain upon the proletarian mystique so propagated in the Soviet Union. The related violations of Soviet laws and standard procedures add another. Workers may be fired legally, but the proper notice must be given by the employer and the local trade union organization must concur. This often has not been the case. A regular plenum of the USSR Supreme Court held that ". . . instances of violations of labor legislation in the dismissal of workers at the initiative of the [plant] administration are being eliminated slowly." The results of an investigation by the RSFSR Procurator's Office indicate that illegal dismissals are "widespread." A third of worker dismissals were illegal, that is, without the concurrence of the local trade union committee. Manpower cuts are cited as one of the main motives for illegal dismissals, with violations of labor discipline and absenteeism being the others.[24] Direct causes of the rise in illegal firings must have been the implicit encouragement the reform offered to directors and the drive for increased productivity. However, an informal constraint remains-- the requirement that the manager hire as many young people as possible (the bronia). Is the manager to have a purely economic role, or is he to possess a "social conscience" or "corporate social responsibility" and be, in effect, an employment agent, too?

An important aspect of the reform does not agree with some of the long-standing social policies of the USSR. This difficulty probably will not be faced squarely until the problems caused become acute or at least more noticeable.

Discipline

A related but more general topic is what new disciplinary measures, if any, the reform allows or encourages managers to adopt in their relationship with workers, short of firing them or docking their pay or bonuses. The matter unavoidably has a certain ambiguity. At the informal level, a worker can more easily lose his place on a housing or vacation list as a result of managerial decision.[25] The reform also has increased management's powers of maintaining labor discipline, and management and higher state functionaries welcome this. For example, one personnel director has said that "the advantages of work according to the new system are obvious. Slovenly workers, slackers, drunkards, and violators of discipline and public order have felt the blow of palpable material damage." A similar attitude was expressed by the chairman of the RSFSR State Committee for the Utilization of Labor Resources, who emphasized a "broader application of material sanctions" toward rolling stones, shirkers, and drunkards. Punishment of workers for nonadherence to scheduled labor routine include the following:

- Transfer of scheduled leave to winter
- Alteration of place in housing priority list
- Deprivation of travel passes to rest homes
- Deprivation of year-end bonus.[26]

It is admitted that such techniques do not work with "some people." Of course, the usual "social" means, such as comrades' courts, are still used to maintain labor discipline. One reason that measures such as these can be applied is that the Soviet labor union fulfills some of the functions of a labor control agency and has not taken an active position in defense of the financial and political interests of laboring people for decades. At present, unions are required actively to support industrial modernization, including widespread automation.[27]

Wages and Bonuses

Under the provisions of the reform, managers may not set wages. The limited experimentation in this regard during early 1965 saw managers raising their own salaries to a disproportionate degree and fixing the wages of other personnel by reference to local conditions. Wage rates are set by the State Committee on Labor and Wages in cooperation with ministries and the Central Trade Union Council. If managers had been allowed to set wages, the generally abhorred tekuchest' rabochei sily (free movement of workers) would have increased more than it has.

The leeway in wages promised to the enterprises by the Statute has not materialized in practice. The wage situation is basically the same as it has been for many years. Not only are the enterprises' powers over wages about as limited as previously, but the much-vaunted right to work is still in reality a duty to work; a great deal of wage differentiation between workers in the same job continues to exist; and workers' wages continue to be far lower than those of the directing strata of Soviet society.[28] The long-standing rationale of a differentiated wage system under "socialism" remains.

E. C. Brown, writing of the pre-reform situation, says that the range of wage rates between the lowest and highest wage grades in "most industries" is 1:1.8 or 1:2 for work under ordinary conditions.[29] The reform may be widening this range, a development toward further material inequality that would be magnified over the long term by the Soviet system of taxation. Highly paid Soviet personnel retain a larger proportion of their incomes than do their counterparts in Western countries.[30] This statement recognizes that the earnings of skilled labor and lower-level managerial personnel and ITR are about the same. It also recognizes that workers' wages have risen slightly in particular places as a result of the reform. But this may have been effected partly by letting some workers go.

If enterprise directors cannot manipulate wages for disciplinary purposes, what of the corresponding uses of bonuses? Here more is possible. The new system has increased the directors' leeway in establishing premiums[31] and in distributing the material incentive fund. The manager or even the head of a shop may, with the "concurrence" of the trade union organization, raise or lower an individual worker's bonus by up to 25 percent.[32] This writer was told in the Soviet Union that the director can do this unilaterally. There is an assumption that personnel problems can be reduced by manipulation of material incentives. As a deputy director of one plant puts it, "the advantages of work according to the new system are obvious. Slovenly workers . . . have felt the blow of palpable material damage." As a As a result, he says, some of these workers "began running all over the place in order to rehabilitate themselves."[33] The new year-end bonus is most easily used for disciplinary purposes. "Good behavior" in all its senses is an "indispensable condition" for its receipt. At one Moscow enterprise ". . . anyone who had even one absence without leave during the year lost the right to remuneration. In the same way there was . . . no remuneration for anyone who was discharged from the plant without legitimate reasons even one day before the end of the year."[34]

Such practices were reported as standard in Leningrad. In addition, workers can be transferred to lower-paid jobs and not receive any bonuses for three months. In one plant visited in the USSR, the reason most stressed for complete denial of this bonus was drunkenness. It was mentioned there that although the decision can be made at an open meeting of a shop's workers, management may unilaterally deny the bonus for many reasons. The "educational" role of such actions was stressed as necessary and desirable.

With the manager's present powers there is nothing to prevent him from reducing his outlay on the year-end bonus through such arbitrary measures as adopting stricter policies in dealing with workers. _Izvestiia_ says that at one plant the bonus money was divided "haphazardly, without relation to anything or any system of indices. It was simply handed out on the basis of emotional and personal reasons." A predilection exists for using this year-end bonus for disciplinary purposes, as is evident from the statement that "shirkers and violators of production discipline forfeit the bonus or receive it in half the amount."[35] In effect, therefore, an additional index of "good behavior" (defined by the enterprise authorities) determines the payment of the year-end bonus.

The "thirteenth wage," although not large, appears to have provided managers with some additional leverage over workers. As one enterprise director writes: "The number of absences without leave dropped by almost 40 percent. More importantly, the losses of working time because of this reason dropped by almost three times. . . it helped to combine personal and social interests correctly."[36]

The use of bonuses led to a controversy over the question of whether material or moral incentives had the greater effect. The then "liberal" journal Novyi mir put the case for the former:

> There is no need whatever to introduce any special educative work against material incentive, to overcome its effects in the consciousness of people. This is . . ., fortunately, hopeless. It is better to look after the proper channeling of material incentives, so that they will lead a man in the same direction as the loftiest moral convictions. The economic reform points to precisely such a course. We need only move along this course, never pausing, never losing our way.[37]

The utility of material incentives to managers is shown by the fact that they were generally in favor of them, as against some academic economists who tended to emphasize the "more essential indices of a socialist economy, . . . its material and spiritual needs."[38]

But by the autumn of 1969 the conservatives began achieving some success in their endeavor to reduce the significance of individually paid incentives, a "structural change" in the incentives system justified by the argument that "such bonuses bear no relation in practice to the results of the enterprises' activity."[39] As a result, more incentive funds are being channeled to incentives distributed collectively, such as social and cultural measures and housing construction. The ideology's (and Russian culture's?) predilection for collectivism, working through old-guard bureaucrats, managers, and apparatchiki may be winning over the economy's needs for greater individual initiative. The bonus situation has returned to one not qualitatively different from the situation prior to the reform. The original proposals for workers' individualized incentives are being abandoned. This may have led to some disillusionment among Soviet workers and may necessitate even more obvious disciplinary means. However, mitigating steps have been taken, such as the exemption of the lowest paid from payment of the income tax and the raising of the minimum monthly wage.

Besides the political implications of the manager's use of bonuses, others exist and merit brief comment. Bonuses have not been large, and perhaps "insignificant,"[40] but nevertheless have been used in an attempt to slow the high rate of free movement of workers between enterprises. A worker generally receives the year-end bonus only if he has an unbroken term of service of a certain length at his present enterprise. In addition, the bonus is not paid fully unless the worker has been at the enterprise for more than seven years.

It seems also that workers with less than a year or a year and a half of service at their present enterprise receive no year-end bonus.[41]

COUNTERVAILING FORCES?

The Trade Unions

The very fact that workers' wages are being raised and the lowest-paid workers are being exempted from the modest and regressive Soviet income tax indicates that Soviet workers' views and feelings are of some concern to the political leadership. They comprise, of course, a grouping whose general dissatisfaction would be a severe hindrance, and even a potentially revolutionary force, particularly since they are the "class" on which the Soviet political system's legitimacy rests. Accordingly, much of Soviet domestic policy and propaganda is directed at the working class, and more so today than before. One goal is to derive support, as did Khrushchev, from "working class conservatism." An unavoidable contradiction in such a policy is that it may elicit a desire for meaningful participation in the making of decisions, something the Party leadership cannot agree to without relinquishing the "vanguard" theory.

Recently the trend is to increase the percentage of workers in the Party, which has been about 38 in recent years (these were workers at the time of joining). Of course, only about 8 percent of industrial workers are Communists. But reportedly 57.3 percent of the persons who joined the Party as candidate members in 1972 were workers.[42] The political weight of Soviet workers today is partially determined by the role of the trade unions in defending and expressing worker interests. The theory underlying Soviet unions' role is well-known: the interests of the proletariat are the same as those of the Party and state, and thus a clash cannot occur. The trade unions are to serve as a "school of administration, . . . and by their daily work bring conviction to the masses" and "spur the members to high productive efforts."[43] Stalin carried this much further, merging the Central Council of Trade Unions with the state's Ministry of Labor and giving the Council the Ministry's former administrative tasks.

The principal task now performed by unions is the determination of how bonuses shall be used. The unions are not rubber stamps, says David Lane. He and Mary McAuley show that conflict between workers and management occurs--for instance, on grading of jobs and dismissals--and that the "union committee plays an important part in resolving the conflict of interests." D. J. R. Scott expresses a similar viewpoint, calling the unions a "useful partial opposition, not against the purposes of the regime as a whole but against the short-term and narrowly production-oriented actions of plant managers and their less august supervisors. . . ." Abraham Katz, writing at the beginning of the reform, saw no significant change in the unions' role but suggested a possibility of a more active one, since the proposed increase in incentives and the firing of personnel would create issues for bargaining. This may occur. In Czechoslovakia in the mid-1960s, although a different case in many respects, the increase in dismissals brought trade union organs into conflict with management and even tended to revitalize them.[44]

What did several years of reform do to the role of the Soviet unions? Early 1970 saw the beginning of a production drive unprecedented during the Brezhnev-Kosygin regime and the emphasizing of a tightening of labor discipline and reliance upon "moral" incentives. The origin could only have been an internal or external problem of great magnitude: falling productivity, fear of ideological "erosion," or concern with China.

The new statute on the rights of trade union committees of September 1971 did not add any new rights. The unions' old role was affirmed more strongly than other matters in which they might have some influence. In a key issue, appointment of executive personnel, management remains substantially independent. Indeed, at least a fourth of the new statute is devoted to the powers of management. In addition to this symbolic diminution of the trade unions, others can be cited, such as the ending of trade union representation on the top level of the Central Election Commission in 1974.[45]

The speeches of A. N. Shelepin, Politburo member, give some indication of official goals for the unions. In his speech to the unions' 15th congress, he spoke about improving working conditions, making work more interesting and less tense, increasing consumer-goods production, introducing more advanced technology and automation into industrial production, and increasing both discipline and workers' participation in production decision-making. Shelepin did speak favorably of increasing material incentives, but tied their increase to a rise in labor productivity and warned of underestimating the worth of moral incentives. With the advent of the 1970s the unions' role in facilitating and quickening the introduction of automation, new technology, and management methods became salient. For example, Brezhnev said, "It is now particularly important [for unions] to study the advanced methods of . . . business management"; and Grishin called increasing the rate of technical reequipping of enterprises the unions' "most important task." Other functions that have received attention in the press are the application of "influence" against violators of labor discipline and the "education and mobilization" of workers to raise labor productivity.[46]

The trade unions have been manifestly unable to prevent illegal dismissals of workers. As a Soviet writer complains:

> Without the agreement of the trade union kollektiv, not a single worker may be dismissed. Yet trade union organs of enterprises often allow themselves to be led by the directors. In 1966 in Cheliabinsk oblast alone, the people's courts reinstated more than 300 workers who had been illegally dismissed by administrations.[47]

That the courts' involvement was necessary for reinstatement shows the uselessness of the Soviet trade union organizations in protecting workers' basic interests. In many societies the matter rarely would go to the courts; it would be decided between the union and the management, possibly after a strike, an activity allowed only very rarely in the USSR, and then briefly before being suppressed. Although Lenin considered some strikes in the USSR as justifiable and Yugoslavia allows strikes and may even legalize them, there is no prospect of this in the USSR.[48]

Participation

The beginning of an increase in unemployment and the movement to make workers learn additional jobs (the "Shchekino" experiment) both raise the possibility that workers are more desirous of protecting their interests. If the social problems caused by the economic reform are not mitigated, pressure will be felt from at least some of the workers for institutional changes in the enterprise. Given the continued existence of a powerful net of controls, such pressure cannot have much effect. Nevertheless, discussion concerning how to increase the voice of the workers in enterprise affairs occurs--for instance, a scheme of cadre appointments based upon examination by a board in which workers would have a role. Competitive selection of cadres in a construction trust in Krasnoyarsk (Krasnoiarskaluminstroi) has been described, and it seems that the board can also discuss whether an incumbent cadre ought to be removed. A further step in the same direction was made in advocating greater worker participation in the production process by adding the right of periodic election of "certain officials" in the arrangement just mentioned. Although the election of managers is said to be "premature," elections of other cadres "would aid the promotion of young specialists who display initiative and would further develop democratic methods in the management of factories."[49]

These suggestions are not on a par with the Yugoslav reality of workers' councils or the West German idea of Mitbestimmung ("codetermination"), of course. Nevertheless, though the exact way in which the working class is to share in administration is not yet clear, the fact that the issue is still open and being discussed shows both the power of a Marxian ideal and the fact that a contradiction continues to exist in the manager's relationship with his workers. For example, the fact that the subject of workers' electing managerial personnel is discussed indicates that the subject cannot be avoided. However, most managers, although they admit that such influence from below is desirable, reject its institutionalization in a way that it limits edinonachalie. But the Marxian concept of reformed work cannot be openly discarded, since to do so would allow the issue to be raised by "new left" opposition because it has a Soviet precedent in the Workers' Control set up after the Revolution.

Certainly the workers' situation is better today as a result of the improvements of the mid- and late-1950s, as McAuley points out,[50] but the progress that has been attained is probably less than what many workers would prefer. The economic reform leaves many Soviet workers in a less secure position. And, although there are tendencies that might alleviate this situation somewhat, they have not progressed far. Thus, the manager's powers over his workers are greater than formerly.

This situation cannot exist forever, even in a society partly insulated from revisionism and from the societies of Western Europe in which attempts are being made "to modify or abolish authoritarianism in industry" and "transfer . . . decision-making to employees," a process sometimes labeled "industrial democracy." This has not yet come into its own, but it is spreading (more rapidly in Europe than in the United States) and ultimately will pose yet another challenge to the official Soviet line that socialism exists in the USSR.[51]

Another challenge is that of a "mature working class." Although a mass of ex-peasants or farmers can be manipulated politically by a resourceful government, their sons and grandsons are less susceptible to such tactics and have a political viewpoint of their own that they try to actualize. As Zygmunt Bauman puts it, a thoroughly urban, better-educated, and more politically aware "new class" of workers now exists in Eastern Europe. McAuley, writing of the USSR, cites the existence of a "more stable, self-generating industrial labor force." The workers' level of education is certainly rising. In one metallurgical plant in the Chelyabinsk area during the decade 1959-69, the number of workers with a secondary education increased by 250 percent.[52] The Soviet drive to increase consumer goods and keep food in good supply, flawed as it is, indicates a concern over the possible political effects of an angry proletariat like that of Poland during the winter of 1970-71. In other words, a serious continuing problem arises out of "the very class in whose name the elite claims to rule," potentially placing the official legitimacy of the system in jeopardy. At some point workers' "participation in administration" may have to be made more meaningful in the Soviet factory. The present form, the standing or permanent production conference, is oriented much more to plan fulfillment than to incorporating workers' views into decision-making.[53]

THE AVAILABILITY OF LABOR

The seemingly simple requirement for a productive industry of having the necessary workers on the job harbors several related complexities and often is not met. Besides a labor shortage of sorts, a definite degree of dissatisfaction with jobs exists among a large percentage of workers. It is expressed in several ways, from drunkenness and pilferage to the very common flight from one job to another, causing serious difficulties for Soviet planners and industrial managers. A poll of workers in 1969 that asked "Are you intending to leave or change your job?" found that 35 percent of those queried answered in the affirmative.[54]

The Demographic Context

Soviet demographers speak of an "unfavorable demographic situation" in general. Since there are no longer any large unutilized pools of easily mobilized labor (formerly peasants and women) and "administrative measures" are no longer fully in use, workers often cannot readily be made available in a given planet. True, the 18-34 age group appears to be increasing, but youth itself offers a special set of problems for the planners of industry. Also, although the total manpower available might appear sufficient, it is migrating generally to the south, where a surplus of labor already exists, thus causing a "negative migration balance." The USSR is coming to be a land of two different population areas: the West and East with a decreasing rate of population growth, and the Southeast with a sharply rising rate of growth.[55]

The population is growing, but this in itself does not alleviate the shortage of labor in particular places. One demographer speaks of a "rapidly aging" population and an "unprecedented" decline in the birth rate in the Russian republic. During 1950-67 the overall birth rate declined by 34.8 percent.[56] Although others give a different rate, all writers cite a decline, both in the birth rate and in the reproduction index. As a result, the Director of the Central Institute for Labor Resources has been led to declare: "If, during the 9th FYP, the birthrate does not increase, after 1985 we can expect not an increase but a decline in the quantity of labor available."[57]

It is therefore not surprising that the current drive to increase labor productivity receives so much attention. It has been calculated that the growth of labor productivity in industry by only 1 percent will increase output as much as would adding 300,000 people to the work force.[58] Births are being encouraged as well. Family allowances for children have been raised, and all working women are now to have fully paid maternity leave regardless of their length of service.

Labor Shortage and Labor Turnover

The shortage of labor in Soviet industry is of course not solely the result of a curve for a falling birth rate crossing that of a rising industrial growth rate. It results as well from specific policies of the state's planners and also from particular patterns of behavior engaged in by large numbers of persons of working age.

Besides an insufficiency of workers, many plants are plagued by a high degree of labor turnover. Whether or not the degree of turnover is greater than that in other industrialized societies is not as important as the fact that in the USSR it is a serious social and economic problem. The shortage itself is commented on widely and in the most serious tones. A high official of the state committee charged with studying and maintaining labor resources states: "If one were to assemble enterprise directors from various branches of industry and ask them what worried them most of all, probably a good half of them would answer the shortage of people."[59]

He blames this problem on the loss of the "territorial aspect," a code term for the sovnarkhozy, and the re-creation of ministries with autarkic goals. The ministries act in a "narrowly departmental way" in siting new enterprises in large cities without regard for the labor supply, creating a "labor shortage for these enterprises before they start operation." Of course, typically for a developed economy, much of the unfulfilled demand is for skilled labor, a factor encouraging a high degree of turnover for workers in this category. Coercive and standard mobilization techniques cannot increase the labor supply because there is no longer a large pool of unused labor.[60]

Besides the "departmental" operations of ministries, other causes can be cited, such as the misuse of manpower. Excessive construction and delays in its completion tie up many workers. Managers' fears that the "ratchet" may be applied to their plans prompt them to keep extra labor on hand. The same effect stems from the unevenness of supply. The organization of agriculture and the level of investment, both capital and social, in it also are involved. There is no objective need for approximately 30 percent of the Soviet labor force working the land. The introduction of the zveno ("link") system in agriculture would release labor, as would the dissolution of the collective farms, admittedly a most unlikely prospect.

Besides the policies of the Soviet state, the individual Soviet worker is creating local labor shortages on his own. He is "voting with his feet" (or his motorcycle) for a better job situation. This is particularly true on construction projects, where many workers break their contracts and leave without even picking up their labor books. For example, of one group of 215 workers recruited by Orgnabor (the organized labor recruiting service) for a project in the Ukraine, only 116 completed their terms of work. One-quarter to one-third of the workers in Moscow and the Upper Volga region leave their jobs annually.[61] No attempt is now made to control this flow or to trace people who have walked off the job. The reasons why workers leave their jobs are varied. Higher pay is not always a factor. Often working conditions and safety practices are uppermost. Sometimes the time spent in commuting is mentioned. Other contributing factors include an insufficiency of housing (particularly in Siberia), too little mechanization of low-paid work, unsubstantiated promises made by management, and the chance to improve one's pay by changing jobs. As one city Party secretary notes: "In certain places the freedom of action resulting from the economic reform is utilized harmfully. . . . Certain enterprises seem to be competing in an attempt to outdo one another in regard to wages."[62] A most ironic contributing factor is the contradictory policy of continuing to build new plants while existing ones lack sufficient workers.

The dimensions of the problem can be perceived easily. First, in any year the "mobile labor force" is composed of approximately four million persons, whereas Orgnabor handles only 130,000 persons per year. The First Party Secretary of Azerbaidzhan has complained of a labor turnover rate of 25 percent, said to be higher than in 1965. In 1973 Izvestiia used Kuibyshev oblast as an example and noted:

> At some enterprises . . . one fifth of all employees quit their jobs in 1971. Over 18,000 individuals passed through the job placement office alone, about 11,000 of them having been away from work for a week to a month. . . . Hundreds of thousands of working days were thus lost, and this at a time when a manpower shortage has forced equipment to operate at less than capacity.... .[63]

This "fluidity" of labor undercuts Soviet "planning" and raises the need for remedial action. Many suggestions have been advanced in hopes of putting together a solution. They range from such general statements such as the equalization of living standards over the country as a whole to enforcing through new laws a prohibition upon managers hiring workers not in possession of their labor books or requiring workers to conclude contracts with their employer for periods of "at least six months or a year." (But a similar rule for workers recruited by Orgnabor has never been effective.) Most suggestions seem to be general ones, including raising the level of automation and mechanization; increasing labor productivity and social investment in rural areas; hiring women and retired persons for part-time work (here United States practice is cited); providing new housing, schools, stores, and other social amenities to fill the needs of workers at new plants; correlating the labor demands of new enterprises being built in the same area; and encouraging work done at home and on farms.[64] An interesting set of programs, begun to a slight degree, is the releasing of workers as a result of the application of automation, retraining them with pay during the training period, and directing them to work for which they are suited through a new system of job exchanges. This set of measures is facing opposition from the advocates of the reintroduction of additional "administrative measures" directed against letany ("flitters").[65]

The call for a tougher stance has not taken hold as general policy but remains confined in its application to specific, local instances. Some effort also is being expended to apply methods used in the West in attempting to fit workers to jobs rationally and, hopefully, lastingly. This is based on a policy of utilizing psychological means of coping with social problems while continuing to reject Freudian psychoanalytic theory on the ground that it ignores social factors. Vocational guidance and occupational aptitude examinations are examples, but as yet are applied only in a very limited way. Their widescale and effective use would require greatly increased social investment, a qualitative change in national priorities, and the introduction of such radical measures as job rotation, the limitation of assembly-line techniques, and the creation of democracy in the plant. Even in the West these concepts have been given scant attention, although some are now being applied.

The as yet unsolved fundamental problem is providing a post-Stalinist system of getting trained workers to places where they are needed and making their stay attractive. In order to create a new labor situation in which these conditions will be met, the Soviet central planners are proceeding on different tracks, including using automation to increase labor productivity and setting up labor exchanges and retraining programs for the placement of the workers who have lost their jobs in this process. These policies have not been coordinated, however, nor do they offer an immediate solution. For one thing, the labor exchanges are being established only now, years after the economic reform began. In addition, the excess of demand on the Soviet labor market hinders attempts to plan labor resources because this mobile labor force is not under the control of the central planning authorities. One unintended consequence is unemployment (by which is meant the nonemployment of a person willing and able to work who was previously employed).

THE REFORM, AUTOMATION, AND UNEMPLOYMENT

The Problem

One of the social processes set in motion by the reform is unemployment and the consequent need, given the assumptions of the Soviet ideology, to eliminate it. That the reform is causing social problems is recognized in the USSR. Indeed, conferences have been held on the theme "social problems of the economic reform." An important social aspect of the reform is the decrease in the work forces of converted enterprises. It is accepted that "as the reform develops, surpluses of manpower will increase"--that is, unemployment will occur. It can no longer be said that "the Soviet worker . . . has no fear of unemployment." No doubt it is the new right to fire more easily that one manager means when he says, "The plenum [of September 1965] . . . has untied our hands."[66]

The firing of workers need not necessarily lead to unemployment in an economy like that of the USSR. However, the demand for labor there, high as it is, in mainly for skilled labor and for persons to fill jobs in the growing new service sector. Since so many jobs in the USSR have long been for unskilled workers, such as loaders and unloaders, the present large-scale application of automation and other new technology is freeing many unskilled workers, who in the absence of a nationwide and effective system of retraining, labor exchanges, and unemployment compensation are becoming a small "reserve army of the unemployed," although perhaps only for a few months. Thus there is no inconsistency between the simultaneous demand for labor and the existence of unemployment. This result is not unique in Communist Eastern Europe. Economic reforms in Czechoslovakia and Yugoslavia led to unemployment. In Yugoslavia a record 9 percent reported unemployment appeared. (It would have been greater without the large-scale migration of Yugoslav workers to West Germany, Sweden, and elsewhere.) The same phenomenon appeared elsewhere as reforms of varying kinds were tried (for instance, in Poland). In Czechoslovakia dismissed workers had trouble finding new jobs in an economy that was being reordered, like that of the Soviet Union, to emphasize labor productivity, quality, and profits. This had political consequences.[67]

What is new is the scale of unemployment. Some degree existed in the Soviet Union during the 1920s, following 1953 and Stalin's death, and again just prior to the beginning of the reform (1965). In addition, "forms of 'partial,' 'concealed,' or 'frictional' unemployment, together with frequent periods of idle-standing in factories, have all played their part in the life of the Soviet working man." There are no unemployment relief payments; the dismissed worker has received no more than two weeks' wages or two weeks' notice.[68] The reform intensified the phenomenon and created a new double-edged problem, since it had long been an axiom that unemployment did not exist in the Soviet Union, although, as E. C. Brown says, "Soviet denial of unemployment is, in considerable part, a matter of definition." Since 1930 no relief has been provided for the unemployed unless "enforced absenteeism" obtains (that is, unjust dismissal or arrest on a criminal charge later proved false).[69]

The decline in the number of workers employed in the enterprises converted to the new system is general. Soviet sources often state explicitly that this is occurring. For example: "The economic reforms ... will lead in a number of works to a reduction in the number of personnel." The process was apparent even in 1966. A top Soviet economist cites a difference of 0.8 percent below the planned increase in workers for reformed enterprises.[70] One journal gave some limited unemployment figures when it noted in 1967 that the reform was causing the "hidden dismissal of workers" in a situation of "shrinking" job opportunities as the reform spread throughout industry. In Rostov on Don the number of persons seeking employment rose from 7,900 in 1965 to 10,100 in 1966. Thus, turnover was becoming unemployment, with an average of 30 days lost between jobs and much more in retraining (when it exists) and adjusting to new jobs.[71]

A large-scale release of workers occurred at the Svetlana obedinenie in Leningrad, where 4,400 positions were eliminated as a result of various reform measures. Eight hundred and fifty of these positions were removed during one year. As to what happened to these displaced workers, it is stated only that "further improved and more thorough social planning must provide an answer." According to one enterprise director writing in 1973, "Some people stay unemployed for years"--some of them, interestingly, making their own employment on a small-scale private enterprise basis. "Great tact [and] the ability to convince" the workers that no such problem exists is required of Party organizations.[72] Perhaps the number of unemployed would be as high as a few million if registration schemes similar to those in effect in Western Europe and the United States were adopted. (Of course the anti-parasite laws would hinder registration, as would the stigma imposed by the ideology.) It would be fascinating and important to know what percentage of Soviet unemployed resulted from the implementation of the reform. One of the main causes of unemployment is a "spin-off" of the reform: automation and the wide application of new labor-saving technology in production.

Automation

The automation of production processes is an increasingly important aspect of Soviet industry, and it is being introduced rapidly and widely. One reason the Soviet Union is bringing in private foreign firms to build key new plants is to have automated production lines in them that will, it is hoped, serve as sources for a continuing Soviet effort along the same lines. Automation in Soviet industry antedates the reform, but the reform has fostered its rapid and wide application. Although initially in this process many displaced workers found other work within the same plant, this solution eventually becomes impossible because it runs into the constraints of later stages of automation (plants operated by a few or even one worker) and various social limitations. Studies have shown that in metallurgical and machinery plants during 1960-62, up to 20 percent of the workers were discharged. This level of retention does not seem to be possible now.[73]

The application of automation is part of a plan to reduce the over-utilization of labor in Soviet industry, particularly in intra-plant transport and auxiliary work. Pravda, commenting on the ninth plan, stated: "The replacement of manual labor with mechanized labor . . . will be conducted on a broad scale." The Party plant organizations are heavily involved in this, even utilizing "everyday supervision."[74] The state machinery is committed as well. In 1969 the USSR Council of Ministers adopted a resolution on the "accelerated development" of automated lines for several branches, with the aim of quadrupling the production of such lines in four years. The number of workers using automated machine tools and other automated devices rose by 245 percent during 1959-69, while the number involved with mechanized work increased by 172 percent.[75]

It is too early to evaluate the total effects of automation. The press presents its social effects as beneficial to the worker (citing, of course, the lighter work of those who are retained). The economic effects also are not clear. Quantifiable results are said to be "still small" in relation to the Soviet economy's requirements for them. Poor planning is cited. There seems, also, to be a lack of workers qualified to handle the new systems, and accordingly a new system of production education is called for.[76]

Eventually a complex of measures will be required to deal with the social effects of automation if they are to be handled adequately. Studies have indicated that although automation reduces physical strain for workers, it may raise the level of nervous and mental strain.[77] Only a few reservations concerning the effects of automation have been expressed in the USSR. Of course, as H. A. Simon points out, "the level of employment in a society is not related in any direct or necessary way to the level of automation in that society"; and it is even probable that automation ultimately produces some socially desirable effects. However, this would be so only when "the social and economic institutions are . . . moderately well adapted to their functions of regulating production and distribution."[78] These conditions may not yet apply to the Soviet Union, particularly in terms of coping with the challenges posed by an emerging post-industrial society.

THE SHCHEKINO EXPERIMENT

Another factor contributing to unemployment is the practice of retaining in an enterprise only those workers who are able to master several jobs, firing the others, and using the share of the wage fund thus obtained for higher wages for the workers who remain in exchange for productivity agreements. The pertinent elements are the following:

- Devising and introducing "progressive work norms"
- Combining jobs
- Extending duty zones
- Mechanizing labor-intensive work.[79]

This pattern began at the Shchekino chemical combine in Tula oblast in the Ukraine during 1967, and has been a widely publicized model for much of Soviet industry since the Party Central Committee approved the experiment and its results in the fall of 1969. The pattern is now officially part of the reform; Shchekino has been praised for "creatively implementing the economic reform." _Izvestiia_ says that it "lies wholly within the channels of the economic reform."[80] This is another example of changing and broadening of the reform.

It appears that at least 12-13 percent of the combine's work force of approximately 8,000 was let go by 1972. The layoffs are continuing; by 1973, 1,268 persons had been "freed" (825 workers and 243 engineers). Claims are made for an increase in labor productivity of 167 percent by early 1973, with an increase of 15.5 percent during 1972. Output is said to have increased by 83 percent over the three years 1968-70. Economies of the wage fund also resulted, possibly of more than 1 million rubles, with half going to workers retained and the rest going to ITR and management as premia. By 1971 the combine entered the second, more intensive stage of the experiment, the goal being to increase output, productivity, and profits by more than 1.5 times over six years while maintaining the present personnel strength. This may be possible with additional automation and high morale of the work force.[81]

The number of workers who had difficulty finding new work is not known, even approximately. Fragmentary references indicate that nearly 500 former workers were transferred to construction sites in the Moscow region.[82] Even in 1969 the model was being applied in 23 other enterprises, with strong backing from high political levels. An example that has received some publicity is the Chelyabinsk metallurgical plant, where 1,305 persons were released over three years. In one cold-rolling shop, 6 of 35 workers were dismissed (approximately 18 percent), the 29 remaining receiving 20 percent more than the basic rate of pay. Of the 211 who had been discharged, 193 were sent to "places where the shortage of cadres is most acute" (the far north, eastern Siberia?). It seems that much of the oil-refining and petrochemical industry was affected by 1972. Other examples exist.[83]

However, the pattern is not necessarily the wave of the future. S. Novozhilov, the Deputy Chairman of the State Committee on Labor and Wages, has pointed out that implementing it in its present form may be "hasty" in some instances; enterprises already working near maximum efficiency cannot reduce staffs greatly. Shchekino seems to have been very overstaffed. Nevertheless, pressure to go forward is noticeable.[84] Enterprises near those that adopt the pattern are criticized for not immediately following suit. But it is not clear how far the experience can be implemented in industries not having continuous-flow processes like those in the petrochemical industry.

The experience does stand out as an unusual example of a rare Soviet lead in innovation in industrial life. Comparable American examples are rare.[85] A significant change in industry that is directed at increasing productivity and profits has been made palatable to the efficient workers. It seems a latter-day version of P. Stolypin's wager on the "hardy and the strong." The workers who were less able or unwilling to accept the new demands seem to have joined a strange category--socialist casualties of the post-industrial age. There will no doubt be more of them. As early as 1965 a poll of recently hired workers in four large plants in Gorky revealed that 12 percent had been out of work more than one month and that 16 percent had not been employed for up to 30 days.[86]

AMELIORATION OR SOLUTION?

Despite the lack of long-term means to cope with unemployment, a number of proposed solutions for the problem have appeared. Some of them involve the creation of new institutions and regularized procedures. In addition, a beginning is being made in the study of the reasons for unemployment and of possible ways to find jobs for dismissed workers.

One writer suggested the organization of a state service to keep records concerning unemployment and to distribute manpower resources--"a state organization for the redistribution of the work force," or labor exchanges. Another interesting proposal was to pay men undergoing retraining after dismissal. This may be a covert plea for the reinstitution of unemployment benefits. (For long only two weeks' severance pay was given.) This was justified by citing the paying of former drivers of steam locomotives about half their previous earnings while they were undergoing retraining as electric train engineers.[87] In order to eliminate some difficulties in transferring workers from one industry to another, a standardized system of general training of workers was advocated. As usual, suggestions for the development of local industries and public services, and also the expansion of industrial construction in the smaller cities, appeared. One economist proposed

> . . . study of methods of forecasting supply and demand for labor ahead of time; . . . a hierarchical state information service on labor requirements; a nationwide system for the retraining of labor resources; study of the question of the possible absorption of the personnel being released in the sphere of agriculture and personnel services. . . .[88]

At present, steps are being taken to institutionalize the regularization of worker dismissals, the retraining of those dismissed, and the expeditious and proper placement (and relocation) of the unemployed. No clear line of development seems to have occurred in regularizing dismissals, although the workers who remain apparently are better paid than before the reduction in force. Their housing and vacation benefits also have improved. Of course, these are the "most skilled and experienced cadres."[89]

There is recognition that the legal relations between workers, enterprises, and the new local agencies for job placement need clarification. The most positive proposal would eliminate the onus and legal difficulties connected with the loss of a position by recording in the dismissed worker's labor book "dismissed because of elimination of the job due to the introduction of new technology."[90] Related suggestions include advance warning of termination, severance pay, and the transfer of vacation time and seniority earned.

Plans for retraining those dismissed in connection with automation are now in preparation. There is recognition that the problem of rational distribution and use of labor cannot be solved without action in this regard. Although K. Novikov speaks of the need for "systematic" retraining, this has not progressed much beyond study. Some limited change is apparent for workers and white-collar employees "released as a result of improvements in the administrative apparatus." Since 1970 these personnel have received "average earnings" for up to three months while being retrained.[91] Much more is being done on the problem of placing dismissed workers. Although in the recent past this function was performed by the local Party organization and other agencies, such as offices of the Soviets, it was not carried out efficiently. Too many agencies were engaged in finding jobs and assigning people for there to be any uniformity of policy. This deficiency was coupled with the lack of precise knowledge about the factors causing fluidity and the ideological proclivity to minimize the employment problem.

The new departments of local Soviets charged with labor resources are of questionable effectiveness. They are not yet a part of the new hierarchical system of republic-level state committees for labor resources ordered established by a joint resolution of the Central Committee of the CPSU and the USSR Council of Ministers of December 22, 1966.[92] These committees operate labor exchanges that formerly were virtually nonexistent (in 1966 there were only two in the whole USSR, one in Armenia and the other in Gorky). They also are to replace Orgnabor. The exchanges or bureaus were authorized for every city of over 100,000 population in the Russian republic. However, they have been dealing with only a small fraction of the fricitionally unemployed, and lack executive power.[93] In addition, a new Department of Labor Resources has been set up within the USSR Gosplan to study labor resources on a national scale and to organize an inter-republic information service. Significantly, no new nationwide scheme of unemployment compensation exists. (There was a patchwork system prior to 1930.)

In the "next few years" (blizhaishie gody) the new agencies are to relieve enterprise management completely of the task of finding jobs for dismissed workers, a difficult goal to attain. In 1968 the new agencies in the RSFSR alone received applications from more than 600,000 people (up from 243,000 in 1967).[94] Proposals for solutions have called, among other things, for requiring enterprises planning to dismiss workers to give the labor agencies several months' notification, and for granting the new agencies the right to issue binding orders to enterprises on hiring policy.[95] (This last proposal could lead to the reimposition of central control over the size of the enterprise's work force, a partial negation or "correction" [?] of the reform.)

Recent reports indicate that some of the new employment exchanges or bureaus have had some success in reducing time spent unemployed. The bureau in Kaluga succeeded in cutting the average time locally between jobs from 24 to 13 days. In addition, turnover has been reduced somewhat. Following the principle that "order begins with control," it was made difficult for a plant to hire anyone other than a person referred to it by a bureau, although by early 1974 it seems that the free market in labor was too important to production to be easily limited.[96] Ideological considerations preclude the possibility of adopting the imaginative attempts at solving unemployment allowed by the Hungarians and Yugoslavs, particularly the latter. Some limited temporary relief would be derived by allowing Soviet workers to go to East Germany or even Western Europe for work. Some 100,000 Hungarian workers went to East Germany in the late 1960s, and about 300,000 Yugoslavs were in Western Europe.

THE YOUNG WORKERS

One of the most important questions for the manager-worker relationship is that of the young worker--a fashionable or even faddish topic in all discussions of mature industrial or post-industrial societies. Nevertheless, it has real significance for the future pattern of authority and communication in Soviet industrial enterprises. High school graduates tend to spurn blue-collar work, preferring to enter higher education (not easy in the USSR) or take some sort of white-collar work. The pyramid of job desires is the reverse of the pyramid of existing jobs.[97] A more-educated work force also necessitates a greater use of explanation and justification for orders.[98] This is analogous to the general drift of things in Western Europe and the United States.

Many young workers are in an undesirable work situation and consequently are dissatisfied; those who have finished high school find it difficult to accept the menial jobs often given them, especially when these jobs are likely to be automated out of existence in the near future. Indeed, there are jobs for only a fraction of high school graduates.[99] The situation of the young workers was brought home to this writer while touring a large Soviet industrial plant that manufactures electric generators. Noticing that all the workers were in their forties or over, I asked, "Where are the young workers?" and was told, "Oh, they're over making the little stuff." Seniority and its perquisites are common, of course, but they can be overemphasized. Some discussions of youth in industry reveal that a notable percentage of new young workers have come into industry from a sheltered and perhaps overly academic background, with little or no preparation for the unreformed realities of the Soviet production line. It should be no surprise that some do not fit in or accept the worker's role. These workers are not counted in establishing productivity figures, thus making them more acceptable to managers.

It is plain that the Soviet labor force is involved in some of the same processes common to labor forces in the West. One of these is the dissatisfactions, including boredom, generated by modern industrial processes, particularly automated ones. Serious discussion of the technical revolution and its social consequences is now under way in the Soviet Union. Suggestions for coping with and alleviating the problems of the young worker include providing better and more realistic information for youth about job opportunities (implying the development of guidance counseling in the schools?); fitting new worker and job more closely, partly through the use of psychological testing;[100] the use of industrial sociology (as begun in the United States four or more decades ago) to improve the work environment; and, some say, indoctrinating students on work as a duty, thus deemphasizing the vague promises of work as a right while at the same time elevating the prestige of blue-collar work. In addition, some steps have been taken to strengthen the legal protection of the Soviet worker although it is not clear how the "additional restrictions" on illegal dismissals of workers that the new Fundamentals on Labor Legislation are said to offer actually are working out.[101] However, without workers' interest groups having some role in the making of labor legislation and a lot more besides, legal prescriptions for the protection of the worker are likely to be widely flouted. The correction of abuses after the fact is not an answer.

CONCLUSION

Several related aspects of the Soviet economic reform as it affects the worker have been discussed. It is evident that managers retain strong powers vis-a-vis their workers and have some new ones; that although incentives for workers have been increased in value and made more numerous, it is difficult for the worker to gain much from them; that the reform has exacerbated certain problems connected with the Soviet labor force (notably fluidity of workers and unemployment); and that although some proposals for solution have been advanced, the effect of their recent implementation is not yet clear.

Despite the concern of the political elite for the workers, the efforts of Party organizations to encourage managers to engage in socialist competition and to "make more efficient use of labor resources" (firing some workers) by copying the Shchekino model and adding more automation reveal a powerful, politically based push for conditions that might make the workers' condition a more demanding one.

If the economic reform brought the workers some easily visible, tangible benefit, it might help mobilize them to work harder. Such a benefit may appear, but it has not yet done so. Since the reform has benefited management most, with the weight of the Party allowing this in deed although not in word, it is just possible that the classic relationship between employer and wage earner may begin to reemerge, this time under Soviet-style socialism. This occurred in Czechoslovakia, where the reform tended to revitalize the trade union organs as a sort of "countervailing power" against the concentration of new powers in management's hands.

Perhaps one way to give workers a real "stake" in the new arrangement would be to make premia or bonuses a larger share of workers' total wages. This, however, would appeal only to those who are already motivated to work faster and better, and would come into conflict with the widespread desire for egalitarianism that exists and to a degree has been met in the USSR. If bonuses have already been used to their maximum effect, then only a systemic change might motivate the workers further.

If the Soviet state is unable to solve the social problems caused by the economic reform, pressure likely will be felt from at least some of the workers for institutional changes in the enterprise, and perhaps beyond. Given the continued existence of a powerful net of politically based, all-encompassing controls, it is unlikely that such pressure will have much result. Although an "amorphous social force" can have some effect, at least in precipitating talk, certainly the election of managers is "premature," as is even that of staff people. There is no sign of workers' councils.

It is evident that many Soviet workers are in a less secure position than formerly as a result of the reform. And, although there are tendencies that might alleviate this situation somewhat, they have not progressed far. The manager's powers over his workers are greater than formerly, and the present course of "progressive" Soviet discussion of the managerial relationship with workers does not posit a fundamentally new set of power relationships within the enterprise that would be favorable to worker interests. The manager has gained the most in the manager-worker relationship, and therefore in this relationship the model has been confirmed much more than it has been negated. Thus "moderate modernizing," not "liberalizing," has been the basic principle or process at work. Soviet industrial organization and its operating principles are still based upon "capitalistic" or classical industrial structures, such as the division of labor and the appropriation of surplus value, although this fact is ibscured by ideological rhetoric and formulations. Without the institutionalization of a new conception of industrialized society and its needs and capabilities that will allow the prediction and solution of social problems such as those of the workers, the economic reform will only produce further social problems.

NOTES

1. See Emily Clark Brown, Soviet Trade Unions and Labor Relations (Cambridge, Mass.: Harvard University Press, 1966) and Leonard Joel Kirsch, Soviet Wages (Cambridge, Mass.: M.I.T. Press, 1972), esp. Ch. VII.

2. N. Rodionov, "Partiinie komitety i sblizhenie nauki s proizvodstvom," Kommunist 9 (June 1970): 18; Moscow Domestic, April 14, 1971, 15:30 (FBIS, April 15, 1971, p. J1); Gertrude E. Schroeder, "Soviet Economic Reform at an Impasse," Problems of Communism 20, no. 4 (July-August 1971): 46; and New York Times, December 14, 1972, and February 4, 1973, citing Ekonomicheskaia gazeta and Izvestiia, respectively. Also see V. Moev, "Forward in Reverse," Literaturnaia gazeta 46 (November 12, 1969): 10, translated in FBIS, November 20, 1969, p. C5.

3. Abram Bergson, "Development under Two Systems," World Politics 23, no. 4 (July 1971): 593; and Jan S. Prybyla, "The Soviet Economy: an Overview," Current History 63, no. 374 (October 1972): 178.

4. Milovan Djilas, The Unperfect Society (New York: Harcourt, Brace & World, 1969), p. 188; and Zbigniew K. Brzezinski, Between Two Ages (New York: Viking, 1970), p. 152.

5. Pravda, September 5, 1971; translated in CDSP 23, no. 36 (October 5, 1971): 2. Also see Sotsialisticheskaia industriia, July 1, 1969, p. 1. Some of the newspaper's personnel were drawn from the staff of Ekonomicheskaia gazeta. I spoke to some of the editorial staff in July 1969.

6. Ekonomicheskaia gazeta 5 (1968): 12, citing the head of the Ukrainian Gosplan. Cited in Michael Ellman, Economic Reform in the Soviet Union (London: Political and Economic Planning, 1969), p. 317, note.

7. Christian Duevel, "Comparison of October Slogans--1970-1971," Radio Liberty Dispatch, October 21, 1971, p. 3; and his "Comparison of October Slogans--1969-1970," October 21, 1970, p. 5.

8. Pravda, September 5, 1971 (translated in CDSP 23, no. 36 [October 5, 1971]: 3-4); Pravda, December 9, 1972; Izvestiia, October 14, 1972 (excerpted in CDSP 24, no. 41 [November 8, 1972]: 20); and Pravda, September 27, 1972 (condensed in CDSP 24, no. 39 [October 25, 1972]: 26).

9. See Moscow domestic Russian, November 27, 1970, 16:00 (FBIS 3 [November 30, 1970]: B17-18); Pravda, March 1972 (reported in New York Times, March 21, 1972); and Keith Bush, The Implementation of the Economic Reform, Research Paper no. 36 (Munich: Radio Liberty, 1970), p. 11.

10. Kirsch, op. cit., pp. 151-52.

11. V. V. Godunov, Vvedenie v teoriiu upravleniia (Moscow: "Ekonomika," 1967), p. 62.

12. A. M. Birman, Nekotorye problemy nauki upravleniia narodnym khoziaistvom (Moscow: "Ekonomika," 1965), p. 85.

13. Jerry Hough, The Soviet Prefects (Cambridge, Mass.: Harvard University Press, 1969), pp. 82, 86.

14. A. Akhundov, "Sovetskii khoziaistvennik," Kommunist 17 (November 1965): 31; and an interview with the head of the promotdel of Pravda vostoka (Tashkent), June 7, 1969. Akhundov was then the First Secretary of the Party organization in Azerbaidzhan.

15. Birman, op. cit., p. 85; and V. Zhuravlev, "Distsiplina truda na predpriiatii," Sotsialisticheskii trud 4 (April 1967): 94.

16. See, for example, the speeches of A. Snechkus, the First Secretary of Lithuania, in Sovetskaia Litva, December 8, 1970; and of V. Tolstikov (former Party Secretary of Leningrad), Leningrad Domestic Russian, February 6, 1969, 15:00 (FBIS, March 24, 1969, p. C3).

17. A. Plokhotnikov, "'Kak reshat' vopros o kadrakh?" Partiinaia zhizn' 9 (May 1968): 32, quoted in J. P. Hardt and T. Frankel, "The Industrial Managers," in H. G. Skilling and F. Griffiths, eds., Interest Groups in Soviet Politics (Princeton, N.J.: Princeton University Press, 1971), p. 197. Also see Izvestiia, January 30, 1971, p. 1.

18. See, for example, E. Zaleski, Planning Reforms in the Soviet Union, 1962-1966 (Chapel Hill: University of North Carolina Press, 1967), p. 153; and Abraham Katz, The Politics of Economic Reform in the Soviet Union (New York: Praeger, 1972), pp. 136-37.

19. Izvestiia, March 19, 1967, p. 2; and P. Bunich, in Ekonomika i matematicheskie metody 6 (November-December 1966): 805, quoted in "Clear Warning of Unemployment," Radio Liberty Dispatch, January 25, 1967.

20. Theodore Frankel, "Economic Reform: A Tentative Appraisal," Problems of Communism 17, no. 3 (May-June 1967): 34.
21. Pravda, October 6, 1965, p. 2. The author is director of the important Lenin Nevsky machine-building plant.
22. N. P. Fedorenko, "Reforma v promyshlennosti . . .," Planovoe khoziaistvo 4 (April 1967): 8.
23. A. Dumachev, I. Chuev, and A. Kurilov, "Kazhdomu kollektivu--chetkuiu perspektivu," Ekonomicheskaia gazeta 17 (April 1967): 15; Sotsialisticheskai industriia, June 1, 1971, p. 1; and Moskovskaia pravda, November 21, 1970, p. 1.
24. Izvestiia, September 21, 1969, p. 4; and Iu. Leonov, "Illegal Dismissals," Sotsialisticheskaia zakonnost' 3 (March 1969) (JPRS 48,026 [May 13, 1969]: 37-38).
25. Trud, August 13, 1969, p. 1; and G. I. Zinchenko and M. N. Laptin, Zainteresovannost', otvetstvennost' i distsiplina (Moscow: "Znanie," 1966), p. 71.
26. Zhuravlev, op. cit., p. 96; and K. Novikov, "Problemy effektivnogo ispol'zovaniia trudovykh resursov," Kommunist 13 (September 1969): 103 (translated in CDSP 21, no. 38 [October 15, 1969]: 3-7). See also Pravda, October 10, 1970, p. 3.
27. John N. Hazard, The Soviet System of Government (4th ed., rev.; Chicago: University of Chicago Press, 1968), p. 195; Sovetskaia Rossiia, April 18, 1965; and see the speech by V. A. Kirillin to the plenum of the AUCCTU (All-Union Central Council of Trade Unions) in October 1968, in Trud, October 2, 1968.
28. Kirsch, op. cit., p. 149; and Arvid Brodersen, The Soviet Worker (New York: Random House, 1966), p. 103.
29. Brown, op. cit., p. 298. This agrees with Alec Nove, The Soviet Economy (rev. ed.; New York: Praeger, 1966), p. 122.
30. Brodersen, op. cit., pp. 104, 111.
31. Kirsch, op. cit., pp. 146, 151.
32. Article 8 of "Tipovoe polozhenie o premirovanii rabotnikov promyshlennykh predpriiatii, perevodimykh na novuiu sistemu planirovaniia i ekonomicheskogo stimulirovaniia proizvodstva," Ekonomicheskaia gazeta 8 (February 1967): 9-10. This is the fundamental normative document on bonuses.
33. Zhuravlev, op. cit., p. 96. Zhuravlev is the deputy director for personnel of the important Lenin-Nevskii machine-building plant in Leningrad. Also see Iu. Margulis, Finansy SSSR 9 (September 1967): 45-50; JPRS 43,514 (November 30, 1967): 34.
34. I. Kurtynin, "Kollektivnaia otvetstvennost' . . .," Sotsialisticheskii trud 5 (May 1967)
35. See the article by G. Popov, Leningrad's First Secretary, in Pravda, February 8, 1970. Izvestiia, October 1, 1969, p. 5 (translated in CDSP 21, no. 40 [October 29, 1969]: 22). Also see

A. Brailovskii and M. Abramson, "Novaia sistema v deistvii," Planovoe khoziaistvo 7 (July 1966): 53.

36. Izvestiia, October 1, 1969, p. 5, on the Moscow thermal equipment plant.

37. O. Latsis, "Net iskliucheniia bez pravila," Novyi mir 4 (April 1967): 172.

38. Oktiabr' 8 (August 1968): 191-202; JPRS 46,495 (September 23, 1968): 1-20.

39. Izvestiia, October 22, 1969, p. 3; (translated in CDSP 21, no. 43 [November 19, 1969]: 26). Interestingly, views favoring increases in material incentives continued to be expressed, as in Izvestiia, February 11, 1971, p. 3.

40. See the complaints in Sovetskaia Belorussia, October 20, 1970, pp. 2-3. Also see I. Kvachakhiia, "Material'naia zainteresovannost'...," Zaria vostoka (Tbilisi), September 7, 1966, p. 3 (JPRS 39,108 [December 14, 1966]: 85); "Vnedriat' novuiu sistemu, sovershenstvovat' pokazateli planirovaniia," Planovoe khoziaistvo 7 (July 1966): 32; and A. P. Koloshin, in Promyshlennost' Belorussii, January 1969, pp. 10-18 (JPRS 47,721 [March 26, 1969]: 10-11).

41. Brailovskii and Abramson, op. cit., p. 53. Also see L. Ovseevich and P. Grodinskii, "Nekotorye problemy perekhoda na novuiu sistemu planirovaniia," Planovoe khoziaistvo 6 (June 1966): 69.

42. Pravda, February 19, 1973, p. 1; reported in New York Times, February 20, 1973. Also see David Lane, Politics and Society in the USSR (New York: Random House, 1971), pp. 135 (Table 8A), 136; and Solomon M. Schwarz, "Education and the Working Class," Survey no. 65 (October 1967): 34.

43. V. I. Lenin, "Polnoe sobranie sochinenii," Collected Works XXXII (Moscow: Gos.iyd-vo polit. lit-ry, 1965), p. 20; and John N. Hazard, Communists and Their Law (Chicago: University of Chicago Press, 1969), pp. 370, 372-73.

44. See Lane, op. cit., pp. 304-15; Mary McAuley, Labour Disputes in Soviet Russia: 1957-1965 (Oxford: Clarendon Press, 1969), pp. 97, 124-27, 160; D. J. R. Scott, "Resistance and Opposition," Survey no. 64 (July 1967): 41; Katz, op. cit., p. 193; and Vaclav Holesovsky, "Labor and the Economic Reform in Czechoslovakia" (Amherst: Labor Relations and Research Center, University of Massachusetts, April 1968), pp. 10, 24. (Mimeographed.)

45. See "Statute on the Rights of Factory, Plant and Local Trade Union Committees," Pravda, September 29, 1971, pp. 1-2; (translated in CDSP 23, no. 39 [October 26, 1971]: 15-18). Also see Pravda, March 31, 1974.

46. Trud, March 21, 1972, pp. 4-8 (excerpted in CDSP 24, no. 13 [April 26, 1972]: 1-9); the Pravda editorial of June 7, 1972, p. 1; Moskovskaia Pravda, January 12, 1971, p. 2; Pravda, September 5, 1971, pp. 1-2 (translated in CDSP 23, no. 36 [October 5,

1971]: 1-4, esp. 4); Sovetskaia Estoniia, September 29, 1970, p. 1; "Stiffer Labor Discipline in the Soviet Union," Radio Liberty Dispatch, March 12, 1970; and Trud, April 18, 1969, pp. 1-2.

47. Izvestiia, March 19, 1967, p. 2.

48. See Pravda, January 16, 1922. Quoted in "Yugoslav TU Leader Defends Workers Strikes," Radio Free Europe Research Report, September 7, 1972.

49. Sovetskaia Rossiia, March 25, 1967, p. 2; F. Rudich, "Poednannia derzhavnikh . . . ," Kommunist Ukraini 7 (July 1967). The article is analyzed in R.R.G., "A Small Step Towards Industrial Democracy?" Radio Free Europe Research Report, September 21, 1967. And see S. Ploss, ed., The Soviet Political Process (Waltham, Mass.: Ginn, 1971), p. 156.

50. McAuley, op. cit., pp. 66, 72-73.

51. David Jenkins, "Democracy in the Factory," Atlantic 231, no. 4 (April 1973): 79; and Bulletin (of the Federal Republic of Germany), February 6, 1973, pp. 28-29, and February 7, 1974, p. 3.

52. See Zygmunt Bauman, "Twenty Years After," Problems of Communism 20, no. 6 (November-December 1971): 50-51; McAuley, op. cit., pp. 73, 251; and N. Rodionov, op. cit., p. 21.

53. Pravda, September 11, 1971, p. 1 (editorial); and Trud, February 25, 1971, p. 2.

54. Trud, July 25, 1969; cited in Radio Free Europe Research Report, February 3, 1970, p. 5.

55. V. Guseinov and V. Korchagin, "Questions of Labor Resources," Voprosy ekonomiki 2 (February 1971) (translated in CDSP 23, no. 18 [June 1, 1971]: 6); Sotsialisticheskaia industriia, July 19, 1969, p. 2; E. V. Kasimovskii, "Productivity of Labor and the Effective Use of Labor Resources in the 9th Five Year Plan," Ekonomika i organizatsiia promyshlennogo proizvodstva 1 (January 1972): 74-89 (discussed in R.R.G., "Labor Resources to Decrease After 1985?" Radio Free Europe Research Report, May 5, 1972, p. 4); Novikov, op. cit., p. 100 (translated in CDSP 21, no. 38 [October 15, 1969]: 3-7); and V. Perevedenchev, "Migratsiia naseleniia i ispolizovanie trudovykh resursov," Voprosy ekonomiki 9 (September 1970): 34-43, esp. 5 (translated in CDSP 23, no. 2 [February 9, 1971]: 1-6), and discussed in "Migration Against the Plan? (II)," Radio Free Europe Research Report, October 12, 1970.

56. D. Valentei, "Pressing USSR Population Problems," Ekonomicheskie nauki 1 (January 1969): 53-59.

57. R.R.G., "Labor Resources to Decrease after 1985?" op. cit., p. 1.

58. Moscow domestic, November 8, 1969; FBIS, November 18, 1969, p. C12.

59. Sotsialisticheskaia industriia, November 11, 1969, p. 2. See also Pravda, June 15, 1971; and Voprosy ekonomiki 7 (July 1968): 15.

60. Sotsialisticheskaia industriia, March 15, 1972, p. 2 (translated in CDSP 24, no. 11 [April 11, 1972]: 15); Alexander Eckstein, "Economic Development and Political Change in Communist Systems," World Politics 22, no. 4 (July 1970): 490-91; and Radjanska skola 6 (1971): 8 ff (cited in "Labor Shortage Threatening Soviet Economy?" Radio Free Europe Research Report, August 2, 1971, p. 2).

61. Rabochaia gazeta, February 16, 1971, p. 3, and May 25, 1971, p. 3; and McAuley, op. cit., p. 122.

62. See Bakinskii rabochi, August 31, 1969, p. 1; Sovetskaia Litva, September 23, 1970, pp. 2-3; Pravda, August 21, 1970, p. 2 (translated in CDSP 22, no. 34 [September 22, 1970]: 17); Izvestiia, January 31, 1973, p. 4 (condensed in CDSP 25, no. 5 [February 28, 1973]: 28); Hans-Jurgen Wagener, "Labor Mobility in the Soviet Union," Radio Liberty Dispatch, March 10, 1969, p. 5; and E. G. Antosenkov, ed., Opyt issledovaniia peremeny truda v promyshlennosti (Novosibirsk: Nanka, 1969).

63. Trud, August 22, 1971; New York Times, March 29, 1971; Izvestiia, January 31, 1973; and Guseinov and Korchagin, op. cit., p. 6.

64. Pravda, October 2, 1969, p. 3 (translated in CDSP 21, no. 40 [October 29, 1969]: 20-21); Guseinov and Korchagin, Izvestiia, December 19, 1971, p. 6 (condensed in CDSP 23, no. 51 [January 18, 1972]: 15-16); Ekonomicheskaia gazeta 43 (October 1968): 15 (JPRS 46,840 [November 8, 1968]: 34); Pravda, October 31, 1971, p. 3 (excerpted in CDSP 23, no. 44 [November 30, 1971]: 23).

65. Pravda, February 27, 1972, p. 2.

66. A. Zaitsev, "Social Problems of the Economic Reform," Ekonomika Sovetskoi Ukrainy (Kiev) 5 (May 1967) (JPRS 42,238 [August 16, 1967]: 48); Paul Hollander, Soviet and American Society: A Comparison (New York: Oxford, 1973), p. 232; and Pravda, October 6, 1965, p. 2.

67. See Carmelo Mesa-Lago, "Unemployment in a Socialist Economy: Yugoslavia," Industrial Relations 10, no. 1 (February 1971): 49, and his "Unemployment in Socialist Countries" (unpublished Ph.D. diss., Cornell University, 1968). See also Holesovsky, op. cit., pp. 8, 10.

68. Robert Conquest, ed., Industrial Workers in the USSR (New York: Praeger, 1967), pp. 21-30, 34; and J. B. Sorenson, Life and Death of Soviet Trade Unionism (New York: Atherton, 1969), pp. 222-25. See also Keith Bush, "Propaganda Considerations Impede Alleviation of Unemployment," Bulletin of the Institute for the Study of the USSR 14, no. 4 (April 1967): 26.

69. Emily Clark Brown, "Continuity and Change in the Soviet Labor Market," Industrial and Labor Relations Review 23, no. 2 (January 1970): 172; and Conquest, op. cit., p. 22.

70. Izvestiia, March 19, 1967, p. 2; Bunich, loc cit.; Frankel, op. cit., p. 34; and Brown, "Continuity and Change," p. 180. Also see Fedorenko, op. cit., p. 8. Fedorenko is the Academician-Secretary of the Economics Department of the USSR Academy of Sciences.

71. Brown, "Continuity and Change . . .," p. 177.

72. A. Dumachev et al., op. cit., p. 15; Pravda, February 11, 1973, p. 2 (excerpted in CDSP 25, no. 6 [March 7, 1973]: 21); and Sovetskaia Belorussiia, November 10, 1970, p. 2.

73. Brown, "Continuity and Change . . .," p. 178.

74. Pravda, February 15, 1971, p. 1, and June 20, 1971, p. 1.

75. Izvestiia, September 27, 1969, p. 3 (translated in CDSP 20, no. 39 [October 22, 1969]: 2); and O. Safranov, "Nekotorye itogi perepisi professional'nogo sostava . . .," Vestnik statistiki 9 (1970): 21 ff. (cited in "The Changing Vocational Structure in Soviet Industry," Radio Liberty Dispatch, October 28, 1970, p. 2).

76. See, for example, Sotsialisticheskaia industriia, July 3, 1969, p. 2; Pravda, July 30, 1971, p. 3 (translated in CDSP 23, no. 30 [August 24, 1971]: 13; and S. Batyshev, "Podgotovka kvalifitsirovannykh rabochikh v usloviiakh nauchno-tekhnicheskoi revoliutsii," Kommunist 17 (November 1971): 32-43.

77. Deutsche Zeitung, February 4, 1972, translated in German Tribune, March 9, 1972, p. 4.

78. P. Balandin in Novyi mir 3 (March 1968): 266-70; and H. A. Simon, The Shape of Automation (New York: Harper & Row, 1965), pp. 94, 22.

79. Moscow Domestic Russian, October 9, 1969, 2:00.

80. Pravda, October 9, 1969, and February 13, 1971, p. 2; and Izvestiia, October 12, 1969, p. 5 (partially translated in CDSP 21, no. 41 [November 5, 1969]: 4, 33).

81. Keith Bush, "The Implementation of the Soviet Economic Reform," Radio Liberty Research Paper no. 36 (1970): 31; Sotsialisticheskaia industriia, June 2, 1972, p. 2. Also see P. Sharov, the director of Shchekino, in Pravda, February 5, 1973, p. 2 (excerpted in CDSP 25, no. 5 [February 28, 1973]: 29); Pravda, February 13, 1971, p. 2; Brown, "Continuity and Change . . .," pp. 180-81; and Pravda, February 13, 1971, p. 2.

82. Neva 8 (1968): 136 (cited by Bush, "Implementation . . .," p. 33; and Pravda, January 14, 1970, which mentions 4,500 being made redundant at Shchekino.

83. Sovetskaia Rossiia, November 16, 1969, p. 1; Pravda, February 13, 1971, p. 2, and June 8, 1972, p. 2; Sovetskaia Estoniia, March 18, 1969, p. 3; Pravda, March 24, 1972, p. 3.

84. Trud, February 13, 1970; Literaturnaia gazeta 46 (November 12, 1969): 10; and Ekonomicheskaia gazeta 1 (January 1973): 8.

85. See Jenkins, op. cit., pp. 79-80.

86. Izvestiia, October 7, 1965. Reported in R.R.G., "The Labor Exchange Proposal," Radio Free Europe Research Report, October 11, 1965, p. 2.

87. See Fedorenko, op. cit.; Planovoe khoziaistvo 11 (November 1968): 16; Trud, September 16, 1969; Literaturnaia gazeta, March 22, 1972, p. 10 (translated in CDSP 24, no. 11 [April 12, 1972]: 14); and M. Sonin, "Nekotorye problemy . . .," Voprosy ekonomiki 8 (August 1966): 36.

88. S. Batyshev, "The Worker's Diploma," Sotsialisticheskii trud 3 (March 1967) (JPRS 41,507 [June 21, 1967]; A. Kurskii, "Itogi khoziaistvennoi reformy za 1966 g . . .," Voprosy ekonomiki 4 (April 1967): 31; and P. Bunich, Ekonomika i matematicheskie metody 6 (November-December 1966).

89. Pravda, October 12, 1969, p. 2.

90. L. Koniakin and V. Soifer, Sovetskaia iustitsiia 23 (December 1967); (translated in CDSP 20, no. 7 [March 6, 1968]: 6).

91. Novikov, op. cit., p. 103; and Guseinov and Korchagin, op. cit., p. 5.

92. Sobranie postanovlenii SSSR no. 1 (1967): 1; and Sotsialisticheskii trud 11 (1968): 91 ff.

93. Trud, October 9, 1969; and Kommunist 13 (September 1969): 106. Cited in Bush, "Implementation," p. 13.

94. Novikov, op. cit., pp. 105-06.

95. Koniakin and Soifer, op. cit., p. 7.

96. Trud, January 29, 1972, p. 2 (condensed in CDSP 24, no. 6 [March 8, 1972]: 6-7), and discussed in New York Times, February 8, 1972). See also Trud, March 7, 1973; and Andreas Tenson, "The Curtailment of the Powers of Public Employment Agencies," Radio Liberty Dispatch, July 9, 1973.

97. See an article by G. Kulagin, the general director of the Sverdlov machine-tool obedinenie in Leningrad, in Pravda, June 18 and 19, 1971, p. 3; discussed in New York Times, June 20, 1971, p. 3, and condensed in CDSP 23, no. 24 (July 13, 1971): 9-10. Also see Izvestiia, December 12, 1971, p. 1 (excerpted in CDSP 23, no. 50 [January 11, 1972]: 27); and the series of abstracts in CDSP 25, no. 2 (February 7, 1973): 13-14.

98. Interview with the head of a Soviet city newspaper's promotdel; and Izvestiia, August 31, 1972, p. 2 (condensed in CDSP 24, no. 35 [September 27, 1972]: 19-20).

99. M. Garin et al., Izvestiia, March 7, 1968, p. 5 (translated in CDSP 20, no. 11 [April 1, 1969]: 6-9); E. Antosenkov, Izvestiia, October 18, 1968; Zarya Vostoka, June 5, 1969; Bakinskii

rabochii, June 4, 1969; and Trud, March 9, 1969, p. 2. See also articles in CDSP 25, no. 43 (November 21, 1973): 8-11.

100. Pravda, August 8, 1972, p. 2; condensed in CDSP 24, no. 32 (September 6, 1972): 13, 18. See also Izvestiia, March 4, 1972, p. 5 (condensed in CDSP 24, no. 9 [March 29, 1972]: 22); and Pravda, August 28, 1971 (excerpted in CDSP 23, no. 35 [September 28, 1971]: 23-24).

101. See Vedemosti verkhovnogo soveta SSSR, 1970, no. 29, p. 265 (for the law), and Pravda and Izvestiia, July 17, 1970, pp. 2-4 (translated in CDSP 22, no. 34 [September 22, 1970]: 1-11); Izvestiia, December 3, 1970, p. 2 (for the implemental decree); Trud, November 25, 1970, p. 4 (for the present penalties for violation of labor discipline); and S. Ivanov, "Novyi zakon o trude," Kommunist 2 (January 1971): 59-69 (FBIS, March 4, 1971, pp. J10-J20 (for a commentary).

CHAPTER 6

THE MANAGER-MANAGER RELATIONSHIP

INTRODUCTION

The one major role relationship of the Soviet industrial manager remaining for discussion is that with other managers--that is, in institutional terms, the contacts and obligations of enterprises vis-a-vis one another. "These relationships run in two directions. In one of these, enterprises figure as sellers: they dispose of their products. In the other, they act as buyers: they purchase the means of production they require for the manufacturing process."[1]

This relationship is very important for the Soviet economy, since "the majority of industrial enterprises do not sell their goods [directly] to the state, but to other industrial enterprises or trading organizations. This [represents] the major part of the internal market of industry."[2] Of course, not all the institutions involved in this two-way process are enterprises in the legal sense. Some, for example, are units of the state supply and distribution network. Nevertheless, enterprises are the type of organization that is most frequently involved.

Despite the initial expression of high hopes for the development of this relationship, it is receiving less attention in the USSR than are the other relationships of the Soviet manager and enterprise; and, as might be expected, it is undergoing the least change. Most Soviet discussions on the industrial aspects of the reform are concerned with the relationship of the manager to his superiors, to Party organizations, or to subordinates. One probable reason for the secondary position of the manager-manager relationship is the unwillingness of decision-makers to allow much development of uncontrolled economic ties among enterprises. But this relationship is also one in which substantive changes would produce far-reaching, even systemic, effects on the Soviet economy and perhaps on the political system as well. At the least, if enterprises were to have a significant amount of freedom in their interrelationships, centralized economic direction and control would be effectively weakened and the question of their continued existence would arise. This possible outcome is being guarded against by interests that want to bring the economy and polity through the present rationalization fundamentally unchanged.

The possibility of fundamental change has been broached openly by a Soviet economist who recognizes that "the expansion of direct economic ties . . . provides the real possibility of a change-over from excessive regulation from above . . . of industrial enterprises . . . to a limited number of key indices that will ensure the required . . . development of the entire socialist economy."[3] A functionary of the Ukrainian Gosplan decries enterprises' lack of the right "to come to terms directly" and their having to turn to main administrations (glavki) for supply, marketing, and deliveries "on all questions" of inter-enterprise supply, even when the enterprises are only a few blocks from one another. "Such ties can scarcely be called direct. It is essential to work out a new system for formulating deliveries which will provide for direct [and] actual ties between suppliers and consumers, with minimal involvement of the soiuzglavsnabsbyty" ("all-Union main supply-marketing administrations").[4]

Basic goals of the reform pertinent here are connected with the new main indicators of success: sales and profits. Sales are inextricably connected with the mutual ties of enterprises and are now being presented as a fundamental indicator for the evaluation of the activity of enterprises. "The evaluation of the activity of the enterprise on the basis of production sold has become a most important element in the new system of management," and the commodity sales indicator is a "mighty economic lever" inspiring collectives to improve the quality of products. It has been noted that "under the reform, volume of sales was to be second only to profits as a managerial goal." Some say it was first.[5]

Besides the stress on the importance of sales, other goals connected with the manager-manager nexus were emphasized at the time of the reform's introduction. Profit, of course, is one. It also is desired that the producing enterprise develop new products of greater use to its customer enterprises. Another goal is economically based, responsible ties among enterprises. "Business-like relationships, based upon conditions of mutual advantage, ought to exist between suppliers and consumers and between the supplier and the supply organization." But, in a cautious vein reminiscent of the pre-1965 period, this is to be effected through strengthening "discipline" regarding the fulfillment of economic agreements.[6]

A list of the reform's goals pertinent to this relationship is in a joint resolution of the CPSU Central Committee and the USSR Council of Ministers of October 1965. It states that a change is envisioned in the methods of guiding the economy along the following lines: basing the economic relations among enterprises on the principle of mutual material responsibility, developing permanent direct ties between manufacturing and consuming enterprises, and raising the role of economic contracts.[7] Three of what Barry Richman calls "ultimate enterprise objectives" are similar to some of the goals of the reform cited above:

1. ". . . output should consist of items required by customers and should be of the highest possible quality in light of available resources"
2. "Output should be delivered to customers in accordance with a predetermined time schedule"
3. "Material and other supply . . . inputs should be as small as possible."[8]

The goals of profitable sales, economically based direct enterprise ties, mutual material responsibility, and meaningful contracts are all extensions of pre-reform goals for Soviet industrial enterprises. Clearly the goals of the present reform in its inter-manager aspect are meant to answer deeply rooted organizational and economic needs of long standing.

DIRECT TIES

One of the key areas in which enterprises' rights were to expand was inter-enterprise contacts. One of Yevsei Liberman's most fundamental proposals was the free making of contracts by economic units. These were to be more stable, and to be initiated and sustained on the basis of enterprises' mutual advantage. The increase of economic relationships between enterprises would reduce the great gap between many producers and consumers. The long-term policy of trying to create an interdependent economy has been pushed too far. Too many enterprises great distances apart are being forced to deal with one another, thereby putting a great strain on transport and making deliveries costly, delayed, and uncertain. The regionalization reintroduced in 1973 also is meant to reduce the burden of these problems.

There has been some movement toward more "direct ties," in the sense of "contractual relations between producing and purchasing enterprises established directly rather than through the ministries."[9] Soviet economists have stressed their importance. One writes:

> Direct ties between enterprises are a highly effective means of systematically ensuring the diverse interbranch, intrabranch, and territorial proportions in production; which, by virtue of the rapid rate of technical progress, are highly dynamic over time and require constant <u>flexible</u> regulation.[10]

Others have faced the ideological issues directly, arguing, for example, that the institution of the "principle of the predominant rights of customers has nothing in common with the taboo theory of the 'pre-eminence of consumption'" strongly opposed by centralist or conservative economists.[11]

In late 1964 Kosygin meant to make enterprise planning in accordance with direct ties a major feature of the reform.[12] This did not fully materialize, however. Of course, direct ties do affect planning, but now mainly in terms of such minor details as color and style, although by 1973 it was claimed that almost a third of wood products and more than 60 percent of paper production were exchanged through direct ties.[13] This is not happening everywhere. As the Deputy Chairman of the Planning Commission of the North Caucasus economic raion said: ". . . here . . . the activity under the new economic system has not exerted any real influence toward strengthening direct economic ties. The initiative of the plants and factories in this regard often does not find support from the agencies of Gossnab."[14]

Gossnab is the State Committee on Material and Technical Supply, a powerful organization that can limit the development of the manager-manager relationship. For example, through the actions of Gossnab, a furniture enterprise in Rostov is unable to determine with which suppliers it may enter into negotiations. Also, during 1966 it changed the suppliers for the Krasnodar furniture and wood-processing kombinat several times. This practice continued into 1973. The glavki of Gossnab "frequently make arbitrary and unwarranted changes in the economic ties of enterprises, allowing traditional suppliers to be replaced by new and sometimes implausible ones, contrary to the production and economic interests of these enterprises. . . ." In one territorial administration in Lithuania, "dozens of orders issued for output delivery are canceled or changed every day."[15] Thus, direct ties that are freely agreed upon by enterprises often are not allowed to go into effect, much less continue over a long period. Ironically, Gossnab is charged with working toward the "further expansion of rational direct economic ties among enterprises."[16] It was to be an aid to the enterprises, not a controller.

"Direct links" between producing and purchasing enterprises are not now part of the reform at the lowest levels. These contacts are restricted to large-scale deliveries that are made on a continuous basis. One Soviet economist adds cautionary remarks on the limitations still placed on such ties. "It should be remembered," he writes, "that the expansion of direct economic ties between enterprises in no way replaces the system of centralized distribution of the more important means of production that is inherent in the socialist mode of production." Elsewhere he adds that if the establishment of such ties became a "spontaneous process," it would be a "vulgar" development fundamentally contradicting the essence of a planned socialist economy. Another writer notes rigidly that "direct links between organizations under conditions of planned distribution do not arise spontaneously, but are established by appropriate planning organizations."[17]

These objections reveal how potentially important the idea is. It is not surprising, therefore, that there are definite limitations upon the development of this aspect of the manager-manager relationship. These stem from an objection to uncontrolled economic relationships, perhaps with a basis more fundamental than Marxism. Simple lack of acceptance is widespread. As late as 1972 an executive of the Ministry of Light Industry, when told by the director of a garment firm that the "right to draw up the plan on the basis of the orders filled by trade" would do the most for increasing production of the articles with the greatest consumer demand, replied with astonishment, "You can't be serious!"[18] An interesting question (although one not answerable) is to what degree cautionary remarks are made freely.

Despite these limitations, expansion of direct ties has occurred in places other than those already cited. For example, the directors of some of the eight enterprises in the Skorokhod shoe-manufacturing obedinenie in Leningrad decide with the managers of retail, wholesale, and trade organizations "all questions" concerning the output and delivery of articles in terms of styles, colors, quantity, and quality. The decisions are then embodied in "direct contracts" (priamye dogovory), which are concluded not later than five to six months before the beginning of the contract year. It is implied that these contracts are made without direction of higher authorities, although it is likely that they are informed and indicate whether they approve.

Also, Skorokhod and the directors of textile, leather, and other nonaffiliated enterprises decide all questions concerning their economic relations and conclude (by themselves, it seems) direct contracts four to five months prior to the beginning of the contract year. Higher authorities become involved only if changes have been made in the plan indicators as a result of changes in orders by trading organizations. Managers set various norms independently, in conformity with the orders placed with them. After examining these norms, higher agencies are "obligated" to provide enterprises with funds for the materials needed. According to Gertrude Schroeder, by 1970 direct ties applied to over 7,000 producers, over 2,300 suppliers and over 900 products. However, the amount of industrial output affected must fall "far short" of 30 percent, and "according to critics the process remains largely a formality...."[19]

The reform was also to aid managers in other ways. For example, enterprises are now allowed to dispose of excess stocks and old or unused equipment to other enterprises through trade or sale. This formerly was difficult to do legally, although there was a great need for it, since above-norm stocks came to form 45 percent of industry's circulating assets and, while many enterprises had surplus stocks, others did not.[20] Since the reform has begun, a great deal of attention and publicity has been devoted to coping with this problem. For example, fairs displaying excess and used goods and equipment have been widely held, and have facilitated many contacts between enterprises. Contracts make such inter-enterprise ties legally binding and serve economic planning functions.

CONTRACTS AND INTER-ENTERPRISE OBLIGATIONS: IDEAL AND ACTUALITY

Russian political traditions and Soviet political conditions have not allowed legally based contractual agreements to flourish.

"Extensive political regulation from the centre . . . has left little room for contract initiative, . . . [and] totalitarian rule tended to induce a flight from the responsibility of making binding decisions. . . ." In addition, the ideology gave the expansion of production a higher priority than freedom of contract. Nevertheless, the contract between production enterprises has meaningful functions: establishing details, declaring managerial loyalty to the plan (a "moral" function), providing the planners with information they have missed, and perhaps discouraging the maintenance of excessively large inventories as "insurance" against the turn of the "ratchet."[21]

Although there is some tendency toward strengthening the ability of enterprises to make contracts of delivery with each other independently, at present much of this is only verbalization and, in addition, is limited by Gossnab. Initially, the reform did seem to promise enhancement of the contract's role. It was to be "a major instrument for reforming attitudes, and a major means of bringing into play greatly expanded . . . incentives" from managers and workers and "to link production with consumption . . . to enable a reduction in the number of centrally planned products."[22] The origin, justification, and past role of the contract belies this hope for future development. It has served as a means of upholding and facilitating the plan, which is an administrative act become law, by filling in details, such as assortment, through a process of lower-level free association. Each year about 250 million economic contracts are concluded in the USSR.[23]

Certainly the system of contracts requires improvement. At times enterprises having significant relationships lack contracts, a fact occasionally requiring recourse to the state arbitration system (Gosarbitrazh) for the resolution of resulting difficulties. Again, contracts often are drawn up "only after extreme delays at the end of the plan period," at a time when they are no longer needed because of the "overvaluing" of "administrative methods" in management.[24] The head of the legal department of Rospotrebsoiuza sees two "barriers" to direct contracts that must be eliminated--the unprofitability to wholesale organizations of connections with manufacturers and the dependence of the wages of workers in wholesale depots on the amount of wholesale turnover.[25]

A similar need for change is noted by a senior consultant on state arbitration for the USSR Council of Ministers, who says, "It is necessary to decisively change the attitude toward the conclusion of contracts . . . [to] transform them into operative and concrete documents by which . . . deliveries will be influenced." It seems that he wants iron-clad contracts that will always be executed.[26] Some legal progress regarding deliveries resulted from the 1969 statute on deliveries of consumer goods, which specified that contracts include sections on delivery conditions.

Certain legal writers are trying to justify an increase in the importance of contracts. For example, one candidate of legal sciences says it is essential that contracts be concluded within a set period several months prior to the beginning of the contract year. Significantly, he also argues that the contract has a planning role and that a "dialectic" exists between plan and contract. It serves, he says, as the basis of the production plan for goods not centrally distributed. The contract "concretizes" the plan's targets and aids in the basic formulation of indicators of the enterprise's tekhpromfinplan not affirmed by superior agencies.[27] This seems a shallow but nevertheless definite attempt to gain a solid place for the contract in the Soviet economy. More arguments to the same effect are likely. Possibly this emphasis on the contract as a basis of the plan is also a suggestion for a new type of planning--"market socialism," in effect. It is significant that the same writer also suggests that an allocation order (nariad) conflicting with a contract not stand unless it is conformed by Gosarbitrazh.

Implicit criticism of central planning is common. An article on the post-reform experience of the Tallin machine-building plant says that centralized planning tends to make contracts less than highly meaningful. The plant still has to submit "blind" orders for materials in May, although it is not yet known what the next year's product mix will be. That information is released by the superior agency (Soiuzglavkhimneftmash, in this case) only in August. The writer complains that as a result, ". . . once again the men in supply, finance and planning will sit down with their calculators. This is senseless . . . [and] the enterprise operates during the first quarter of the year at its own risk."[28]

Other problems in inter-enterprise ties are related to contracts. "Reformed" enterprises still have only a limited ability to choose their suppliers and to determine the exact specifications of the materials and products they need. Another related difficulty is the lack of economic accountability in supply and marketing.[29] A major difficulty is deliveries that are late or are never made. One ideal of the reform was the prompt transport of undamaged, high-quality goods between enterprises, and between them and supply and distributing agencies. However, contracts do not always serve to effect deliveries of goods as desired. For example, a Soviet source points out that in Kazakhstan "literally all of the enterprises [transferred to the new system] have encountered . . . the dispatch of finished products [that] greatly exceeds the 'travelling' time of the documents . . .,"[30] causing delays in payments to the supplying enterprise.

The formerly omnipresent problem of shturmovshchina ("storming") still appears and delays deliveries. This writer, in Rostov at the end of June 1969, found his visit to Tostsel'mash canceled because it was the "end of the month." "Many suppliers upset the supply period by dispatching a significant part of production in the last days of the month or the quarter." For example, the Moscow tire plant has dispatched to the Vilnius supply base the supplies it contracted for only in the last few days of each quarter. As a result, the supply base has not been able to fulfill its obligation to its customers. A post-reform factor contributing to this type of problem is enterprises' unwillingness to ship if their production for the month is "up to date" (v azhure)-- that is, has already reached the planned figure. In such cases the "excess" products are held back in warehouses as a reserve or "insurance" against poor results in a succeeding month.[31] As a result, customers do not receive on time the goods they have contracted for. The proposed "solution" of making the profit plan exist only in a yearly, not a monthly, form seems, however, no solution at all, since its adoption probably would only lengthen the effects of the problem. (Shipments also are slowed by the still existing practice of railroads' accepting freight only on dates and in amounts that they determine.) One of the solutions proposed for analogous problems in Bulgaria, also engaged in an economic reform, is the making of contracts between not only the managements of enterprises but also between their trade union committees, with material incentives for regular and proper deliveries.[32] A possible solution to the delivery problem in the USSR and the East European countries is the provision of readily tappable alternative sources of supplies. Free contracts might provide this.

Not only the supplying or producing enterprises cause difficulties. Customer or receiving enterprises may well hold up payments to producers and suppliers or simply refuse to accept products, thus disrupting the plan. No effective regulated system of paying for products has been established between purchasers and suppliers. This leads to the nonfulfillment of commodity sales and profit plans and to underpayments into incentive funds, all of which harm enterprises.[33] Moreover, the Ministry of Finance complains that "arrears in payments . . . amount to a considerable sum."[34] Neither Party organizations nor state agencies seem able to eliminate payments difficulties between enterprises. In light of this, it is not surprising that a large free or black market for enterprises still exists. What may be the crowning absurdity is the complaint of one firm that "because of interruptions in raw material deliveries, it is frequently necessary to have materials delivered by airplane."[35]

PROPOSED SOLUTIONS

Various proposals for solutions have been advanced. Some suggest changing the present success indicator of production sold. One group of economists wants the sales plan to be considered fulfilled not when money is (finally) transferred to the current account of the producing enterprise, but when that enterprise has shipped the commodities and the documents have been sent to the bank. A second group holds that fulfillment should be based upon the proportion of money paid into the current account of the producing enterprise.[36]

There appear to be two reasons for dissatisfaction with the new major indicator of production sold. First, a "number of enterprises" are unable to sell their products and thus have not been able to fulfill the sales plan.[37] This has a certain irony, since the sales plan's elimination was a specific target for the reform. Second, there is the "very important" reason of the "survival of the former, ineffective system of material responsibility for violations of contractual agreements." Various implemental statements and directives have not had operative effect.

The subject of ways, proposed and existing, designed to ensure payments necessarily involves penalties for nondelivery or late or irregular deliveries of goods and for nonpayment or delayed payment. Several writers call for stricter sanctions against both the refusal of a buyer to pay for products and against the supplier for late deliveries. The supply agencies are also to bear material responsibility if they are at fault. A strong feeling exists that the institutions of the state must no longer be allowed to create economic difficulties for the enterprises.

The economist A. Birman wants to establish what he calls the "inevitability of payments" by making it normal procedure for an enterprise manager to pay his financial obligations in the chronological order in which they come due. At present, as for decades, the first obligation to be met is the wage fund; and payments due to other enterprises have a definitely lower priority.[38] The intent of Birman's proposal is the creation of a new type of fiscal sense on the part of directors. They would have to keep close track of their enterprises' finances and ensure ahead of time that they could meet the financial demands made upon them. But how is this suggestion to have its intended effect? Birman proposes that an enterprise that continually fails to pay its bills on time face a succession of penalties, ultimately including cessation of operations. This should force the management to accept only sound, realizable plans. However, it goes against the time-honored practice of using "administrative" measures to rectify a failing management.

A state arbiter, in describing the measures actually used to encourage inter-enterprise payments and the fulfillment of obligations, says that whereas in the past, fines paid for the breaking of contracts were "exceedingly small" (chrezvychaino maly) and thus had an "insignificant economic role," since the second half of 1965 the sanctions "have been significantly increased."[39] He adds that this has had "positive results," and it is intended to extend the practice. However, "several problems" of an economic and of a legal nature have arisen. For example, each enterprise fined "exacts them [the fines] from its own suppliers and customers." Therefore, "the material responsibility of enterprises for breaking state and contractual discipline is . . . 'slurred over' [smazyvaetsia] and does not completely attain the desired goal." As a result, the "'balance of fines' is . . . distorting the actual economic results of the work of an enterprise." Fines paid may even be offset by fines received. About half of Soviet enterprises have a "zero or positive fine sheet" and "by no means experience the unfavorable consequences of paying fines," since they are covered by "recoveries."[40] This indicates the limitations of fines for ensuring good economic relations between plants and firms.

One possible solution is a practice followed since 1966 at a vacuum cleaner plant in Moscow. There it is mandatory that 25 percent of the amount of fines paid out be deducted from the bonus funds of the shops responsible. This localization of effect would seem to support the principle that "by [economic] stimulation should be understood not only incentive for good work, but also material responsibility for bad work."[41] A move is also under way to prevent fines and penalties from being included in the cost of production. They must be charged against profits, and therefore they will directly affect the size of the enterprise's incentive fund. Another Gosarbitrazh functionary outlines a number of steps that must be implemented in order to create a high degree of material responsibility among enterprises. He suggests:

> It is necessary to establish economically-based dimensions of penalties, forfeitures and fines so they become actual stimulators of the fulfillment of contracts, to determine the group of responsible persons who are to bear material responsibility, and the size of . . . the reimbursement of losses by the guilty workers, who because of it will lose all or part of their premiums.[42]

This, of course, leads back to the sensitive subject of bonuses and other material incentives, and reveals that the losses caused by managerial errors will be felt by the workers. It is not likely that this would result in elimination of the problem, for it is also caused by management and Party organizations. By 1970 serious discussions raised the question of withholding bonuses specifically from managerial executives and ITR of enterprises that do not live up to contractual obligations. For example, one economist notes, "It is necessary to penalize the executives . . . involved (primarily by material sanctions, such as depriving them of bonus payments . . .)."[43] The slogan "intensifying the enterprises' material responsibility" may be given content and effect by involving management directly. It remains to eliminate ministries' power to exempt enterprises from the payment of fines.

A problem also arises from cancellations of orders, a matter of significant dimensions even among "reformed" enterprises. Customers who cancel orders get off with a "light scare" or small fine. One writer notes, "It is obviously high time to revise these regulations. The customer should bear greater financial responsibility for costs incurred by the manufacturer."[44] The state of affairs of sanctions and penalties for nonfulfillment of contractual obligations was summed up by a professor of economics who wrote: "At present we have no system for establishing the sanctions to be imposed for the violation of contractual obligations and for compensating for the damage caused."[45]

In 1968 new and stringent measures were set forth in a government decree.[46] Briefly stated, it substantially raises penalties for late deliveries and nondeliveries (including for railroads' causing such delays), raises the sanctions imposed for failure to fulfill contractual obligations, and stipulates that customer organizations not paying their bills on time be fined 5 percent of the value of the goods ordered. This unimaginative attempt at a solution promises only harsher penalties, not an alleviation of the underlying difficulties. In any case, the increased penalties have not had much effect. "Even with the increased amounts of penalties and fines . . . these forms of economic sanctions come nowhere near fully covering the losses of enterprises and--this is very important--the degree of coverage is far from equal in the various departments," and the branches of industry with the most complex output are compensated to the least degree.[47]

A related legal question is whether "objective" or "subjective" causes of failure to fulfill obligations are to serve as the criteria for imposition of sanctions. At present the majority of Soviet jurists interpret the fault of an enterprise under the subject aspect of responsibility. This means that "it is natural . . . that the enterprise must bear material responsibility for the nonfulfillment of a contract only when fault is present."[48] As a result, it is exceedingly difficult to "pinch" the material interests of enterprises that in some way fail in their responsibilities to others. Correction would be more likely to occur if enterprises that do not live up to their obligations were automatically and quickly penalized, although not to an undue degree. Under such conditions, managers might learn behavior conducive to the reform's goals.

MINISTRIES, SUPPLY, AND ARBITRATION

Although the ideal of the reform initially assumed that enterprises would have a greater role in inter-enterprise supply than previously, a nationwide centralized network of state supply controls was created that set the tone and real content in matters of supply. This is significant, since "the most serious problem arises with supplies."[49] But perhaps the supply situation, although remaining difficult, is less confusing than it was during the sovnarkhoz period. In 1965 some administrative controls over supplies were transferred from the sovnarkhozy back to the resurrected ministries, with others going to Gossnab. The new ministries are responsible for uninterrupted supply to enterprises and construction projects. They are to distribute and check on the realization of allocated funds and to ensure intra-branch cooperative deliveries.[50] But they have a definite and significant role in supply that they guard jealously, even to the extent of not allowing "their" enterprises to acquire supplies from other ministries' plants. Of course, enterprises can get some scarce supplies through their ministries and Gosplan, while materials that are readily available are provided by Gossnab.[51] The General Statute on USSR Ministries, adopted by Resolution No. 640 of July 10, 1967, of the USSR Councils of Ministers, contains five articles on the ministries' role in supply. At least three of these represent a denial to enterprises of supply powers that may have been theirs (at least implicitly) at the reform's beginning. For example, Article 53 states that the USSR ministry

> ... exercises control over the realization of funded raw materials, fuel, equipment and other material resources and also over the prompt conclusion by the enterprises, organizations, and institutions in the ministry system of contracts for the delivery of output and [over] the fulfillment of contract obligations.[52]

The formulation survived into 1973, when *Pravda* proclaimed that "the raising of the responsibility of suppliers and of the role of direct economic contracts belongs above all to Gossnab SSSR and the branch ministries."[53] The functions of the new Gossnab include making supply plans and distributing products that are not distributed by Gosplan SSSR. It is also to establish long-term direct ties for enterprises, thus reducing Gosplan's role slightly, and to receive many of the supply functions and facilities from the ministries. By 1970, 24 industrial ministries had complied. The advantages cited are elimination of parallelism and duplication of work; more effective use of resources and storage facilities; and stricter control over the movement and quality of deliveries. It is admitted, however, that "the development of an independent system will not actually resolve all the questions of supply and sale."[54]

The government has "considerably expanded the rights of the State Committee for Supply." Gossnab's main tasks are "to plan, calculate material balances for, allocate and physically distribute some 12,000 items for production needs."[55] It also may adopt "changes in assignments as to array and type-size of products ... within the limits of the established overall volume of output and delivery of this production." It is obligated to obtain the agreement of either the appropriate department of a USSR ministry or the Council of Ministers of a Union republic, which indicates that no single supply system in fact exists. It is not known if such agreement is always secured. Even so, the resulting paper work may well cause the slowing down of deliveries and perhaps other deleterious effects. In addition, Gossnab may curtail or stop the production of "products not enjoying demand" and define "lack of demand" in particular cases.

The Chairman of Gossnab points out that the new system has not overcome several "serious deficiencies." One of the problems he singles out is violations of the time periods and "completeness" of deliveries. He also says that a great deal of trans-shipment, the old bogey of the Soviet supply situation, continues to exist. As an example he cites the "senseless" shipment of cement from a plant in Krasnoyarsk to the hydroelectric plant in the same area via "intermediate warehouses." The old practice of hoarding by enterprises also is criticized as a complicating factor in the supply picture. He says:

> The overwhelming share of stocks is located at the customers. This leads to the scattering of material resources among numerous plant warehouses, to incompleteness of stocks and a decrease in maneuverability. For example, at the warehouses of many tens of thousands of customers is found 83.5 percent of the general stocks of rolled metal. For steel pipe the corresponding figure reaches 90. There is an analogous situation in [the case of] many other products.[56]

His comments form a damning indictment of the "new" supply situation.

Gossnab heads a large new territorial network with 56 territorial administrations, 42 in the RSFSR and 14 in the Union republics. This organizational complex is composed of 1,400 lower-level supply organizations that service consumers regardless of their branch affiliation. More than 60 percent of the turnover of all the country's supply agencies is handled by it. Thus, it is evident how limited the opportunities for "direct ties" are. The number of workers in the apparatus has "significantly decreased" in comparison with the number similarly employed by the supply network of the former sovnarkhozy. For the Moscow raion this decrease is 21 percent. This reduction may have been facilitated by the introduction of computers.[57]

If the number of personnel in such administrations does not increase, it would seem that although the new supply system reduces the powers of enterprises, some degree of organizational rationalization is taking place in matters of supply. This will be more significant if the principles of the reform are made to govern the supply network's operations. At least fewer plan indices are set from above. But, although Soviet enterprises have in fact received new powers in dealing with one another, the state retains the major share of powers.

An indication of what the new system can actually mean for inter-enterprise contacts is the fact that "a consignment of goods shipped by the Mayak firm to fulfill a direct contract with a particular customer was intercepted by the wholesale trade organization and sent to a different retail outlet."[58] What may be the other side of the picture was the refusal of the Bolshevik plant to provide products to the Skorokhod obedinenie that had been included in their contract for many years, a refusal that was negated by the action of Gossnab.

There have been numerous statements about the many shortcomings in the operation of the new supply system and its tendency toward regimentation of enterprises. For example, "in the enterprises which are operating according to the new system a number of . . . supply and sales organizations excessively regulate the products list of industrial output."[59] Some are critical of the central supply organs for attempting to exert detailed control over operations that generally work satisfactorily without their aid. "The entire cumbersome control [system] exists in order to catch two percent of the violations."[60] K. N. Rudnev, the very "visible" Minister of Instrument-Making, says that approximately half the output of plants controlled by his ministry is distributed by Gossnab and about a quarter by various organizations and departments, all of which demand additional supplies without even offering the limited security of a legal contract. He asks, "How can there be talk of khozraschet with relations of this sort?"[61] One candidate of economics says that a fundamental supply problem is that "supply . . . activity . . . is frequently viewed as a technological and not an economic process."[62] In addition, since Gossnab "exercises considerable influence over wholesale trading," "under these circumstances it is difficult to visualize much free exercise of managerial authority in wholesale trade." Seventy-nine percent of the industrial managers polled on the supply system said that it had not improved, and almost half of them said supply was their principal problem under the reform.[63]

One of the most radical suggestions for improvement is the implicit rejection of the possibility that a centralized supply system ought to do a great deal. According to proponents of this position:

> . . . production workers will transfer only those functions that an intermediary is capable of fulfilling more cheaply and better than they themselves can do. This will force the workers of the supply administration and its bases to lower the cost of the apparatus, introduce efficient control systems, reduce reporting, and eliminate all the unnecessary administrative functions.[64]

More wholesale trade through an enlarged network of wholesale outlets for industrial items has been urged. At present the effort is still experimental.

The state arbitration system also tends to reduce the powers for independent initiatives that might have accrued to industrial initiatives that might have accrued to industrial enterprises, but its effect is less than that of the supply network. It is widely assumed that the reform presupposes an increase in the importance of the role of the state arbitration system. Some of the ways in which this is to be effected are the "influencing" of enterprises, by threat of larger sanctions, to provide customers with a greater variety of products, and the elimination of "deficiencies" in the work of enterprises that Gosarbitrazh may discover.[65] The example of the Tula arbitration committee in 1967 and 1968 indicates its increased role. Whereas in 1967 it reviewed 3,500 cases, in 1968 it reviewed about 13,500. The increase was occasioned, it is suggested, by the end of state compensation for nondeliveries. Now an aggrieved enterprise has a strong reason to turn to arbitrazh.[66] Again we see a pattern of agency functionaries boosting their own organization and in effect asking for more power.

One writer typical of this group criticizes Gosarbitrazh as not active enough, adding that it is too slow in deciding questions and that "arbitrazh must come to a decision after the first meeting, not postpone it due to insufficiency of evidence from one or another side." Others have a similar attitude and complain about the alleged difficulties of control inherent in a decentralized arbitration system; for instance, the near impossibility of halting the implementation of a "poor decision" unless it is detrimental to the general interests of several constituent parts of the USSR. They favor further centralization and increased supervisory powers by arbitration organs.[67] One arbitrazh official even wants his agency to displace the People's Control Committees and the courts, and to decide "questions of the contract responsibility of the collective and the personal responsibility of officials of enterprises." He sweeps aside the issues of "citizens' rights and legal interests" by referring to the pressing needs of his own agency. Some idea of the scale of arbitrazh's activity can be gained from viewing the work of the 15 arbiters of the Moscow City Soviet Executive Committee during 1970. They handled 21,589 disputes, of which 1,759 were appealed to the chief arbiter with only 85 being reversed. Many of the disputes could have been settled among the parties themselves but for the excuse of losses that arbitration decisions may bring.[68]

It is evident that the system of state arbitration probably will not become less involved in or have fewer supervisory powers over inter-enterprise ties. On the contrary, as the Soviet writers cited and the general tenor of recent Soviet writing on the subject imply, its importance in this respect is likely to increase, as indicated by a resolution of the USSR Council of Ministers of August 7, 1970.[69]

Since enterprises are not being either allowed or forced to cope fully with their mutual obligations, this result may be unavoidable. However, it is unlikely that arbitrazh can resolve important questions of price and quality, since these are results of fundamental systemic decisions. In addition, its technical and economic competence may be lower than required.[70]

SUMMARY AND CONCLUSION

In general, the manager-manager relationship has not developed to a point where managers may freely make long-term commitments with the managers of other enterprises or inter-enterprise obligations are often fulfilled. A significant alteration of this set of ties would necessarily mean the loss of some of the main means of effecting state control over an important part of the economy. At most, some degree of rationalization of the means of centralized state control has occurred. No new departure is in evidence. Rather, enforced conformity to norms of long standing is at the center of the attempt of the Soviet leadership to obtain more effective cooperation and trade among enterprises through the increase in the power and numbers of regulatory agencies.

NOTES

1. Janos Kornai, Overcentralization in Economic Administration (London: Oxford University Press, 1959), p. 147.
2. B. Sukharevskii, "Predpriiatie i material'noe stimulirovanie," Ekonomicheskaia gazeta 49 (December 1965): 13.
3. Iu. Koldomasov, "Razvitie priamykh khoziaistvennykh sviazei . . .," Voprosy ekonomiki 11 (November 1965): 15.
4. A. Emdin, "Supply System Has Key Role in Economic Reform," Ekonomika Sovetskoi Ukrainy 9 (September 1968): 34-38; JPRS 46,765 (October 29, 1968): 13.
5. N. Garetovskii, "Aktual'nye voprosy khoziaistvennoi reformy," Finansy SSSR 1 (January 1967) (JPRS 40,089 [March 2, 1967]: 50-51); Theodore Frankel, "Economic Reform: A Tentative Appraisal," Problems of Communism 26, no. 3 (May-June 1967): 38; and Herbert S. Levine, in Abram Bergson et al., "Soviet Economic Performance and Reform," Slavic Review 25, no. 2 (June 1966): 223, 226.
6. I. Mikuchenis, "Interesy potrebitelei i otvetstvennost' postavshchikov," Planovoe khoziaistvo 3 (March 1966): 88.

7. "V tsentral'nom komitete KPSS i Soveta Ministrov SSSR," Pravda, October 10, 1965, p. 1.

8. Barry M. Richman, Soviet Management (Englewood Cliffs, N.J.: Prentice-Hall, 1965), p. 65.

9. See Frankel, op. cit., p. 33.

10. Koldomasov, op. cit., p. 16. Emphasis added.

11. S. Anufrienko, "Khoziaistvennaia reforma i initsiativa predpriiatii," Voprosy ekonomiki 12 (December 1968): 32.

12. See Abraham Katz, The Politics of Economic Reform in the Soviet Union (New York: Praeger, 1972), p. 110.

13. Pravda, April 9, 1973, p. 1.

14. P. Rivnii, "Inertsiia starogo," Ekonomicheskaia gazeta 15 (April 1967): 16.

15. Ibid.; Iu. Sedushev, "Povyshenie material'noi otvetstvennosti v promyshlennosti," Voprosy ekonomiki 1 (January 1970): 12; Pravda (lead article), April 9, 1973; and Trud, July 3, 1969.

16. Material'no technicheskoe snabzhenie 3 (March 1967); JPRS 41,340 (June 9, 1967): 3. For a veiled criticism of Gossnab's impeding of direct ties, see Ekonomicheskaia gazeta 38 (September 1973): 17; abstracted in CDSP 25, no. 48 (December 26, 1973): 15.

17. Koldomasov, op. cit., pp. 15, 19; and V. Soifer, Sovetskaia iustitsiia 5 (March 1968): 6-7 (JPRS 45,229 [May 1, 1968]: 54).

18. Izvestiia, April 14, 1972, p. 3; condensed in CDSP 24, no. 15 (May 10, 1972): 7-8.

19. N. V. Tsapkina, ed., Firmy i ekonomika (Leningrad: Lenizdat, 1966), pp. 129-31; and Gertrude E. Schroeder, "The 'Reform' of the Supply System in Soviet Industry," Soviet Studies 24, no. 1 (July 1972): 105-06. The percentage figure is from Izvestiia Akademii nauk SSSR, seriia ekonomicheskaia (1971): no. 1, 36.

20. See G. Sireno, "Supply System Must Help Sell Surpluses," Material'no-tekhnicheskoe snabzhenie 7 (1968): 77-81 (JPRS 46,407 [September 11, 1968]: 40); Koldomasov, op. cit., pp. 16-17; and V. Semenov, "Material and Technical Supply Under the New Conditions," Material'no-tekhnicheskoe snabzhenie 6 (December 1966) (JPRS 40,271 [March 15, 1967]: 30-31).

21. Martin C. Spechler, "Decentralizing the Soviet Economy," Soviet Studies 22, no. 2 (October 1970): 223-25.

22. John N. Hazard, Communists and Their Law (Chicago: University of Chicago Press, 1969), p. 356; and Eugene Zaleski, Economic Reform in the Soviet Union, 1962-1966 (Chapel Hill, N.C.: University of North Carolina, 1967), p. 110.

23. See Hazard, op. cit., pp. 327-28, 353-55; and Izvestiia, December 17, 1971, p. 3 (condensed in CDSP 23, no. 50 [January 11, 1972]: 13).

24. I. Korchak, Robochaia gazeta (Kiev), April 18, 1969, p. 3. Korchak is a Chief Arbitrator of USSR Gosarbitrazh (and an I. I. Korchak was a Deputy Procurator of the Ukrainian branch of the Procuracy in 1964).

25. Iu. Ia. L'vovich, "Povysit' dogovornuiu distsiplinu pri postovke tovarov torgovym organizatsiiam," Sovetskoe gosudarstvo i pravo 4 (April 1966): 76-77.

26. M. S. Fal'kovich, "Khoziaistvennyi dogovor i ekonomicheskie otnosheniia predpriiatii," Planovoe khoziaistvo 4 (April 1966): 69-70, 72; and Izvestiia, December 7, 1971, p. 3.

27. N. I. Klein, "Rol' khoziaistvennogo dogovora v formirovanii plana . . .," Sovetskoe gosudarstvo i pravo 6 (June 1966): 41-42, 44.

28. Ia. Tolstikov, "The New Economic System at the Tallin Machine-Building Plant," Sovetskaia Estoniia (Tallin), May 26, 1966, p. 2; JPRS 37,443 (September 6, 1966): 15.

29. O. Latsis, "Net iskliucheniia bez pravila . . .," Novyi mir 4 (April 1967): 171.

30. "A More Businesslike Approach, More Responsibility," Narodnoe khoziaistvo Kazakhstana (Alma-Ata) 10 (October 1966); JPRS 39,487 (January 11, 1967): 4.

31. Mikuchenis, op. cit., p. 87, and "Ekonomike predpriiatii --vseobshchee vnimanie," Ekonomicheskaia gazeta 18 (May 1967): 16.

32. See Harry Trend, "Bulgarian Economic Reforms Fail to Solve Inter-Enterprise Delivery Problems," Radio Free Europe Research Report, October 2, 1967, pp. 1-2.

33. G. Uiboland, "Startuet legkaia industriia," Sovetskaia Estoniia (Tallin), June 1, 1967, p. 2 (JPRS 41,660 [July 1, 1967]: 41); Pravda, May 8, 1969, p. 2; I. Malyshev, "Khoziaistvennaia reforma v deistvii," Partiinaia zhizn' 20 (October 1966): 20; Rivnii, op. cit., p. 16 (writing in April 1967); Garetovskii, op. cit., p. 51; and Keith Bush, "The Reforms: A Balance Sheet," Problems of Communism 16, no. 4 (July-August 1967): 34.

34. "V kollegii Ministerstvo Finansov SSSR," Finansy SSSR 10 (October 1966); JPRS 39,520 (January 13, 1967): 50.

35. Pravda, December 16, 1969. Quoted in Steven J. Staats, "Corruption in the Soviet System," Problems of Communism, 21, no. 1 (January-February 1972): 42.

36. Opyt i problemy stimulirovaniia v novykh usloviiakh (Moscow: Ekonomika, 1966).

37. Ibid., p. 51.

38. A. Birman, "Neotvratimost'," Literaturnaia gazeta 2 (January 11, 1967): 10.

39. F. Rabinovich, "Ot 'balansa shtrafov' k kontroliu rublem," Ekonomicheskaia gazeta 14 (April 1967): 15.

40. F. Rabinovich, "Ekonomicheskoe stimulirovanie i dogovornaia otvetstvennost'," Kommunist 14 (September 1972): 84-85, condensed in CDSP 24, no. 43 (November 22, 1972): 1. And see Pravda, February 13, 1974, p. 2 (abstracted in CDSP 26, no. 7 [March 13, 1974]: 19); and Pravda, September 26, 1969, pp. 2-3.

41. Rabinovich, "Ot 'balansa . . .,"

42. Fal'kovich, op. cit., pp. 71, 72.

43. V. G. Verdnikov, "O planovom kharaktere khoziaistvennogo dogovora," Sovetskoe gosudarstvo i pravo 4 (April 1966): 70; and Rabinovich, "Ekonomicheskoe stimulirovanie . . .," p. 88.

44. Tolstikov, op. cit., p. 17.

45. S. Iampol'skii, Ekonomika Sovetskoi Ukrainy (Kiev) 9 (September 1966); JPRS 39,088 (December 13, 1966): 69.

46. See Izvestiia, November 13, 1967. See also Raymond H. Anderson, "Soviet Sets Fines to Speed Reform," New York Times, November 15, 1967, p. 18. See also M. S. Fal'kovich, "Usilenie material'noi otvetstvennosti po khoziaistvennym dogovoram," Sovetskoe gosudastvo i pravo 8 (August 1968): 121-25; JPRS 46,573 (October 1, 1968): 25.

47. See Sedushev, op. cit., p. 11; and Izvestiia, April 26, 1969, p. 2.

48. F. L. Rabinovich, "Vina kak osnovanie dogovornoi otvetstvennost' sotsialisticheskogo predpriiatiia," Sovetskoe gosudarstvo i pravo 6 (June 1966): 30.

49. Bush, op. cit., p. 35.

50. "Novaia sistema snabzheniia--v deistvii," Ekonomicheskaia gazeta 4 (January 1966): 3.

51. New York Times, January 21, 1973, p. 14; and Izvestiia, January 13, 1972, p. 2 (condensed in CDSP 24, no. 2 [February 9, 1972]: 12. See also Schroeder, op. cit., p. 102; and Sotsialisticheskaia industriia, October 29, 1970, p. 2 (ABSEES, April 1971, p. 106).

52. "Obshchee polozhenie o ministerstvakh SSSR," Ekonomicheskaia gazeta 34 (August 1967): 8.

53. Pravda, April 9, 1973, p. 1.

54. See "Novaia sistema snabzheniia--v deistvii"; Emdin, op. cit., pp. 9-12; and Schroeder, op. cit.

55. Material'no-tekhnicheskoe snabzhenie 3 (March 1967); JPRS 41,340 (June 9, 1967): 2-3. See also Schroeder, op. cit., p. 101; a statute approved by the Council of Ministers in April 1969, in A. F. Rumiantsev et al., eds., Khoziaistvennaia reforma v SSSR (Moscow: Pravda, 1969), pp. 186-91 (discussed in Izvestiia, May 31, 1969, p. 2).

56. V. E. Dymshits, "Obespechenie proizvodstva--zadacha gosudarstvennaia," Ekonomicheskaia gazeta 18 (May 1967): 6-8.

57. I. Luk'ianov, "Snabzhenie v novykh usloviiakh," Ekonomicheskaia gazeta 2 (January 1966): 22. He is head of the Material and Technical Supply Administration. See also N. Aleshin, Material'no-tekhnicheskoe snabzhenie 1 (January 1969) (JPRS 47,666 [March 18, 1969]: 93-94); Schroeder, op. cit., 103-04; and Pravda, January 26, 1973, p. 2 (condensed in CDSP 25, no. 4 [February 21, 1973]: 8-9).

58. Rush V. Greenslade, "The Soviet Economic System in Transition," in U.S. Congress, Joint Economic Committee, New Directions in the Soviet Economy (Washington, D.C.: U.S. Government Printing Office, 1966), Pt. I, p. 14; and Semenov, op. cit., p. 32.

59. A. Kurskii, "Itogi khoziaistvennoi reformy za 1966 g . . .," Voprosy ekonomiki 4 (April 1967): 30.

60. A. Nikitin and V. Seliunin, "Pis'ma ob upravlenii: II. Kontroler ili posrednik?" Ekonomicheskaia gazeta 12 (March 1967): 18.

61. K. N. Rudnev, "Otrasl' vstupaet v reformu," Kommunist 1 (January 1967): 62.

62. A. Aleinik, "The Role of Supply in Raising the Effectiveness of Enterprise Operations," Material'notekhnicheskoe snabzhenie 4 (April 1967); JPRS 41,204 (May 30, 1967): 24.

63. Frankel, op. cit., p. 33; and Ekonomika i organizatsiia promyshlennogo proizvodstva 1 (1970): 103, 105, 107 (cited in Schroeder, op. cit., p. 117).

64. Nikitin and Seliunin, op. cit., p. 19.

65. I. T. Gavrilenko and I. G. Pobirchenko, "Struktura gosudarstvennogo arbitrazha . . .," Sovetskoe gosudarstvo i pravo 6 (June 1966): 47; L'vovich, op. cit., p. 80; and N. G. Egorov, "Boriba s nedostatkami . . .," ibid. 12 (December 1965): 92.

66. Sovetskaia Rossiia, October 23, 1968, p. 2.

67. Mikuchenis, op. cit., p. 88; Gavrilenko and Pobirchenko, op. cit., p. 46; and F. Rabinovich, Izvestiia, February 3, 1972, p. 3 (condensed in CDSP 24, no. 5 [March 1, 1972]: 22).

68. Izvestiia, July 3, 1971, p. 5 (condensed in CDSP 23, no. 27 [August 3, 1971]: 27); and Izvestiia, June 2, 1971, p. 3 (excerpted in CDSP 23, no. 22 [June 29, 1971]: 18).

69. Izvestiia, September 10, 1970, p. 3; CDSP 12, no. 36 (October 6, 1970): 17.

70. Spechler, op. cit., pp. 252-53; and Rabinovich, "Ekonomicheskoe stimulirovanie i dogovornaia otvetstvennost'," pp. 88-92.

CHAPTER 7
MANAGERS AND MANAGEMENT

SIGNIFICANCE, PROBLEMS, AND POLITICS

The system of Soviet industrial administration is now so large and its issues and problems so complex that central decision-making cannot keep up with the decisions that have to be made, thus leaving more up to the industrial managers themselves and increasing their importance. As one writer on economic topics summarizes the situation:

> Today the problem of managing technical progress is essentially the problem of choice. In contrast to past times, when . . . "we squeezed out the last drops," [now] we do not have to make a decision on the basis of a single variant; instead we choose one of several possibilities. One decision is the optimal one.[1]

Other writers, including economists, have stressed that the new situation, including the goal of the "continuous rise in the standard of living of the population," requires management to change over from extensive to intensive methods, to the application of the principles of mathematical economics and the use of computers, and to the most modern and effective principles and systems of management.[2] The present lack of reserves of labor alone, a shock that is still being assimilated by planners, makes good management much more important. The urgency of the ever-rising demands of Soviet consumers, perhaps sharpened by the mass outbursts by disgruntled consumers in Poland in December 1970, requires a qualitatively improved management. As <u>Pravda</u> has put it, the "continuous raising of the standard of living of the people is an objective economic necessity." (The second adjective might well be replaced by "political.") The leading aircraft designer O. K. Antonov has said "the improvement of quality" is the "most important problem" in the economy.[3]

The new emphasis upon consumer goods indicates the arrival of a more complex political situation. The Soviet leadership is appealing to the Soviet citizen as individual consumer. The large-scale purchases of American grain and the trade deals pushed by Brezhnev during negotiations in the United States in June 1973 work toward the same ends. Potentially, a political whirlwind is being fostered that the Party may not always be able to ride. The realization of a qualitatively improved economy requires substantive changes in the principles and methods of operation of the entire structure of industrial management and of the attitudes, knowledge, and capabilities of managerial personnel. At the Twenty-Fourth Congress, General Secretary Brezhnev pointed out that "the growing scale of our economy and its qualitative shifts . . . are making new and higher demands on management and do not permit us to rest content with the existing forms and methods, even if they have served us well in the past." He accordingly called for improvement in management by raising the professional abilities and knowledge of managerial cadres and rapid development of the "science of management" and computer technology. Brezhnev specifically called for a new pattern of decision-making in which most questions would be decided "once and decisively, and not be bounced back and forth from one department to another."[4]

To be realized, this would require significant managerial decentralization and a great increase in managers' knowledge and in their willingness to act on their own initiative on the basis of new principles and goals. Essentially, it would mean that the longstanding hierarchic pattern of managerial rules and bureaucratized indices of success would have to be discarded in favor of flexible guidelines within which managers would have the freedom to make decisions on their own, subject to the requirement of profitable operation. The task is difficult to attain, and not just in the Soviet Union. As Herbert Simon notes, "the environment of the . . . factory manager . . . is not the kind . . . a psychologist would design to produce high motivation." The typical manager responds by creating for his subordinates the same sort of restrictive environment that his superiors have formed for him. "The task of middle managers today is . . . taken up with pace setting, with work pushing, and with expediting."[5] The Soviet managers' work situation has been very much like this. Simon sees the introduction of automation creating a more rational and less authority-ridden environment in which men will work better and with less tension. His guess, as he calls it, remains to be tested.

One fundamental problem starkly confronting management change in the Soviet Union is the dead weight of the combination of the old economic system and the managers formed by it. Although "a new managerial style is needed and is being called for . . . adaptation to the post-Stalin atmosphere is not easy for those whose attitudes and habits have been shaped by Stalinism. . . ."[6] The use of harsh methods would defeat the new emphasis on rationally based spontaneity. Some other way has to be found to inspire lasting change in management.

A major source of difficulties facing attempts at organizational change derives from the fact that most organizational activities are habitual, patterned responses to stimuli--often no real thought precedes action. Adaptation does occur, but rarely as an entirely new program. "In most cases, adaptation takes place through a recombination of lower-level programs that are already in existence."[7]

Nevertheless, policy-makers will still try to change group behavior in order to implement their plans. If attempts at organizational change are inevitable, what is in general the best way--the way with the best chances for success--to go about them? Amitai Etzioni suggests that attempts to change people are "more expensive and usually less productive than approaches that accept people as they are and seek to mend not them but the circumstances around them." This position has recently begun to enjoy some degree of acceptance in the USSR. For example, "To change a manager's psychology and to teach him how to work in a new way is far more difficult than to select the correct structure for the [managerial] apparatus."[8] Of course, such an approach is within the Soviet tradition. Soviet politico-administrative history has seen several attempts to alter circumstances (such as collectivization), but few serious attempts such as seen in China several times, to "reeducate" people into living and thinking a new way. This difference in approach is fundamental and puts its stamp upon politics and society. However, changes of situation are ineffectual if those who are to be affected contrive to maintain previous relationships and attitudes, thereby subverting the attempts at change. Soviet managers and bureaucrats have been adept at this. The possibility of the reform engendering a new stagnation has been suggested. "The result of this may well be at worst some kind of paralysis or at best a set of adjustments that will leave things much as they were before."[9]

Jan Prybyla links organizational change to economic change when he suggests:

> To breathe new life into the Soviet economy what is needed is not just to change the formal organization, but to reduce it; to replace administrative

> coordination with a coordinative mechanism that
> springs from a multitude of decisions taken inde-
> pendently, in response to a common set of price
> signals, the prices themselves reflecting the
> choices of many participants.[10]

He correctly notes that to induce managers to adopt new methods and technologies is "the most difficult question." Building a new structure of relationships, ideals, and goals requires their cooperation; and finishing the job inevitably means attempting to change managerial attitudes and patterns of thinking, despite the low chance of success. As Marshall Goldman points out, "many Soviet managers fear the effects of competition and are reluctant to abandon the . . . climate of fixed markets and stable production quotas in which they have operated."[11] Barry Richman says:

> . . . in the Soviet Union major gains could best
> be achieved by changing the external environment
> of the enterprise. . . . Such major structural
> changes are clearly painful, since . . . they may
> well involve capitalist heresies and bureaucratic
> empire dismemberment. However, the Soviets'
> overwhelming desire for grandeur in the modern
> world may give them little choice in the matter.[12]

The political significance of the changes in management required by the reform are as yet only potential. Nevertheless, certain considerations can be mentioned. For one thing, the changes, to take place, would require making the Soviet industrial manager more a businessman, even an entrepreneur, and less a bureaucrat. The Soviet industrial manager often had to engage in the typical bureaucratic "displacement of goals" and replace officially desired goals with the attainment of such formalized indices of success as the VAL.[13] Of course, in his relations with Party organizations he sometimes entered the world of politics. This was particularly so when he joined "family circles" or local mutual protective groupings.

Giving the Soviet industrial manager a greater decision-making role would mean that the Party-based control system over the economy would have to be loosened. At the least, the points at which it would come into play would be made more distant from the enterprise director. Ironically, this will not be welcomed by all managers, some of whom have appreciated the general controls under which they have long worked for the alibi they offered in the event of difficulties and failures. Similarly, the administrators in the glavki and ministries above the enterprises were not personally affected by enterprise failures. "In the past, a man had nothing to worry about: No matter how well or how poorly the plants subordinate to the chief administration operated, this did not affect his pay." Supposedly, it is to be different now, at least for the functionaries of obedineniia.[14]

Alfred Meyer has called attention to the problems of control posed by modern bureaucratic organization in the USSR, saying: "Soviet government is characterized by that same imbalance between ability and authority and suffers from all that 'tension generated by the conflict between specialization and hierarchy' which seems to trouble all giant organizations in other parts of the world."[15]

This tension has been particularly acute in the Soviet case because of the great demands made by the ideology and its interpreter, the Party. To reduce this, full implementation of the reform would lead to a change in political structure and principles, because the center's powers would be lessened. Significant administrative change has political effects. As Carl Friedrich says, "politics and administration are not two mutually exclusive boxes, or absolute distinctions, but . . . two closely linked aspects of the same process. Public policy . . . is a continuous process, the formation of which is inseparable from its execution."[16] What can happen is that some degree of policy-making, at least for the enterprise or the firm, can be added to the already great internal power granted by edinonachalie. Soviet industrial managers cannot, of course, be a major political grouping in their own right, despite claims to that effect made by a few writers in the West; but they can become a more important "policy group," and accordingly be better able to engage in advocacy with the political leadership.

Jeremy Azrael says that "it is practically certain that the new managers will press for operational autonomy and procedurally stabilized access to the policy process within their own spheres." This does not at all mean they will press for systemic political change in the direction of democracy. Azrael also notes:

> Their composite image of the good society is and is likely to remain one in which such cardinal attributes of the system as the dictatorship of the party, the primacy of the party apparat, the canonization of Marxist-Leninist ideology, the comprehensive institutionalization of collective forms of social and economic organization, and extensive central planning are combined with such "new" attributes as stabilized policy-making procedures, a substantial devolution of authority to specialized functionaries of proven political reliability, and reliance on material and honorific

incentives as the principal means of social
and economic mobilization.

He adds that managerial political aspirations smack "at least as much of continuity as of change."[17] Nevertheless, a new mix of admittedly old elements, coupled with a few genuinely new components in an atmosphere of post-industrialism, ethnic and intellectual dissent, relaxation of international tensions, and the absence of active totalitarian repression, can begin to produce a qualitatively different political system.

In recent decades industrial managers have enjoyed increasing power within their plants and the economy, thus attaining a good position for further, and perhaps qualitatively different increases, in their powers. Although J. Burnham's "managerial revolution" is not in the offing, it is unavoidable that under now-emergent conditions, managers will be brought up still more against "the economic planners at the center or the political controllers."[18] Certainly "the political consequence in strengthening the role of industrial managers requires explanation." Most writers on Soviet politics discuss what the political role of the industrial managers might be, although some treat the managers as part of a larger grouping. Vernon Aspaturian, for example, discusses the "managerial-technical bureaucracy, a structure of production and distribution" that he presents as one of four "political institutional groups" in the Soviet political system.

Others treat industrial managers as an interest group because they lead similar professional lives and share a common set of attitudes. John Hardt and Theodore Frankel present the most important of these shared attitudes as "the demand for greater operational autonomy from ministerial and party interference," "the demand for professionalism," and "the striving for the maximization of personal income via the bonus system."[19] The first two clearly have political implications. They say that professional conferences are one place where group attitudes arise and that bargaining with the ministries and with Party secretaries constitutes interest articulation. Trud has noted that "councils of enterprise directors . . . systematically discuss the most important problems of accelerating technical progress."[20] These arguments show only that managers have a say in technical and operational matters. But this has political significance in a planned economy and a priority-ridden society. And the managers' influence on planning can only rise. The increase in councils of directors and in the importance attached to flexible management are two indications.

However, the Party apparatus has a position easy to protect and a good one from which to counterattack against any assertion of political views or any attempt to change the political system. Indeed, it is probable that divisions among managers preclude such challenges. Managers of light and heavy industry and those of bureaucratic or entrepreneurial bent might have very different views on matters of policy and operations.[21] In addition, the Party holds political legitimacy and also sits astride the nexus of coordinating channels. One force that might be used against the managers is the industrial workers. Managerial rationality, if allowed to proceed unchecked, would try to make the remaining workers expend greater efforts; and the ongoing Shchekino experiment, if carried to its logical extreme, might create the proverbial "industrial reserve army" of Marxism. In view of the political implications of such a development, "the political power is susceptible to tolerating certain economic irrationalities when these are deemed to be a politically rational means of appeasing worker discontent." This is observable in the policy of producing a pattern of income distribution "substantially more egalitarian than it is in the advanced Western countries. . . ."[22] This is not a move of democratic intent, of course; its intention is the same as that described by Lenin in his <u>Imperialism</u> and similar to that of Disraeli and Bismarck earlier. Certain Marxists, Svetozar Stojanovich for example, have noted that egalitarianism in income and the entry of workers into the ruling class do not constitute socialism.[23] A general analogy for the Soviet system might be feudalism, albeit a technocratic one, with a ruling class using the ideology of collective ownership for its own interests.

Although we have been discussing possibility rather than probability, one can develop into the other. Since 1965 or even earlier, the Soviet political leadership has been attempting to institutionalize significant changes in the principles, structure, and operation of the economy in hopes of making it perform more rationally, efficiently, and productively. Many of these changes grow out of the economic reform and closely affect managerial personnel. This process raises the potential of moving Soviet society into a post-industrial stage and, in turn, the need to put Soviet politics on a new basis. At that point, one possible line of development--although not necessarily the most probable one--is a decentralization of major decision-making, and the consequent magnification of the political significance of industrial managers and planners.

THE CHALLENGE

Industrial Management and the Burdens of the Past

The management of Soviet industry has been deeply affected by its long need to function in a milieu permeated by political considerations, notably the military-like view of the economy as a complex of redoubts to be assaulted and taken by storm. This approach, though successful in a narrow sense, had become incapable of directing the more sophisticated economy that emerged in the 1960s. This was inevitable, considering the violation of certain basic economic principles at the inception of Stalin's industrialization drive. Most of industry was operating at a loss, and profits were not an important consideration. Two Czech scholars note: "The original system of management in the socialist order was . . . adapted for the job of handling elementary issues of the class struggle, and it relied on the traditional means of power politics and administration."[24]

A new corps of managers fit only for the process of massive but basic industrialization performed well within this milieu of Stalinism and Taylorism. By the late 1930s many of these managers were representatives of a "new social stratum . . . in process of formation."[25] However, it appears that the professional qualifications of industrial executives, although they had risen greatly since the first plan, dropped after the mid-1950s and deteriorated still further from 1961 to 1964, through losses due to retirement and science, and through reductions in staff. The existence of a "certain discrepancy" between the requirements of production and the capabilities of management that the reform actually widened has been noted by others.[26] This deficiency in managerial knowledge added a new burden to the enterprise director's already burdensome situation.

There are other reasons why his situation is not a completely enviable one. Although he is almost invariably a member of the Communist Party, receives perquisites comparable to those of the Party professional elite, and is granted near-plenary powers over what is often, in effect, his personal domain, the environment in which he works has nevertheless been highly unstable and filled with difficulties. In order to survive, he has been forced to engage in informal and even illegal behavior.[27] This pattern of behavior has made him liable, particularly in the event his enterprise fails to attain its goals, to a range of penalties: demotion, removal, and even public disgrace and imprisonment as a "wrecker" of socialist construction. The manager's working life has been likened to a tightrope act. Harry Schwartz says: "Under this unremitting pressure for production, the managerial bureaucracy sought to produce by every possible means including informal behavior and outright illegalities. . . . The pressure for production never relented."[28]

The reform was meant to lessen the rigors inherent in this situation by allowing the manager a much wider latitude of action through making the process of industrial management and the operation of the industrial enterprise more rational in foundation and routine in operation. Hopefully, the enterprise was to become a more productive operation. The Soviet industrial arrangement had contained "a built-in bias against innovations."[29] The reform, despite limitations on its fullest development, still means more independence for managers and is an approach to the improvement of managerial importance quite different from that of Khrushchev, who tried to increase Party and "people's" control over managers in hopes of making them more productive and efficient.[30]

Current Interference and Limitations

Performance has not matched official intentions. The enterprise and its management continue to face frequent plan changes and "petty tutelage" from the ministries and chief administrations, supervision and interference by the local Party organizations, a scarcity of supplies, and the restriction of contacts with suppliers and buyers. The managers' bureaucratic superiors often act like the autarkic ministries that existed before 1957. One Soviet observer complains:

> The possibilities inherent in the reform [are] impeded by elements of bureaucratism and by relapses into voluntarism . . . this takes the form of presentation of insufficiently substantiated plans to enterprises, arbitrary changes in plan assignments . . . and the unjustified reallocation of sources . . . . ministries, chief administrations and other agencies . . . still do not bear full material and moral responsibility for the harm that they sometimes do to enterprises.[31]

In addition, the Communist Party's apparatchiki continue to intervene actively in production matters, a practice often necessary for fulfilling the plan but that results in the lowering of managers' initiative and sense of responsibility.

Difficulties of Managerial Attitudes and Abilities

Besides outright interference from above, many managers have not accepted or been able to work with the new demands and responsibilities the reform has granted them. Some managers want to be led firmly by a linked chain of orders and directives authoritatively handed down to them by their superiors, and were sorry to see the ministries disappear in 1957. The managers' present difficulties relate to their understanding and application of economics, possession and use of financial and business sense, and capability of managing under the new conditions. A secretary of the Altai Territory Party Committee says that Soviet enterprise directors' ". . . previous experience in economic management has not prepared them for the deft handling of such concepts as profit, profitability and the use of production assets."[32] Their formal education has not been of much help in these matters either. Most of the higher technical schools give their graduates little training in economics. The new conditions require a good understanding of economics. John Armstrong correctly states that "an engineering . . . or technocratic approach toward human problems is more characteristic of Soviet than of Western European administrators" and cites as a cause the fact that "so many" Soviet administrators were trained as engineers.[33] Azrael notes the existence of a similar pattern, saying that ". . . many young Soviet engineers appear to have had difficulty in disengaging themselves from a purely technological perspective and adjusting to the large problems of 'human engineering' that executive responsibility entails."[34]

This is a critical limitation upon the reform's chances of success, but management qualities now take precedence over engineering qualities. For example, it has been stated that "to be a 'manager' under present-day conditions means having a special profession, holding a post that no longer can be held by an engineer. . . ."[35] It is authoritatively stressed today that the Soviet manager be a generalist, be able to oversee the enterprise's work, but also be able and willing to delegate operational tasks to others. The manager's "political qualities" of high idealism and devotion to Communism are still given their due, but only in passing.

Attitudes of some managers also stand in the way of innovation. It is apparent that the reform's introduction of new (although fewer) success criteria is as upsetting to some managers as was the unrealistic stress often given the VAL in the past. Many managers are unable to operate effectively in the new and less authoritarian environment. As one plant director comments:

> It seemed that it was necessary only to enlarge the director's rights and give him the opportunity to feel himself a real boss, and all problems would be solved. But . . . while we have been given the rights, the problems have not disappeared. On the contrary, there are even more of them, not to mention that responsibility has been added.[36]

This is an example of the appearance of "unanticipated consequences," a side effect of attempts at organizational change. The delegation of authority often results in conflict among subunits and a commitment to subunit goals ". . . over and above their contribution to the total organizational program."[37] And, of course, disequilibrium and conflict are greatest during implementation of a policy. The managers' negative reaction is partly a direct outgrowth of some elements in the reform's context. The post-1965 success indicators are not internally consistent and make contradictory demands upon them. It is therefore not surprising to see paralysis of will, reticence to act in a new way, and even occasional opposition. It is possible, however, that the recalcitrance of some managerial personnel in implementing the reform is an expression of a political position. In addition, polls show that many managerial personnel are not satisfied with their work situations.[38]

Similar difficulties in giving managerial personnel new goals and responsibilities are common. For example, R. Cordiner, the former Chairman of the Board of the General Electric Company in the United States, in explaining why his decentralization and reorganization of the management of the company was only partly successful, says, "I thought that a lot of the fellows we took from functional jobs and made general managers would respond to the challenge of being measured. I was wrong."[39] The reorganization caused a lot of "heartaches" and "troubles" for the G.E. managers. The present Soviet reform is having a similar effect upon managers (and their ministerial superiors) who are being required in mid-career to learn new techniques, operate under new conditions in accordance with new principles, and to accept judgment by new and more numerous criteria. This is a strain for those men and women who assume they have reached a safe plateau in society, particularly for those in their fifties and sixties. It is problematical whether many Soviet managers will be able to manage or even work in the new larger industrial associations.[40]

Difficulties of Action

Examples of managers' lack of success in operating in a new manner can be drawn from the experiences for "reformed" enterprises in the chemical industry. In 29 such enterprises the level of productivity of labor dropped during the first year of the reform. Many managers continued to take on the easiest assignments available. One commentator says: "The managers, having easily grasped the most available reserves, do not greatly concern themselves with how to attain the greatest efficiency of production or how better to regulate the mechanism of economic relations."[41]

The Soviet press is full of reports of the old shell game of purely formal fulfillment of plans. As a member of the Academy of Sciences said in 1973: "There are still enterprise executives who,

MANAGERS AND MANAGEMENT

with the tacit consent and sometimes even the approval of the ministries, plan understated indices and then, after achieving these indices without any special effort, take a place among the outstanding enterprises."[42]

Other holdovers from the unreformed past include overstaffing, "storming" (shturmovshchina) to fulfill the plan on time, violation of law, and the widespread use of that venerable Soviet entrepreneurial middleman, the "pusher" or tolkach. And, as Pravda editorialized at the end of 1972, many directors "still react indulgently to the wrecking of the plan, show little initiative, [and] do not fully use the powers granted them."[43]

Overstaffing is still railed against, but managers have always felt, on the basis of experience, that to be realistic they needed as many personnel as they could keep on the payroll, in order to cope with production problems that would inevitably arise. Also, since "an engineer who does not become an administrator can expect no gains in earnings . . . we create unnecessary administrative positions." Many small enterprises have the same administrative structure as much larger ones. Some enterprises register bookkeepers and accountants as laboratory assistants or cleaners on their wage bills.[44] By 1967, on the average "one out of each six or seven people working in industrial enterprises was a worker of the administrative apparatus." Shturmovshchina is still endemic as well, even among many "reformed" enterprises, perhaps since the provision of supplies is still erratic and the motivations for work so deficient.

The tolkach is definitely still with us. No study of Soviet industrial management is complete without his presence. This peripatetic "representative" of the Soviet firm has become almost the Pantagruel of writing in the field. Perhaps the space devoted to his misadventures is a product of "cold warring." Yet one economist after another notes the importance of his diverse functions to Soviet industry. He is par excellence a living example of informalism in bureaucracy and of the performance of functions that cannot be carried out by formal organization. He may be "unspecified." But he is ever on call for the tough job or for solution of the little problem that has brought a great organization to a halt. His milieu is the supply problem and his metier its solution. As for a definition of the role, Joseph Berliner calls the tolkach "the specialist in obtaining all manner of scarce commodities through a combination of influence and gifts." Alfred Meyer calls him "a combination lobbyist and salesman." He may be an element of capitalism, since he obtains things "on the basis of free competition."[45] The role of the "intermediary" in Western business is similar.

Since 1965 the tolkach's numbers may have increased, because a less centralized economy may have a greater need for his services.

Production and sale of new, more complex commodities from previously unused materials ensure an indispensable position for him. This possibility seems particularly implicit in the new relationship of factory managers and retail outlets in light industry. In the Hungarian economic reform tolkachi have been legally institutionalized as "trading companies."[46] Also, many managers and management personnel still do not use their time well. They can waste time on lesser tasks, even exhausting themselves on them, never getting to the main work.

> An analysis by the various branches of industry shows that from 30 percent to 40 percent of all administrative labor expenditures goes into obtaining information on the course of production work, 10 percent to 15 percent into transmitting the information, and 20 percent to 25 percent into analyzing the information.[47]

Obviously, much remains to be done to change Soviet industrial managers as a type. A theoretical framework for the work of management is needed in order to increase the efficiency of industry's operations. It is appropriate to examine the suggestions for solutions, the attempts to implement them, and their effect.

THE RESPONSE

In order to correct management's ineffective response to the reform's demands, the political leadership is introducing changes in four areas: the reform of administrative structure, the introduction of business administration or "scientific management," the initiation of new training programs, and the application of computer technology.

Changes in Administrative Structures and Staffs

One of the most common reactions to an administrative problem is arbitrary reduction in force. This is being applied throughout the administrative structure of industry. Finance Ministry personnel were "horrified" by the snowballing increase in the numbers of managerial personnel and want to cut the total number by 10 percent yearly.[48] In Penza during 1966-69 the industrial management staff increased 20 percent (and that of farm and construction management grew by 32 and 35 percent, respectively). The authorities in Penza in effect avoided implementing recent government orders to cut administrative staff by adding those persons "eliminated" elsewhere in the management apparatus. Thus the staff had been "cut" although its total size remained about the same, a good example of the operation of organizational informalism. Leningrad had similar problems; supposedly eliminated administrative positions reappeared almost immediately.[49]

Of course, some of this furious attempt to thin the bureaucratic ranks may have been misplaced. An enterprise operating under the reform requires a larger administrative staff in order to perform new functions, such as studying the market and finding supplies. This decision to slash the size of administrative staffs in industry across the board was a clumsy, authoritarian approach to a fundamental problem that could have been handled more effectively by furthering the implementation of the reform as originally conceived. Besides the outright cutting of staffs, other means are being used to reduce them, including the provision of up-to-date office equipment and computers. Interestingly, this has not reduced the managerial apparatus but has increased it.[50] The result was predictable; careless introduction of new office machinery cannot bring the results desired without prior rationalization of administrative structures and relationships.

Attempts are also being made for the first time to provide an adequate number of secretaries and stenographers and to improve the means of record-keeping and office communications. Secretarial work is one of the weakest links in industrial administration. Pravda has suggested a fundamental improvement of the image of the secretary, noting that she is not a mere "errand girl" but "specialist in one of the managerial professions" or "auxiliary personnel who serve management," and called for large-scale and systematic training of secretaries.[51] A real drive seems to have been initiated to achieve a broad recognition of the beneficial uses of modern office equipment, from ballpoint pens to dictaphones and copying machines, and the large-scale production of such items.[52] However, as in the case of the secretaries, real change is only about to begin. Some improvement is taking place in record-keeping and communications. The number of primary documents is being reduced; in one ministry 1,174 such documents existing in 1968 have been cut to 128. The goal is the "creation of common and simple forms of primary documentation which will be capable of being processed mechanically and will be identical for all similar enterprises. . . ."[53]

Another method of modernizing the administration is the establishment of simpler administrative structures. In summary, this often involves the replacement of chief administrations by associations. What is significant is the conscious and widely publicized recognition that a proper administrative structure is important for effective administration and management, particularly in a time of rapid technological progress. The American experience is referred to favorably. "The majority of American specialists . . . recognize that without a corresponding apparatus of decision-making the guidance of production activity. . . may only lead to additional difficulties. . . ."[54] It is also noted that an economic organization does much more than produce; "an economic organization is a multipurpose system." The increasing complexity of economic interrelationships and the rising rate of scientific and technical change "pose the task of creating flexible and dynamic management structures capable of ensuring the speedy adoption of optimal decisions." A decidedly new position is citing the limitations of structures "built along lines of a vertical hierarchy" and the consequent fundamental need for a "flexible and dynamic system of 'horizontal' coordination." This naturally suggests the emerging obedinenie.[55] However, Academician V. A. Trapeznikov goes further in advocating that the obedineniia be loose structures of cells in which decisions are taken as far down the hierarchy and as close to the issues of the decision as possible. Trapeznikov emphasizes the need to minimize information loss and perhaps has a quasi-political viewpoint as well.[56]

    Others, notably the advocates of what can be called "computopia," have a very different vision of a network of obedineniia controlled by a national computer network. Another suggestion is to create within each ministry a functional subdivision that would be responsible for increasing the effectiveness of management within the branch. Lenin's plan for the reorganization of control agencies is referred to for support. "The essence of Lenin's plan . . . consisted in the organic combination of control functions with the functions of the rationalization of the managerial apparatus. 'The task of the Workers' and Peasants' Inspection Agency,' Lenin wrote, 'is not only, and even not so much, to catch and expose as it is to know how to put things right.'" He goes on to stress that "what is needed is a systems approach that encompasses all levels and elements from the work sector to the ministry." This call for overall structural change in industrial administration is a direct challenge to the ministries and must have been an advance, although indirect, announcement of the "re-regionalization" of economic organization announced in April 1973.

    Despite shortening of lines of communication, there is no guarantee that blanket reductions in force and the indiscriminate creation of associations will always produce better administration. For one thing, it is possible that the supposedly extra personnel may help an organization overcome bottlenecks and other intermittent but unavoidable difficulties. Interestingly, the resolution of October 1969 has been objected to by a high-level Soviet researcher, who says that "it is a mistake to assume that the whole state managerial system is overstaffed. The approach to managerial staffs must be strictly scientific in each instance."[57] As for the associations, some Soviet commentators consider them to be a new means for strictly controlling enterprise directors through a new form of centralization by taking away the rights recently granted.

Retraining and a New Education

In 1959 a report of the USSR Academy of Sciences stated: "No special provision is made for the training of professional administrators. . . ." It was confidently added that specialized courses of study gave a "sufficient grounding" in administration.[58] Less than a decade later this view was no longer tenable in the Soviet Union. The increased complexity of the industrial process (already alluded to) led to such an overloading of executives with "information" that management required thoroughgoing change. Whether warranted or not, the educational process was turned to in hopes of "qualitatively changing the level of management." By 1970 Pravda proclaimed editorially that "today one cannot rely solely on the ability and practical experience of the economic manager. The cadres of production organizers must be taught the science of management. . . ." It was even stated that the preparation of cadres for the organization of labor and the management of production is the "most important task of the higher schools."[59]

Some rather innovative suggestions have been made. For example, the chairman of one department of political economy cited the need for the teaching of management psychology in every technological course given in a higher school, and in effect called for fundamental changes in managerial assumptions and practices by emphasizing the importance of studying and teaching small group behavior, the psychology of communication and adaptation, teamwork and compatibility, and the general issue of adapting technology to man. This suggests the advent of the "sociologizing" mode,[60] but it is still too early to say whether it is in fact a harbinger of the future or only a suggestion whose time has not yet come. At present, change is under way but overorganized and centrally directed.

Retraining

One of the first applications of the new management education was attempts to retrain the present industrial managers. This is feasible to a degree, although it cannot be as successful as the introduction of a differently educated generation into managerial posts. One quick way to accomplish this would be to purge managers considered unfit for their jobs. This has been done more than once in Soviet history, and has been implied in contemporary statements; but a large-scale purge would be disastrous economically and politically impossible to carry out now. Retraining cannot correct the inappropriateness of managers' previous education. Therefore, short-term acts cannot provide solutions in this sphere and long-term policies must be relied upon.

Long-term policies involve basic changes in the education of engineers (who continue to be the main source of factory directors) and the establishment of completely new courses of managerial study and of institutions to administer them. Nevertheless, some institutionalization of retraining and refresher training courses has taken place, in itself a move against stagnation. The Higher Education Ministry has set up special offices for such courses, and several ministries have established permanent retraining institutes for their executives. The periodic retraining of teachers of engineering is also envisaged.[61] The most prestigious retraining institution is the Institute for the Management of the National Economy, established in Moscow in early 1971 by the State Committee for Science and Technology. Its students are ministers, deputy ministers, directors of glavki and ministerial departments, and executives of obedineniia. Its teaching emphasis is current management methods and the use of computers. Kosygin spoke at its opening ceremony.

A New Education

In the past half-decade there have been many calls for a new type of education for future Soviet industrial managers. At the plenum of September 1965, Kosygin noted that there have been "major shortcomings" in the training of technicians and engineers for industry and that the importance of such training is growing "acutely" under the new conditions. The press has been calling for the systematic teaching of menedzhment without, however, saying what should be taught. A Soviet shipyard director who could not find a widely accepted definition of management exclaims, "There are no textbooks, no scientific research, no methodological aids--nothing!" The Deputy Chairman of the RSFSR Gosplan noted, "There has been a great deal of discussion about the problems of management. It is time to stop talking and do something about it." He added that more training institutions and teachers are needed and that high-level scientists and executives should be persuaded to teach in schools of administration.[62]

A beginning, but only that, is being made in engineering instruction. Some engineering schools now are reversing the traditional Soviet practice of producing narrow practitioners for specific jobs. A fundamental problem has been that although an engineer can become a "captain of industry . . . he does not even know the rudiments of administrative work."[63] Another new departure is deemphasizing descriptive lectures and giving practical, sometimes independent, work experience a place in the curriculum, in hopes of making study more purposeful and knowledge more closely attuned to industrial practice. An interesting suggestion involves the formal search in higher schools for students who have a decided talent for managerial work and their placement in courses of study differing from those of students preparing for research or production line work.[64] In order for this idea to have results, it will be necessary to pay junior managerial personnel salaries comparable with those of their counterparts in research work.

Other measures include the establishment of new specialties that will provide support for a new field of management, such as economic cybernetics, which has been introduced at several higher educational institutions, including Moscow, Leningrad, and Kiev universities. Related fields are automated management systems; record, document, and data systems; and mathematics of large-scale systems.[65] It will be necessary, of course, to get graduates of these new fields into industry.

New institutions to provide managerial training have been established. (The USSR had management training institutes in the 1920s that are now being cited in justifying the creation of new training centers without, of course, any mention of their disintegration before the Stalinist tide.) Although the East European countries are leading the USSR in this matter, the latter is attempting to acquire knowledge of the latest Western, particularly American, practices in management training and to duplicate them in new institutions. One way this knowledge has been acquired is by sending young Soviet citizens to study in management schools in the United States, such as M.I.T.'s Sloan Institute and the Harvard Business School.[66] This practice probably will continue. I have spoken with a Scientific Secretary of the Academy of Sciences' Central Mathematical-Economic Institute whose desk was literally covered with brochures of Western management training programs. D. M. Gvishiani, Kosygin's son-in-law, has cleverly justified the use of Western managerial practices and theories thus:

> In the words of Lenin, state-monopoly capitalism is the fullest material preparation for socialism. The organizational experience of the administration of large-scale production acquired under capitalism thus must be critically assimilated by the new society. Therefore, bourgeois

theories of administration likewise, which reflect this experience, cannot simply be rejected. They must be critically reworked.[67]

A former student at the Harvard Business School now heads a new management school at Moscow's prestigious Plekhanov Institute (the Faculty of the Planning of Industrial Production, Moscow Institute of National Economy). It provides a year's intensive training modeled upon that at Harvard to engineers who have had at least five years' experience in industry. Other such schools are now being established and are aided by institutes that do research on enterprise management and associated fields: USSR Gosplan's Scientific Research Institute for the Organization of Management and Norms, the Central Statistical Administration's Scientific Research Institute for Planning Computer Centers and Systems of Economic Information, the Voznesenskii Finance-Economics Institute in Leningrad, and the Ordzhonikidze Engineering-Economics Institute in Moscow.

One of the interesting features of the new management instruction is business gaming. At Leningrad University students are initiating processes of production management in games such as "reform," "industry-trade complex," and "limited resources."[68] This kind of exercise has had some institutional results, notably the new Soviet-brand "R&D firm" that solves problems for productive enterprises. Some of these were founded by scientifically trained Komsomol and trade union members, notably "Torch" in Novosibirsk, "Innovator" in Baku, "Neva" in Leningrad, and "Spark" in Tomsk. Reputedly they have performed well, partly because they are not subject to the usual state controls, an advantage they may be losing as the state bureaucracy, particularly the State Bank and the Ministry of Finance, strives to control them. "Torch" had to shut down, even though it was remarkably innovative and profitable. It seems that a genuine fear of the effects of profits was a factor in the reaction against them, as was a dislike of their flexibility and their slighting of procedures. Their advantages over Academy and ministerial institutes were extolled in the pages of Literaturnaia gazeta. One of their defenders noted:

> These firms are right at the junction between science and production. Moreover, their staffing is based not on an "ironclad" staff list, but on the subject matter of the research. The firms keep almost no one "in reserve"; rather, they call in whoever is necessary. Thus, in a sense . . . their staff is practically unlimited. . . .
> Their existence is determined not by reports, but by their output.[69]

By 1973 it seemed that the R&D firms would be merged into the existing industrial structure. However, by combining them with the new obedineniia, it was hoped to preserve their advantages while containing them within established Soviet patterns.[70] It is still too early to say whether their effectiveness survives in their new organizational forms.

It is apparent that a beginning is now being made in creating a network of institutionalized courses of study in modern managerial techniques and in supporting fields. Difficulties abound, two of the obvious ones being the acquisition of qualified teachers and enough suitable texts, although several useful books have been published in the past few years.[71] The results of this will be apparent only after many years, if not decades, and will develop most fruitfully only if the overall organizational setting is changed properly as well.

The New Manager as Ideal Type

The goal of creating a new, efficient industrial manager is a major concern of the present Soviet political leadership. The Party leadership astutely recognizes that the strength of its rule depends on the authority and power of key subordinate elites. Every political elite requires lower-level groupings that radiate its power and gather political information for it. As a writer in Kommunist says in an article on the role of industrial managers in Soviet society during the reform period: "The Party is constantly concerned about improving the style of leadership--for its impact on the masses is intensified precisely by the authority of the leaders it promotes."[72]

Citing an authoritative Western view of the manager and his present role and comparing Soviet goals with it reveals how much the Soviets have decided to change a type of management fit mainly for basic industrialization. David Ewing says, "The manager is commonly defined as one who gets results primarily through people. . . ."[73] Similar definitions have been given in the USSR. In the 1920s a Soviet writer on management theory stated: "The good organizer does nothing himself. He has the ability to induce others to execute the entire work, leaving to himself only basic general guidance [rukovodstvo] and general supervision [kontrol']."[74] Much more recently, another Soviet writer has said that "the task of management consists . . . in bringing people's subjective activity into line with the requirements of objective law-governed patterns and progressive tendencies."[75] This "people-orientation" is not the rule in the USSR. In the United States, the teaching of engineering skills has been superseded by the teaching of problem-solving skills, values, and general attitudes; "the big issues have less and less to do with techniques of work and more and more . . . with the purposes of work, co-ordination of work, standards, creativity, and equity." One American writer says the main issue is change itself: "The essential task of modern management is to deal with change."[76] A Soviet statement parallels these: "The main function of an executive is to make decisions, and to perform it well he must be conversant with psychology, sociology, and jurisprudence, besides having a knowledge of engineering and economics. He must also be trained to solve problems, work with people and analyze the information that reaches him."[77]

Contemporary Soviet statements like this are permeated with an anti-bureaucratic feeling, almost an animus; a renewed Soviet emphasis on rationality, efficiency, and productivity; and, significantly, an implication that decentralized, quasi-independent, and even entrepreneurial behavior should be the new norm for Soviet industrial managers.

Ultimately, of course, such a point of view comes into conflict with the bureaucratic essence of the Party and the ethos and operational rules of the Soviet polity as presently constituted. Whether this opposition will be made explicit depends on factors that may not yet be present. The quest for a more creative management will at least lead to a struggle over still further change in management. A new conception of human organization comes to be an issue. "Initiative, flexibility, creativity, adaptability are the qualities now required [in management]. . . ." This will demand "not only a different kind of manager but a different organizational structure," based on collaboration and reason, that rejects bureaucratic forms and procedures and the idea that man must be coerced, controlled, and directed in order for him to work.[78] This formulation, change-oriented as it is, neglects to consider the possibility that managers in post-industrial societies may have to devote a good part of their efforts to effect changes desired by employees and interest groups.

This "convergence" of Soviet and American views shows an attitudinal base for the creation of a new type of Soviet industrial manager. The Soviet leadership and the new conditions demand that managers as a group now have qualities that formerly either were not emphasized or were considered unnecessary. These include a knowledge of economics and the ability to apply it in managing the enterprise; a financial sense; an ability to motivate people to do consequential work (an ability to manage); a willingness to compete; an enthusiasm for improving a plant's performance, taking on the production of new items, and engaging in routinized innovation; and a capacity for empirical study of the context in which an enterprise operates, particularly the market and the social dynamics of the workers and labor force at large. All this taken together is a standard that even the managers with a new education will not be able to meet in all its aspects. But it nevertheless constitutes an authoritative demand for a new manager that will have appreciable effect and create long-term political questions.

It is likely, however, that the Party ideologues will try to retain an "ideological-organizational" or political role for the industrial managers so as to uphold ultimate Party supremacy. In an article on guidelines for the Party's education system in 1972, Pravda called for paying "special attention" to the "ideological tempering and economic training of executive cadres."[79] It is possible that the "new Soviet manager" will be basically the same as the old but covered with a thin veneer of orientation to a few new goals that are subscribed to only at the operational level. Change in organizations is not always conducive to the introduction of a new order. "Old orders may be maintained as well as transformed by originality and innovativeness."[80]

Developments in Yugoslav industrial management since 1971 testify to the ability of ideological political elites to reimpose their own views of ends and means on organizations even after a few decades of standing apart from operational activities.[81] The goal there now seems to be a "technobureaucracy" that is ideologically correct as well as economically productive, technologically effective, and administratively efficient. This may contain a hidden pitfall for the ideologues. If the ideology becomes "de-Marxized" in an environment of ready transference of the best specialists into the Party apparatus, the bureaucrats might be able to rule mainly as a "technobureaucracy" with an ideology of their own. This might yet occur in the USSR.

Despite this possibility, the Soviet Party leadership is emphasizing the new management as a completely desirable goal. A successful outcome in this sphere, however, requires a further improvement in Soviet economics itself. Several significant concepts have not received much attention: opportunity cost, cash flow analysis, theory of capital investment, marginal and equilibrium economics, and the law of diminishing returns.[82] The new conditions require even more. The Minister of Finance says that in addition to increased economic and managerial skills, personnel must acquire an appropriate financial sense. He adds that the economic and financial services of both the enterprises and the ministries must be strengthened and their roles made more significant.[83] This, however, may be a concealed plea for greater powers for financial agencies.

It is also desired that managers have broad administrative capabilities. A former Moscow Party Secretary says that "in the new conditions the question of teaching our cadres the skills to manage production scientifically assumes particular acuteness."[84] The former First Secretary of Azerbaidzhan says: "Economic cadres must manage in a new way. This means that cadres themselves ought to change in many ways and acquire new qualities," such as "business qualities." He also asserts that two "types" of plant directors are leaving the scene: the "unthinking executor" of orders and the type that overcomes economic obstacles "high-handedly or with an onslaught" (nakhrapom ili natiskom). A new broader "type," he says, is coming to the fore--one able to "cogitate" and act in accordance with scientific data and advanced practices. He explains the need by arguing that ". . . in the new conditions the one who reaches the finish line will be he who masters commercial nerve, he who is nimble, economically calculating and at the same time introduces innovation."[85]

These new emphases show a concern for some of the qualities often attributed to businessmen operating in a competitive environment. Of course, the Soviet manager has always been calculating, but heretofore in a primarily bureaucratic and political way. The stress on economics, commercialism, and innovation signifies a desire to produce a manager with a new style of operation and new capabilities. This is being facilitated by recent changes in popular attitudes. The term delovye liudi had a definitely pejorative meaning, "suggesting something like black market operators," until seven or so years ago, when it became neutral, denoting people engaged in industry or commerce. It is now suggested that "organizational-managerial work" be recognized as a specialty because, "according to Lenin's judgment," it is "the most complex art," a clear implication that the Soviet industrial manager should become similar to his Western counterpart.[86]

Transformation along this line is strongly pushed. As an apparatchik in Sverdlovsk puts it, "Managerial cadres are the most qualified category of workers. Therefore their incorrect use and improper assignment is a waste of social labor. This determines the necessity of the rational organization of the labor of the administrative apparatus of enterprises and above all of its managers."[87] Industrial managers are to have well-defined responsibilities, spend less time in meetings and conferences, devote much less time to the preparation of written reports, and stop performing secretarial duties. This last requirement is the corollary of the new stipulations that superior organizations demand fewer reports from managers.

Another of the new requirements for managers is that they engage in empirical study of their operations, particularly to find out what consumers want. Some studies of the "Party sociology" school indicate that the unavailability of goods or their poor quality acts as an "anti-stimulant" on people's work and therefore is an "important social problem." A. Birman says that the "paramount" demand of the reform on the manager is the "need to look at one's own enterprise

MANAGERS AND MANAGEMENT 269

with the eyes of the consumer of its production."[88] In addition to analyses of the market, managers are also to use sociological studies of the workers, in order "to anticipate social processes in the production collective."[89]

It is, of course, too early to tell whether a new corps of Soviet managers can measure up to the diverse elements contained in the new ideal. Certainly, the manager will continue to be a powerful figure. Despite some idealistic theorizing that with the approach of Communism, directors will be "elected at general meetings of the collective," one-man management is as strong as ever; and, if the director's new powers to "hire and fire" are considered, is in fact stronger than it has been for decades. But despite the manager's undoubted importance, he is still a cog in an only partly reformed industrial system. Soviet discussions on creating a new type of managerial behavior along the order of that sketched above continue to emphasize what might be called "rules-materials" thinking instead of "people-profits" thinking. Of course, since industrial decision-making is still a field in which the Party apparatus operates, there is built-in politicized limitation on managerial development.

Another limitation is the difficulty of receiving significant economic rewards for innovation and creativity. This is not to say that managers who attain the goals set for them are not well rewarded, since they are (for instance, large "personal" salaries and bonuses). These rewards, however, considerable as they are beside the pay of ordinary workers, have been provided for the attainment of particular indices of success set from above. Such indices often do not measure innovation and actual profitability. Some general suggestions for indices of a new type have been made. For example, Academician V. A. Trapeznikov has suggested the replacement of all present success indicators by one new one, the rate of scientific and technical progress; and the economist B. Sukharevskii has called for managerial success indicators that would reflect not only the end results of production but particularly the relative degree to which economic growth is realized by the use of intensive and extensive factors. Suggestions like this are temporarily shunted aside by the glittering hopes reflecting from the computer.[90]

Cybernetics and Computers

Since the fundamentals in this area have been covered elsewhere, it remains to summarize the major considerations, to discuss recent developments, and to indicate the probable results of these for Soviet management. In recapitulation, the application of computers to planning is part of a grand effort to salvage the present economic system through making central planning a realistic and paying proposition by simulating the behavior of a decentralized market. The "computopia" envisaged is meant to "assure retention of centralized political control without loss of economic efficiency."[91] This goal, however, is not feasible. Cybernetics and computers cannot in themselves rationalize an economic system.

Nevertheless, the application of computer technology to industrial management proceeds under Party pressure and perhaps a modicum more sensibly than it did initially. Leningradskaia Pravda has editorialized: "The science of management is now the most necessary and most promising branch of knowledge. . . . It is particularly a question of utilizing computer technology."[92]

A bit later, at the Twenty-Fourth Party Congress, Brezhnev stated: "It is necessary to make more extensive use of methods of economico-mathematical modeling, systems analysis . . . to create more rapidly sectoral automated management systems, considering that in the future we shall have to create a state-wide automated system for collecting and processing information."[93]

This whole drive has a definite ideological and strategic significance that is an inherent and unavoidable part of any major Soviet policy. Academician V. Marchuk stated: "Today computer equipment is becoming one of the chief motive forces of technical progress and tomorrow it might become a decisive factor in the competition of social systems."[94]

Lately some Soviet commentators have written cautionary statements, sometimes based upon Western and American experience, on the uses of computer technology in management. For example, in 1973 the head of a department of the USA Institute warned that if management is not thoroughly improved prior to computerization, "computers will simply 'mechanize' all . . . shortcomings."[95]

Although in 1969 the United States had about 72 percent of the total number of computers in the world (68,000 units) and the reasonable prediction that by the mid-1970s almost all computers in the United States will be third- and fourth-generation machines, with two-thirds to three-quarters being used in production processes, this achievement was attained at great expense and with many difficulties. For example, IBM, the giant of the American computer industry, developed the software for its System 360 two years behind schedule and got it operating well four years late; RCA had to get out of the computer business altogether, reporting an extraordinary loss of $490 million (remaining as high as $250 million after an estimated tax recovery); several of the "dwarfs" of the industry have had severe problems; maintenance costs of computers alone ran almost $1 billion in 1970; and absurdities have abounded.[96] Possibly, because of this experience, the USSR might be able to avoid certain pitfalls of computer application in industry. But despite the knowledge of other countries' experience and some recognition of the capacity for greater productivity that computerization allows, it seems probable that the path the USSR is traversing in its application of computers to industrial processes and their management is no less rocky than it has been in other countries. Besides, the USSR is still behind. "Backwardness" can have its advantages, of course, and a flourishing trade with the West may allow a speeding up of economic development; but this can occur, if it does, no earlier than the late 1970s. Even the purchase of Western computers does not in itself bridge the gap. The IBM 360, which the USSR has ordered, is a third-generation machine of the early 1960s. In addition, most Soviet machines are second-generation units with severe operational problems due to the deficiencies of peripheral equipment (called the "Achilles' heel" by some Soviet scientists), a severe lack of software, and a shortage of computer specialists.[97]

Despite the authoritative push for progress that is bearing some results, the multiplicity of bureaucratic agencies involved in operationalizing the effort makes the process of implementation a slow one. At least nine different nationwide agencies are actively engaged in the drive for the introduction of automated management systems (ASU, avtomatizirovannye sistemy upravleniia) in industry. For example, the supplying of computer centers is "uncoordinated" because the "Central Statistical Administration distributes punch-card machinery, the U.S.S.R. Ministry of Communications distributes some of the data-preparation apparatus, the Ministry of Culture accepts statements of requirements for magnetic tape . . . ," and the USSR Ministry of Higher and Specialized Secondary Education devises training programs.[98] As a result, there is no definite center of responsibility but a patchwork of unrelated bureaucracies working at cross purposes. In effect, the organizational situation is one of all "dwarfs" and no "giants."

This multiplicity of structural units, so common in modern efforts at change, poses the dangers of "reinventing the bicycle" through the production and proliferation of commonplace computers, thus inhibiting consequential development. It has already produced at least four different families of computers that are "neither program--nor data--compatible."[99] Two methods of mitigating the difficulties that are likely to follow are the building in of competition in the designing and production of computers and their associated equipment and software, and the designation of a single, powerful, top-level coordinator for the entire effort. These are within the historical parameters of Soviet industrial development; the production of combat aircraft is an example. There have been calls for a super-agency to ensure uniformity or at least compatibility among all systems. Not surprisingly, some writers argue for centralization under their own agencies.[100] Undoubtedly attempts at solution will entail the inter-bureaucratic tug-of-war typical of Soviet administration.

CONCLUSION

This chapter has dealt with the topics most important for the present state and dynamics of Soviet industrial management. After presenting some of the main elements of the managerial environment, such as the economic reform and the political implications of the topic, the problems of management were presented as a challenge and the ways in which they are being approached as a response. If the response was described as problem-ridden and often deficient, as well as occasionally intelligent and appropriate to the challenge, this is not an indication of incipient failure. Soviet management has overcome many obstacles that once seemed insuperable. The accomplishments of the Soviet "military-industrial complex" indicate that when a problem is given high priority by political authority, resources appropriate and sufficient for its resolution are available. However, the successful management pattern of military production has not been transferred to the sphere of nonmilitary goods.[101]

Although "cadres decide everything," it is doubtful that the orientation and retraining programs for managers that now exist will fundamentally change the present generation of industrial managers. The limited results of educational efforts in effecting organizational change have been mentioned. The chances for success in the short term are therefore slim. "So long as the Stalin generation [of managers] dominates . . . the entrepreneurial problem is at best only partly soluble. . . ."[102] Another reason for the unwillingness of many managers to innovate is their lack of definite material incentives to do so, and the consequent nonentrepreneurial attitude thus engendered. Recent sociological research shows that dissatisfaction with pay and the degree of independence granted by the reform are widespread among white-collar workers.[103] On the other hand, the atmosphere of managerial action and, more important, the rules of the game have changed. Although the older managers may not be willing or able to understand this, some managers will take cognizance of these and other changes and act in ways appropriate to the goals of the reform.

But the best managers, even with massive amounts of information and a smoothly functioning administrative system, cannot transform the productive process without also solving the problems of the workers. These will have to be viewed in their own terms but resolved in conjunction with the reform of management and the economy as a whole. For example, although industrial sociology is a current fad in the USSR, management often does not utilize its findings. Neither the former artificial maintenance of full employment nor the present reductions in force is a sufficient solution.

What is essential for effective management, although still not in evidence, is a decisive reordering of assumptions, methods, and priorities in the economy as a whole--necessarily based, given the politicized nature of Soviet economics, upon a new political decision at the highest level to reorient the key relationships among the major institutions of the Soviet system, particularly the Party, the ministries, and the experts. This would have to resolve the different and partly opposing demands and claims of ideology, bureaucracy, and science. Such a process cannot develop fully until after the system reaches a widely apparent crisis that cannot be handled by the old methods.

NOTES

1. Izvestiia, January 27, 1972, p. 3; excerpted in CDSP 24, no. 4 (February 23, 1972): 27.
2. See, for example, the long editorial in Pravda, December 12, 1970; the directives of the Twenty-Fourth Party Congress on the ninth five-year plan in Sotsialisticheskaia industriia, February 14, 1971, pp. 1-6 (particularly p. 6); and Pravda, April 17, 1973, p. 2.
3. Pravda, December 12, 1970, p. 1; and Pravda Ukrainy, April 5, 1970 (quoted in ABSEES, July 1970, p. 103).
4. Pravda, March 31, p. 7.
5. Herbert A. Simon, The Shape of Automation (New York: Harper & Row, 1965), p. 109.
6. Jeremy R. Azrael, "Politics and Management," Survey 49 (October 1963): 95-96.
7. James G. March and Herbert A. Simon, "Decision-Making Theory," in Oscar Grusky and George A. Miller, eds., The Sociology of Organizations (New York: Free Press, 1970), p. 100, reprinted from March and Simon's Organizations (New York: Wiley, 1958).
8. Amitai Etzioni, "Human Beings Are Not Very Easy to Change After All," Saturday Review, June 3, 1972, pp. 45-46; and Pravda, May 13, 1973, p. 3 (translated in CDSP 25, no. 19 [June 6, 1973]: 27).
9. Gertrude E. Schroeder, "Soviet Economic 'Reforms,'" Soviet Studies 20, no. 1 (July 1968): 14.
10. Jan S. Prybyla, "The Soviet Economy: An Overview," Current History 63, no. 374 (October 1972): 176.
11. Marshall I. Goldman, "Economic Revolution in the Soviet Union," Foreign Affairs 45, no. 2 (January 1967): 325.

12. Barry M. Richman, Soviet Management (Englewood Cliffs, N.J.: Prentice-Hall, 1965), p. 256.
13. See Robert Merton, Social Theory and Social Structure (rev. and enl. ed.; Glencoe, Ill.: Free Press, 1957), p. 155; and Peter Blau, Bureaucracy in Modern Society (New York: 1956), pp. 86-91.
14. Pravda, May 13, 1973, p. 3.
15. Alfred G. Meyer, The Soviet Political System (New York: Random House, 1965), pp. 214-15. The phrase quoted is from Victor A. Thompson, Modern Organizations (New York: Knopf, 1961), pp. 6, 78.
16. Carl J. Friedrich, "Public Policy and the Nature of Administrative Responsibility," in Francis Rourke, ed., Bureaucratic Power in National Politics (Boston: Little-Brown, 1965), p. 167.
17. Jeremy R. Azrael, Managerial Power and Soviet Politics (Cambridge, Mass.: Harvard University Press, 1966), pp. 167, 170-71, 162-63.
18. Daniel Bell, The Coming of Post-Industrial Society (New York: Basic Books, 1973), p. 94; and John N. Hazard, "The Politics of Soviet Economic Reform," in Alexander Balinky, ed., Planning and the Market in the USSR (New Brunswick, N.J.: Rutgers University Press, 1967), p. 79.
19. Vernon V. Aspaturian, "Social Structure and Political Power in the Soviet System," a paper prepared for the 1963 Annual Meeting of the American Political Science Association, September 4-7, 1963, pp. 15, 14; and John P. Hardt and Theodore Frankel, "The Industrial Managers," in H. Gordon Skilling and Franklyn Griffiths, eds., Interest Groups in Soviet Politics (Princeton, N.J.: Princeton University Press, 1971), pp. 183-87, 194-200.
20. Trud, March 15, 1969, p. 1.
21. See Skilling's summation in Skilling and Griffiths, op. cit., pp. 386, 396.
22. Zygmunt Bauman, "Twenty Years After: The Crisis of Soviet Type Systems," Problems of Communism 20, no. 6 (November-December 1971): 53; and Jerry F. Hough, "The Soviet System: Petrification or Pluralism?" Problems of Communism 21, no. 2 (March-April 1972): 39.
23. See Svetozar Stojanovich, Between Ideals and Reality, translated by G. S. Sher (New York: Oxford University Press, 1973), pp. 47-51.
24. Ota Klein and Jindrich Zeleny, "Dynamics of Change: Leadership, the Economy, Organizational Structure, and Society," Ch. ix in R. Barry Farrell, ed., Political Leadership in Eastern Europe and the Soviet Union (Chicago: Aldine, 1970), p. 218.
25. Solomon M. Schwarz, "Plant Managers," Ch. ix in Gregory Bienstock et al., Management in Russian Industry and

Agriculture (Ithaca and New York: Cornell University Press, 1948), p. 120. Also see Azrael, Managerial Power and Soviet Politics.
  26. I. G. Kurakov, Voprosy filosofii 3 (March 1970): 75-85; translated in CASP 11, no. 6 (June 1970): 16. Also see, for example, S. Gurenko, Izvestiia, July 10, 1970, p. 3; (translated in CDSP 22, no. 28 [August 11, 1970]: 19-20). Gurenko is chief engineer of a machine-building plant.
  27. Alec Nove, "Economic Policy and Economic Trends," in A. Dallin and T. B. Larson, eds., Soviet Politics Since Khrushchev (Englewood Cliffs, N.J.: Prentice-Hall, 1968), p. 81. Also see Joseph S. Berliner, Factory and Manager in the USSR (Cambridge, Mass.: Harvard University Press, 1957); and David Granick, Management of the Industrial Firm in the USSR (New York: Columbia University Press, 1954).
  28. Richman, op. cit., pp. 163-64; and Harry Schwartz, The Soviet Economy Since Stalin (Philadelphia and New York: Lippincott, 1965), p. 23.
  29. Harry G. Shaffer, "What Price Economic Reforms?" Problems of Communism 12, no. 3 (May-June 1963): 20. On innovation, see Joseph Berliner, Economy, Society and Welfare (New York: Praeger, 1972), pp. 115-17; and Peter F. Drucker, Management (New York: Harper & Row, 1974), pp. 755-88.
  30. See Rush V. Greenslade, "Khrushchev and the Economists," Problems of Communism 12, no. 3 (May-June 1963): 30-31.
  31. V. Afanasev, Pravda, December 4, 1969, p. 3; (partially translated in CDSP 21, no. 49 [January 6, 1970]: 19). See also "Letters from a Ministry," Pravda, December 1969 (translated in CDSP 21, no. 52 [January 27, 1970]: 18-21, 44); and Pravda, February 16, 1971, p. 2. The author is First Secretary of Kalinin raikom.
  32. M. Vasil'ev, "Direktor za partoi," Izvestiia, May 14, 1967, p. 5.
  33. Pravda, September 17, 1968, p. 2; and John A. Armstrong, "Sources of Administrative Behavior: Some Soviet and Western European Comparisons," American Political Science Review 59, no. 3 (September 1965): 654.
  34. Azrael, Managerial Power and Soviet Politics, p. 153.
  35. V. Lisitsyn and G. Popov, "O kadrakh upravleniia," Planovoe khoziiastvo 5 (May 1968): 3. See also A. A. Godunov, Vvedenie v teoriiu upravleniia (Moscow: "Ekonomika," 1967), pp. 63, 64. The citation is from D. M. Gvishiani, Sotsiologiia biznesa (Moscow: Sotsialno Ekonomicheskoi Literatury, 1962), pp. 98-99. Gvishiani is a son-in-law of Premier Kosygin and a Deputy Chairman of the State Committee on Science and Technology.

36. V. Firsov, "Novizna," Literaturnaia gazeta, February 1, 1966, p. 1. He is director of the Lenin Neva machine-guilding plant in Leningrad.

37. See March and Simon, op. cit., pp. 36-47. For empirical evidence see Jerald Hage and Michael Aiken, Social Change in Complex Organizations (New York: Random House, 1970), pp. 100-04.

38. Iu. F. Bukhalov and E. A. Iakuba, eds., Rol' obshchestvennosti v upravlenii proizvodstvom (Kharkov: Kharkov University Press, 1968), p. 82. On a poll taken at the Kharkov tractor plant.

39. New York Times, October 14, 1967.

40. See A. G. Aganbegian, "Progress in Management and the Management of Progress," Komsomolskaia pravda, July 30, 1970, p. 2 (translated in CASP, II, 7, 7); and N. Fedorenko and P. Bunich, "Association Spells Progress," Pravda, February 9, 1970, p. 2 (translated in CDSP 22, no. 6 [March 10, 1970]: 8, 10).

41. Pravda, April 6, 1969, p. 2.

42. Pravda, March 3, 1973, pp. 2-3; condensed in CDSP 25, no. 9 (March 28, 1973): 8. Also see Sovetskaia Belorussiia, March 7, 1969, p. 1; and Izvestiia, April 25, 1973, p. 3.

43. Pravda, December 13, 1972, p. 1. Also see Literaturnaia gazeta 6 (1973): 11.

44. Literaturnaia gazeta 9 (February 26, 1969): 10-11 (translated in CASP 1, no. 10 [March 1969]: 10); Pravda, December 9, 1971, p. 3 (People's Control Sheet No. 169; translated in CDSP 23, no. 49 [January 4, 1972]: 42); Pravda, October 31, 1969, p. 1; Bakinskii rabochii, December 17, 1970, p. 2 (cited in ABSEES, April 1971, p. 105); F. A. Savenkov, "Ratsionalizatsiia struktury i shtatov apparata upravleniia proizvodstvom," Sovetskoe gosudarstvo i pravo 3 (March 1967): 28; and Pravda, September 17, 1968, p. 2.

45. Berliner, Factory and Manager in the USSR, p. 319; Meyer, op. cit., p. 232; Herman Achminow, "Covert Capitalism in the USSR," Bulletin of the Institute for the Study of the USSR 7, no. 3 (March 1960): 17; and Wilbert Moore, The Conduct of the Corporation (New York: Random House, 1962), p. 268.

46. See Ekonomicheskaia gazeta 14 (April 1969): 16; Pravda, January 21, 1971; Pravda, December 4, 1972, p. 3 (translated in CDSP 24, no. 49 [January 3, 1973]: 13); Izvestiia, January 21, 1971, p. 3 (abstracted in CDSP 23, no. 4 [February 23, 1971]: 17); and Leslie Szeplaki, "A Progress Report on Socialist Economic Reforms: The Hungarian Experience," A.S.T.E. Bulletin 12, no. 1 (Spring 1970): 3.

47. Izvestiia, September 26, 1967, p. 2.

48. Komsomolskaia pravda, December 20, 1968, p. 2; (translated in CDSP 20, no. 52 [January 15, 1969]: 14-15).

49. See Izvestiia, March 27, 1970, p. 4; and Leningradskaia pravda, February 2, 1971, p. 2. The resolution on reduction of the

managerial apparatus is in Pravda and Izvestiia, October 24, 1969, p. 1; reproduced in CDSP 21, no. 43 (November 19, 1969): 8.

50. V. Batysheva and K. Grishin, "Leninskie printsipy khoziaistvennogo rukovodstva," Planovoe khoziaistvo 1 (January 1970); 11.

51. Izvestiia, March 26, 1969, p. 3; and Pravda, March 17, 1973, p. 2 (condensed in CDSP 25, no. 11 [April 11, 1973]: 20-21).

52. See Sotsialisticheskaia industriia, October 1, 1970, p. 2; and Pravda, September 8, 1971, p. 2 (condensed in CDSP 23, no. 36 [October 5, 1971]: 7).

53. Sotsialisticheskaia industriia, October 29, 1969, p. 2; and Ekonomicheskaia gazeta 5 (February 1969): 11-12.

54. B. Z. Mil'ner, "Vliianie tekhnicheskogo progressa na struktury upravleniia," S.Sh.A. (-U.S.A.) 9 (September 1971): 24. The author visited Litton industries and refers to the work of J. W. Forrester.

55. Izvestiia, May 13, 1973, p. 3; (translated in CDSP 25, no. 19 [June 6, 1973]: 1-3, 9). This article is also by Mil'ner.

56. For Trapeznikov's views see Literaturnaia gazeta, May 13, 1970, p. 10; cited in ABSEES 2 (October 1970): 102.

57. Kurakov, op. cit., p. 14.

58. "The Teaching of Administrative Sciences in the Higher Educational Establishments of the Union of Soviet Socialist Republics: Report of the Academy of Sciences of the USSR," International Review of Administrative Sciences (1959): no. 4, 452. Quoted in John A. Armstrong, "Tsarist and Soviet Elite Administrators," Slavic Review 31, no. 1 (March 1972): 17.

59. Trud, March 27, 1969, p. 3; Pravda, March 13, 1970, p. 1 (condensed in CDSP 22, no. 11 [April 14, 1970]: 14); and Izvestiia, March 19, 1970, p. 3 (condensed in CDSP 22, no. 11 [April 14, 1970]: 13).

60. Izvestiia, March 11, 1973, p. 3; excerpted in CDSP 25, no. 10 (April 4, 1973): 28. Also see Bell, op. cit., pp. 42-43.

61. Pravda, April 14, 1970, p. 3; Pravda, April 16, 1971, p. 2 (condensed in CDSP 23, no. 15 [May 11, 1971]: 47); Pravda, July 10, 1971, p. 3 (translated in CDSP 23, no. 28 [August 10, 1971]: 27).

62. See A. N. Kosygin, "Ob uluchshenii upravleniia . . .," Pravda, September 28, 1965, p. 1; Ekonomicheskaia gazeta 36 (September 1967): 31; and V. Lisitsyn, Literaturnaia gazeta 11 (March 12, 1969): 10 (translated in CASP 1, no. 10, 7).

63. V. Andreev, Izvestiia, October 15, 1970, p. 5. Andreev is Rector of the Ulyanovsk Polytechnic Institute. Also see Literaturnaia gazeta 9 (February 26, 1969): 10-11 (CASP 1, no. 10 [March 1969]: 10); and Trud, March 27, 1969, p. 3.

64. Pravda, July 7, 1971, p. 3 (condensed in CDSP 23, no. 27 [August 3, 1971]: 31); Izvestiia, August 4, 1971, p. 3 (condensed in CDSP 23, no. 31 [August 31, 1971]: 17-18); Pravda, February 8, 1972, p. 2 (condensed in CDSP 24, no. 6 [March 8, 1972]: 25-26); and Izvestiia, July 31, 1970, p. 3 (translated in CDSP 22, no. 31 [September 1, 1970]: 15-16).

65. Izvestiia, August 15, 1970, p. 5; excerpted in CDSP 22, no. 33 (September 1970): 20.

66. For an article by a former Soviet student at Harvard see V. Ozira, Literaturnaia gazeta 41 (October 9, 1968): 11; (translated in CASP 1, no. 6 [November 1968]: 15). Ozira heads the new faculty at the Plekhanov Institute.

67. See D. M. Gvishiani, Organizatsiia i upravlenie (Moscow: Nanka, 1970), p. 123; reviewed in Pravda, October 19, 1970, p. 2, and in Izvestiia, October 11, 1970, p. 3. For analysis and comment based on American management, see S. Sh. A.: Organizatsionnye formy i metody upravleniia promyshlennym korporatsiiami (Moscow, 1972), and S. Sh. A.: Sovremennye metody upravleniia (Moscow, 1971).

68. See Izvestiia, October 31, 1970, p. 5; partially translated in CDSP 22, no. 44, 4, 16.

69. Literaturnaia gazeta no. 24 (June 9, 1971): 10 (abstracted in CDSP 23, no. 29 [August 17, 1971]: 13); and no. 26 (June 24, 1970) (abstracted in CASP 2, no. 7 [September 1970]: 7).

70. Trud, April 5, 1973, p. 2; abstracted in CDSP 25, no. 18 (May 23, 2973): 16-17.

71. For example, A. V. Gutshtein, Upravlenie promyshlennym predpriiatiem i kibernetika (Moscow: "Ekonomika," 1969); A. A. Godunov, op. cit.; B. D. Vladimirskii et al., Deiatel'nost' promyshlennogo predpriiatiia v novykh usloviiakh (Moscow: "Ekonomika," 1967); O. A. Deineko, Nauka upravleniia v SSSR (Moscow: "Ekonomika," 1967).

72. A. Pershin, "Avtoritet rukovoditelia," Kommunist 1 (January 1971): 75.

73. David Ewing, The Managerial Mind (New York: 1964), p. 11. See also his "The Russians Yearn for the Managerial Mind," Harper's, January 1965, pp. 67-72.

74. P. M. Kerzhentsev, Printsipy organizatsii (Petrograd, 1922), p. 11; quoted in Godunov, op. cit., p. 67.

75. V. Afanasev, Pravda, December 4, 1969, pp. 2-3.

76. Ewing, The Managerial Mind, pp. 155-56; and Max Ways, "Tomorrow's Management," Fortune, July 1966, p. 84.

77. Ozira, op. cit., p. 11.

78. Ways, op. cit., pp. 85, 87, 148.

79. Pravda, September 6, 1972, pp. 2-3; condensed in CDSP 24, no. 36 (October 4, 1972): 19.

80. Herbert Kaufman, The Limits of Organizational Change (University: University of Alabama Press, 1971), p. 8.

81. Slobodan Stankovic, "Role of Enterprise Directors in Yugoslavia," Radio Free Europe Research Report, April 4, 1973, p. 2; and Vjesnik u srijedu (Zagreb), March 7, 1973.

82. See Barry M. Richman, Management Development and Education in the Soviet Union (East Lansing: Michigan State University Press, 1967), Ch. VI, particularly pp. 141, 147.

83. V. Garbuzov, "Finansy: ekonomicheskie stimuly," Ekonomicheskaia gazeta 41 (October 13, 1965): 4.

84. N. Yegorychev, "Razvivat' kommunisticheskof tvorchestvo mass," Pravda, October 4, 1965, p. 3.

85. A. Akhundov, "Sovetskii khoziaistvennik," Kommunist 17 (November 1965): 23-25.

86. Michael Connock, "Birth of the Soviet Businessman," Financial Times (London), November 8, 1967, and I. Slepov, "Voprosy nauchnoi organizatsii truda," Planovoe khoziaistvo 12 (December 1965): 13.

87. V. Mazyrin, "Organizatsiia truda rukovoditelei predpriiatii," Planovoe khoziaistvo 2 (February 1966): 58, 62.

88. L. Velikanova, Literaturnaia gazeta 50 (December 10, 1969): 11 (translated in CASP 2, no. 3 [March 1970]: 31); and A. Birman, "Sut' reformy," Novyi mir 12 (December 1968): 198.

89. E. Vannakh, Sotsialisticheskii trud 5 (May 1968) (translated in CASP 1, no. 6 [November 1968]: 17); I. Golembiovsky, Izvestiia, October 28, 1969, p. 4; and I. Titarenko, Pravda, April 24, 1968, p. 2.

90. See V. A. Trapeznikov, Literaturnaia gazeta, May 13, 1970, p. 10 (abstracted in ABSEES 2 [October 1970]: 102, and partially translated in CDSP 22, no. 3 [February 17, 1970]: 8-9). For Sukharevskii's idea see Pravda, December 3, 1970, pp. 2-3.

91. Alexander Eckstein, "Economic Development and Political Change in Communist Systems," World Politics 22, no. 4 (July 1970): 493; and Egon Neuberger, "Libermanism, Computopia, and the Visible Hand," American Economic Review: Papers and Proceedings, May 1966, pp. 131-44.

92. Leningradskaia Pravda, January 5, 1971, p. 1.

93. FBIS Supp. 16, March 30, 1971, p. 22.

94. Izvestiia, April 10, 1969, p. 3.

95. Mil'ner, op. cit., p. 23.

96. Some of the statistics are from Internationale Wirtschaft no. 40 (1969) and EDP Industry Report, March 18, 1970, pp. 16-19. Cited in R.R.G., "A Soviet Study of the World Computer Market," Radio Free Europe Research Report, March 8, 1973; and in Vestnik Statistiki no. 1 (1973). And see K. D. Fishman, "Programmed

Disaster: The Story of RCA's $490 Million Computer Debacle," Atlantic 229, no. 5 (May 1972): 33-42.

97. For discussions of these problems in 1973 see Pravda, January 16, 1973, p. 1 (condensed in CDSP 25, no. 3 [February 14, 1973]: 13); and Pravda, January 8, 1973, p. 2 (translated in CDSP 25, no. 1 [January 31, 1973]: 1-3).

98. Pravda, October 9, 1972, p. 2; (translated in CDSP 24, no. 41 [November 8, 1972]: 6-7).

99. Pribory i sistemy upravleniia 11 (1968): 1-2; quoted in Kathryn M. Bartol, "Soviet Computer Centres," Soviet Studies 23, no. 4 (April 1972): 616.

100. Kommunist 2 (January 1974): 63-76 (abstracted in CDSP 26, no. 11 [April 10, 1974]: 9-10); Vestnik statistiki 5 (May 1968): 75-82 (translated in CASP 1, no. 6 [November 1968]: 11); Izvestiia, March 8, 1974, p. 2 (translated in CDSP 26, no. 10 [April 3, 1974]: 1-3); and ibid., March 21, 1974, p. 2 (condensed in CDSP 26, no. 12 [April 17, 1974]: 1-4).

101. A. J. Alexander, R & D in Soviet Aviation (Santa Monica, Calif.: RAND, 1970), p. 27; and Robert W. Campbell, "Management Spillovers from Soviet Space and Military Programmes," Soviet Studies 23, no. 4 (April 1972): 586-607.

102. Azrael, "Politics and Management," p. 96.

103. In Bukhalov and Iakuba, op. cit., p. 82; and the first issue of Ekonomika i organizatsiia promyshlennogo proizvodstva (Novosibirsk), summarized by Keith Bush in a Radio Liberty dispatch of August 4, 1970.

CHAPTER 8

THE INCOMPLETE REFORM: EFFECTS AND SIGNIFICANCE

FUNDAMENTAL SIGNIFICANCE

The central question is whether Soviet industrial management has undergone a qualitative change in the direction postulated by the Party-state resolution of October 1965. The answer must assume that in affairs involving large, long-standing structures backed by powerful authority, systemic change is extremely rare. No organization lives up to the goals set for it. This is even more true during attempts at organizational change.

A more realistic question is to what extent change took place and what the political, economic, and social implications of this change are. The view that the reform was too limited to have significant effects can be rejected. The important administrative and social changes and problems that resulted, and the extensive public discussions that have filled the pages of Soviet newspapers and journals, preclude the possibility that the reform was "just another reorganization"--although, of course, many persons in the Soviet Union thought that this was all the reform should be.

Although the Soviet economic reform has not been as far-reaching as most of those under way in Eastern Europe, it has been meaningful in the very different Soviet political context. The de-Stalinization of the Soviet economy, although not a dismantling of the centrally planned economy oriented to the attainment of politicized ends, much less a liberalization of Soviet society, is no insignificant step. Although it has no doubt been taken partly to increase the Soviet Union's strategic might, it is inevitably a first step in a series that has ultimately profound significance. "Space and military activities have created an interest group with a real material interest in modernized management and planning techniques. . . ."[1] A Stalinist edifice must stand complete or eventually face the threat of the erosion of its constituent parts and its replacement by a new political system. Whereas Khrushchev struck a limited blow at the mythology and ideology of Stalinism, the Brezhnev-Kosygin leadership has begun to remove parts of the Stalinist economic structure as well. Qualitative change, though still slight, is already under way in the Soviet economy. There is "a very gradual erosion of those forces--surely the dominant forces of recent decades--that emphasize priority for industrial growth over other interests."[2]

The reform's significance lies in its role as an initiator of significant sociopolitical change whose full extent and final form will be clearly visible only in the future. Its implementation has set in motion waves of economic and social change, and perhaps ultimately political change as well, whose magnitude cannot but grow to such an extent that it cannot be contained either by readjustments or by massive countervailing forces because the Communist Party, the motor of the Soviet system, has itself become part and parcel of the process of reform. Perhaps this is the reform's main political significance: the inextricable involvement of the "super-coordinating" institution precludes a halt or retreat in the process of reform. The Party has "engaged." Now it can only "push on."

RESULTS AND EFFECTS

General Considerations

Although the plan of organization involves discussion of economic, social, and political matters, these categories are not at all exclusive. "The conventional division between economics and political science cannot be preserved in a study of the Soviet-type system."[3] But since in the USSR the political category is often dominant, especially when its continued preeminence is threatened, it is particularly important to specify exactly how the political sphere's dominance is being affected by the economic reform.

One way to begin is to consider whether the reforms of 1965 can be expected to serve the leadership's objective of increased and higher-quality production. Also, can the Soviet consumer anticipate economic progress measured in terms that he can appreciate--acceptable goods on the shelves of retail outlets? Many in the Soviet leadership and a great many Soviet economists and other specialists have written, naturally, as if there were a definite connection between the political and economic spheres of activity. The problem remains, of course, that neither Marx nor anyone since has been able to predict the exact connection, much less directly translate changes in one area into corresponding changes in the other.

Economic Effects

Despite its limitation, the reform may produce some definite economic progress, at least for a time, even though in its present form it will ultimately fail to attain the results set for it in the fall of 1965. Of course, it is difficult to differentiate economic effects and gains brought about by measures of the reform or originating in "reformed" sectors from the results and progress attained by the rest of the economy. Nevertheless, the changes in norms and climate are leading to some particular economic improvements. For example, as a result of the changes set in motion there have been ". . . significant savings in labor costs; and economizing on capital resources has also been spurred, though with less visible effect. [Also,] a good beginning has been made on cutting down consumer goods inventories."[4]

Other economic gains are possible. For example, perhaps now there will be less investment in projects of little general effect. The sovnarkhozy were prone to mestnichestvo in this, as in several other respects. Although many official statements and press comments are generally too favorable to be in full agreement with reality, others are more credible. Judging from these, it seems that the reform is valued for its effect in increasing labor productivity, permitting a better use of reserves, and accelerating the assimilation of technology. This may indicate the leadership's main intentions for it and one way in which its introduction has been justified to conservatives.[5] By July 1970, 40,000 industrial enterprises, producing 92 percent of gross industrial output and 95 percent of industry's profits, had been transferred to the new scheme of operation. This encompasses approximately 85 percent of all enterprises. Complete transfer is scheduled to take place by the end of 1975.[6]

However, since formal transfer does not mean complete operation by the principles and procedures of the reform, it will still be in the process of application in the late 1970s and even beyond. In addition, even full implementation, as presently conceived, ceases to yield appreciable payoffs after a period; and the principles and measures of the reform often are either not fully applied or are gravely flawed during implementation. As a result, both Soviet and foreign observers point out serious deficiencies in the reform process. The chief of the USSR Gosplan's section for the introduction of the reform critically notes that "the economic mechanism of the reform is still not operating in an integrated [fashion] and at full strength." And the director of one of the first 43 enterprises to be transferred says that in 1965-70, "trail-blazers" of the reform exhausted their reserves and were not able to maintain the higher growth rates they were trying to attain because no thorough "restructuring" of the industrial system took place.[7] By 1968 it became clear that plants that had adopted the reform had been unable to sustain their initial momentum. The situation had not improved appreciably by 1973. The consensus among non-Soviet analysts is that the reform's economic results have been slim and that, in addition, most of the old problems of the Soviet economy remain, on about the same scale and with about the same effect as prior to 1965.[8]

In addition, the growth rate of the Soviet economy has slowed. Whereas formerly it was at the top of the "medium-growth" group of economies--including the United States, France, West Germany-- since the late 1960s it has been near the bottom of this group. It seems probable that, without thoroughgoing qualitative change, the growth rate of the Soviet GNP will increase 2-4 percent yearly. The rate of growth of industrial output alone, although above 8 percent, also has generally declined, even though the rates for certain favored industries, such as petrochemicals and automobiles, are higher.[9] Besides the exhaustion of reserves, other problems include new demands created by the reform that are difficult to meet. The new goal of giving buyers a wider choice of better products necessitates the maintenance of more diversified inventories of higher-quality goods. Also, the increased stress on attaining profits poses another demand difficult to attain in a context of continued authoritative pressure for quantity.

This general presentation of the economic picture after ten years of reform does not preclude creation of a larger, more diversified, and more productive economy. Some notable successes may be visible--for example, the attainment of results in certain fields so superior that non-Soviet companies will go to the Soviet Union for the technology involved. But these are likely to be isolated cases. The export balance is still shaky; very little (about 1 percent) of Soviet exports to developed countries is machinery. The Soviet Union will continue to be a significant importer of technology and even complete plants for years to come.[10]

To put the economic situation briefly, despite the top-level decision in the directives for the ninth plan (1971-75) to make the production of consumer goods (group B) increase faster than producer goods (group A), the Soviet reform in its economic dimension is limited to the more productive use of resources and a quite selective change in fundamental rules and major institutions, and it has definitely avoided the creation of a regulated market. In short, the central purpose, major institutions, and defining characteristics of the economy remain unchanged although its instruments are being modernized and given some additional freedom to operate and maneuver. The result is a modified Stalinist economy.[11] The maximum utilization of this change in economic structure and rules depends upon developments in the social and political spheres.

THE INCOMPLETE REFORM 285

Social Effects

A major thesis here is that the reform is having effects other than purely economic ones, and that these may be the more significant for the Soviet system taken as a whole. Any change in this network of politicized human affairs, variously labeled "totalitarian," "administered," and "movement-regime," is bound to affect other parts of the system.

Specifically, here we summarize changes in the main relationships of the Soviet industrial manager, changes in these managers themselves and in their operations ("management"), and changes in society at large that have resulted from the implementation of the reform. Two of the four managerial relationships examined here are clearly in the social sphere: the manager-worker and the manager-manager. The manager-Party relationship is quite politicized. The manager-superior relationship is partially social and partially political, as is the topic of management. This can be presented in a simple diagram.

FIGURE 8.1

Results of the Reform by Topic

Societal	Political
manager-worker	manager-Party
manager-manager	

manager-superior

managers and management

What has and has not been changed in these relationships and in Soviet management can be summarized briefly. In the relationship between managers and superiors, the leadership wanted to enlarge the managers' sphere of independence and increase their initiative, but within a framework of state retention of central control over the most important goals of the enterprise: products, profits, and sales. Accordingly, it reduced the number of goals the enterprise must attain from more than 30 to 8 or 9. But the ministries and chief administrations have maintained several of the former enterprise success indicators and may even have invented new ones.

Not to be outdone, the Ministry of Finance has continued to maintain authority over enterprise personnel matters and the State Bank has worked to keep and even increase its powers over credit.

As a result, managers clearly are not much more independent vis-a-vis their superiors. True, they are operating in a different situation; but, although some constraints are gone, others have been added. This indicates that some institutions of the Soviet state are strong enough to impede the implementation of orders of the political leadership. The recent regionalization of parts of Soviet industrial administration is a blow directed against the state bureaucracy by the Party leadership. Although the Party apparatus will give the bureaucrats pause, the latter will retain sufficient strength to give it serious concern again. This is part of the pattern of Russian and Soviet administrative history. As Alf Edeen states the issue, "The delicate problem the present leaders have to tackle is to strike a nice balance between the bureaucracy's need for stability and consistency and society's growing need for innovation and new administrative techniques."[12]

The manager-worker relationship is the one in which the manager has increased his powers the most, mainly at the expense of the worker. Significantly, this is the aspect of the reform from which social problems may come. (Perhaps the manager's gains here make up for what he has not gained vis-a-vis his superiors.) In this sphere the ideal has been effected to some degree. Managers now have greater powers over their subordinates in terms of wages, material incentives, and even employment. With these powers managers have a better chance, although no guarantee, of meeting some of the new demands made upon them. It is not surprising that the workers have had to give when the bureaucratic superstructure could retain many of its prerogatives. It is possible, although not probable, that the trade unions or the people's courts may limit the use of managers' newly gained powers over the workers. However, this could not materialize without high-level Party approval, which would be forthcoming only if grave social problems result. It is probable, instead, that various organizational means will be established to lessen the impact of the unemployment that is occurring. The labor exchanges and retraining are only beginning to be applied, however. The taking of steps to alleviate the impact of automation and other spin-offs of the reform (such as the Shchekino pattern) indicates that the Soviet system still has some degree of adaptability in the face of social problems. The extent of this adaptability as the post-industrial society evolves will be a significant and even crucial sociopolitical question.

Another possible problem arising in the manager-worker relationship might be apathy or outright dissatisfaction on the part of workers if incentives are not increased significantly. Thus far this has not happened, although average wages have risen (but in an economy in which the stock of consumer goods is increasing more slowly). Young workers pose a special problem, and a meaningful degree of "workers' control" is as far from existing as ever. The crucial question is how long the new industrial working class of the Soviet Union will be satisfied with its situation. A Polish-, Hungarian-, or Czech-type crisis is not unthinkable. The new urban industrial workers "would certainly have something to say" if they were asked "how they would run their factory, local community, or country"; and "they can no longer be easily manipulated simply by administering a bigger dose of carrot or stick."[13]

The relationship among managers in terms of supply seems to have changed least, partly because the model called for little change and partly because contracts and the idea of "direct ties" have not developed significantly. In addition, the degree of fulfillment of obligations among enterprises has not increased perceptibly. The creation of long-lasting and freely made inter-enterprise ties could lead to the rise of an organized interest group of enterprise managers. Thus far this important body of professionals has not enjoyed much cohesion.[14] A factor limiting the development of the manager-manager relationship is the establishment of a powerful and centralized state supply system that limits inter-enterprise ties regarding supply. Another limiting factor seems to be the inability of the arbitration system to cope with the litigation and need for coordination that further decentralization would require.

The area of management, broadly defined, was a major target for change in the reform. Here real effort is being expended, and it will have some significant results with the passage of time and the departure of the older generation of managers who were molded in the fires of Stalinist industrialization. Several problems will impede thorough change in management, however, One is the quandary of indecision into which some managers have been put by the new freedoms allowed them by the reform--for instance, the reduction in the number of success indices and the raising of the earning of profit to the status of a major goal. These have put new goals and new problems before managers.

The adversary relationship between the managers and the planners, ministerial bureaucrats, and Party secretaries remains, because there has been no change in the political order as it affects the economy. An atmosphere of mutual suspicion also remains because of the tautness of planning, the politicized nature of goals and supervision, and the continued threat of the application of the "ratchet." A manager is only being politically realistic in not using all his reserves. Managers cannot run enterprises profitably and most productively in conformity with bureaucratized and politicized regulations. Also, once accustomed to a partly covert mode of action, they cannot readily use a completely overt, authorized system even if it is generally more rational than the old. Accordingly, industrial management does not unreservedly support the present reform. The advantages it confers are not sufficient to motivate managers to the degree desired by the leadership. The attempt to create a new type of industrial manager who works with better methods in a more rational management structure will no doubt bring a measurable payoff; but it is unlikely to result in a substantially more innovative or productive management without changes in the Soviet system as a whole, particularly political and social changes. Accordingly, it is appropriate to consider what relevant changes of a political nature have taken place since 1965.

Political Effects

The most pertinent question is what change has taken place in the manager-Party relationship. Here tensions are not as apparent as they once were. This may be due more to the atmosphere surrounding this aspect of the reform--Party organizations are to stand aside and allow the reform to progress--rather than to any elimination of Party rukovodstvo. Of course, such guidance is not supposed to be eliminated, but instead to become less arbitrary in application, although functions such as control of appointments, enforcement of goals and priorities, and intervention in operations remain. A long-term difficulty exists, however. In engaging actively in the support of the reform, the Party is in fact ensuring a failure to realize its goals. Instead of creating an economy that functions without requiring close guidance by powerful noneconomic forces and considerations, it is carrying one of the former "crutches" into the future. Of course, this is done because many in the Communist Party apparatus are naturally trying to maintain the Party's preeminent position in the Soviet polity. Nevertheless, it cannot but have undesired economic effects, such as undue caution among managers, the constant presence of politicized goals in the economy, and a lack of rational, spontaneous economic processes. The effect of the reform on the manager-Party tie has been to create some additional "distance" in the relationship but not to change it significantly. If this distance is maintained, the political effect will be greater, particularly if the new breed of managers (ironically, desired by the Party apparatus) claims a greater role for its specialized knowledge.

In sum, if the set of areas in which change was posited in 1965 is considered as a whole, it is clear that change has not been great.

Despite claims by Soviet leaders that the manager's place in the industrial process has been thoroughly altered, it remains essentially what it was under Khrushchev's system of decentralized direction, and even what it was under Stalin's ministerial centralism. The manager has not acquired greatly increased powers to make decisions except in relation to the work force. However, this relative stability of the manager's role, to be expected in a system as old and as highly structured as the Soviet's, does not tell the whole story, because the atmosphere and context in which Soviet industrial management operates has changed.

While the roles and relationships remain essentially unchanged, the implications of this fact demand attention, for there has been a vigorous effort to change them. The intent is present, but the results are only beginning to appear--and randomly at that. The questions coming to the fore because of this fact are several; the primary one is whether the Soviet political leadership, working through its most powerful institutions, is unable to effect organizational changes, and particularly basic alterations, in the manager's relationships. Has bureaucracy triumphed over politics? Indeed, is it forcing a change in the Soviet political system, demonstrated by the relative impotence of a leadership determined to effect change? An examination of the reasons for so slight a change in the face of both acknowledged objective necessity and an authoritatively expressed will for change is in order.

CAUSAL FACTORS

One general reason for organizations' lack of propensity to change is simple inertia. It is very difficult to give a new direction to a complex of relationships. "The Soviet economy, bound up as it is with the daily life of 240 million people, has an enormous inertia. . . ."[15] In addition, the Russian organizational tradition is a force setting parameters that limit change. Whereas "English industrialization resulted principally from the struggle of a rising entrepreneurial class . . . in Russia interaction among social classes which was connected with industrialization was continually subject to autocratic intervention and autocratic controls." In a memorandum to the emperor in 1899, Sergei Witte wrote of the centrality of "plan and system" in the administration of the Russian state. In early 1900, in another memorandum to Nicholas, he emphasized that if "industrialization was to succeed, the paramount need was for central direction."[16] This tradition was so powerful even after the Revolution, that a Stalin who could again give it expression was almost unavoidable. The Communist Party has perpetuated and stabilized some important Russian political traditions and practices. It is possible that the central issue for change in the USSR is a cultural one.

Economic Factors

The economic factors favoring the reform include the immense natural resources of the country, the great number of heavy industrial plants and their machinery and productive capacity, and the availability of fuel, power, transportation, and communications. These are not an insignificant result of primitive Stalinist industrialization. However, the shift of emphasis to chemicals, electronics, and light industry that was begun during the Khrushchev years provided a base for wide-ranging further development upon which the reform model could depend to a degree.

On the negative side and operating against the reform are the accumulation of great disproportions in the Soviet economy, a still backward agricultural sector much larger than those in comparable economies, and the need to modernize the large existing industrial stock. The increasing technological gap between the USSR and Western Europe, Japan, and the United States is also an important limitation. (The gaps in application of computers and nuclear power plants are two striking examples.)[17] To this set of limitations must be added that of prices not representing the relative values of commodities. Factors relating to economic operations are the lack of standards for performance and of incentives that will motivate economic behavior desired by the leadership.[18]

Social Factors

How are organizational and administrative factors facilitating and limiting the reform's implementation? Crucial here is the degree of the state bureaucracy's and Soviet managers' acceptance and furtherance of the reform, which poses a differentiated offering of rewards and losses to various groups. The institutionalized groups are best placed to affect the outcome--for instance, the ministerial and planning bureaucracy, whose actions in impeding and altering the reform's implementation have been described. The power of this vast industrial establishment to alter Party policy in its domain to suit its own purposes has been amply documented. The basis of this ability also has been shown in general, in comparative perspective, and in the case of Soviet industry specifically. It is clear that "conflicts of interest and articulation in the Soviet Union, denied a special political sphere of operation tend to give a political coloration to processes ostensibly executive and administrative in character, that is, to generate a distinctive crypto-politics."[19]

Ironically, Soviet analysts understand the process well but are intellectually disarmed by their unwillingness to transfer what they see as a scourge of capitalist society to Soviet socialism. One Soviet scholar has said of bureaucratic politics in the United States, "The bureaucracy is transformed into its own type of self-contained force which has its own interests separate from the interests of the . . . political leadership." "Parkinson's Law" is known and given a particularly Russian definition: "Any organization possessing power strives to expand the boundaries of its jurisdiction."[20] This connection between administration and politics indicates that the two types of administration contrasted by Jerry Hough, the "Weberian" and the "developmental," are different only in degree. Any system of administration will contain, for example, unintended consequences and informal behavior that are, in effect, statements of value preference. "Bureaucrats are always semi-administrators and semi-politicians."[21]

This sort of behavior by elements in the Soviet bureaucracy can be effective. For example, "Even if the 'steel-eaters" lobby can no longer dictate policy . . . it is still strong enough to prevent other groups from reaching their goals. . . ."[22] The ways in which this obstruction has been accomplished since 1965 have been described and some of the reasons why it occurred have been given. Others, however, should be cited in order to clarify the reasons behind this pattern of resistance. A fundamental problem is the impossibility of making any set of general goals the working goals of an organization. Goals are cultural constructs, whereas organizations are social systems. The former are more consistent, while the latter are multifunctional and cannot bend all their efforts to the performance of one function, particularly one new to them. If an organization were to put most of its effort into the attempt to achieve goals, it could not perform maintenance functions necessary for its survival. Organizations can assimilate elements of change in the nature of their structures, thus transforming the changes into supports for themselves. Although an organization can change somewhat, the "basic principle" is the "preservation of the character of . . . [its] system."[23] The state bureaucracy has so acted in altering the goals and substance of the reform in its own interest. Other reasons for the obstruction include decentralizing while giving the state bureaucracy an implemental role and avoiding the creation of a market economy.

Since the bureaucracy has been opposed to any significant changes, the contradiction inherent in the reform leads to such problems as goal bifurcation, organizational lethargy, and outright sabotage.[24] Another impediment of the reform is its imposition from above. Creativity may be amenable to plan, but only if the plan conforms to existing conditions. A. P. Fedoseyev, a Doctor of Sciences and Lenin Prize laureate, says that advance planning in the Soviet Union "inevitably leads to a collision with those new things which you are hoping to achieve. . . . This planning, of course, generates a terribly nervous atmosphere. . . ."[25] When this atmosphere permeates entire government departments, it spreads an attitude of blind adherence to rules, whatever the conditions and professed goals actually call for. In addition, reorganizations directed by persons specializing in administrative fields tend to be more nearly successful than those run by persons in other fields. Most Soviet industrial administrators are engineers who have not had administrative training. Also, reorganizations concentrating on administrative problems accomplish more of their goals than those aimed at programmatic changes and changes in professional behaviors. The Soviet reform was aimed at the latter kinds of changes and therefore suffered from an initial handicap. Also, reorganizations imposed from above usually encounter "substantial opposition" from within the agencies concerned.[26]

The presence of "bureaupathology" shows that the generalizations and hypotheses of students of bureaucracy and organization in societies very different from the Soviet Union's stand up when applied to the organizational aspects of the implementation of the Soviet economic reform; it also demonstrates that specialists in management, organization, and bureaucracy (including the politics of bureaucracy) have pointed to real problems of organizational change. In short, the contemporary Soviet experience with organizational change is not unique. However, knowledge of the literature on organizations probably would not have saved the initiators of the Soviet reform from many pitfalls. Contemporary knowledge of processes pertinent to the organizational aspects of the economic reform is not yet definite enough to allow its successful application. In addition, it is not at all clear that what students of organization have dubbed "correct" or "best" at the operational, structural, or theoretical level could solve the problems of Soviet organizational change if it were adopted. The effective context of Soviet organizational life is much larger than that ordinarily covered by organization theory. Most pointedly, the political sphere is still crucial. This is not to say that students of organizations have not considered political factors. They have, but these cannot be controlled on the basis of organization theory. Major sources of the reform's limited implementation are political, not organizational (it being understood that the two categories are not completely separable).

Bureaucracies, properly led and given good operating situations, including attractive incentives, can overcome some obstacles to change on their own. This is particularly true of a "planning bureaucracy" that deals primarily with quantitative, not qualitative, decisions. A major problem is the failure of the Soviet political system to take "advantage of the potential creativity of an economic bureaucracy." Development requires a "balanced bureaucracy in a balanced policy," and accordingly "development of the bureaucracy and polity may be necessary preconditions for sound growth of the economy."[27] Joseph Berliner notes that "bureaucracies that deal primarily with qualitative categories are more likely to act conservatively, and bureaucracies that deal primarily with quantitative decisions are more likely to act creatively." The insertion of political (qualitative) goals may reduce an organization's capacity for change. He considers two major sources of the conservatism of the planning bureaucracy to be the "absence of a satisfactory set of quantitative indicators of the relative values of commodities as implied in the Party's preferences" and the "fact that the incentives system is tied to a criterion of performance that motivates behavior not consistent with Party preferences."[28]

Other societal limitations on the reform include factors having to do with managers and management, engineers and ITR, and the workers. Essentially, the "line" implementors of the reform, the managers, are neither trained to implement the changes called for nor ready or willing to see the leadership's goals realized. In addition, the process of management is still so tied to the previous style and content of the economy that the addition of new methods and means, such as computers, will require a decade and more to show appreciable effect. The human problem of management has been stated well by one Soviet lawyer who writes on industrial management:

> Not everyone--be it a work superintendent or a minister--finds it easy to adapt to the new style. . . . Not everyone wants to grow accustomed to such a style of work, and there are some who refuse to because they cannot. No one is venturing to launch an overt attack upon the decisions of a Party plenary session, but there are some who, either deliberately or because of the old ways of thinking, fulfill these decisions formally, trying to leave the substance unchanged.[29]

A new goal, in this case innovation through implementation of the reform, cannot be handled well by an organization unless it first divests itself of some of its former major goals. This has not been allowed on political grounds.

The resistance of ITR and workers to the reform is probably due to insufficient incentives. The reform has not increased workers' bonuses much, unless of course workers involved in a Shchekino-type experiment are considered. But this can refer to only some workers of an enterprise, the less adaptable being let go, a situation raising the complicating issues of unemployment and new and costly means of coping with it, some of which are ideological irritants. The ITR currently are angered by pay scales they consider too low compared with those for workers, and over the feeling of alienation common to professionals and scientists who work in bureaucratized situations where they can neither fully apply their specialized knowledge nor enjoy the meaningful participation to which they feel entitled. The dilemma of "autonomy versus integration" and alienation from work are common to organizations employing scientists and engineers. The current stress on "concrete," short-term, "practical" research increases the tension.[30]

Political Factors

The Present Political Context

By 1970 or 1971 the political climate in the Soviet Union had become tense and overtly ideological through the Party leadership's attempt to increase the degree of conformity to its wishes in many spheres of Soviet life. No doubt the seemingly sudden development of "socialism with a human face" in Czechoslovakia, in which an innovative economic reform had a central role, provoked second thoughts about changes in the Soviet economy. The ceiling of permissible independent activity was lowered perceptibly. The result was an atmosphere that was semi-totalitarian in effect and intent without being Stalinist in means, no outright terrorizing or massive application of violence being present. This more restrictive political atmosphere is noticeable in all fields, but its manifestation in regard to economic and scientific research probably best suggests how it might affect the economic reform. The discussion of the harsh climate for literary and artistic experimenters, minority nationalists and Jews, and religious people in general is so well known that repetition is not required to show the restricted context in which the reform proceeds.

Generally, a fear of the possible power of expertise in post-industrial society motivates the attempt to control scientists' work closely and to denigrate its possible role as a provider of indicators for general policy-making, a role that would limit the Party generalists' power. This fear may be a reaction to an undercurrent of independence and possible opposition to general Party dominance within the scientific community.[31] A. Sakharov is not an isolated example of the Soviet scientist turned political philosopher and formulator of alternative public policy. This perspective and the action flowing from it also involve criticism and curtailment of theoretical research work that does not promise an immediate industrial or military payoff. As *Pravda* editorialized:

> Among the most important tasks of economic science is the pursuit of concrete research. . . . The development of economic science is inseparably linked with the strict observance of the principle of party-mindedness in researching economic processes and the irreconcilable struggle against bourgeois, revisionist and dogmatic theories.
>
> The effectiveness of scientific work depends to a high degree on the work of the Party organizations of the scientific research institutions.[32]

This is nothing new, of course, but its maintenance at a time when innovation, professionalism, and research are needed more than ever constricts the economy. Sometimes the criticism of scientists is polemically political, as when the authoritative I. Aleksandrov says that dissident intellectuals and "mercenary ignoramuses" are "lurking behind the mask of scientists," an assertion that (once formulated within leading circles of the Party) can be used against independent-minded scientists who by definition must be dissidents.[33]

The general drift of policy on intellectual and cultural matters was confirmed by the Twenty-Fourth Party Congress in the spring of 1971. The appearance of Yevsei Liberman's book early in the year, containing something akin to a recantation of his earlier major premise for the development of the economy, may be seen as a definite clue to the Party's fundamental policy regarding the economic reform. The watchword was centralization and the fear was of "market socialism." Liberman praised the former and damned the latter as close to "anarcho-syndicalism" (a term used against revisionist Marxists). Liberman was even quoted by a Moscow Tass broadcast as saying that "Soviet Jews . . . will never think in the same terms as Zionist extremists." His enlistment in this propaganda effort may have been an indication of personal peril.[34]

At the Twenty-Fourth Congress Brezhnev called for continued economic reform, but centrally planned and controlled on the basis of computerization.[35] This position regarding the reform can be characterized as an "optimistic engineering" approach. Its bases had been expounded throughout the reform period by many writers representing a strong current of conservative but modernizing opinion. The point had been made, for example, that the "establishment of economic ties between socialist enterprises on the basis of a 'free choice of partners,' the development of intra-branch competition, the weakening of centralized price formation . . . belittles the economic role of the socialist state." In addition, it had been stressed that the "functions of a socialist state with respect to economic control cannot be interpreted as purely administrative and superstructural." It was even derisively asked, "Can you imagine effectively organized economic circulation if forty or fifty thousand enterprises are going to be involved in output sales?"[36] What seems to be at the bottom of such opposition to a new type of economy is a fear that decentralization means anarchy, political as well as economic, a point that has been often made in diverse places.

This is an implicit but definite indication that this study's thesis of the active connection of the economic, social, and political spheres in the USSR has adherents there. The centralized authoritarian pattern of the Russian state has been widely accepted as both normality and necessity. Criticism of economic decentralization has been raised to a more general level and made more ideological by the attacks upon the Polish praxiologists and the Yugoslav neo-Marxists, groups that have called for more reliable and effective social and economic organization. Some Soviet writers have charged that this is a non-Marxist search for greater efficiency for its own sake.[37] The recent defense of econometrics against its Soviet critics is not a change in the general context of socioeconomic action. It only confirms the strength of the new overall Party policy for the economy, centralized planning (though less detailed than prior to 1965) based upon mathematical analysis and prognostication utilizing computers.[38]

A major reason for this confused picture and for the inability of the reform to overcome bureaucratic and ideological resistance is that no thorough ideological justification of the reform was ever made by the leadership. If ideology is neglected within an ideological political system, it becomes a decided and perhaps decisive hindrance to change, "an invincible weapon in the hands of vested interests resisting change."[39] In other words, the legitimacy conferred by use of the ideology passes by default to the elitist resistance to Party policy. This failing is perhaps to be expected from a Politburo composed mainly of engineers and technicians. As a result, the ideological climate came to contain an element hostile to the reform that seemed, or could be made to seem, ideologically correct.

In short, the political context emphasized centralism and negativism in regard to change to such a degree that the creativity and

THE INCOMPLETE REFORM

independence required by the reform model could not flourish. On top of this, besides the Party leadership itself being in favor of the restrictive situation just described, it put its energies abroad into a foreign policy that was a mirror image of its general domestic goals: it expended its strength in attempts to contain China, beat back revisionism within the Communist states of East-Central Europe, and expand its military and diplomatic reach. Without concentrated effort directed from on high, change encounters great difficulties in a Soviet-type society. Of course, more than context is limiting the reform's implementation. Political limitations of a more active nature are at work.

The Politics of Elitist Interests

A fundamental problem is that the leadership has been unable to get major interests to accept the reform as it was originally formulated, partly because those interests are related with the leadership and mutually supportive of it--at times even to the point of necessity. In other words, the leadership of the post-Stalin USSR depends upon the support of various key interest groups for the performance of tasks it sets for the system and, to some degree, for its own continued political preeminence. As the revisionist Marxist philosopher Leszek Kolokowski says, "The Party as a whole, in a single-party system, is a reflection of the various tendencies operating in the community...."[40] (This point is carried to an extreme by the East European bon mot to the effect that "there is no military-industrial complex in the USSR, it itself is a military-industrial complex.")

This relationship between the political leadership and major interests makes policy choices crucial. "Organization theory in public administration is a problem in political strategy; a choice of organization structure is a choice of which interest or which value will have preferred access or greater emphasis." Soviet scholars are aware of this. One Soviet writer on administration notes, "The resolution of economic questions requires in the first place a political approach." In the USSR, as elsewhere, interests contend and conflict with each other and also affect public policy, although politicalized coercion is endemic. However, "since coercion is merely another term for the suppression of interests, these will exist and be articulated to the extent that the coercive content of the regime is not total."[41] In any case, a figure important to the reform presents a "classic" statement on the formation of interest groups in connection with the reform. S. Novozhilov says that "people from different economic institutions approach the reform from different angles. People in charge of planning and administration press the need for greater centralization while the many managers of enterprises expect decentralization and a greater freedom for decision-making."[42] Several questions arise: what interests have to be "taken care of" in implementing the Soviet economic reform; how they are being considered, how successful this effort is, and what the implications of this are for the Soviet political system.

The course of the implementation of the reform was the result of a struggle and perhaps a compromise between the positions of those who wanted definite change and those who wanted little or no change in economic and industrial organization and its guiding principles. The leadership made concessions to some of the groupings opposed to reform by watering down the original "Liberman proposals." The sets of attitudes involved numbered more than two. A picture of only reformers and conservatives would be simplistic; but it is unrealistic to think of the various positions as a continuum, because the differences were important. While those wanting no change could be lumped together, they could be subdivided into ideological stand-patters ("Stalinists") and those fearful of change either because of personality or because of a fear of personal material loss ("classic bureaucrats").[43] Those wanting change also could be subdivided, perhaps into three main groupings: "econometrician-computopians"; "moderate marketeers" (close to the "optimalists" and wanting a slow, incremental, or experimental approach to the adoption of new principles and organizational forms); and "ideological marketeers" (desiring a rapid, complete economic change to the degree present in Yugoslavia).

This means that at least five main orientations to economic reform exist; but since these positions rarely are expressed without some approval of elements in other positions, the actual discussions have been less clear than this construct might suggest. For example, "all interest groupings appear to accept . . . the legitimacy of the monopoly of national policy-making by the higher organs of the Party."[44] Also, both conservatives and reformers (of all shades) are agreed that shortages and other economic problems exist. However, the former say these can be eliminated through further development of the existing economy, while the latter say the economy must be transformed, not just developed, for these problems to disappear. It would seem that the main operational contention is between the "classic bureaucrats" and the "econometrician-computopians," the latter apparently having "sold" their view to the dominant grouping in the political leadership, with the "Stalinists" being allowed to voice their views to the extent necessary to keep the two kinds of "marketeers" on the defensive, although not to such a degree that their views are not expressed or argued.

Examination of the views of the "marketeers" almost requires using characterizations of them written by the "Stalinists." Here

THE INCOMPLETE REFORM   299

what may be present is not group activity but "individual lobbying and protest."[45] One economist spoke of "certain writers" who "counterpose various forms of incentive . . . to the functions of control, make artificial distinctions between administrative and economic methods . . . and virtually reduce the functions of planned control to . . . a kind of 'self-regulating economy,' depriving socialist planning of its directive character." He went on to single out and criticize an economist named R. Belousov for saying "It is enough to establish the volume of capital investment, credit rates, payment into production funds, and a number of other norms in order to guarantee the proportional development of the economy." Significantly, what is being criticized, albeit indirectly, is the reform model of 1965. Others spoke of "rightist revisionists . . . attempting to represent centralized planning as bureaucratic administration" and even struck out at alleged "advocates of the Sik model" of Czechoslovak reform, who, it was further alleged, really favor a "capitalist commodity economy."[46] Some of this is typical Soviet hyperbole of the kind developed extensively during the 1930s, but the censure of the USSR's leading economics institute in 1971 for not adhering to the Party line and the demand that Voprosy ekonomiki "improve" its content indicate that there was a basis to the charges. The struggle between groupings of economists was resolved in favor of the econometricians, although the hardliners could not have been entirely dissatisfied.[47]

The military as well must be concerned over the effect that the economic reform will have on its interests. A colonel writing on the topic stresses increased efficiency as the main goal of the Soviet reform but intimates the limits of change tolerable to the military by criticizing the Czech reforms of 1967-68 and particularly decrying the "throwing overboard" of "such fundamental socialist principles" of economics as democratic centralism, state planning and socialist competition. . . ."[48]

Still another grouping among which there may be an objection to certain measures of the reform is the working class. Certainly their work situation is less enviable now because of the new pressures to produce, which for the first time include the prospect of dismissal. Although workers' pay is rising, there seemed to be no particular official concern for them until the Polish worker outbreaks of December 1970 led the Soviet leadership to "draw conclusions" and reduce the cost of some consumer goods and express greater concern about the workers' situation. And, although the trade unions have not been champions of worker interests, they may be showing some resistance, judging from the criticism of some of them for not "resolving questions" of the reform's implementation.[49]

Again, the major grouping resisting the reform is within the state bureaucracy. It is particularly important because it can act politically as a legitimate and institutionalized organization and can be, although with difficulty, maneuvered by its leaders to some degree. As Andrew Janos points out: "Normally, the politics of communist parties is the politics of organizations and not of autonomous groups." In addition, the head of an administrative department in a hierarchy is a "boss" whose authority over his subordinates derives not from the services he performs for them as a group but from his control over "rewards, promotions and punitive sanction. . . . He cannot be regarded as a representative of the group." What we see, then, is the working out of a process of bureaucratic politics that is limiting the implementation of the reform, that is, the "bargaining along regularized channels among players positioned hierarchically within the government."[50]

This study has presented many examples of inter-bureaucratic competition and conflict among bureaucratic agencies. There are at least two reasons for this. First, the understandable desire of bureaucrats and their organizations to recover their former positions in relation to the enterprise managers and the Party. Second, an attempt on the part of these bureaucratic agencies to take advantage of the officially sponsored and fairly relaxed atmosphere of increased rights and initiative of enterprise managers and of a more rational, pragmatic approach to problems in order to improve their own power positions and relationships vis-a-vis other bureaucratic actors in the economic policy milieu. The groupings that are economically valuable and have entrenched positions will have a better chance than ever to indulge in the familiar Soviet variety of inter-bureaucratic politics and carry it to new lengths. This may even come to have a general political effect. The result may well be a reform implemented not in accordance with the model but in conformity with the final balance of forces among the bureaucracies involved. In this the enterprise, and perhaps even the larger obedinenie, is likely to come off less than second best. Thus, the reform's implementation is being seriously hampered not only by a stikhiinyi ("spontaneous") process caused by normal bureaucratic caution and the difficulty of adjusting to new requirements, but also by a soznatel'nyi ("conscious") process of bureaucratic struggle for improved power positions.

The fact that the political leadership allows this to occur, although it does make efforts to mitigate it, shows that the Soviet political system has changed from the type portrayed by the totalitarian model, at least for tens of thousands of people in various social elites who are able to use their governmental institutions in defense and pursuit of their own interests. The "anaemic compromise" of 1965, as Michel Tatu calls the reform model, was further compromised. It is clear that groupings, particularly those enveloped in the cocoons of the state bureaucracy, were able to express their views in both consequential action and the press, and to force the central leadership to respond to the issues, thus fulfilling some of the defining requirements of interest groups. It seems obvious that these groupings have constituted interest groups by their actions against the reform, expression of their views being superfluous in some cases since the actions were, in effect, meaningful political communication.

This has powerful implications for the topmost political leadership. It is unable to enforce the reform model effectively or to prevent its sabotage. Of course, since professed organizational goals cannot be fully realized, the leadership obviously has been playing a losing game. But what is significant is that this game, with its modest goals, is being lost to such a degree. It must be that the existing relationships among the Soviet oligarchs actually encourage this and that, in T. H. Rigby's words, a "situation most supportive of the oligarchical principle" exists.[51] This can be put differently: that economic reform and rationality will be pursued and established by the political leadership only insofar as this rationality contributes to its self-preservation. In this interpretation it is assumed that each "oligarch" encourages the groupings owing him allegiance to act in a manner most conducive to his political well-being. Marx is turned on his head once more.

This perspective raises the old issue of whether the political process can ultimately triumph over social and economic change. Certainly, it has as good a chance in the Russo-Soviet (or Tsarist-Leninist) state as it has ever had. The case is presented well by the Dutch economist Willem Keizer, who states:

> Where economic and political rationality conflict, the decision in favour of either depends on the contribution each makes to this aim [self-preservation]. It would appear as if thus far the leadership has valued the contribution of political ends and rationality more highly than it values the contribution that economic ends and rationality could make. . . . As the supreme aim of the Soviet politico-economic system is primarily of an ideological/political nature, there is no imperative reason why the quest for economic rationality should lead to the transformation of the entire system.[52]

The possible defect in this reasoning lies, of course, in the meaning of the "ideological/political nature" of the Soviet system. If the leadership's ideology were to change, as the current stress on scientific rationality and mathematical means seems to reveal, then the system would indeed face the possibility of its transformation.

Some sort of victory was won by the "moderate-modernizers" at about the time of the Twenty-Fourth Party Congress in the spring of 1971 or within the two years following. Its effects were evident by the spring and summer of 1973, when, for example, conservative economists were severely criticized in Pravda (June 4), the new regional obedineniia were instituted (April), the visit of Brezhnev to the United States took place (June)--despite the opportunities offered to Soviet conservatives and ideologues by the publicizing of the Watergate affair--and the Soviet government's move to consummate several economic and trade deals with private American firms occurred. It seems likely that a new set of major political considerations, perhaps even the rudiments of a new implicit or "unarticulated" ideology, motivates the Soviet Politburo.

> They are not . . . averse . . . to giving socialism a more technocratic face so long as the turn to technocracy enhances their power, improves economic performance, and preserves the dominant position of the Party in the political system. . . . Scientific management may be the New Course and technocracy the New Face of [Soviet] socialism in the 1970s.[53]

The changes in the membership of the Politburo that took place in April 1973--specifically the addition to it of the leaders of the armed forces, the secret police, and the Foreign Ministry (Andrei Grechko, Yuri Andropov, and Andrei Gromyko)--strongly suggest that the oligarchical nature of the Politburo has been significantly increased. The changes reduced the influence of the Party apparatus in the Politburo, only 4 national Party secretaries being among the 16 full members. They also further reduced the significance of the traditional Soviet ideology and attenuated the influence of the ideologues. The state bureaucracy, speaking quite generally, was strengthened by the addition of Grechko and Gromyko, although Andropov may be considered a "Party hack" type despite his heading a state agency. These changes signify the "stretching" of the Politburo to accommodate the increasing diversity and complexity of the Soviet political system. Their effect on the future course of the economic reform cannot, of course, be judged. It is likely that the three new members will go along with a cautious advance within the present channels allowed to the reform, while the new candidate member, G. V. Romanov, the First Party Secretary of Leningrad, may want a greater rate of progress.[54]

THE SIGNIFICANCE AND IMPLICATIONS OF
THE SOVIET ECONOMIC REFORM

Although the economic reform has not yet induced a systemic change in the Soviet way of life, it is still better to apply intelligence and knowledge to the limit of possibility and face this issue than to err on the side of caution and accept what has thus far occurred as finality. Accordingly, some general discussion of the future of the Soviet system is worthwhile. It is obvious that the Soviet economy is still a command economy locked in the Russian tradition of administration and policy-making, and that etatism is not in question. The changes contemplated and those occurring do not yet involve the existence of central planning and the imposition of politically set priorities for the economy. Indeed, the priorities for the Soviet economy may always be politically based. They are becoming more so for "capitalist" economies. Everywhere production is considered too important to be left to the producers. The reform as presented in 1965 posits changes that, according to one economist, "concern only the nature and volume of edicts to be effected by the centrally appointed supervisory agencies of the enterprises . . . and particularly the mechanisms to be established for 'identifying' [checking and comparing] the performance of the enterprises."55

In this view the reform is, in Egon Neuberger's phrase, "more legacy than reform." But this is true only in the narrowest of economic senses. Politically and socially the reform concerns far more than this. It offers a "last chance" to show that the Soviet system as presently constituted can clothe and comfort its people. The reform is an attempt to reconcile the old pattern of political control of socioeconomic processes with the need of an emerging post-industrial society for increased rationality in production processes. The goal is to raise the economy's growth rate and improve its products without weakening political controls or changing the political system. However, some of the changes being adopted--the introduction of automated production processes, the encouragement of managers to work with fewer directives from above and to be more forthcoming and cooperative in their relations with other enterprises, the transformation of the authoritative ministries into accounting, planning, and research agencies, and the reduction of the intensity and perhaps the scale of the Party's involvement at the operational level in industry--are outside the Russo-Soviet tradition and, therefore, raise the prospect of systemic change because they clearly cannot be thoroughly executed within the present sociopolitical framework. Although the main lines of the reform as presently formed better fit the characterization of "technocratization" than "marketization," it is fairly clear that a full return to the former command economy is precluded by the new goals of the leadership and many in the industrial elite, if not by the distance already traveled and the fact that the command economy variant has exhausted its possibilities for the Soviet Union. A Soviet economy that will be more like those of developed "Western" societies of the future is unavoidable.[56]

Although the ultimate results of the reform cannot be foreseen, certain questions of fundamental importance can be considered. First, is this reform the ultimate of its type or is further reform probable or inevitable? Second, if further reform is assumed and probable, at what point and in what way do economics affect politics? Put another way, can further economic reform be carried out without affecting political relationships, either as a whole or selectively?

The results of this study support the conclusions of several other non-Soviet writers on the reform who say that it is not going to produce significant economic results of the type desired and that, accordingly, further reform is necessary and even inevitable. Considerations of prestige alone will push in this direction. Further organizational and behavioral changes are necessary if the goals of the present reform are to be realized and because, once such a Stalinist command economy is modified (as it has been), further adjustments are continually necessary to cope with the unavoidable effects of the initial modifications. These will outrun the ability of the "supercoordinator" to coordinate. Also, once the Party gives up some areas of decision-making to the technical experts, who cannot be transformed by co-opting, "the reform as it progresses intensifies the process and calls for its extension into new areas such as law and sociology."[57] For example, the unemployment and decrease in the work force caused by the change in the manager-worker relationship will necessitate, at least with the passage of time, the establishment of means within the economy to use the labor thus displaced. One possible solution would be the larger-scale establishment of service enterprises, perhaps partly or wholly based upon private ownership. This stage has already been reached in Yugoslavia. Emigration is also a possibility, although a less likely one. The establishment of employment information centers and labor exchanges is a significant development stemming partly from the reform. The provision of unemployment insurance and the appropriate ideological adjustments will have to occur as well.

Similarly, the reduction in the number of success indicators of enterprise management may eventually lead to a further decrease in their number, although a replacement of those now in use by economically more sophisticated indicators also is possible. Of course, in the short run ministries have increased their number by "additional indicators." These will be eliminated by some "zig" in the

THE INCOMPLETE REFORM 305

continuing reform. The pace chosen depends partly upon the attitudes held by the Soviet leadership and also upon the relative powers of opposed groupings within the state bureaucracy and the Party apparatus at the moment of greatest need to act.

Thus, it is apparent that the reform must be reformed thoroughly, although it is barely possible instead that with the development of a nationwide network of computer centers, if it could be made effective, a centrally directed economy might be workable to a degree.[58] Thus, given the present seeming practicality of some central controls, no basic economic transformation is probable. However, reform up to the point of a free market with a rational price system cannot be dismissed as an ultimate necessity. Given the cast of the economic and other experts with dominant influence in the Politburo, "Whenever the government has economic difficulties and seeks expert advice, the advice will be to liberalize further."[59] This group, however, must also contend with the advice of the proponents of computopia, who will ask for more and better computers. Eventually, however, the decisive change once suggested by Oscar Lange may be necessary in order to prevent the "vested interests" from sabotaging the reform. Such a prospect may become unavoidable if the defects long existing in the Soviet economy are finally to be eliminated. But when this point will be reached cannot now be stated, although sudden changes have been the typical response to the recurring crises of Soviet and Russian history.

Besides the social changes just mentioned, others of equal or greater significance are likely, and perhaps even unavoidable. The reform and the present stage of development of the Soviet economy have made organizational tasks more complex, a characteristic that tends to lead to the debureaucratization of authority relations within organizations. This process cannot end there, but will tend to expand into Soviet society at large. Change in the education of scientists, engineers, and technicians is one means. And, since process industry has more delegation and decentralization than large-batch and mass-production industry, as the former type becomes more important and as the goals of industry become less set, there will be a corresponding change in patterns of management and perhaps in sociopolitical relations as well.[60] Of course, possibilities such as these may seem only theoretically inherent in current Soviet life.

Nevertheless, one of the most important requirements of economic change in the USSR, as it was in old Russia, is anterior consequential sociopolitical change. If the desire for a new economy is strong enough, change in the other spheres will be both allowed and even fostered. This, too, is in the Russian tradition, but at a low level of magnitude. The post-industrial society may not allow the continued insulation of one social sphere from another. Putting it another way, the continued existence of "sybsystem autonomy," with its opportunities for politicking and implemental discretion, cannot be allowed to continue indefinitely in its present form without its having institutional results. The "Anti-Party Group" of 1957 may well have been correct; once the Stalinist edifice is modified, its continued modification to the point of qualitative change is unavoidable. The timing and form are unclear. However, as yet the Soviet economic reform of 1965 is an economic and technical partial reorientation of industrial life that lacks a new comprehensive or systemic view of human and organizational relationships and their effects. Without a new conception of modern industrialized society leading to the prediction of problems and their rational resolution, measures such as the economic reform cannot succeed and may lead only to renewed arbitrariness.

The connection between the political and economic spheres in the USSR and the effects upon this of the economic reform cannot, of course, be answered in any definitive sense. However, the question has come to have a close and direct relationship to actual events because of recent Czech, Yugoslav, and Polish history and the changes now beginning to occur in the USSR. In light of the course of West European and American history over the past 150 years (the period of the working out of the social and political effects of the industrial revolution) and of East European history since 1956, it cannot be denied that socioeconomic changes have political effects other than those intended by the political leadership and even going against their interests.[61] The political structure must consider the political consequences of the desire for a more productive society if that desire is a serious one. As two Czech writers note:

> Man can be forced . . . to function as simple laborpower. . . . But no one will be induced to engage in creative activity . . . if he is not committed freely, of his own will. And . . . no elite will be capable of opening up the sources of science, technology, and culture adequately to meet the demands of a complete transformation of the productive forces of human life.[62]

Of course, as the pressure for political response increases, the leadership may decide to clamp on the lid of totalitarianism again. However, that would be an admission of failure that would cost heavily in prestige and economic growth, would go against the leadership's new implicit ideology, and would necessitate a furious and enervating struggle within the political elite itself. One of the forces that makes the reimposition of totalitarianism unlikely is the

THE INCOMPLETE REFORM

politics of Soviet bureaucracy. Perhaps "bureaucratism" in the USSR--that is, the assertion by state bureaucrats of their powers-- is "objectively" a necessary precondition for future general liberties within the Soviet system. Such an assertion of bureaucratic powers, if continuous, works against the "charismatic" rule of the ideologues and the totalitarian ideology. Factions and bureaucratic freedoms, being a source of conflict, tension, and disagreement, produce by their operations some of the dialectics necessary for political change toward a less centrally directed system. Their defect may be, of course, that in the event of their balancing one another, they will produce only a stasis or Soviet-type immobilism characteristic of situations where interest groups have been allowed to play a politics of the "pure game" type. One result of continued inter-bureaucratic conflict may be a "layering effect" like that of French politics. All issues, conflicts, and groups continue to exist without any decisive political change ever having occurred, despite the turbulence of politics. The structure of politics in this case can be likened to a medieval palimpsest, with the outlines of the old "layers" still visible through the new and continuing to have a determining effect on the whole. That is, the tension between ideology, bureaucracy, and modernization will remain unresolved. The common disorderliness of political structures, principles, and processes suggests this.

The fact that institutional and ideological changes have not yet occurred in response to the pressures engendered by the process of reform does not mean that they will not occur. Ideas and institutions often continue past the point where objectively they are no longer necessary. The end of the Soviet movement regime awaits the forced recognition that it has reached its limit and that a new approach to the problems of human society is required. The implementation of the new perspective and practice awaits a Soviet leadership able to devise a vision of further change and communicate it to the cautious bureaucracies and populace in such a way that the changes called for are accepted. This vision has been only partly devised and partly communicated. The coming years will witness the further development of the reform and its results. Whether these are effectively introduced will suggest how adaptable the Soviet political system and the Soviet Communist Party are.

Although, as some writers argue, a possibility may exist that the Soviet system can be modernized without either crises or liberalization, this perspective assumes an omnicompetence and predictability on the part of politicians that general historical experience does not suggest is realistic and a rather limited conception of modernization.[63] The rejection of this general argument does not suggest that qualitative change is imminent, but that such change is likely despite the repression of the voicing of some new ideas in the Soviet Union today. The long-term division between existence and thought so characteristic of Russian history cannot be maintained indefinitely in the face of the growing consequences of the introduction of elements of the post-industrial society. The tension between the demands flowing from the attempt to modernize Soviet society and the resistance of ideologues and conservative functionaries will affect Soviet politics for a long time to come. The reform has thus set in motion a major current of Soviet political life.

NOTES

1. Robert W. Campbell, "Management Spillovers from Soviet Space and Military Programmes," Soviet Studies 23, no. 4 (April 1972): 590.

2. Jerry F. Hough, "The Soviet System: Petrification or Pluralism?" Problems of Communism 21, no. 2 (March-April 1972): 38.

3. S. Wellisz, The Economies of the Soviet Bloc (New York: McGraw-Hill, 1964), p. 8.

4. Theodore Frankel, "Economic Reform: A Tentative Appraisal," Problems of Communism 16, no. 3 (May-June 1967): 41. Frankel cites A. V. Bachurin in Trud, January 17, 1967.

5. For example, see the statements by A. Snechkus, the First Secretary in Lithuania, and T. Kiselev, Chairman of the Council of Ministers of Belorussia, in Trud, February 25, 1971, p. 2, and on Moscow Radio, February 3, 1971; and N. Tarasov, the Minister of Light Industry, on Moscow Radio, July 17, 1969.

6. See Sotsialisticheskaia industriia, September 26, 1970, p. 2; and Pravda, April 11, 1971 (the directives of the ninth five-year plan).

7. Sotsialisticheskaia industriia, loc. cit.; Pravda, August 22, 1970, p. 2; and New York Times, April 28, 1968.

8. Jan S. Prybyla, "The Soviet Economy: An Overview," Current History 63, no. 374 (October 1972): 178, 180; and Franklyn D. Holzman, "Some Notes on Over-Full Employment Planning, Short-Run Balance, and the Soviet Economic Reforms," Soviet Studies 22, no. 2 (October 1970): 255, 258-59.

9. Gertrude E. Schroeder, "Soviet Economic Reform at an Impasse," Problems of Communism 20, no. 4 (July-August 1971): 36-46; and Keith Bush, "Soviet Economic Growth: Past, Present and Projected," Radio Liberty Dispatch, April 4, 1973, pp. 3, 8-9.

10. From New York Times, September 17, 1972; and a presentation by Marshall I. Goldman at the Russian Research Center, Harvard University, March 3, 1971.

11. Willem Keizer, The Soviet Quest for Economic Rationality: The Conflict of Economic and Political Aims in the Soviet Economy (Rotterdam: Rotterdam University Press, 1971), pp. 224, 251; Eugene Zaleski, Planning Reforms in the Soviet Union, 1962-1966 (Chapel Hill: University of North Carolina Press, 1967), p. 181; and Gregory Grossman, "A Comment," Survey no. 70-71 (Winter/Spring 1969): 167.

12. Alf Edeen, "The Administrative Intelligentsia," Survey no. 65 (October 1967): 69.

13. Zygmunt Bauman, "Twenty Years After: The Crisis of Soviet-Type Systems," Problems of Communism 20, no. 6 (November-December 1971): 50-51, 593 ("the New Proletariat").

14. John N. Hazard, "The Politics of Soviet Economic Reform," in Alexander Balinky, ed., Planning and the Market in the USSR: The 1960's (New Brunswick, N.J.: Rutgers University Press, 1967), pp. 80-84; and John P. Hardt and Theodore Frankel, "The Industrial Managers," in H. Gordon Skilling and Franklyn Griffiths, eds., Interest Groups in Soviet Politics (Princeton, N.J.: Princeton University Press, 1971), pp. 171-208.

15. Michael Ellman, Economic Reform in the Soviet Union (London: Political and Economic Planning, 1969), p. 316.

16. Reinhard Bendix, Work and Authority in Industry (New York: Wiley, 1956), pp. 15, 20, 435; and Theodore H. von Laue, Sergei Witte and the Industrialization of Russia (New York: Columbia University Press, 1963), pp. 182, 186.

17. See the articles by V. Pavliuchenko and I. Pashko in Voprosy ekonomiki, July 1970, pp. 23-32, 33-42.

18. See Joseph S. Berliner, "Bureaucratic Conservatism and Creativity in the Soviet Economy," paper presented at the Annual Meeting of the American Political Science Association, New York City, September 6-10, 1966, p. 18.

19. T. H. Rigby, "Crypto-Politics," Survey no. 50 (January 1964): 183.

20. S. B. Marinin, S.Sh.A.-USA.: Politika i upravleniia (Moscow: Meyhdunarodnie olnosheniia, 1967), p. 67; and V. Seliunin, "The Inverted Pyramid," Moskva 1 (January 1968) (abstracted in CASP 1, no. 3 [June 1968]: 5). I am also indebted to Paul Cocks, "Communist Bureaucracy and Party Control: An Analytical Framework in Comparative Perspective," a paper presented at the Russian Research Center, Harvard University, April 27, 1971.

21. Fred W. Riggs, "Bureaucratic Politics in Comparative Perspective," paper presented at the Annual Meeting of the American Political Science Association, Washington, D.C., September 2-7, 1968.

22. Michel Tatu, Power in the Kremlin (New York: Viking, 1970), p. 431.

23. Based upon Amitai Etzioni, "Two Approaches to Organizational Analysis," in Oscar Grusky and George A. Miller, eds., The Sociology of Organizations (New York: Free Press, 1970), pp. 218-21; Daniel Katz and Robert Kahn, "Open-Systems Theory," in ibid., pp. 151-55; and Morton H. Halperin, "Why Bureaucrats Play Games," Foreign Policy 2 (Spring 1971): 70-90.

24. See Alexander Eckstein, "Economic Development and Political Change in Communist Systems," World Politics 22, no. 4 (July 1970): 492.

25. Interview with Anatoli Fedoseyev Broadcast by Radio Liberty September 24-25, 1971 (New York: Radio Liberty, 1971), p. 4.

26. Frederick C. Mosher, ed., Governmental Reorganizations: Cases and Commentary (Indianapolis, Ind.: Bobbs-Merrill, 1967), p. 514.

27. Berliner, op. cit., p. 11, and Riggs, op. cit., p. 21.

28. Berliner, op. cit., p. 18.

29. O. Latsis, "Net iskliucheniia bez pravila," Novyi mir 4 (April 1967): 171.

30. George A. Miller, "Professionals in Bureaucracy: Alienation Among Industrial Scientists and Engineers," in Grusky and Miller, op. cit., pp. 503-04, 514-15. Miller cites William Kornhauser, Scientists in Industry (Berkeley: University of California Press, 1962), pp. 195-96. Also see Pravda, February 3, 1971, p. 1; (partially translated in CDSP 23, no. 5 [March 2, 1971]: 11).

31. See the critique of Daniel Bell's article, "The Electronic Civilization," By Iu. Ostrovitianov in Literaturnaia gazeta 17 (April 23, 1969): 12-13; abstracted in CASP 2, no. 1 (April 1969): 4-5.

32. See Pravda, February 3, 1971, p. 1. Views such as this were criticized by V. P. Shelest, the physicist son of P. Ye. Shelest the former Politburo member, in Literaturna Ukraina, May 5, 1970.

33. Pravda, December 17, 1970; October 13, 1970.

34. See Yevsei Liberman, Ekonomicheskie metody povysheniia effektivnosti obshchestvennogo proizvodstva (Moscow: "Ekonomika," 1970). The statement attributed to Liberman was broadcast in English on January 21, 1971.

35. Pravda, March 31, 1971, pp. 6-7.

36. See Pravda, November 3, 1970; D. Allakhverdian and E. Slastenko, "Khoziaistvennaia reforma i nekotorye problemy upravleniia . . .," Voprosy ekonomiki 3 (March 1968): 16-25 (JPRS 45,234 [May 2, 1968]: 6); and Pravda, September 22, 1968, p. 2. Also see Zaleski, op. cit., p. 95.

37. See "Polemics Against Polish and Yugoslav Theoreticians," Radio Free Europe Research Report, January 27, 1971, citing articles by A. Rybalko and I. M. Savel'ev in Ekonomika radianskoi Ukrainy 9 (1970) and in Filosofskie nauki 5 (1970), respectively.

38. See Pravda, June 4, 1973.
39. Ernst Halperin, "Beyond Libermanism," Problems of Communism 26, no. 1 (January-February 1967): 47-48. Halperin notes that when Tito announced the Law on Workers' Self-Management in 1950, he claimed he was giving the factories to the workers and beginning the withering away of the state. (Borba, June 27, 1950.)
40. Leszek Kolokowski, interview in Encounter, October 1971, p. 46. Also see Herbert Marcuse, Soviet Marxism (New York: Columbia University Press, 1958), pp. 107-19.
41. Wallace S. Sayre, "Premises of Public Administration: Past and Emerging," Public Administration Review 18, no. 2 (Spring 1958): 104, quoted in Felix A. Nigro, Modern Public Administration (New York: Harper & Row, 1965), p. 149; V. V. Godunov, Vvedenie v teoriiu upravleniia (Moscow: "Ekonomika," 1967), p. 186; and Francis G. Castles, "Interest Articulation: A Totalitarian Paradox," Survey no. 73 (Autumn 1969): 118.
42. Literaturnaia gazeta, April 8, 1970, p. 12; abstracted in ABSEES 1 (July 1970): 114.
43. On "classic bureaucrats" see Robert D. Putnam, "The Political Attitudes of Civil Servants in Western Europe," British Journal of Political Science 3, no. 3 (July 1973): 259-61.
44. Philip D. Stewart, "Soviet Interest Groups and the Policy Process," World Politics 22, no. 1 (October 1969): 45.
45. Andrew C. Janos, "Group Politics in Communist Society," in S. H. Huntington and C. H. Moore, eds., Authoritarian Politics in Modern Society (New York: Basic Books, 1970), p. 442.
46. See the articles by S. Starostin in Ekonomicheskaia gazeta 13 (March 1969): 42; A. Yefimov, ibid. 14 (April 1969): 3; and A. Motylov, ibid. 11 (March 1969): 28.
47. See New York Times, January 18, 1972.
48. Kommunist Vooruzhennykh sil' 21 (November 1968) (JPRS 47,065 [December 12]: 34).
49. See Pravda, January 14, 1971, p. 4; New York Times, March 3, 1971; N. Garetovskii, "Ekonomicheskie interesy i ekonomicheskaia politika v sotsialisticheskom obshchestve," Kommunist 10 (July 1972): 37-49; and Trud, May 21, 1969, p. 1.
50. Janos, op. cit., pp. 446-47; and Graham T. Allison, "Conceptual Models and the Cuban Missile Crisis," American Political Science Review 63, no. 3 (September 1969): 707.
51. T. H. Rigby, "The Soviet Leadership: Towards a Self-Stabilizing Oligarchy?" Soviet Studies 22, no. 2 (October 1970): 181.
52. Keizer, op. cit., p. v.
53. Paul Cocks, "Comment," Survey 19, no. 2 (Spring 1973): 157-58. I am indebted to Professor George Kline, speaking on the philosophy of Leszek Kolokowski, for the concept of an "unarticulated ideology." Smith College, November 4, 1971.

54. See *Pravda*, April 17, 1971, p. 2.

55. Nicolas Spulber, *Socialist Management and Planning* (Bloomington: Indiana University Press, 1971), p. 3.

56. The terms are from Radoslav Selucky, *Economic Reforms in Eastern Europe* (New York: Praeger, 1972); and Egon Neuberger, "Central Planning and Its Legacies," in A. Brown and E. Neuberger, eds., *International Trade and Central Planning* (Berkeley: University of California Press, 1968).

57. R. W. Campbell, "Economic Reform in the USSR," *American Economic Review* 58, no. 2 (May 1968): 558.

58. See Benjamin N. Ward, *The Socialist Economy* (New York: Random House, 1967), p. 180.

59. Rush V. Greenslade, "The Soviet Economic System in Transition," U.S. Congress, Joint Economic Committee, *New Directions in the Soviet Economy*, Pt. I, p. 16.

60. See John Brewer, "Organizational Patterns of Supervision . . .," and Joan Woodward, "Technology and Organization," in Grusky and Miller, op. cit., pp. 347 and 273-83, respectively.

61. See Zvi Gitelman, "Beyond Leninism: Political Development in Eastern Europe," *Newsletter on Comparative Studies of Communism* 5, no. 3 (May 1972): 18-43, particularly 25-30.

62. Ota Klein and Jindrich Zeleny, "Dynamics of Change: Leadership, the Economy, Organizational Structure, and Society," in R. Barry Farrell, ed., *Political Leadership in Eastern Europe and the Soviet Union* (Chicago: Aldine, 1970), p. 211.

63. George Fischer, *The Soviet System and Modern Society* (New York: Atherton, 1968), p. 13.

BIBLIOGRAPHY

This bibliography does not include some items cited or quoted only once and those items cited only in notes.

BOOKS AND MONOGRAPHS

Albrow, Martin. Bureaucracy. New York: Praeger, 1970.

Alekhin, A. P., et al. Pravovoe polozhenie ministerstv SSSR. Moscow: Iuridicheskaia Literatura, 1971.

Alexander, Arthur J. R & D in Soviet Aviation. Santa Monica, Calif.: The RANK Corporation, 1970.

Almond, Gabriel, and Powell, G. Bingham. Comparative Politics: A Developmental Approach. Boston and Toronto: Little-Brown, 1966.

Arakelian, A. Industrial Management in the USSR. Translated by Ellsworth L. Raymond. Washington, D.C.: Public Affairs Press, 1950.

Armstrong, John A. The Soviet Bureaucratic Elite: A Case Study of the Ukranian Apparatus. New York: Praeger, 1959.

_____. The European Administrative Elite. Princeton, N.J.: Princeton University Press, 1973.

Azrael, Jeremy R. "Political Profiles of the Soviet Technological Intelligentsia and Managerial Elite." Ph.D. dissertation, Harvard University, 1961.

_____. Managerial Power and Soviet Politics. Cambridge, Mass.: Harvard University Press, 1966.

Balinky, Alexander, ed. Planning and the Market in the U.S.S.R.: The 1960's. New Brunswick, N.J.: Rutgers University Press, 1967.

Belkin, V. B., and Kholodnaia, G. N. Osnovy organizatsii i ekonomiki promyshlennogo proizvodstva. Moscow: "Vysshaia Shkola," 1964.

Bell, Daniel. The Coming of Post-Industrial Society. New York: Basic Books, 1973.

Bendix, Reinhard. Work and Authority in Industry. New York: Wiley, 1956.

Bergson, Abram. The Economics of Soviet Planning. New Haven and London: Yale University Press, 1964.

Berliner, Joseph S. Factory and Manager in the USSR. Cambridge, Mass.: Harvard University Press, 1957.

_____. Economy, Society and Welfare: A Study in Social Economics. New York: Praeger, 1972.

Berman, Harold J. Justice in the U.S.S.R. Rev. ed. New York: Vintage Books (Random House), 1963.

Bienstock, Gregory; Schwarz, Solomon M.; and Yugow, Aaron. Management in Russian Industry and Agriculture. Edited by Arthur Feiler and Jacob Marschak. Published for the Institute of World Affairs of the New School for Social Research. Ithaca and New York: Cornell University Press, 1948. (First published in 1944.

Birman, A. Nekotorye problemy nauki ob upravleniia narodnym khoziaistvom. Moscow: "Ekonomika," 1965.

Blau, Peter M. The Dynamics of Bureaucracy. Chicago: University of Chicago Press, 1955.

Brodersen, Arvid. The Soviet Worker: Labor and Government in Soviet Society. New York: Random House, 1966.

Brown, Emily Clark. Soviet Trade Unions and Labor Relations. Cambridge, Mass.: Harvard University Press, 1966.

Brzezinski, Zbigniew. Between Two Ages: America's Role in the Technetronic Era. New York: Viking, 1970.

Bush, Keith. *The Implementation of the Soviet Economic Reform.* Radio Liberty Research Paper No. 36. Munich: Radio Liberty, 1970.

Chandler, Alfred, Jr. *Giant Enterprise: Ford, General Motors, and the Automobile Industry.* New York and Burlingame, Ind.: Harcourt, Brace and World, 1964.

Chapman, Brian. *The Profession of Government.* London: Allen & Unwin, 1959.

Churchward, L. G. *Contemporary Soviet Government.* New York: American Elsevier, 1968.

Cohn, Stanley H. *Economic Development in the Soviet Union.* Lexington, Mass.: D. C. Heath, 1970.

Communist Party of the Soviet Union. *Spravochnik sekretaria pervichnoi partiinoi organizatsii.* 2nd ed. Moscow: Izdatel'stvo Politicheskoi Literatury, 1967.

Conquest, Robert. *Power and Policy in the U.S.S.R.: The Study of Soviet Dynastics.* London and New York: Macmillan and St. Martin's, 1962.

_____, ed. *Industrial Workers in the USSR.* New York: Praeger, 1967.

Crossman, R. H. S. *The Myths of Cabinet Government.* Cambridge, Mass.: Harvard University Press, 1972.

Dallin, Alexander, ed. *Politics in the Soviet Union.* New York: Harcourt, Brace and World, 1966.

Djilas, Milovan. *The Unperfect Society.* New York: Harcourt, Brace and World, 1969.

Drize, I. D., et al. *Opyt i problemy stimulirovaniia v novykh usloviiakh.* Moscow: "Ekonomika," 1966.

Drucker, Peter F. *Management.* New York: Harper & Row, 1974.

Ellman, Michael. *Economic Reform in the Soviet Union.* London: Political and Economic Planning, 1969.

Fainsod, Merle. How Russia Is Ruled. Rev. ed. Cambridge, Mass.: Harvard University Press, 1963.

Fedorov, T. K. Pamiatka po nauchnoi organizatsii truda i proizvodstvo. Moscow: "Ekonomika," 1966.

Fischer, George, ed. Science and Ideology in Soviet Society. New York: Atherton, 1967.

_____. The Soviet System and Modern Society. New York: Atherton, 1968.

Galbraith, John K. The New Industrial State. Boston: Houghton-Mifflin, 1967.

Godunov, V. V. Vvedenie v teoriiu upravleniia (sistema promyshlennogo proizvodstva). Moscow: "Ekonomika," 1967.

Graham, Loren R. Science and Philosophy in the Soviet Union. New York: Knopf, 1972.

Granick, David. Management of the Industrial Firm in the USSR: A Study in Soviet Economic Planning. New York: Columbia University Press, 1954.

_____. The Red Executive: A Study of the Organization Man in Russian Industry. Garden City, N.Y.: Anchor Books (Doubleday), 1961.

Grigor'ev, B. V. Upravlenie gosudarstvennym promyshlennym predpriiatiem v SSSR. Moscow: Izdatel'stvo Moskovskogo Universiteta, 1966.

Gross, Neal; Mason, Ward; and McEachern, Alexander. Explorations in Role Analysis: Studies of the School Superintendency Role. New York: John Wiley and Sons, 1958.

Grusky, Oscar, and Miller, George A. The Sociology of Organizations: Basic Studies. New York: Free Press, 1970.

Gvishiani, D. M. Sotsiologiia biznesa: Kriticheskii ocherk amerikanskoi teorii menedzhmenta. Moscow: Sotsialno Ekonomicheskoi Literatury, 1962.

Hage, Jerald, and Aiken, Michael. Social Change in Complex Organizations. New York: Random House, 1970.

Hangen, Welles. The Muted Revolution: East Germany's Challenge to Russia and the West. New York: Knopf, 1966.

Hazard, John N. The Soviet System of Government. 3rd ed. Chicago: University of Chicago Press, 1964.

_____. Communists and Their Law. Chicago: University of Chicago Press, 1969.

Hollander, Gayle D. Soviet Political Indoctrination. New York: Praeger, 1972.

Hough, Jerry Fincher. "The Role of the Local Party Organs in Soviet Industrial Decision-making." Ph.D. dissertation, Harvard University, 1961.

_____. The Soviet Prefects: The Local Party Organs in Industrial Decision-making. Cambridge, Mass.: Harvard University Press, 1969.

Karpov, A. G.; Zholkevich, A. E.; and Nikitin, D. N. Khozraschet pronikaet vsiudu. Moscow: "Ekonomika," 1966.

Katz, Abraham. "The Politics of Economic Reform in the Soviet Union." Unpublished draft. Mimeographed. Cambridge, Mass.: Center for International Affairs, Harvard University, May 1967.

_____. The Politics of Economic Reform in the Soviet Union. New York: Praeger, 1972.

Kaufman, Herbert. The Limits of Organizational Change. University: University of Alabama Press, 1971.

Keizer, Willem. The Soviet Quest for Economic Rationality: The Conflict of Economic and Political Aims in the Soviet Economy, 1953-1968. Rotterdam: Rotterdam University Press, 1971.

Kirsch, Leonard J. Soviet Wages: Changes in Structure and Administration Since 1956. Cambridge, Mass.: MIT Press, 1972.

Kornai, Janos. Overcentralization in Economic Administration: A Critical Analysis Based on Experience in Hungarian Light Industry. Translated by John Knapp. London: Oxford University Press, 1959. First published in Budapest by Kozgazdosagi es Jogi Kiadovallalat, 1957.

Lane, David. Politics and Society in the USSR. New York and London: Random House and Weidenfeld and Nicolson, 1971.

_____. The End of Inequality? Stratification Under State Socialism. London: Penguin, 1971.

Liberman, E. G. Ekonomicheskie metody povysheniia effektivnosti obshchestvennogo pro'zvodstva. Moscow: "Ekonomika," 1970. Published in the United States as Economic Methods and the Effectiveness of Production. Translated by Arlo Schultz. Edited by Leonard J. Kirsch. White Plains, N.Y.: International Arts and Sciences Press, 1971; Garden City, N.Y.: Doubleday and Company, 1973.

_____. Economic Methods and the Effectiveness of Production. Translated by Arlo Schultz. Edited by Leonard J. Kirsch. Garden City, N.Y.: Doubleday (Anchor Books), 1973.

Leonhard, Wolfgang. The Kremlin Since Stalin. New York: Praeger, 1962.

Lewin, Moshe. Political Undercurrents in Soviet Economic Debates: From Bukhaim to the Modern Reformers. Princeton, N.J.: Princeton University Press, 1974.

March, James G., and Simon, Herbert A. Organizations. New York and London: John Wiley & Sons, Inc., 1958.

Maslova, I. S. Vysvobozhdenie rabochei sily v promyshlennosti SSSR i ee ratsional'noe ispol'zovanie. Moscow: Izdatel'stvo Moskovskogo Universiteta, 1967.

McAuley, Mary. Labour Disputes in Soviet Russia: 1957-1965. Oxford: Clarendon Press, 1969.

Merton, Robert K. Social Theory and Social Structure. Rev. and enl. ed. Glencoe, Ill.: Free Press, 1957.

Meyer, Alfred G. The Soviet Political System: An Interpretation. New York: Random House, 1965.

Moore, Wilbert E. The Conduct of the Corporation. New York: Random House, 1962.

Mosher, Frederick C., ed. Governmental Reorganizations: Cases and Commentary. Indianapolis, Ind.: Bobbs-Merrill, 1967.

Naumenko, M. V novykh usloviiakh khoziaistvovaniia. Moscow: Profizdat, 1967.

Nedosekina, N. Organizatsiia raboty profgruppy. Moscow: Profizdat, 1967.

Nigro, Felix A. Modern Public Administration. New York: Harper & Row, 1965.

Nove, Alec. The Soviet Economy: An Introduction. 2nd rev. ed. New York: Praeger, 1969.

_____. An Economic History of the U.S.S.R. Baltimore: Penguin, 1972.

Osborn, Robert J. Soviet Social Policies: Welfare, Equality, and Community. Homewood, Ill.: Dorsey Press, 1970.

_____. The Evolution of Soviet Politics. Homewood, Ill.: Dorsey Press, 1974.

Parry, Geraint. Political Elites. London: Allen & Unwin, 1969.

Pevsner, A. G., and Subotskii, Iu. V. Pravovye osnovy upravleniia promyshlennost'iu. Moscow: "Ekonomika," 1966.

Ploss, Sidney I. Conflict and Decision-making in Soviet Russia: A Case Study of Agricultural Policy, 1953-1963. Princeton, N.J.: Princeton University Press, 1965.

_____. Soviet Politics Since the Fall of Khrushchev. Philadelphia: Foreign Policy Research Institute, University of Pennsylvania, 1965.

_____, ed. The Soviet Political Process: Aims, Techniques and Examples of Analysis. Waltham, Mass.: Ginn, 1971.

Richman, Barry M. "Informal Managerial Practices and Formal Enterprise Goals in Soviet Industry." Ph.D. dissertation, Columbia University, 1962.

_____. Soviet Management: With Significant American Comparisons. Englewood Cliffs, N.J.: Prentice-Hall, Inc., 1965.

_____. Management Development and Education in the Soviet Union. East Lansing: Michigan State University Press, 1967.

Rigby, T. H. Communist Party Membership in the USSR, 1917-1967. Princeton, N.J.: Princeton University Press, 1968.

Rourke, Francis, ed. Bureaucratic Power in National Politics. Boston: Little-Brown, 1965.

Rumiantsev, A. F.; Mikhailov, M. V.; and Pravotorov, G. B., eds. Ekonomicheskie zakony i rukovodstvo khoziaistvom: Ekonomicheskaia propoganda v sovremennykh usloviiakh. Moscow: "Ekonomika," 1966.

Schapiro, Leonard. The Communist Party of the Soviet Union. New York: Random House, 1960.

Schopflin, George, ed. The Soviet Union and Eastern Europe. New York: Praeger, 1970.

Schwartz, Harry. The Soviet Economy Since Stalin. Philadelphia and New York: J. B. Lippincott Company, 1965.

Selucky, Radoslav. Economic Reforms in Eastern Europe. New York: Praeger, 1972.

Semigorelov, N. S. Metody partiinogo rukovodstva khoziaistvom. Moscow: "Ekonomika," 1967.

Shkorupeev, I. S., and Singur, G. N. Khoziaistvennaia reforma i ministerstvo. Moscow: "Ekonomika," 1968.

Shore, Peter. Entitled to Know. London: Macgibbon and Kee, 1966.

Simon, Herbert A. The Shape of Automation for Men and Management. New York: Harper & Row, 1965.

Skilling, H. Gordon, and Griffiths, Franklyn. Interest Groups in Soviet Politics. Princeton, N.J.: Princeton University Press, 1971.

Solo, Robert A. Economic Organizations and Social Systems. Indianapolis, Ind.: Bobbs-Merrill, 1967.

Spulber, Nicolas. Socialist Management and Planning: Topics in Comparative Socialist Economics. Bloomington and London: Indiana University Press, 1971.

Stewart, Philip D. Political Power in the Soviet Union: A Study of Decision-Making in Stalingrad. Indianapolis and New York: Bobbs-Merrill, 1968.

Stojanovich, Svetozar. Between Ideals and Reality: A Critique of Socialism and Its Future. Translated from Serbian by Gerson S. Sher. New York: Oxford University Press, 1973.

Tatu, Michel. Power in the Kremlin: From Khrushchev to Kosygin. Translated from French by Helen Katel. New York: Viking, 1970.

Thompson, Victor A. Modern Organizations. New York: Knopf, 1961.

Tsapkina, N. V., ed. Firmy i ekonomika. Leningrad: Lenizdat, 1966.

U.S. Central Intelligence Agency, Directorate of Intelligence, Office of Research and Reports. An Evaluation of Experimental Economic Reforms in the Consumer Industries of the USSR. Washington, D.C.: Central Intelligence Agency, December 1965.

Von Laue, Theodore H. Sergei Witte and the Industrialization of Russia. New York: Columbia University Press, 1963.

Ward, Benjamin N. The Socialist Economy. New York: Random House, 1967.

Wellisz, S. The Economies of the Soviet Bloc. New York: McGraw-Hill, 1964.

Wilczynski, J. Socialist Economic Development and Reforms: From Extensive to Intensive Growth Under Central Planning in the USSR, Eastern Europe, and Yugoslavia. New York: Praeger, 1972.

Zaitsev, B. I., and Sonin, I. E. Glavnyi inzhener zavoda, ego funktsii i metody raboty. Moscow: "Ekonomika," 1967.

Zaleski, Eugene. Planning Reforms in the Soviet Union, 1962-1966: An Analysis of Recent Trends in Economic Organization and Management. Translated from French and edited by Marie-Christine MacAndrew and G. Warren Nutter. Chapel Hill: University of North Carolina Press, 1967.

_____. Planning for Economic Growth in the Soviet Union, 1918-1932. Translated from French and edited by Marie-Christine MacAndrew and G. Warren Nutter. Chapel Hill: University of North Carolina Press, 1971.

Zinchenko, G. I., and Laptin, M. N. Zainteresovannost', otvetstvennost' i distsiplina. Moscow: "Znanie," 1966.

ARTICLES, DOCUMENTS, PAPERS, REPORTS, SPEECHES, AND STATUTES

Akhundov, A. "Sovetskii khoziaistvennik." Kommunist 17 (November 1965): 22-31.

Aleinik, A. "The Role of Supply in Raising the Effectiveness of Enterprise Operations." Material'no-tekhnicheskoe snabzhenie 4 (April 1967): 17-22. JPRS 41, 204 (May 30, 1967): 24-31.

Alekseev, G. "Partiinaia organizatsiia promyshlennogo predpriiatiia." Kommunist 13 (September 1972): 62-73.

Alfeevna, N. "Pervye resul'taty." Kommunist 1 (January 1966): 32-35.

Allakhverdian, D., and Slastenko, E. "Khoziaistvennaia reforma i nekotorye problemy upravleniia promyshlennost'iu." Voprosy ekonomiki 3 (March 1968): 16-25. JPRS 45,234 (May 3, 1968): 1-13.

Amalrik, A. "Will the USSR Survive Until 1984?" Survey 73 (Autumn 1969): 47-79.

Anderson, Raymond H. "Soviet Sets Fines to Speed Reform." New York Times, November 15, 1967, p. 18.

_____. "Profit Plan on Soviet State Farms Termed Success." New York Times, November 21, 1967, p. 20.

Andreev, V. "Doverie partii okryliaet." Pravda, October 6, 1965, p. 2.

Anufrienko, S. "Khoziaistvennaia reforma i initsiativa predpriiatii." Voprosy ekonomiki 12 (December 1968): 25-34.

Ar'kov, P. "Kakim byt' proizvodstvennomy obedineniiu?" Ekonomicheskaia gazeta 10 (March 1969): 10. JPRS 47,819 (April 10, 1969): 137-39.

Armstrong, John A. "Sources of Administrative Behavior: Some Soviet and Western European Comparisons." American Political Science Review 59, no. 3 (September 1965): 643-55.

_____. "Tsarist and Soviet Elite Administrators." Slavic Review 31, no. 1 (March 1972): 1-28.

Artemov, Iu. "Povysit' stimuliruiushchuiu rol' sistemy premirovaniia." Planovoe khoziaistvo 9 (September 1965): 53-56.

_____. "Increase the Effectiveness of Material Stimulation at the Expense of Profits." Finansy SSSR 2 (February 1967): 43-47. JPRS 40,434 (March 28, 1967): 47-54.

Aspaturian, Vernon V. "Social Structure and Political Power in the Soviet System." Paper prepared for delivery at the Annual Meeting of the American Political Science Association, New York City, September 4-7, 1963.

_____. "Moscow's Options in a Changing World." Problems of Communism 21, no. 4 (July-August 1972): 1-20.

Aver'ianov, K. "The Rights and Duties of a Socialist Enterprise." Kommunist (Yerevan), November 24, 1965, p. 2. JPRS 33,600 (January 5, 1966): 74-78.

Azrael, Jeremy R. "Politics and Management." Survey 49 (October 1963): 90-101.

Baibakov, N. "O gosudarstvennom plane razvitiia narodnogo khoziaistva SSSR na 1966 god." Pravda, December 8, 1965, pp. 1-3.

_____. "Vnedrenie khoziaistvennoi reformy--vazhneishaia zadacha." Pravda, November 4, 1966, pp. 2-3.

Balbekov, S. "Ekonomicheskoe obozrenie: Million v avangarde." Pravda, May 27, 1966, p. 2.

_____. "Fakty i vymysly: O nashei khoziaistvennoi reforme i ee zarubezhnykh kritikakh." Pravda, July 17, 1967, p. 2.

Bartol, Kathryn M. "Soviet Computer Centres: Network or Tangle?" Soviet Studies 23, no. 4 (April 1972): 608-18.

Batyshev, S. "The Worker's Diploma." Sotsialisticheskii trud 3 (March 1967): JPRS 41, 507 (June 21, 1967): 91-94.

Batysheva, V., and Grishin, K. "Leninskie printsipy khoziaistvennogo rukovodstva." Planovoe khoziaistvo 1 (January 1970): 3-12.

Bauman, Zygmunt. "Twenty Years After: The Crisis of Soviet-Type Systems." Problems of Communism 20, no. 6 (November-December 1971): 45-53.

Beliaev, V. "V dobryi chas." Pravda, January 8, 1966, p. 2.

Belobzhetskii, I. "Finance Organ Realization and Control Index." Finansy SSSR 3 (March 1969): 78-84. JPRS 47,971 (May 5, 1969): 48-59.

Bergson, Abram. "Development Under Two Systems: Comparative Productivity Growth Since 1950." World Politics 23, no. 4 (July 1971): 479-617.

──────; Erlich, Alexander; Levine, Herbert S.; et al. "Soviet Economic Performance and Reform: Some Problems of Analysis and Prognosis." Slavic Review 25, no. 2 (June 1966): 222-46. A round-table discussion.

Berliner, Joseph S. "The Informal Organization of the Soviet Firm." Quarterly Journal of Economics 66 (August 1952): 342-65. Reprinted in Holzman, Franklyn D., ed. Readings on the Soviet Economy. Chicago: Rand McNally and Company, 1962.

──────. "The Situation of Plant Managers." In Soviet Society: A Book of Readings, edited by Alex Inkeles and Kent Geiger, pp. 361-81. Boston: Houghton Mifflin Company, 1961.

──────. "Marxism and the Soviet Economy." In Issues of World Communism, edited by Andrew Gyorgy, pp. 188-207. Princeton, N.J.: D. Van Nostrand Company, Inc., 1966.

──────. "Innovation and Economic Structure in Soviet Industry." Paper presented at the joint session of the American Economic Association and the Association for Comparative Economics on Innovation and Public Enterprise: East and West, New York, N.Y., December 30, 1969.

Birman, A. "Mysli posle plenuma." Novyi mir 12 (December 1965): 194-213.

_____. "Khoiziaistvennaia reforma i 'puskovoi impul's'." Pravda, March 9, 1966, pp. 3-4.

_____. "Neotvratimost'." Literaturnaia gazeta 2 (January 11, 1967): 10.

Blau, Peter. "The Comparative Study of Organizations." In The Sociology of Organizations, edited by Oscar Grusky and G. A. Miller, pp. 175-86. New York: Free Press, 1970. Reprinted from Industrial and Labor Relations Review 18, no. 3 (April 1965): 323-38.

"Bol'shie vozmozhnosti bol'shie perspektivy." Ekonomicheskaia gazeta 14 (April 1967): 23-24.

Braginsky, B., and Pekarsky, L. "The Key to Partnership." Komsomolskaia pravda, April 3, 1969, p. 2. See FBIS. Daily Report (Soviet Union), April 15, 1969, pp. C2-C5.

Brailovskii, A., and Abramson, M. "Novaia sistema v deistvii." Planovoe khoziaistvo 7 (July 1966): 50-55.

Bratus', S. N. "Sootnoshenie administrativnykh i ekonomicheskykh metodov v regulirovanii khoziaistvennykh otnoshenii." Sovetskoe gosudarstvo i pravo 3 (March 1966): 24-34.

Breyev, M. "Sistema metodov planirovaniia." Planovoe khoziaistvo 10 (October 1968): 28-39. JPRS 46,942 (December 2, 1968): 45-58.

Brown, Emily Clark. "Continuity and Change in the Soviet Labor Market." Industrial and Labor Relations Review 23, no. 2 (January 1970): 171-90.

Brzezinski, Zbigniew K. "The Nature of the Soviet System." In Ideology and Power in Soviet Politics, edited by Z. K. Brzezinski, pp. 65-94. New York: Praeger, 1962. Originally appeared in Slavic Review 20, no. 3 (October 1961): 351-68.

_____. "The Soviet Political System: Transformation or Degeneration." Problems of Communism 15, no. 1 (January-February 1966): 1-15.

Bush, Keith. "The Progress of the Industrial Reforms: A Review of the Measures to Raise Soviet Economic Efficiency Through Decentralization and Emphasis on Profitability and Sales Indexes as Success Criteria [and] a Discussion of the Negative Factors Influencing the Reform." Radio Liberty Research Paper No. 7, 1966.

_____. "The First Year of the Industrial Reforms: An Evaluation of Progress by 673 Enterprises Converted to the Profit System in 1966 and a Discussion of Its Shortcomings Under Soviet Conditions." Radio Liberty Research Paper No. 13, 1967.

_____. "Birman on Economic Inevitability." Radio Liberty Dispatch, January 26, 1967.

_____. "Propaganda Considerations Impede Alleviation of Unemployment." Bulletin of the Institute for the Study of the USSR 14, no. 4 (April 1967): 25-28.

_____. "The Reforms: A Balance Sheet." Problems of Communism 16, no. 4 (July-August 1967): 30-41.

_____. "An Appraisal of the Soviet Economic Reform." In U.S. Congress, Joint Economic Committee. Soviet Economic Performance: 1966-67, pp. 129-44. Washington, D.C.: U.S. Government Printing Office, 1968.

_____. "Soviet Economic Growth: Past, Present and Projected." Radio Liberty Dispatch, April 4, 1973.

Campbell, Robert W. "Economics: Roads and Inroads." Problems of Communism 14, no. 6 (November-December 1965): 23-33.

_____. "Economic Reform in the USSR." American Economic Review 58, no. 2 (May 1968): 547-58.

_____. "Management Spillovers from Soviet Space and Military Programmes." Soviet Studies 23, no. 4 (April 1972): 586-607.

Castles, Francis G. "Interest Articulation: A Totalitarian Paradox." Survey no. 73 (Autumn 1969): 116-32.

Chadaev, Ia. "Tsentralizovannoe planirovanie i initsiativa mest." Kommunist 18 (December 1965): 26-35.

_____. "Reforma v deistvii." Planovoe khoziaistvo 6 (June 1967): 47-50.

Chelnokov, V., and Rybin, V. "Partner predpriiatii." Izvestiia, February 5, 1967, p. 2.

Chernov, I. "Bank v novykh usloviiakh." Kommunist 8 (May 1966): 94-98.

"Clear Warning of Unemployment." Radio Liberty Dispatch, January 25, 1967.

Collegium. "V Kollegii ministerstva finansov SSSR." Finansy SSSR 3 (March 1967): 94-96. JPRS 41,437 (June 16, 1967): 50-55.

Communist Party of the Soviet Union, Central Committee. "Ob uluchshenii upravleniia promyshlennost'iu, sovershenstvovanii planirovaniia i usilenii ekonomicheskogo stimulirovaniia promyshlennogo proizvodstva." Pravda, October 1, 1965, pp. 1-2.

Connock, Michael. "Birth of the Soviet Businessman." Financial Times (London), November 8, 1967.

"The Council of Directors--a New Managerial Device." Radio Free Europe Research Report, January 11, 1971.

Council of Ministers, USSR. "Obshchee polozhenie o ministerstvakh SSSR." Ekonomicheskaia gazeta 34 (August 1967): 7-9.

Cousins, Norman. "Notes on a 1963 Visit with Khrushchev." Saturday Review 47, no. 45 (November 7, 1964): 16-21, 58-60.

Davies, R. W. "Planning a Mature Economy in the USSR." Economics of Planning 6, no. 2 (1966): 138-53.

Denhardt, Robert B. "The Organization as a Political System." Western Political Quarterly 24, no. 4 (December 1971): 675-86.

Dolgikh, V. "Partiinye komitety i organy narodnogo kontrolia." Kommunist 8 (May 1972): 76-86.

Donaldson, Robert H. "The 1971 Soviet Central Committee: An Assessment of the New Elite." World Politics 24, no. 3 (April 1972): 382-409.

Dozortsev, V. "Ekonomicheskoe stimulirovanie tekhnicheskogo progressa." Kommunist 4 (March 1966): 26-34.

Drogochinsky, N. "Ekonomicheskaia reforma i sovershenstvovanie upravleniia narodnym khoziaistvom." Planovoe khoziaistvo 11 (November 1970): 36-46. Partially translated in CDSP 23, no. 4 (February 23, 1971): 7.

Drucker, Peter F. "The Surprising Seventies." Harper's 243, no. 1454 (July 1971): 35-39.

Duevel, Christian. "Toward Workers' Self Management or Tighten Party Control?" Radio Liberty Dispatch, May 5, 1967.

_____. "'Pravda' Reinterprets Party Leadership of Soviets and Mass Organizations. Radio Liberty Dispatch, December 13, 1967.

_____. "Sharpening Conflict Between Soviet Industrial Management and Party Apparat." Radio Liberty Dispatch, June 6, 1968.

_____. "Brezhnev's Secret Report." Radio Liberty Dispatch, January 29, 1970.

_____. "'Partiinaia zhizn' Is Critical of Party and Government Leadership of the Economy." Radio Liberty Dispatch, March 16, 1970.

_____. "Comparison of October Slogans--1969-1970." Radio Liberty Dispatch, October 21, 1970.

_____. "A Dubious Experiment: The 'Enlarged Party Committee.'" Radio Liberty Dispatch, November 3, 1970.

_____. "Proposed CPSU Statutes Changes Strengthen Authoritarian Rule." Radio Liberty Dispatch, April 6, 1971.

Dumachev, A.; Chuev, I.; and Kurilov, A. "Kazhdomu kollektivu-- chetkuiu perspektivu." Ekonomicheskaia gazeta 17 (April 1967): 15-16.

Dymshits, V. E. "Obespechenie proizvodstva--zadacha gosudarst- vennaia." Ekonomicheskaia gazeta 18 (May 1967): 6-8.

Dzarasov, S. "O metodakh upravleniia sotsialisticheskim khoziaistvom." Voprosy ekonomiki 10 (October 1968): 29-39. JPRS 47,041 (December 9, 1968): 11-23.

Eckstein, Alexander. "Economic Development and Political Change in Communist Systems." World Politics 22, no. 4 (July 1970): 479-95.

Edeen, Alf. "The Administrative Intelligentsia." Survey 65 (October 1967): 61-74.

Edinovich, I. "Ekonomicheskaia reforma i khoziaistvennyi raschet." Den'gi i kredit 12 (December 1966): 48-49.

Egorov, N. G. "Boriba s nedostatkami v deiatel'nosti predpriiatii i organizatsii--odna iz osnovnykh zadach gosarbitrazha." Sovetskoe gosudarstvo i pravo 12 (December 1965): 92-93.

"Ekonomicheskaia teoriia i khoziaistvennaia praktika." Planovoe khoziaistvo 11 (November 1968): 3-10.

"Ekonomike predpriiatii--vseobshchee vnimanie." Ekonomicheskaia gazeta 18 (May 1967): 16-17.

Emdin, A. "Supply System Has Key Role in Economic Reform." Ekonomika Sovetskoi Ukrainy 9 (September 1968): 34-38. JPRS 46,765 (October 29, 1968): 9-16.

Emel'ianov, P. "Luchshe ispol'zovat' prava." Trud, March 22, 1967, p. 2. JPRS 40,806 (May 1, 1967): 1-2.

Etzioni, Amitai. "Two Approaches to Organizational Analysis: A Critique and a Suggestion." In The Sociology of Organizations: Basic Studies, edited by Oscar Grusky and George A. Miller, pp. 215-25. New York: Free Press, 1970. Reprinted from Administrative Science Quarterly, September 1960, pp. 257-78.

_____. "Human Beings Are Not Very Easy to Change After All." Saturday Review, June 3, 1972, pp. 45-47.

Fal'kovich, M. S. "Khoziaistvennyi dogovor i ekonomicheskie otnosheniia predpriiatii." Planovoe khoziaistvo 4 (April 1966): 69-72.

_____. "Usilenie material'noi otvetstvennosti po khoziaistvennym dogovoram." Sovetskoe gosudarstvo i pravo 8 (August 1968): 121-25. JPRS 46,573 (October 1, 1968): 24-33.

Fedorenko, N. "Reforma v promyshlennosti: Pervye itogi, problemy povysheniia ee deistvennosti." Planovoe khoziaistvo 4 (April 1967): 5-17.

Feshbach, Murray. "Manpower Management." Problems of Communism 22, no. 6 (November-December 1974): 25-33.

Filippov, V. "Nekotorye voprosy osushchestvleniia khoziaistvennoi reformy." Ekonomicheskaia gazeta 51 (December 1965): 8-9.

Firsov, V. "Navstrechu XXIII s"ezdu KPSS: Novizna," Literaturnaia gazeta, February 1, 1966, p. 1.

"Former G.E. Chief Tells How I.B.M. Won on Computers." New York Times, October 14, 1967, p. 36.

"Galbraith Offers Industry a Maxim." New York Times, December 12, 1966.

Gal'perin, S., and Shabanov, A. "Zakonomernost' i problemy." Sovetskaia Belorussiia, May 25, 1967, p. 2. JPRS 41,496 (June 21, 1967): 6-10.

Garbuzov, V. "Finansy i ekonomicheskie stimuly." Ekonomicheskaia gazeta 41 (October 13, 1965): 4-5.

Garbuzov, V. F. "O gosudarstvennom biudzhete SSSR na 1966 god i ob ispolnenii gosudarstvennogo biudzhete SSSR na 1964 god." Pravda, December 8, 1965, pp. 4-5.

Garetovskii, N. "Aktual'nye voprosy khoziaistvennoi reformy." Finansy SSSR 1 (January 1967): 31-39.

Gatovskii, L. "Edinstvo plana i khoziaistvennogo rascheta." Kommunist 15 (October 1965): 34-48.

Gavrilenko, I. T., and Pobirchenko, I. G. "Struktura gosudarstvennogo arbitrazha na uroven' zadach novoi khoziaistvennoi reformy." Sovetskoe gosudarstvo i pravo 6 (June 1966): 45-47.

"Glavk or 'Firm'?--The Controversy over Economic Control Apparatus." Radio Free Europe Research Report, August 26, 1970.

Goberman, I. "Stimuly, prava, initsiativa." Pravda, October 1, 1965, p. 3.

Goldman, Marshall I. "Living Standards and Consumer Goods." Problems of Communism 5, no. 9 (September-October 1960): 32-41.

_____. "The Economy at the Crossroads." Survey 57 (October 1965): 125-31.

_____. "Economic Revolution in the Soviet Union." Foreign Affairs 45, no. 2 (January 1967): 319-31.

Gorlin, Alice C. "The Soviet Economic Associations." Soviet Studies 26, no. 1 (January 1974): 3-27.

Graham, Loren R. "Cybernetics in the Soviet Union." Survey 52 (July 1964): 3-18.

_____. "Cybernetics." In Science and Ideology in Soviet Society, edited by George Fischer, pp. 83-106. New York: Atherton, 1967.

Granick, David. Personal interview at the Russian Institute, Columbia University, August 22, 1967.

Greenslade, Rush V. "Khrushchev and the Economists." Problems of Communism 12, no. 3 (May-June 1963): 27-32.

Grigor'ev, V. "Problemy nauchnoi organizatsii upravleniia sotsialisticheskoi promyshlennost'iu." Voprosy ekonomiki 8 (August 1955): 148-50.

Gritsenko, P. F., and Prischchepa, G. P. Tekhnologiia i organizatsiia proizvodstva (Kiev) 5 (May 1966): 4-7. JPRS 38,945 (December 5, 1966): 42-47.

Grossman, Gregory. "Innovation and Information in the Soviet Economy." American Economic Review 56, no. 2 (May 1966): 118-30.

_____. "The Economic Reforms: A Balance Sheet." Problems of Communism 15, no. 6 (November-December 1966): 43-55.

Guzhkov, I. Finansy SSSR 7 (July 1968): 7-15. JPRS 46,495 (September 23, 1968): 36.

Hardt, John P., and Frankel, Theodore. "The Industrial Managers." In Interest Groups in Soviet Politics, edited by H. G. Skilling and F. Griffiths, pp. 171-208. Princeton, N.J.: Princeton University Press, 1971.

Hazard, John N. "The Politics of Soviet Economic Reform." In Planning and the Market in the USSR: The 1960's, edited by Alexander Balinky, pp. 65-88. New Brunswick, N.J.: Rutgers University Press, 1967.

Hodnett, Grey. "The Obkom First Secretaries." Slavic Review 24, no. 4 (December 1965): 636-52.

_____. "Khrushchev and Party-State Control." In Politics in the Soviet Union: 7 Cases, edited by Alexander Dallin, pp. 113-64. New York: Harcourt, Brace and World, 1966.

Hoffmann, Erik P. "Social Science and Soviet Administrative Behavior." World Politics 24, no. 3 (April 1972): 444-71.

Holesovsky, Vaclav. "Labor and the Economic Reform in Czechoslovakia." Mimeographed. Labor Relations and Research Center, University of Massachusetts, Amherst, April 1968.

Hough, Jerry F. "The Soviet Concept of the Relationship Between the Lower Party Organs and the State Administration." Slavic Review 24, no. 2 (June 1965): 215-40.

_____. "Reforms in Government and Administration." In Soviet Politics Since Khrushchev, edited by Alexander Dallin and Thomas B. Larson, pp. 23-40. Englewood Cliffs, N.J.: Prentice-Hall, 1968.

_____. "The Prerequisites of Areal Deconcentration: The Soviet Experience." In Spatial Dimensions of Development Administration, edited by James J. Heaphey, pp. 132-75. Durham, N.C.: Duke University Press, 1971.

_____. "The Soviet System: Petrification or Pluralism?" Problems of Communism 21, no. 2 (March-April 1972): 25-45.

_____. "The Bureaucratic Model and the Nature of the Soviet System." Journal of Comparative Administration 5, no. 2 (August, 1973): 134-67.

Inkeles, Alex. "Models and Issues in the Analysis of Soviet Society." Survey 60 (July 1966): 3-17.

"In the Collegium of the USSR Ministry of Finance." Finansy SSSR 11 (November 1968): 94-96. JPRS 47,666 (March 18, 1969): 72-78.

"In the Collegium of the USSR Ministry of Finance." Finansy SSSR 3 (March 1969): 92-95. JPRS 47,971 (May 5, 1969): 66-71.

Iurna, V. "Sovershenstvovat' vedomstvennyi kontrol'." Sovetskaia Litva (Vil'nius), September 10, 1966, p. 2. JPRS 39,108 (December 14, 1966): 89-91.

Ivanov, V. "Organizatsiia i planirovanie material'no--tekhnicheskogo snabzheniia na sovremennom etape." Voprosy ekonomiki 2 (February 1966): 61-66.

Jenkins, David. "Democracy in the Factory." Atlantic 231, no. 4 (April 1973): 78-83.

Johnson, A. Ross. "Polish Perspectives, Past and Present." Problems of Communism 20, no. 4 (July-August 1971): 59-72.

"K vysokoi effektivnosti obshchestvennogo proizvodstva." Ekonomicheskaia gazeta 16 (April 1967): 17-18.

Kaminskas, K. A. "Mesto proizvodstvennykh obedinenii v sisteme upravleniia promyshlennost'iu." Vestnik Moskovskogo Universiteta (series XII, law) 3 (1966): 54-63.

Karinskii, S. S. "Khoziaistvennaia reforma i voprosy oplaty truda." Sovetskoe gosudarstvo i pravo 7 (July 1967): 31-38.

Karpenko, I. "Chto takoe khorosho." Izvestiia, July 30, 1965, p. 3.

Karpov, A. "Stimuly, poisky, rentabel'nost'." Pravda, February 11, 1966, p. 2.

Kaser, Michael. "Planned Economies Under Reform." In The Soviet Union and Eastern Europe: A Handbook, edited by George Schopflin, pp. 291-300. New York: Praeger, 1970.

Katsuk, M., and Onipko, N. "Bor'ba s mestnichestvom." Sotsialisticheskaia zakonnost' 11 (November 1960): 47-50.

Katz, Daniel, and Kahn, Robert L. "Open-Systems Theory." In The Sociology of Organizations: Basic Studies, edited by George A. Miller, pp. 149-58. New York: Free Press, 1970. Reprinted from The Social Psychology of Organizations, pp. 14-29. New York: Wiley, 1966.

Kaufman, Herbert. "Organization Theory and Political Theory." American Political Science Review 58, no. 1 (March 1964): 5-14.

Kazankova, K. "Nekotorye itogi raboty po novomy." Finansy SSSR 11 (November 1966): 11-15. JPRS 39,693 (January 30, 1967): 13-20.

Keep, John. "The Soviet Union and the Third World." Survey 72 (Summer 1969): 19-38.

Khalidetskii, G. "Direktor." Ekonomicheskaia gazeta 36 (September 1967): 31.

Kheifets, S. "Mestnaia promyshlennost' i kontrol' finorganov." Finansy SSSR 2 (1967): 25-29. JPRS 40,434 (March 28, 1967): 21-28.

Khovin, A. "Opyt uchit, podskazyvaet." Ekonomicheskaia gazeta 11 (March 1969): 10. JPRS 47,888 (April 18, 1969): 42-44.

Khrushchev, N. S. "O programme Kommunisticheskoi Partii Sovetskogo Soiuza." Izvestiia, October 19, 1961, p. 6.

Klatt, Werner. "The Politics of Economic Reforms." Survey 70/71 (Winter/Spring 1969): 154-65. Followed by "A Comment" by Gregory Grossman, pp. 165-68.

Klein, N. I. "Rol' khoziaistvennogo dogovora v formirovanii plana proizvodstva tovarov narodnogo potrebleniia." Sovetskoe gosudarstvo i pravo 6 (June 1966): 38-44.

Koldomasov, Iu. "Razvitie priamykh khoziaistvennykh sviazei i sovershenstvovanie raspredeleniia sredstv proizvodstva." Voprosy ekonomiki 11 (November 1965): 14-25.

Kolobashkin, G., and Proshko, Ia. "Kombinat--vygodnaia forma upravleniia." Partiinaia zhizn' 23 (December 1965): 38-41.

"Kommunist i proizvodstvo." Pravda, January 9, 1966, p. 1.

Konova, M. "Kredit banka i pribyl' predpriiatiia." Sovetskaia Estoniia (Tallin), September 7, 1966, p. 2. JPRS 39,108 (December 14, 1966): 92-95.

Korbe, G. "Nauchno obosnovannye normativy--voshneishee uslovie raboty po novomy." Planovoe khoziaistvo 12 (December 1965): 53-56.

Korzimov, O. "About Shortcomings in Planning." Den'gi i kredit 9 (September 1968): 46-49. JPRS 46,956 (November 26, 1968): 31-33.

Kosygin, A. N. "Ob uluchshenii upravleniia promyshlennost'iu sovershenstvovanii planirovaniia i usilenii ekonomicheskogo stimulirovaniia promyshlennogo proizvodstva." Pravda and Izvestiia, September 28, 1965, pp. 1-4.

_____. "Sotsial'no-ekonomicheskoe razvitie sovetskogo mnogo-natsial'nogo gosudarstva." Kommunist 17 (November 1972): 15-41.

Kotov, F. "Sovremennaia organizatsiia planirovaniia i puti ee sovershenstvovaniia." Planovoe khoziaistvo 10 (October 1968): 3-18. JPRS 46,984 (December 2, 1968): 25-44.

"Kredit i effektivnost' proizvodstva." Ekonomicheskaia gazeta 20 (May 1967): 9-10.

Kulagin, G. "Obedinenie predpriiatii i ministerstvo." Kommunist 3 (February 1966): 82-91.

_____. "Reservy reformy." Pravda, August 9, 1967, p. 2.

Kul'vets, P. "Mezhotraslevye proizvodstvennye sviazi v promyshlen-nosti." Kommunist (Vil'nius) 3 (March 1969): 21-27. JPRS 47,931 (April 28, 1969): 46-54.

Kurskii, A. "Itogi khoziaistvennoi reformy za 1966 g. i nekotorye problemy ee dal'neishego osushchestvleniia." Voprosy ekonomiki 4 (April 1967): 28-38.

_____, and Slastenko, E. "Nekotorye itogi perevoda gruppy predpriiatii na novuiu sistemu." Voprosy ekonomiki 10 (October 1966): 3-18. JPRS 39,334 (October 30, 1966): 48.

Kurtynin, I. "Kollektivnaia otvetstvennost' i trudovaia distsiplina." Sotsialisticheskii trud 5 (May 1967): 33-36.

Kutsevol, V. "Ekonomicheskii poisk." Kommunist 17 (November 1965): 32-40.

Kux, Ernst. "Technicians of Power Versus Managers of Technique." In The Soviet Political Process, edited by Sidney Ploss, pp. 145-83. Waltham, Mass.: Ginn, 1970.

Kuzin, M. "Voprosy shtatnoi raboty." Finansy SSSR 9 (September 1965): 7-12. JPRS 34,122 (February 14, 1966): 7-16.

_____. "Polozhenie o predpriiatii: Smeta, struktura, shtaty." Ekonomicheskaia gazeta 3 (January 1967): 20.

Kuznetsov, O. "U nas v banke pol'nyi poriadok!" Trud, August 27, 1966, p. 2. JPRS 38,068 (October 10, 1966): 31-34.

Kvachakhiia, I. "Material'naia zainteresovannost' i khoziaistvennaia reforma." Zaria vostoka (Tbilisi), September 7, 1966, p. 3. JPRS 39,108 (December 14, 1966): 85-91.

Kvasha, Ia. V. "Kontsentratsiia proizvodstva i melkaia promyshlennost'." Voprosy ekonomiki 5 (May 1967): 26-31.

Larrabee, F. Stephen. "Bulgaria's Politics of Conformity." Problems of Communism 21, no. 4 (July-August 1972): 42-52.

Latsis, O. "Net iskliucheniia bez pravila: Zametki ob ekonomike stroitel'stva." Novyi mir 4 (April 1967): 158-72.

Lazerev, B. M. "Gosudarstvennoe proizvodstvennoe predpriiatie i ego administratsiia." Sovetskoe gosudarstvo i pravo 5 (May 1966): 12-21.

Lentrinskii, F. Ekonomika Sovetskoi Ukrainy (Kiev) 6 (June 1966): 1-12. JPRS 38,276 (October 21, 1966): 18-28.

Leonov, Iu. "Illegal Dismissals." Sotsialisticheskaia zakonnost' 3 (March 1969): 13-16. JPRS 48,026 (May 13, 1969): 36-41.

Leont'ev, L. "Plan i khoziaistvennaia initsiativa." Pravda, April 29, 1966, pp. 2-3.

Lepeshkin, A. I. "O razmezhevanii kompetentsii mezhdu organami Soiuza SSR i soiuznykh respublik v oblasti rukovodstva narodnym khoziaistvom." Sovetskoe gosudarstvo i pravo 6 (June 1966): 3-11.

Levine, Herbert S. "Industry." In Prospects for Soviet Society, edited by Allen Kassof, pp. 291-317. New York: Praeger, 1968.

Liberman, E. G. Ekonomika i matematicheskie metody 5 (September-October 1968): 690-701. JPRS 46,891 (November 18, 1968): 5-19.

Liberman, Ye. "Plan, priamye sviazi i rentabel'nost'." Pravda, November 21, 1965, pp. 2-3.

⸺. "Report of a Roundtable Discussion on the Soviet Economic Reform." Renascita (Rome) 23, no. 52 (December 31, 1966): 13-14. JPRS 39,731 (February 1, 1967): 19-20.

Liberman, Yevsei. "The Soviet Economic Reform." Foreign Affairs 46, no. 1 (October 1967): 53-63.

Lisitsyn, V. "Problemy upravleniia sotsialisticheskim khoziaistvom." Planovoe khoziaistvo 4 (April 1965): 39-49.

Loshchenkov, F. "Samostoiatel'nost', initsiativa, otvetstvennost'." Kommunist 15 (October 1965): 49-57.

Luk'ianov, I. "Snabzhenie v novyh usloviiakh." Ekonomicheskaia gazeta 2 (January 1966): 21-22.

L'vovich, Iu. Ia. "Povysit' dogovornuiu distsiplinu pri postovke tovarov torgovyn organizatsiiam." Sovetskoe gosudarstvo i pravo 4 (April 1966): 76-81.

Majstrenko, I. W. "The Difficulties of the New Reform." Bulletin of the Institute for the Study of the USSR 14, no. 4 (April 1967): 19-24.

Malyshev, I. "Khoziaistvennaia reforma v deistvii." Partiinaia zhizn' 20 (October 1966): 14-20.

Maniushis, I. "Vsemerno povyshat' effektivnost' promyshlennogo proizvodstva." Sovetskaia Litva (Vil'nius), November 5, 1966, pp. 1-2. JPRS 39,607 (January 20, 1967): 6-13.

Mantsurov, G., and Selivanova, T. "Effekt budet narastat'." Ekonomicheskaia gazeta 15 (April 1967): 10.

March, James G., and Simon, Herbert A. "Decision-Making Theory." In The Sociology of Organizations: Basic Studies, edited by Oscar Grusky and George A. Miller, pp. 93-102. New York: Free Press, 1970. Reprinted from Organizations, pp. 137-50, 169-71. New York: Wiley, 1958.

Masiagin, A. "Kommunisty zavoda." Kommunist 2 (January 1966): 19-27.

Material'no tekhnicheskoe snabzhenie 3 (March 1967): 1-4. JPRS 41,340 (June 9, 1967): 1-6.

Mazurov, K. T. "Ob uluchshenii upravleniia promyshlennost'iu." Pravda, October 2, 1965, pp. 2-3.

Mazyrin, V. "Prganizatsiia truda rukovoditelei predpriiatii." Planovoe khoziaistvo 2 (February 1966): 58-62.

Mesa-Lago, Carmelo. "Unemployment in a Socialist Economy: Yugoslavia." Industrial Relations 10, no. 1 (February 1971): 49-69.

Mikuchenis, I. "Interesy potrebitelei i otvetstvennost' postavshchikov." Planovoe khoziaistvo 3 (March 1966): 87-88.

Mil'ner, B. Z. "Vliianie tekhnicheskogo progressa na struktury upravleniia." S. Sh. A. 9 (September 1971): 23-34.

Miskin, S. "Rychagi i tormoza." Literaturnaia gazeta 12 (March 22, 1967): 10.

Mochalova, A. "Nedostatki eshche ne izzhity." Den'gi i kredit 12 (December 1966): 44-47.

Mzhavanadze, V. "Pervichnaia organizatsiia i partiinyi komitet." Pravda, August 14, 1965, p. 2.

Naidis, I. "Zavodskoi kollektiv, partorganizatsiia, direktor." Kommunist 18 (December 1965): 43-49.

Nash, Edmund. "Recent Changes in Labor Controls in the Soviet Union." In U.S. Congress, Joint Economic Committee. New Directions in the Soviet Economy, pp. 849-71. Washington, D.C.: U.S. Government Printing Office, 1966.

Nekrasov, O. "Otraslevoi printsip upravleniia promyshlennost'iu i tekhnicheskii progress." Voprosy ekonomiki 11 (November 1965): 3-13.

Nikitin, A., and Seliunin, V. "Pis'ma ob upravlenii: II. Kontroler ili posrednik?" Ekonomicheskaia gazeta 12 (March 1967): 18-19.

Nikolaev, K. K. "Gluboko vnikat' v ekonomiku." Ekonomicheskaia gazeta 5 (February 1966): 7-8.

──────. "Partiinoe rukovodstvo narodnym khoziaistvom v novykh usloviiakh." In Ekonomicheskie zakony i rukovodstvo khoziaistvom, edited by A. F. Rumiantsev et al., pp. 43-54. Moscow: "Ekonomika," 1966.

"Novaia sistema snabzheniia--v deistvii." Ekonomicheskaia gazeta 4 (January 1966): 3.

Nove, Alec. "Revamping the Economy." Problems of Communism 12, no. 1 (January-February 1963): 10-16.

──────. "Some Thoughts While Reading the Soviet Press." Soviet Studies 17, no. 1 (July 1965): 97-102.

Novikov, I. "Razvivat' initsiativu i otvetstvennost' mestnykh organov." Pravda, October 14, 1965, p. 2.

Novikov, K. "Problemy effektivnogo ispol'yovaniia turdovykl resursov." Kommunist 13 (September 1969): 99-108.

"Novyi etap reformy." Den'gi i kredit 5 (April 1967): 3-8.

Nuriev, Z. "Rukovodit' ekonomikoi, ne podmeniaia khoziaistvennye organy." Kommunist 16 (November 1965): 59-67.

"O gosudarstvennom plane razvitiia narodnogo khoziaistva SSSR na 1966 god." Pravda, December 8, 1965, pp. 1-3.

Olsienkiewicz, Henryk. "The Dialectics of Soviet Economic Revisionism." Bulletin of the Institute for the Study of the USSR 12, no. 6 (August 1965): 19-25.

Orlov, A. "Kto otvechaet za plan." Izvestiia, March 19, 1967, p. 2.

Ososkov, V. "Kommunisty v proizvodstvo." Partiinaia zhizn' 19 (October 1965): 22-31.

Ostrovskii, S. "On the Combination of Centralized Branch Management with Territorial Planning." Ekonomika Sovetskoi Ukraini (Kiev) 12 (December 1966): 17-23. JPRS 46,221 (March 10, 1967): 1-10.

Ovseevich, L., and Grodinskii, P. "Nekotorye problemy perekhoda na novuiu sistemu planirovaniia." Planovoe khoziaistvo 6 (June 1966): 60-70.

"Partiinaia demokratiia i otvetstvennost' kommunista." Kommunist 10 (July 1966): 3-13.

Pekarskii, L. "Ekonomicheskie problemy povysheniia kachestva produktsii." Voprosy ekonomiki 3 (March 1967): 153-55.

Pershin, A. "Avtoritet rukovoditelia." Kommunist 1 (January 1971): 69-79.

Petrov, N. "Partiinaia organizatsiia ministerstva." Kommunist 1 (January 1972): 43-55.

Platonov, N. "Usiliiami kollektiva." Ekonomicheskaia gazeta 9 (March 1966): 20.

Ploss, Sidney I. "Interest Groups." In Prospects for Soviet Society, edited by Allen Kassof, pp. 76-103. New York: Praeger, 1968.

──────. "Politics in the Kremlin." Problems of Communism 19, no. 3 (May-June 1970): 1-14.

──────. "Deadlock in the Party Presidium." In The Soviet Political Process, edited by Sidney I. Ploss, pp. 213-19. Waltham, Mass.: Ginn, 1971. Originally published in New Leader, October 16, 1961, pp. 19-22.

_____. "Examples of Analysis: The Politics of Policy Since Stalin." In The Soviet Political Process, edited by Sidney I. Ploss, pp. 123-44. Waltham, Mass.: Ginn, 1971.

_____. "The Rise of Brezhnev." In The Soviet Political Process, edited by Sidney I. Ploss, pp. 271-95. Waltham, Mass.: Ginn, 1971.

"Polozhenie o predpriiatii." Ekonomicheskaia gazeta 24 (June 1966): 19.

Popov, G. "Problemy sovershenstvovaniia metodov upravleniia sotsialisticheskoi ekonomiki." Kommunist 2 (January 1974): 63-76.

Portes, Richard D. "The Tactics and Strategy of Economic Decentralization." Soviet Studies 23, no. 4 (April 1972): 629-58.

Poskanov, A. "Khoziaistvennaia reforma i kredit." Pravda, November 19, 1965, p. 3.

"Posledovatel'naia leninskaia politika partii: Pretvorim v zhizn' resheniia sentiabr'skogo Plenuma TsK KPSS," Partiinaia zhizn' 15 (October 1965): 3-10.

"Povysit' rol' pravovoi nauki v sovershenstvovanii khoziaistvennogo rukovodstva." Sovetskoe gosudarstvo i pravo 12 (Debember 1965): 3-11.

Protserov, S. "Prava i otvetstvennost' predpriiatii." Planovoe khoziaistvo 1 (January 1966): 62-66.

Prozorov, V. "Kto on, glavnyi inzhener?" Pravda, August 22, 1967, p. 3.

Prybyla, Jan S. "The Soviet Economy: An Overview." Current History 63, no. 374 (October 1972): 175-80, 186.

Rabinovich, F. "Ekonomicheskoe stimulirovanie i dogovarnaia otvetstvennost'." Kommunist 14 (September 1972): 82-92. Condensed in CDSP 24, no. 43 (November 22, 1972): 1-4.

Rabinovich, F. L. "Vina kak osnovanie dogovornoi otvetstvennost' sotsialisticheskogo predpriiatiia." Sovetskoe gosudarstvo i pravo 6 (June 1966): 30-37.

_____. "Ot 'balansa shtrafov' k kontroliu rublem." Ekonomicheskaia gazeta 14 (April 1967): 15.

Rabinovits, M. "Bank i prepriiatie." Den'gi i kredit 12 (December 1965): 26-30.

Radio Free Europe. "Experimental Establishment of Industrial Centrals." Situation Report, Rumania 36, April 11, 1969.

Raman, M. "Ekonomicheskaia rabota v novykh usloviiakh." Kommunist Sovetskoi Latvii (Riga) 5 (May 1967): 42-48. JPRS 42,225 (August 15, 1967): 1-11.

"Reforme--'zelenuiu ulitsu'!" Ekonomicheskaia gazeta 24 (June 1967): 30.

Rigby, T. H. "Crypto-Politics." Survey 50 (January 1964): 183-94.

_____. "The Soviet Leadership: Towards a Self-stabilizing Oligarchy?" Soviet Studies 22, no. 2 (October 1970): 167-91.

_____. "The Soviet Politburo: A Comparative Profile, 1951-71." Soviet Studies 24, no. 1 (July 1972): 3-23.

Riggs, Fred W. "Bureaucratic Politics in Comparative Perspective." A paper presented at the Annual Meeting of the American Political Science Association, Washington, D.C., September 2-7, 1968.

Rivnii, P. "Inertsiia starogo." Ekonomicheskaia gazeta 15 (April 1967): 15-16.

Rodionov, N. "Partiinie komitety i sblizhenie nauki s proizvodstvom." Kommunist 9 (June 1970): 14-25.

R.R.G. (R. Rockingham Gill). "Governmental Changes in USSR." Radio Free Europe Research Report, October 4, 1965.

_____. "New Enterprise Statute Extends Powers of Soviet Managers, Reduces Those of Moscow." Radio Free Europe Research Report, October 29, 1965.

_____. "An Economist Replies to Kosygin." Radio Free Europe Research Report, January 31, 1966.

_____. "Juvenile Unemployment Rising." Radio Free Europe Research Report, April 20, 1967.

_____. "A Profitable Proposal for Improving Incentives." Radio Free Europe Research Report, June 12, 1967.

_____. "A Small Step Towards Industrial Democracy?" Radio Free Europe Research Report, September 21, 1967.

_____. "Brezhnev Again on Economic Problems." Radio Free Europe Research Report, April 14, 1970.

_____. "'Problems of Philosophy' Versus the Computer Lobby." Radio Free Europe Research Report, December 12, 1971.

_____. "Kosygin on the 1973 Plan." Radio Free Europe Research Report, November 15, 1972.

Rudich, F. "Poednannia derzhavnikh i gromads'kikh zasad v upravlinni virobnitstvom." Kommunist Ukraini 7 (July 1967): 75-82.

Rudnev, K. N. "Otrasl' vstupaet v reformu." Kommunist 1 (January 1967): 57-63.

Rumiantsev, A. "Ekonomicheskaia nauka i upravlenie narodnym khoziaistvom." Kommunist 1 (January 1966): 42-54.

_____, and Bunich, P. "Khoziaistvo i sistema upravleniia." Izvestiia, November 16, 1967, p. 2.

Ryavec, Karl W. "Soviet Industrial Management: Challenge and Response, 1965-1970." Canadian Slavic Studies 5, no. 2 (Summer 1971): 151-77.

Rzheshevskii, V. "Pribyl' i pooshchrenie." Pravda, June 8, 1967, p. 2.

Savenkov, F. A. "Ratsionalizatsiia struktury i shtatov apparata upravleniia proizvodstvom." Sovetskoe gosudarstvo i pravo 3 (March 1967): 23-30.

Schaefer, Henry. "Soviet Associations and Comecon Integration." Radio Free Europe Research Report, September 23, 1970.

Schroeder, Gertrude E. "Soviet Economic 'Reforms': A Study in Contradictions." Soviet Studies 20, no. 1 (July 1968): 1-21.

_____. "Soviet Economic Reform at an Impasse." Problems of Communism 20, no. 4 (July-August 1971): 36-46.

_____. "The 'Reform' of the Supply System in Soviet Industry." Soviet Studies 24, no. 1 (July 1972): 97-119.

Schwarz, Solomon M. "Education and the Working Class: Expansion and Advance." Survey 65 (October 1967): 15-34.

Scott, D. J. R. "Resistance and Opposition." Survey 64 (July 1967): 34-44.

"Sedulus." "The Soviet Economic Dilemma." Radio Liberty Dispatch, April 28, 1970.

Sedushev, Iu. "Povyshenie material'noi otvetstvennosti v promyshlennosti." Voprosy ekonomiki 1 (January 1970): 50-62. Condensed in CDSP 22, no. 11 (April 14, 1970): 9-12.

Seton, Francis. "Economic Planning in Communist Societies." In The Soviet Union and Eastern Europe: A Handbook, edited by George Schopflin, pp. 279-90. New York: Praeger, 1970.

Shaffer, Harry G. "What Price Economic Reforms? Ills and Remedies." Problems of Communism 12, no. 3 (May-June 1963): 18-26.

Shafikov, G. "Glavnoe--effektivnost' proizvodstva." Pravda, October 16, 1965, p. 2.

Shechter, Jerrold L. "Report from Moscow." Fortune, May 1970, pp. 105-06.

Shepetovskii, V., and Pavlovskii, V. "Vospitanie rabotnikov apparata ministerstva." Partiinaia zhizn' 4 (February 1966): 43-48.

Shkurko, S. "Material'noe pooshchrenie rabotnikov." Ekonomicheskaia gazeta 8 (February 1966): 21-22.

Shreiber, I. "Bankovskii kontrol' rublem." Den'gi i kredit (January 1966): 39-44.

Shulman, Marshall D. "The Future of Soviet Studies in the United States." An address to the American Association for the Advancement of Slavic Studies Annual Meeting, Columbus, Ohio, March 26, 1970. Slavic Review 29, no. 3 (September 1970): 582-88.

Sinitsa, M. "Tsentralizovannoe rukovodstvo i initsiativa mass." Partiinaia zhizn' 2 (January 1966): 8-14.

Sitnin, V. "Khoziaistvennaia reforma i peresmotr optivykh tsen na promyshlennuiu produktsiiu." Kommunist 14 (September 1966): 37-46.

Slepov, I. "Voprosy nauchnoi organizatsii truda." Planovoe khoziaistvo 12 (December 1965): 9-13.

Smagalov, T. "The Stride of the Economic Reform." Narodnoe khoziaistvo Kazakhstana (Alma-Ata) 6 (June 1968): 3-5. JPRS 46,391 (September 10, 1968): 1-6.

Smolinski, Leon. "What Next in Soviet Planning?" Foreign Affairs 42, no. 4 (July 1964): 602-13.

──────. "The Soviet Economy: In Search of a Pattern." Survey 66 (April 1966): 88-101.

──────. "Towards a Socialist Corporation: Soviet Industrial Reorganization of 1973." Survey 20, no. 1 (Winter 1974): 24-35.

Sonin, M. "Nekotorye problemy povysheniia effektivnosti ispol'zovaniia trudovykh resursov." Voprosy ekonomiki 8 (August 1966): 28-40.

"Sovershenstvovat' rukovodstvo promyshlennost'iu." Partiinaia zhizn' 19 (October 1965): 5-10.

"Sovershenstvovat' stil' i motody raboty finansovykh organov." Finansy SSSR 10 (October 1966): 3-7. JPRS 39,520 (January 13, 1967): 1-6.

Spechler, Martin C. "Decentralizing the Soviet Economy: Legal Regulation of Price and Quality." Soviet Studies 22, no. 2 (October 1970): 222-54.

Staats, Steven J. "Corruption in the Soviet System." Problems of Communism 21, no. 1 (January-February 1972): 40-47.

Stankovic, Slobodan. "Yugoslav Press and Radio Analyze Economic Reforms in Eastern Europe." Radio Free Europe Research Report, May 22, 1967.

Stepin, A. "Rukovodiashchii printsip zhizni i deiatel'nosti leninskoi partii." Kommunist 6 (April 1969): 37-47.

Stewart, Philip D. "Soviet Interest Groups and the Policy Process: The Repeal of Production Education." World Politics 22, no. 1 (October 1969): 29-50.

Sukhanov, V. "Ekspertiza prigodnosti." Sovetskaia Rossiia, March 25, 1967, p. 2.

Sukharevskii, B. "Predpriiatie i material'noe stimulirovanie." Ekonomicheskaia gazeta 49 (December 1965): 12-14.

Sukharevsky, B. "Reforma: Opyt i problemy." Pravda, April 12, 1967, pp. 2-3.

Szamuely, Tibor. Untitled article (part of the series "The USSR Since Khrushchev"). Survey 72 (Summer 1969): 51-69.

Szeplaki, Leslie. "A Progress Report on Socialist Economic Reforms: The Hungarian Experience." A.S.T.E. Bulletin 12, no. 1 (Spring 1970): 1-12.

Szuprowicz, B. O. "East Europe: The Search for Computers." East Europe 21, no. 4 (April 1972): 2-6.

Tatu, Michel. "Soviet Reforms: The Debate Goes on." Problems of Communism 15, no. 1 (January-February 1966): 28-34.

Tikhomirov, Iu. A. "Razvitiefunktsii upravlencheskikh organov." Sovetskoe gosudarstvo i pravo 1 (January 1966): 26-34.

Tolskikov, Ia. "Medovyi mesiats' mashinostroitelei." Sovetskaia Estoniia (Tallin), May 26, 1966, p. 2. JPRS 37,443 (September 6, 1966): 14-18.

Tolstov, V. "Shtatnye i vneshtatnye." Partiinaia zhizn' 22 (November 1965): 38-41.

BIBLIOGRAPHY 347

"To the New System of Planning and Economic Initiative." Material'no-tekhnicheskoe snabzhenie 4 (April 1967): 1-4. JPRS 41,204 (May 30, 1967): 12-17.

Trend, Harry. "Bulgarian Economic Reforms Fail to Solve Inter-Enterprise Delivery Problems." Radio Free Europe Research Report, October 2, 1967.

_____. "Soviet Economic Reorganizations Influenced by the Need to Preserve Top Jobs." Radio Free Europe Research Report, August 12, 1970.

Trifonov, G. "Rezhim ekonomii i partiinye organizatsii." Ekonomicheskaia gazeta 23 (June 1967): 19-20.

"Trudom slaven chelovek." Pravda, August 22, 1965, p. 1.

Tsantis, Andreas C. "Political Factors in Economic Development." Comparative Politics 2, no. 1 (October 1969): 63-78.

TsK KPSS i Sovet Ministrov SSSR. "V tsentral'nom komitete KPSS i sovete ministrov SSSR." Pravda, October 10, 1965, p. 1.

Uibokand, G. "Startuet legkaia industriia." Sovetskaia Estoniia (Tallin), June 2, 1967, p. 2. JPRS 41,660 (July 1, 1967): 40-43.

U.S. Congress, Senate. "Assessment of 24th Communist Party Congress." Congressional Record, 94th Cong., 2nd sess. (January 18, 1972): E62-E74.

USSR. "Polozhenie o predpriiatii." Ekonomicheskaia gazeta 24 (June 1966): 19.

_____. "Tipovoe polozhenie o premirovanii rabotnikov promyshlennykh predpriiatii, perevodimykh na novuiu sistemu planirovaniia i ekonomicheskogo stimulirovaniia proizvodstva." Ekonomicheskaia gazeta 8 (February 1967): 9-10.

_____, Council of Ministers. "Polozhenie o sotsialisticheskom gosudarstvennom proizvodstvennom predpriiatii." Ekonomicheskaia gazeta 42 (October 20, 1965): 25-29.

_____, Supreme Soviet. "Zakon SSSR o vnesenii i dopolnenii v tekst konstitutsii (osnovnogo zakona) SSSR." Pravda, October 3, 1965.

_____. "Zakon SSSR ob izmenenii sistemy organov upravleniia promyshlennost'iu i preobrazovanii nekotorykh drugikh organov gosudarstvennogo upravleniia." Pravda, October 3, 1965, p. 1.

"V kollegii Ministerstvo Finansov SSSR." Finansy SSSR 10 (October 1966): 94-96. JPRS 39,520 (January 13, 1967): 45-51.

"V tsentral'nom komitete KPSS i Soveta Ministrov SSSR." Pravda, October 10, 1965, p. 1.

Valentei, D. "Pressing USSR Populations Problems." Ekonomicheskie nauki 1 (January 1969): 53-59. JPRS 47,708 (March 25, 1965): 23-31.

Vasil'ev, M. "Direktor za partoi." Izvestiia, May 14, 1967, p. 5.

"Vazhnyi etap v razvitii sotsialisticheskoi ekonomiki." Pravda, October 4, 1965, p. 1.

Veduta, N. "Nauka upravliat'." Pravda, November 15, 1967, p. 2.

Verdnikov, V. G. "O planovom kharaktere khoziaistvennogo dogovora." Sovetskoe gosudarstvo i pravo 4 (April 1966): 63-70.

"Vernym kursom." Pravda, October 10, 1965, p. 2.

"Vnedriat' novuiu sistemu, sovershenstvovat' pokazateli planirovaniia." Planovoe khoziaistvo 7 (July 1966): 31-41.

Vorob'ev, V. K. "Bank Official Outlines Broader Role for Credit." Den'gi i kredit 7 (July 1968): 3-15. JPRS 46,597 (October 4, 1968): 1-21.

Vvedensky, G. A. "The Industry of the Irkutsk Oblast." Bulletin of the Institute for the Study of the USSR 16, no. 12 (December 1969): 12-15.

Ways, Max. "Tomorrow's Management: A More Adventurous Life in a Free-Form Corporation." Fortune, July 1966, pp. 84-87, 148, 150.

"White-Collar Communism." Economist 221, no. 6426 (October 22-28, 1966): 366.

Yagodkin, V. "Partiinaia zhizn' v nauchnykh kollektivakh." Kommunist 11 (July 1972): 51-64. Abstracted in CDSP 24, no. 41 (November 8, 1972): 9-11.

Yam'polskii, S. Ekonomika Sovetskoi Ukrainy (Kiev) 9 (September 1966): 10-19. JPRS 39,088 (December 13, 1966): 60-71.

Yegorychev, N. "Razvivat' kommunisticheskoe tvorchestvo mass." Pravda, October 4, 1965, pp. 2-3.

Yelistratov, P. M. "Organizovat', a ne podmeniat': Zametki o stile i metodakh partiinogo rukovodstva." Pravda, February 17, 1966, p. 2.

Zaikin, A. D. "Premirovanie rabotnikov predpriiatii, pereshedshikh na novye usloviia khoziaistvovaniia." Sovetskoe gosudarstvo i pravo 6 (June 1967): 93-96.

Zaitsev, A. "Social Problems of the Economic Reform." Ekonomika Sovetskoi Ukrainy (Kiev) 5 (May 1967): 51-54. JPRS 42,238 (August 16, 1967): 48-54.

Zaitsev, I., and Pronin, I. "Kommissii po kontroliu deiatel'nosti administratsii." Partiinaia zhizn' 14 (July 1967): 30-35.

Zakharov, B. "Voprosy povysheniia urovnia ekonomicheskoi raboty na predpriiatii." Planovoe khoziaistvo 10 (October 1965): 35-41.

Zaluzhnii, V. "Biurokratismu ne mesto v apparate upravleniia." Pravda, September 8, 1965, p. 3.

_____. "Trud i vremiia." Izvestiia, September 26, 1967, p. 2.

_____. "Ideinost' khoziaistvennogo rukovoditelia." Kommunist 7 (May 1968): 85-95.

Zhuravlev, V. "Distsiplina truda na predpriiatii." Sotsialisticheskii trud 4 (April 1967): 94-96.

Zotov, N. "Novaia sistema v deistvii." Den'gi i kredit 9 (September 1966): 3-9.

INDEX

Academy of Sciences, USSR, 18, 261
"additional conditions," 81
administirovanie, 58
administration. (See bureaucracy)
administrative structure, 68
Afanasev, V., 104
Aganbegian, A., 18-19, 20
agriculture, 290
Akhundov, A., 47
Aleksandrov, I., 295
Allakhverdian, D., 87
allocation order (nariad), 231
allocations, 44
all-Union industrial associations (promyshlennye obedineniia), 117
amalgamation. (See obedinenie)
Amalrik, A., 92, 147
Andropov, Yuri, 302
anti-Party group, 160, 306
Antonov, O. K., 247
armed services (U.S.), competition among, 85
Armenia, 212
Armstrong, J., 63, 82-83, 146, 255
Aspaturian, V., 251
association (industrial). (See obedinenie)
autarky, 134
automation, 208-09, 303
Azrael, J., 8, 145, 251, 255

Baibakov, N., 101
Bell, D., 124
Belousov, R., 299
Benediktov, I., 23
Berliner, J., 177, 257, 293

"big systems," 71
Birman, A., 190-91, 234, 268-69
birth rate, 202-03
Bismarck, O., 252
black market, 233
blat, 9
Brest, 122
British civil service, 62
Bolshevichka (obedinenie), 26, 80, 239
bonuses, 81-82, 189, 195-98, 294; year-end, 196
Brezhnev, L., 5, 19, 56, 63, 65, 72, 76, 116, 120, 132, 159, 162, 165, 167, 169, 178, 189, 199, 247, 270, 282, 295, 302
bronia, 43, 194
branch management, 56
Brown, E., 95, 207
budgets, program, 33
Bulgaria, 134-35, 232
Bunich, P., 78
bureaucracy, bureaupathic behavior, 87; campaign against, 159-61; capabilities, 292-93; change in, 305-06; criticism of, 266; elitism, 11-12; goals, 291-92; informalism, 9; Leninist style, 4; managerial, 11; monistic, 9; Polish, 87; politics of, 8-9, 10-11, 58-59, 66, 134, 136, 146, 291, 299-300, 306-307; powers, 33, 290-93; reform, 12; reorganizations, 292; size, 64; Tsarist tradition, 12, 302, 303, 305; United States, 291

INDEX

"bureaucratism," 160-61, 175
bureaucrats, view of reform, 36; sovnarkhoz, 36
"bureaupathology," 8
Burnham, J., 251

cabinet, Labour, 66-67
Campbell, R., 148
capitalism, 3
"career-line isolation," 63
Central Committee (CPSU), 65-66; plenum of, 18; membership, 66
Central Institute for Labor Resources, 203
Central Statistical Administration, 19, 22, 85, 104, 114, 271; and computers, 69
Central Trade Union Council, 195
centralization, 19, 116-18
Chapman, B., 10, 135
Chelyabinsk, 201; tractor plant of, 156
chief economist, 41-42
chief engineer, 41-42
China, 248
"classic bureaucrats," 298
classifiers, 105
clerical facilities, 74
"co-determination" (Mitbestimmung), 201
combines, 120
communication, 82-83
Communist Party (CPSU), 4-5, 11, 251, 265, 307; and enforcement, 154-55, 170; and ideology, 267; and interests, 297-302; and ministries, 39, 158-65; and obedineniia, 133, 174-75; and operations, 155-56, 170-71; and planning, 296-97; and politics of reform, 147-51; and research, 295; and state bureaucracy, 286; and sociology, 173, 268; and trade unions, 166; and workers, 198; apparatchiki of, 66, 145-47, 153, 159, 166; as tolkach, 173-74; cadres' work of, 154-55, 169; dualism in, 25; goals and priorities of, 157, 173-74; goals of in reform, 152-53, 282; ideological work of, 156-57, 171-73; leadership of, 300-01, 302, 307-08; politics of, 299-300; role in industrial management, 21-22, 37-39, 253, 269; rukovodstvo of, 288-89; statutes of, 162-63
computers, 58, 68-72, 269-72, 293; and bureaucracy, 271-72; application of, 270; costs of, 271; foreign sources of, 71; in planning, 269-70; in United States, 271; late generations of, 71; limitations of, 270, 271; linkage of, 105-06; problems of, 71; proliferation of, 105; significance of, 270; sources of, 271; systems of, 71
computing centers, network of, 69-70
"computopia," 270, 305
comrades' courts, 24, 160, 195
Conquest, R., 3, 148
consumer goods, 246-47, 284; cost of, 299
consumers, 18, 26, 268
contracts, 22, 44-45, 229-31; failure to fulfill, 236; in planning, 231; sanctions for violation of, 234
Control Data Corporation, 75
Cordiner, R., 256
corporations (U.S.), competition among, 85
corruption, 20

cost reduction, 32-33
costs, 22
Council of Directors, 72, 128-29, 175, 251
Council of Ministers (USSR), 28, 65, 66, 78-79, 160, 208, 212; and Gosbank, 113; of Kazakhstan, 79; of Lithuania, 86
Cousins, N., 160
creativity, 306
credits, 18, 111-13
Crossman, R., 66
crypto-politics, 290-91
Cuba, Soviet policies, 23
Cultural Revolution, 158-59
Cybernetics, 68-72, 104, 269-72; and computers, 58; see also computers
Czechoslovakia, 294; reforms in, 88-89, 299

Dagestan, 170
decentralization, 2-3, 35, 110, 116-18; limits of, 57
decision-making, 247, 259
deliveries, 232
Department of Labor Resources, 212
depreciation deductions, 33
direct production relations, 26
director (enterprise). See manager
Disraeli, B., 252
Djilas, M., 176, 187
Donaldson, R., 63
Drucker, P., 60, 133
druzhiny. See people's militia
dual executive, 63, 151
Duevel, C., 65

"econometrician-computopians," 298
econometrics, 296
economic democracy, 19

economics, and political science, 282; and politics, 306-07
Economics Institute of the USSR Academy of Sciences, 109
economies of scale, 20
Edeen, A., 286
edinonachalie, 39, 40, 250
Elektrosila (obedinenie), 83
elites, 12
Ellman, M., 104
emigration, 304
enlarged party committee, 168
enterprises (industrial), autonomy of, 77-78; budgets of, 21; councils, 40; functions of, 31; merging of, 117-18; size of, 35; small, 123; staffs of, 21; statute for, 27-28, 132; success indicators of, 26
engineers, training of, 262-63
Etzioni, A., 248
Ewing, D., 265
excess stocks, 230
export balance, 284

Fakel, 171
fairs (industrial), 230
family allowances, 203
"family relationships," 20-21
Fedorenko, N. K., 105, 107
Fedorenko, N. P., 64, 193
Fedoseyev, A., 292
feudalism, 252
filialy (branches), 123
Finansy SSSR, 114, 115
fines, 90, 234, 235, 235-36
firm. See obedinenie
Fischer, G., 63, 151
Ford, H., 46
foreign policy, 296-97
forms, 105
Frankel, T., 251
Friedrich, C., 250

INDEX
353

Galbraith, J., 4, 149
Garbuzov, V., 114
General Electric Co., 256
General Motors Corp., 46
Georgia, 162
German Democratic Republic, 118; and innovation, 119
glavki (chief administrations), 30, 119
Glushkov, A., 71, 76, 104
GOELRO, 68
Goldman, M., 249
Gorky (city), 210, 212
Gosarbitrazh, 23, 231, 232-33, 235, 240-41; and fines, 90; and price and quality, 241; cases handled, 240-41; criticism of, 240; role of, 45-46
Gosbank, 19, 21, 83, 110-14, 264, 285; bribery of officials of, 113; local offices of, 112; number of offices, 110-11; role in credit, 31, 111-14; role of, 33; sanctions of 112-13; take-over of enterprises, 110-11
Gosplan, 20, 65, 82, 85, 86, 91, 101-10, 160; and computers, 69, 104; and supplies, 237; criticism of, 108; deputy chairman of, 123; leadership of, 101-02
Gosplan (Azerbaidzhan), 121
Gosplan (North Caucasus raion), 228
Gosplan (RSFSR), 20, 78, 79
Gossnab, 29, 38, 45, 84, 230, 236-39; plan changes by, 228; structure of, 238-39
Graham, L., 68-69, 71-72
Granick, D., 145-46
Grechko, A., 302
Greenslade, R., 91
Gromyko, A., 302

Grossman, G., 106
growth (industrial), 18, 29
Gvishiani, D., 263-64

Hammer and Sickle plant, 155
Hardt, J., 251
Harvard Business School, 263
Hough, J., 40, 61, 62, 65, 66, 149, 150, 157, 177, 291
Hungary, 130

I.B.M. See International Business Machines Corp.
"ideological marketeers," 298
ideology, 10, 92, 230; centralist inclination of, 110; "unarticulated," 302
incentives, 18, 22, 43; material, 188; "moral," 188-89; utility of, 197; year-end bonus, 189
"industrial centrals" (Romanian), 118
industry, cost of administration of, 60; large-batch, 305; operation of, 18; organization of, 23-24; organizational structure of, 60; process, 305
inefficiency, 59
information, 76; control of, 71; flows of, 68
informalism, 19
innovation, 47, 106
Institute for Management of the National Economy, 76, 262
institutional pluralism, 57
intelligentsia (specialist), 91
inter-branch relations, 86, 89
Inter-Departmental Committee on Economic Reform, 102
Inter-Departmental Council for the Study of Demand, 109
interest, 18, 25-26, 33; rate of, 57
interest groups, 12, 297, 302

International Business Machines
  Corp., 75, 270, 271
investment, 18
ITR (inzhinerno-tekhnicheskie
  rabotniki), 40-42, 56, 293-
  94; wages of, 195

Janos, A., 300
jury, 27

Kaluga, 213
Kantorovich, V., 18
Katz, A., 57, 77-78, 80, 199
Keizer, W., 64, 301
Kharkov tractor plant, 167
khozraschet, 29, 60, 106,
  134, 239
Khrushchev, N., 2, 3, 9, 24,
  25, 26, 57, 65, 78, 91,
  117-18, 157, 160, 165, 171,
  191, 198, 254, 282; removal
  of, 26
Kirilenko, A., 76
Kirillin, V., 76, 77
Kirov, 122
Kolokowski, L., 297
Kolomna textile machine-
  building plant, 82
komandirovki, 83
kontrol' rublem, 21, 111
Korotchenko, D. S., 63
Kosygin, A., 1, 6-8, 18, 19,
  20, 21, 23, 30, 32, 33, 34,
  35, 47, 48, 56, 76, 109,
  147, 167, 189, 228, 262,
  263, 282; report of at
  1965 CC plenum, 27
Krasnoyarsk, 238
Kuibyshev, 204
Kulindorov, 122
Kusbass, 193
Kux, E., 145

labor, in industry, 40; overstaffing, 42-43; productivity
  of, 2, 42, 124, 186-87

labor exchanges, 43, 210
Lane, D., 62, 198
Lange, O., 305
La Palombara, J., 11
Latvian SSR, Chairman of Coun-
  cil of Ministers of, 32
law, and industry, 89-90, 304
Lenin, V., 4, 11, 25, 40, 48,
  59, 119, 164, 252, 260, 263,
  270
Leningrad University, 264
Lennauchtekhsnab, 171
Leont'ev, L., 18
Levine, H. S., 29, 70
Liberman, Ye., 17, 20, 25, 32,
  45, 82, 109-10, 227, 295,
  298
Libermanism, 25, 26, 58
Lithuania, First Party Secre-
  tary of, 172
loans, for enterprises, 112
local industry, 36
localism. See mestnichestvo
Lomako, P., 101
lumbering, 20
Lysenkoism, 68

McAuley, M., 198, 201
Malenkov, G., 23, 160
management, 293; and class
  struggle, 253; and computers,
  270-72; and economics, 267;
  and post-industrial society,
  266-67; change in, 249, 281-
  82; definition of, 265-66; engineering approach, 255;
  gaming, 264; in past, 253-
  54; in U.S., 265; in Yugoslavia, 267; mathematical
  methods, 70; multi-stage
  system of, 19-20; new schools
  of, 1, 261-62, 263-64; new
  specialties in, 263; office
  machinery in, 259-60; overstaffing in, 257, 258, 260-61;
  paper work of, 259; personnel,

21; principles of, 18-19; R&D firms, 264-65; responsiveness of, 41; secretaries in, 259; structure of, 41, 258-60; style of, 248

managers, 19; and change, 46-48, 248, 249; and economics, 255; and edinonachalie, 39, 40, 189-92, 250; and employees' salaries, 42; and labor discipline, 194-95; and labor legislation, 192; and Party, 37-39, 251, 253; and past, 252-54; and planning, 251; and politics, 135, 145-47, 249-52; and social research, 268-69, 272; and subordinates, 40-43; and suppliers and customers (other managers), 22-23, 44-45, 225-41; and workers, 186-216 (Ch. 5), 251-52, 272; as grouping, 287; assistants of, 41-42; attitudes of toward reform, 256, 257-58, 287-88; bonuses of, 235; contracts among, 229-31; Councils of (Councils of Directors), 72; demands on, 255; "direct ties" among, 228, 229, 238; election of, 40, 269; environment of, 247-48; experience and education of, 46-47, 48, 260-65, 272-73; firing of workers, 192-94; illegal behavior of, 253-54; incentives of, 272; indecision of, 287; initiative of, 37; new requirements of, 42, 265-69; powers of, 31, 269, 288-89; problems of, 21; purge of, 262; qualities of, 246, 247; qualifications of, 253, 254-56, 266, 267-68; relationship with superiors, 29-32, 254; relationships of, 6-8, 285-88; responsibility of, 36; rewards of, 269; sanctions of, 191; security of, 24; staffing powers of, 42; thinking and attitudes of, 31, 254-56; use of, 47-48, 268; work of, 258

Mao Tse-tung, 159
market, under socialism, 23, 87, 106, 110, 231
market prices, 57
"marketization," 304
Marx, K., 301
Marxism, 229, 252
Matskevich, V., 65
Mayak (obedinenie), 26, 238-39
Mazurov, K., 34, 103
mestnichestvo, 19, 25, 35
Meyer, A., 250, 257
Mikoyan, A., 23
military, and reform, 299; expenditures on, 29
ministers, 61-62; and managers, 62; as political grouping, 62-63; backgrounds of, 63-64; "departmental view" of, 66; minister of finance, 34; socialization of, 63-64

ministries, actions against other ministries, 84-86; and enterprise plans, 81-84; and khozraschet, 73; and Party, 158-61; and politics, 80-81, 160; combinations of, 121; functions of, 31-32, 57-58, 80; general statute on, 237; informalism in, 81; interference in enterprise operations, 81-84; legal services of, 90; limitations of, 33, 119; number of, 57; reestablishment of, 27, 30; salaries of functionaries of, 73-74, 89; staff or apparatus of, 30-31, 56-57, 60-65, 75-77; structure and

operations of, 67-68, 72-78, 86-89; supply offices of, 84
Ministry, of Communications, 39, 104, 271; of Culture, 271; of Domestic Services (Georgia), 74; of Finance, 19, 21, 33-34, 80-81, 114-16, 233, 264, 285-86; of Food Industry (Estonia), 68; of Food Industry (Moldavia), 72; of Foreign Affairs, 302; of Higher Education, 271; of Industrial Construction Materials, 75, 79; of Instrument Making, 29, 72, 74, 103, 124; of Light Industry, 229; of Machine Building for Construction, 76, 167; of Machine-Tool Building, 120; of Nonferrous Metallurgy, 79; of Oil and Gas Extraction, 127; of Trade, 108
"moderate marketeers," 298
Mosca, G., 57, 150, 151
Mosher, F., 148

nationalities question, 128
nationalized industries (British), competition among, 85
"negative power," 59
Nemchinov, V., 25, 88
Neuberger, E., 303
New Course, 23, 302
New Economic Policy (NEP), 3, 35, 119
"new left," 201
Nikolaevsky, B., 147
Nizhny Tagil, 168
nomenklatura, 169
NOT (nauchnaia organizatsiia truda), 47-48

Nove, A., 62, 77, 82; on clarical personnel, 74
Novikov, K., 212
Novosibirsk Economics Institute, 18-19
Novozhilov, S., 210, 297

obedineniia, 5, 30, 41, 57, 116-35, 260; administirovanie of, 133; and councils of directors, 129; and efficiency, 122-23; and enterprises and ministries, 118, 131; and Party, 128, 132-33, 174-75; and R&D, 124; and repairs, 124; and technology, 124; definition of, 125-26; effects of, 128, 129-30, 131, 132; elimination of, 120; firing of workers by, 127; formalism in, 131; heads of, 129-30; implications of, 133-35; number of, 130-31; number of enterprises in, 127; opposition to, 132; origins of, 119-20; output of, 130-31; politics of, 136; reasons for, 120-25; relationship to sovnarkhozy, 35; role of, 35; Shchekino variant, 131; specialization and cooperation of, 123; types of, 126-27, 129-30
October slogans, 166, 188
Office of Management and Budget (U.S.), 34
operations research, 77
opposition, political, 66
"optimalists," 298
orders, cancellation of, 235
Ordzhonikidze Engineering-Economics Institute, 264
organization theory, 298
Orgnabor, 204, 205
output (industrial), 18, 22, 32

INDEX

Pares, B., 12
"Parkinson's law," 65, 125, 291
participation, of workers in management, 200-02
partiinost', 66
Party Congress, Twenty-Fourth, 39, 63, 77, 104, 161, 162, 166, 167, 247, 270, 295, 302
payments, 232
Penza, 258
people's assessors, 26
People's Control Committee (KNK), 64, 80, 171, 240
people's militia (druzhiny), 24, 160
performance criteria, 290
Pervukhin, M., 160
Peter the Great, 3
planning, bargaining in, 102; by territorial and local agencies, 90-91; by weight, 108; difficulties of, 246; market-type, 103; "most important products," 102-03; national computer network in, 104-06; optimality in, 103; "ratchet" in, 20, 80; role of, 32-33; "stimulation" in, 109-10
plans: "alien," 20; changes in, 109; "easy," 84; ninth plan, 29, 284; "ratchet" in, 20; seven-year plan, 18; "tautness" of, 69
Plekhanov Institute, 264
Ploss, S., 160
Poland, 130, 201-02, 246; workers of, 299
Polish praxiologists, 296
Politburo, 9, 65, 302, 305; members of, 151, 296
political culture, 11-12
political science, 26
political system, 4-5
politics, 5, 11, 273; and economics, 298, 301, 306-07; change of, 307-08; climate of, 294-97; in France, 307; interests in, 297-302
Popov, G., 70
post-industrial society, 92, 287, 294, 303, 305, 308
prices, 19, 106, 290; "contractual prices," 109
Procurator, 194
producer goods, 284
productivity, 24; measurement of, 60
profits, 2-3, 4, 24, 32-33, 57; conceptions of, 87-89; "free profit balance," 89; plan for, 232, 233; "unused remainder" of, 115
Prybyla, J., 248-49
public administration. See bureaucracy

quality, 246-47

Radio Corporation of America (RCA), 270
rationalization, 68
recentralization, 2-3, 35
Red October plant, 83
reform (economic), and bureaucracy, 290-93, 296; and GNP, 284; and military, 299; and Party, 282; and unemployment, 205-08, 304; announcement of, 27-30; chances for failure of, 248; contradictions in, 36; criticism of, 87, 108; economic effects of, 283-84; effect on managers, 256; future of, 304-05, 307-08; goals of, 30-32; groups and, 298; history of, 23-27; implementation of, 2, 27, 29,

59, 298, 305; in Eastern Europe, 206, 207, 281; "legacies" in, 303; limitations of, 289-302; managerial attitudes toward, 256, 257-58, 287-88; number of enterprises on, 283; political effects of, 288; politics of, 59, 147-51, 175-76, 272-73, 282; significance of, 36, 281-82, 303-08; slow-down of, 284; social effects of, 285-88; success indicators in, 256, 304; transfer of enterprises to, 27-30, 78-79
regionalism, 57, 90-91, 121, 122
reorganization, limits of, 292
republics, role of, 34-35
research, 295; firms for, 264-65
Richman, B., 227, 249
Rigby, T., 59, 63, 65, 151, 301
"right opportunist theoreticians," 87
Romania, 118
Romanov, G., 133, 302
Rostov, 165, 167; obkom of, 172
Rostsel'mash, 83, 232
Rudnev, K. N., 239
Rumania. See Romania
Rumiantsev, A., 8
Rybinsky machine-building plant, 154

Saburov, M., 160
Sakharov, A., 295
sales, 32; plan for, 233
Schapiro, L., 24, 159
Schroeder, G., 81, 91, 187, 230
Schwartz, H., 253

Scientific Research Institute for the Organization of Management, 264
scientific technical revolution, 76-77
scientists, 295
Scott, D. J. R., 63-64, 198-99
secret police, 187
secretarial schools, 74
Secretariat (Party), 65
Seton, F., 57
Shabad, T., 129
Shchekino (obedinenia), 84, 168, 173, 200, 209-10, 252, 286
Shelepin, A., 199
Shelest, P., 59, 168
shturmovshchina, 9, 21-22, 232, 257
Shulman, M., 5
Sigma obedinenie, 125
Sik, O., 299
Simon, H., 117, 209, 247
Skorokhod obedinenie, 229, 239
Sloan Institute (at MIT), 263
Snechkus, A., 166
social sciences, 104
soiuzglavsnabsbyty, 226
Solo, R., 150
Soviets, 35; placing of workers by, 212
sovnarkhozy, 19, 20, 22, 24, 25, 26, 34-35, 56, 57, 63, 283; dissolution of, 27, 30
Spulber, N., 119
Stalin, J., 3, 4, 17, 23, 61, 198, 253, 289
Stalinism, 92, 253
Stalinists, 298
standard of living, 246, 247
State Bank. See Gosbank
State Committee, 20, 27, 61; for Science and Technology, 75, 160-61, 262; for the Utilization of Labor Resources, 194; on Labor and Wages, 195, 210

INDEX

Stewart, P. D., 146
Stojanovich, S., 252
Stolypin, P., 210
strikes, 200
Stroibank, 155
subsystem autonomy, 305-06
success indicators, 3, 19, 32, 269, 304; additional conditions, 4; sales and profits, 226
Sukharevskii, B., 269
supplies, 18, 236-39, 287; and Gossnab, 45; hoarding of, 238
Supreme Council of the National Economy, 101
Suslov, M., 172, 177-78
Sverdlov obedinenie, 107
Sverdlovsk, 268
Svetlana obedinenie, 193, 207
Szamuely, T., 61-62

Tallin machine-building plant, 231-32
Tatu, M., 76, 300
Taylorism, 68, 253
Tbilisi, 168
"technocratization," 303
technology, 2, 290; utilization of, 56
Terebilov, V., 90
three-link system, 67, 127
Tolkach, 9, 156, 163, 257; functions of, 257; numbers of, 257
Tomsk, 83
totalitarianism, 300
trade unions, 40, 198-200, 299; and dismissals, 200; agreements between, 232
traditions, political, 230
transshipments, 238
Transcaucasus, 121
Trapeznikov, V., 26, 71, 260-61, 269

Treasury (British), 34
"Triangle," 42
trusts, 119-20
Tullock, G., 10
two-link system, 68

Ukraine, 146
unemployment, 1, 173, 192, 205-06, 304; benefits, 211; consequences of, 57; means for solution, 211-13
United States, 265, 302; grain of, 247; R&D in, 123

VAL, 2, 20, 81, 91, 107, 116
Vereinigungen Volkseigener Betriebe (VVB in GDR), 118-19
Vietnam, 189
Voprosy ekonomiki, 121, 299
Voprosy filosofii, 104
Voznesensky, N. A., 23
VSNKh, of 1920s, 121

wages, 195-98; as index, 42; wage funds, 4, 32, 42, 234
Weber, M., 106
Whitehall, 67
Wilson, H., 66
Witte, Sergei, 3
work, attitudes toward, 213
workers, 42-43, 286-87; and automation, 208-09; and managers, 186-216 (Ch. 5); as "mature working class," 201-02; availability of, 202-03; combination of jobs of, 173; dissatisfactions of, 213-14; educational level of, 191; firings of, 192-94; housing of, 204; legal protection of, 214; placing of, 212; political significance of, 215-16; retraining of, 211; rights and powers of, 26; satisfactions of, 43-44;

shortage and turnover of, 203-06; young workers, 213-14
workers' councils, 26; in Yugoslavia, 200
work force, reductions in, 42-43

Yangiyul, 155
Yugoslavia, 89, 298, 304; free capital market in, 111; neo-Marxists of, 296
Zhigalin, V., 78

ABOUT THE AUTHOR

KARL W. RYAVEC is Associate Professor of Political Science at the University of Massachusetts at Amherst, where he has been teaching Soviet and comparative politics since 1964. He is currently editing a volume of original articles on the Communist Party of the Soviet Union and is pursuing his interest in bureaucracy and administration in Leninist states.

Professor Ryavec has published articles in several journals, including <u>Soviet Studies</u>, <u>Slavic Review</u>, <u>Canadian Slavic Studies</u>, and <u>Western Political Quarterly</u>.

He earned his M.A. and Ph.D. at Columbia University, from which he also received the Certificate of the Russian Institute. He spent a year at the Russian Research Center, Harvard University, as a Research Fellow and has done research in the USSR and Yugoslavia.

RELATED TITLES
Published by
Praeger Special Studies

INPUT/OUTPUT ANALYSIS AND THE SOVIET ECONOMY:
An Annotated Bibliography
        Vladimir G. Treml

SOVIET AGRICULTURAL POLICY: Toward the Abolition
of Collective Farms
        Stephen Osofsky

DEVELOPMENT REGIONS IN THE SOVIET UNION,
EASTERN EUROPE, AND CANADA
        Edited by Andrew F. Burghardt

ECONOMIC REFORMS IN EASTERN EUROPE: Political
Background and Economic Significance
        Radoslav Selucky

SOVIET ECONOMY IN REGIONAL PERSPECTIVE
        Edited by V. N. Bandura and
        Z. L. Melnyk

THE POLITICS OF ECONOMIC REFORM IN THE
SOVIET UNION
        Abraham Katz